500 PALEO RECIPES

Hundreds of Delicious Recipes for
Weight Loss and Super Health

DANA CARPENDER

FAIR WINDS

PRESS

BEVERLY, MASSACHUSETTS

© 2012 Fair Winds Press
Text © 2012 Dana Carpender

First published in the USA in 2012 by
Fair Winds Press, a member of
Quayside Publishing Group
100 Cummings Center
Suite 406-L
Beverly, MA 01915-6101
www.fairwindspress.com

16 15 14 13   7 8 9

ISBN: 978-1-59233-532-9

Digital edition published in 2012
eISBN: 978-1-61058-614-6

Library of Congress Cataloging-in-Publication Data available

Cover design by Kathie Alexander
Page layout by Sporto

Printed and bound in U.S.A.

The information in this book is for educational purposes only. It is not intended to replace the advice of a physician or medical practitioner. Please see your health care provider before beginning any new health program.

This book is dedicated to my volunteer recipe testers:

Lynda Vander Voort, Heidi L. Bayer, Lisa Meagher, Arleen Skidmore, Julie McIntosh, Saskia van der Zanden, Regina Mulligan, Yvonne Mitchell, Lisa E. Gonzalez, Mary H. Erickson, Katy Kopczynski, Lisa Coker, Tammera Lowe, Wendy McCullough, Rebecca Jaxon, Heather Doiron, Kathryn Hanft, Robert and Jennifer Larrabee, Kim Eidson, Mary Braun, Michelle Gylanders, Ashley E. Durgin, Kimberly Carpender, Nancy A., Deb O'Connor, Mary Braun, Brian E. George, Burma Powell, Carmen Ganter, Kay Ideker, Heather Westerberg, Keri Bucci, Lisa Gonzalez, Sherri Attoe, Marilyn McCormack, Mary Erickson, Amy Dungan, Amy Alexander, Jillian Tully, and Maria Vander Vloedt.

I couldn't have done it without you. I always knew my readers were the best, and you have proved it. Your hard work and enthusiasm made this possible, and you have my sincere gratitude. Guys, you rock.

And, as so many times before, to my husband Eric. From grocery store runs and taste-testing, to editing and proofreading, to bailing me out of computer trouble yet again, his contributions to my work are not just invaluable, they're indispensable. All that, and he's just plain nice to have around the house.

CONTENTS

INTRODUCTION

Why This Book?

It's no secret that I've been a low carber for the better part of two decades now. My story and my recipes are out there for all the world to see (and thank you very much to all of you who have taken a look). So why a paleo book?

It's been clear to me for a while that, despite occasional turf wars, the low-carb movement and the paleo movement are kissin' cousins. Both focus on animal foods. Both avoid grains, potatoes, and sugar. Both make liberal use of vegetables.

The difference has been that low carbers, especially newbie low carbers, often use "crutch" or "bridge" foods—low-carb breads and tortillas, bake mixes, pastas, protein bars, and the like. These products are generally highly processed and often sources of gluten, soy, or both. While I felt, and continue to feel, that some of these products have a place in helping to wean people from their old, carb-laden diets, I know them to be a double-edged sword. I suspect that many cases of low-carb "failure" have occurred because people have relied on these products as staples, instead of basing their diets on those foods that are naturally low in carbohydrate.

(I will insert, parenthetically, that Dr. William Davis, in his excellent book *Wheat Belly*, asserts that there are proteins in gluten that are opioids, and physically addictive. The difference between these opioids and the ones we consider "drugs" is that instead of getting you high, wheat opioids make you hungry. This makes low-carb bread, tortillas, and pastas dangerous double-edged swords indeed.)

But my email, my blog responses, and my Facebook encounters with low carbers around the world tell me that there is a shift occurring. I hear from more and more people who are shunning soy products, who avoid gluten, who are seeking out grass-fed meat and dairy and wild-caught fish. More and more, I hear from people who have quit using artificial sweeteners. (The Sweetener Wars are the bane of my existence, quite honestly. No matter what sweetener I use in a recipe, someone will complain.) Huge numbers of people have dropped processed protein bars, soy-based cereals, diet soda, and are "eating clean."

In other words, low carbers are trending toward paleo.

Many of the recipes in my previous books are paleo-friendly, but many are not. Indeed, my own eating habits have shifted over the years, to the point where there are recipes in my own books that I would no longer be willing to eat. I've gone gluten free, no longer eating even low-carb bread or tortillas, yet quite a few of my old recipes call for these items, or ingredients such as vital wheat gluten, wheat germ, and wheat bran. Some use canola oil, which I haven't touched in years. Others use commercial mayonnaise, but I now make my own, because the jarred stuff is replete with soy oil and other such nastiness.

Not so with this book. Here you will find no gluten, no grains of any kind, no soy, no omega-6-heavy processed oils, no processed specialty products. You will find animal protein and animal fats in many guises, bushels of vegetables, and quite a lot of fruit. Nuts and seeds, too. And, of course, herbs and spices galore. Have fun exploring!

What Is Paleo?

There was a learning curve to this book, and quite a lot of the problem was that there is no clear definition of *paleo*. With low-carb recipes, there is one simple metric: How many grams of carbohydrate per serving? But there is considerable disagreement as to which foods are paleo and which are not. I had to make a few decisions regarding what *I* thought constituted the modern paleolithic menu.

It bears pointing out that unless you eat only locally hunted and gathered wild foods, you're not really eating the same as Ogg. (Or Grok, with a tip of the hat to blogger and author Mark Sisson, of *The Primal Blueprint*. His prototypical caveman is named Grok, and his excellent blog, *Mark's Daily Apple*, has the cheer "Grok on!") Given that most of us are going to eat cultivated foods, and may very well eat foods that are not local to our area (she said, a cup of tea at hand—not many tea bushes in southern Indiana), it behooves us to define our terms.

The first paleo nutrition book I read—possibly the first written—was *Neanderthin*, first self-published by Ray Audette in 1995, coincidentally the year I went low carb. Audette had suffered from rheumatoid arthritis and diabetes but found that with his paleo diet all symptoms vanished. His rule was simple and straightforward: *If you can't gather a food with a sharp stick and a rock, and eat it raw, it's not really food.* Audette said that the big shift in the human diet came when people started using a new technology—cooking—to render otherwise toxic foods fit to eat. Or at least, make them nontoxic enough that people didn't immediately get ill. To Audette, that was the real line—can you eat it raw?

Note that Audette didn't say that you must eat all your food raw, but rather that you shouldn't eat things that are toxic when eaten raw. Most of us cook our meat, but steak tartare, carpaccio, and sashimi have been enjoyed for centuries. Despite recent hysteria regarding eggs, as recently as my childhood, eggnog made with raw eggs was considered a healing, strengthening food for invalids and children. (Be honest: Did you ever refuse to lick the cookie dough off the beater because it had raw egg in it? Didn't think so.)

On the other hand, if you eat any quantity of uncooked grain, raw legumes, or potatoes you'll get a good bellyache. It was only the discovery of cooking that put these into the category of "food," starting the Agricultural Revolution. That revolution, in turn, gave us civilization, but it did so at the cost of degrading our health in numerous ways and shortening our life spans. (It also was the beginning of environmental degradation, but that's a discussion for another book.)

"Can you eat it raw?" has been a guiding principle while exploring this way of eating.

While the shift from hunting and gathering to agriculture, and hence from a diet of meat and vegetables to one of grains and beans, can be seen as the first, and perhaps greatest, nutritional "sin," there are a couple of other, far more recent dietary shifts that have had a drastic, deleterious effect on health.

It was about 300 years ago that European colonization of tropical islands, and slavery, made mass, commercial sugar production practical, and sugar cheap enough for the masses. It was disastrous for the slaves, for ecosystems, and for human health, all three.

Defenders of sugar like to point out that it's "natural," and that our bodies can use glucose for fuel. This is true. But the first rule of toxicology is "dose is everything." Ask yourself what would happen if you increased your water intake 3,700 percent? (Don't try it. You can die from hyperhydrosis, because—like sugar—it is possible to get too much water.)

3,700 percent: That's roughly how much our sugar consumption has increased over the past 300 years, from 4 pounds (1.8 kg) per person per year in 1,700, to over 150 pounds (68 kg) per year, or a little under a half a pound (227 g) a *day*. (And someone's eating more, folks, because I'm eating less.)

Even more jaw-dropping, I've seen estimates that paleolithic man ate roughly 20 teaspoons (117 g) of sugar per year, one assumes in the form of honey, since there was no refined sugar. If this is so, the average American is eating more sugar in a day than our hunter-gatherer ancestors ate in a year, and consumes more sugar in six weeks or so than Ogg ate in a lifetime.

Accordingly, another basic principle of paleo nutrition is to shun separated, concentrated sugars, especially table sugar and corn syrup.

Even more recent has been the switch from traditional fats like lard, tallow, schmaltz (chicken fat), coconut, and palm oils to vegetable oils. This really only occurred in the twentieth century, when oil-seed interests promulgated the ill-conceived notion that these oils, previously foreign to the human diet, were somehow safer and more nutritious than the fats humankind had been eating since the caves.

This was a drastic mistake. Rather than preventing heart disease, it turns out these oils promote inflammation in the body, causing a host of ills, from cancer to arthritis to—ironically—heart disease. The great problem turns out to be an imbalance in unsaturated fatty acids, especially the omega-6 versus the omega-3 polyunsaturated fatty acids. This is why omega-3-rich fish oil has shown so many beneficial effects: It helps to balance out the omega-6/omega-3 ratio. However, it's just as important that we stop flooding our bodies with excess omega-6 fatty acids. Hence, a paleo diet eliminates polyunsaturated vegetable oils. (And no canola oil, because it's highly processed, and anyway, it's a genetically manipulated version of a toxic oil long used for varnish—*varnish*, fercryingoutloud.)

These, to me, are the core principles of a paleo diet:

- No grains, beans, or potatoes, nor anything that must be cooked to be edible. Especially no gluten and no soy.
- No refined or separated sugars.
- No polyunsaturated vegetable oils.

These, which Kurt Harris of the *Archevore* blog calls "neolithic agents of disease," are the don'ts. Add one "do":

- Eat plenty of animal protein and animal fats. There is no such thing as a vegetarian paleo diet.

Similarly, Robb Wolf, author of *The Paleo Solution*, lists his dos and don'ts:

DO EAT	DON'T EAT
Fruits	*Dairy*
Vegetables	*Grains*
Lean meats	*Processed food and sugars*
Seafood	*Legumes*
Nuts and seeds	*Starches*
Healthy fats	*Alcohol*

There are refinements, and we'll get to those in a moment. But I confidently state that if you do these things, and these things alone, you'll improve your health. To bring up the old ⁸⁰⁄₂₀ wheeze, this is the 20 percent of the change that will bring you 80 percent of the results. Yes, I made those percentages up. I stand by the statement that these are by far the most important dietary changes you can make.

Now, for those refinements:

- As much as possible, eat fresh, rather than packaged, foods—fresh meats, poultry and fish, fresh vegetables, fresh fruits.

- Avoid additives—eating fresh foods will dramatically reduce your intake of additives right there.

- Choose grass-fed beef and lamb, pasture-raised pork and chicken, pastured eggs, and wild-caught fish as much as you can. Some of you will have issues with availability, others with cost. Still, these foods are nutritionally superior to conventionally raised foods. In particular, they have a vastly better omega-6/omega-3 ratio than their conventionally raised counterparts. Animal fat from grass-fed or pasture-raised animals is health food.

- Similarly, choose organically raised fruits and vegetables as much as possible. Of course, if you have the time and space, gardening is the ultimate way to get fresh organic produce. If you have a local farmers' market, they are a wonderful source of organic produce, offering all sorts of varieties that you won't find at the grocery store. And let me stick in a plug here for backyard poultry farming— we love our chickens. They lay wonderful eggs, they're endlessly amusing, and they turn ticks into food, which around here is no small thing. Backyard chickens are rapidly growing in popularity for a good reason.

- Gauge your carbohydrate intake by your waistline and your blood sugar. Paleo isn't strictly low carb, allowing for starchy root vegetables, winter squashes, and a wider variety of fruit than most low carbers eat. This does not mean that if you've got blood sugar and/or obesity trouble, you can throw caution to the winds and say "It's paleo! That means I can eat all the (insert high-carb food here) I want!" You may be able to fool your mind, but you will never fool your body.

- Get some sun. Without fortification, food sources of vitamin D are rare. It's really more a hormone than a vitamin, and your body's trigger to make that hormone is sun shining on your skin. America's obsession with sunscreen has led to a host of vitamin D deficiency– related problems, from depression to cancers. Your ancestors ran around in the sun all day, naked or mostly naked.

- Get enough sleep. I say this as a lifetime insomniac, and I know all too well that for some it's more easily said than done. But if you're staying up late to watch TV or catch up on housework, cut it out. Create a proper sleep environment, as dark and quiet as possible, and consider an eye mask and earplugs if you live in the city. Remember that Ogg not only didn't have a television, he also didn't have much in the way of light once the sun went down, so he went to bed. Extending the day with artificial light has had consequences we understand poorly, if at all.

- Exercise, but think about how your ancestors used their bodies. Ogg didn't run marathons. He probably didn't run much at all, except when chasing prey or being chased *as* prey, and then he didn't jog, he ran like hell, but quit as soon as he safely could. On the other hand, Ogg walked a lot—looking for food, stalking prey, following the herds with the seasons. He lifted and carried, because how else are you going to get the antelope back to the cave? He climbed, both to access food and to get out of harm's way.

Paleo or Not Paleo?

As I said, there is a lot of disagreement on what is and is not paleo. Please understand, I come to the whole thing, as I did to low carbing, from the perspective of a cook. I want the widest range of flavors and textures I can possibly get while enjoying the benefits of dietary discipline. Here are some things that some people accept as paleo, and others do not:

Fatty meat. Loren Cordain, one of the pioneers of the paleo movement, originally insisted on lean muscle meats only, recommending that you discard the fat, the skin, and any other rich bits of the carcass. Quite honestly, this boggles me. I cannot imagine that having done the work and taken the risk to hunt and kill a mammoth, a deer, a bear, a wild boar, that our ancestors didn't eat every scrap of the thing. Yes, game is leaner than farm-raised meat, but we know that hunter-gatherers prized the marrow, the brain, the spinal cord, the kidney fat—every fatty bit they could find. And not all game is naturally very lean, especially in the autumn "grease season."

The fatty parts of the carcass have nutritional value not found in the muscle meats. Skin, for instance, is a rich source of gelatin, very nutritious stuff. Discarding the skin skews the amino acid balance that would be gained by eating the whole carcass. Gelatin is fantastic for your bones and skin, and is anti-inflammatory to boot. So eat your chicken and turkey skin, and your pork rinds and cracklings. Skin is paleo.

Marrow is a terrific source of fat-soluble vitamins, not to mention brain-building DHA and EPA. (That it basically tastes like meat-flavored butter only sweetens the deal.) There's a reason why predators go for the marrow first.

From a personal perspective, I have seen my health improve as I have increased fat as a percentage of my calories. Accordingly, I have not shunned fatty cuts of meat in this book. Loren Cordain, by the way, has said that he's reconsidered his position regarding fatty meat.

Salt. Some paleo peeps shun salt altogether. But despite demonization, salt is an essential nutrient; a serious deficiency will kill you. The question is, would our hunter-gatherer ancestors have had access to salt?

Surely they would have been aware of mineral-rich areas. Places where the soil is salty, known as "salt licks," draw game from far around, and would have been prime hunting grounds. Seeing animals licking the ground, Ogg would have tasted the soil. I find it likely that salt deposits would have been discovered this way.

Anyone who lived near salt water would have known that the white stuff left behind by drying tide pools had the coveted flavor. For that matter, those who lived by bodies of salt water would have gotten plenty of salt eating raw clams, mussels, oysters, and other shellfish.

I suspect that anywhere that salt could be found, our ancestors found it and ate it. We know that salt was one of the earliest trade commodities. Is it so hard to believe that nomads whose travels brought them near a salt cave or salt water would take salt along, both for their own use and to trade with other tribes?

Like the omega-6 fatty acids, the question is quantity. By avoiding processed, packaged foods, you will automatically remove most of the salt from your diet. There is also the issue of balance; sodium needs to be balanced with potassium. If your intake of vegetables, fruits, pork, and fish, all rich in potassium, increases, you will need enough sodium to balance itto balance it. Too, while high-carbohydrate diets cause the body to retain sodium, carbohydrate restriction allows the body to eliminate sodium properly. In *The Art and Science of Carbohydrate Restriction*, researchers Stephen Phinney and Jeff Volek state that people who cut out concentrated carbohydrates often find themselves weak and tired, not from lack of carbs, but from lack of sodium.

I see little reason to ban the saltshaker, and while I have kept added salt to the minimum needed to get the flavor I wanted in these recipes, I did not leave the salt out altogether. Blame my cook's instincts. Feel free to omit the salt if you like.

Be aware that my stance on salt is informed by the fact that my husband, Eric, has actually been diagnosed—twice—with *hyponatremia*, too little sodium in the blood. He had been sprinkling salt on his eggs and meat,

but we eat so little processed food, and so few carbs, that apparently he wasn't keeping up with his body's need. Counterintuitively, his hyponatremic state was accompanied by slightly *elevated* blood pressure.

We eat our salt. However, we eat good salt—see the Ingredients section for more information.

The exception seems to be the Inuit. They lived on an Ornish-defying diet of fatty meat, blubber, and fish, and did very well on it, but they disliked salt. I have only a guess as to why this might be—that eating saltwater fish as a staple of their diet gave them all the sodium they needed. That is, I repeat, a guess.

Alcohol and vinegar. Some paleo folks allow for alcohol and vinegar, some do not. I have used them here, though I have avoided, for the most part, grain-derived alcohol and vinegars. (I have one recipe that calls for a teeny bit of bourbon. But I'm telling you, it's wonderful, and the distilling process leaves little of the grain lectins and none of the carbohydrate behind.)

Wild yeasts are everywhere; carbohydrates ferment. Park rangers tell stories of bears finding fruit that has fermented on the bush or vine, and eating enough to get drunk. If bears did it, so did Ogg. He didn't have bottles of the stuff around the cave, but they are not foreign substances that are toxic unless cooked. (Alcohol is toxic if you drink enough of it, but half a cup of wine in a dish to be shared by four people does not strike me as dangerous.)

Vinegar is the natural end-product of alcohol, unless it is distilled first. At my old house, we had an apple tree in the backyard, and there is no question that some of the apples that fell to the ground smelled of vinegar. Do you think a hungry caveman would have passed them up? I don't.

I have used a number of kinds of vinegar in these recipes, most apple cider vinegar, red and white wine vinegars, and both dark and white balsamic vinegars. In particular, there are numerous recipes where a little balsamic vinegar lends the touch of sweetness needed without additional sweetening. I hadn't tried white balsamic vinegar before this book, and it has become one of my favorite ingredients. My favorite moderately priced balsamics are from Colavita.

Dairy. My email tells me that the biggest exception people are making to the paleo plan is including dairy products, especially raw, grass-fed dairy. Mark Sisson's "primal" diet is largely paleo-plus-quality-dairy.

The argument against dairy in a paleo diet is that Ogg probably didn't chase down and milk wild buffalo and sheep. The argument for dairy is that human beings are mammals, so the components of milk are not foreign to our bodies, and also that milk is edible raw. Paleoanthropologists believe mankind was a herder before he was a farmer, and that makes sense. It's not a huge leap from following a flock as prey to controlling that flock. I wonder, too, if the first discovery of cheese didn't happen when someone killed a suckling animal, and discovered coagulated milk in its stomach. That could have happened long, long before anyone started dairying, and might well be where humankind got the idea that ruminants kept for milk could provide food over and over, rather than just once.

I am of the unshakeable opinion that butter and cheese make everything taste better. Further, I myself have never noticed any health problems from eating dairy, though I should mention that I am from English and Dutch stock, both with a long, long history of dairy consumption. Grass-fed dairy products are an excellent source of many nutrients, especially the fat-soluble vitamins A, E, and K. The fat in butter includes lauric acid, which kills yeasts and fungi, and conjugated linoleic acid (CLA), a cancer fighter that also helps lessen abdominal obesity. I will very likely continue to include butter, cream, and cheese in my diet, especially raw, grass-fed, local dairy.

But I've published a whole pile of recipes that include dairy, and that otherwise suit a primal plan. In this book, I've gone dairy free, for all of you folks who have decided you're better off without it. If you are more primal than paleo, feel free to sneak some butter, cream, and cheese into these recipes. I certainly won't be hurt.

How Paleo Is Paleo?

I am not a purist. Indeed, one of my most popular blog articles is titled "Why I'm Not a Purist." As I said, I think that if you skip the grains and especially gluten grains, eliminate separated sugars, shun polyunsaturated vegetable oils, and avoid soy and other legumes, you'll get at least 80 percent of the value of a paleo diet. Remember, we're not going to replicate the caveman diet; we can't. We're not going to replicate the caveman lifestyle, either. Most of us have jobs that call for the same actions or inaction at least 40 hours a week, something Ogg never imagined. Most of us wouldn't give up central heat, air-conditioning, or artificial lighting, either.

What we're trying to do is avoid those parts of the modern diet that actively and profoundly have metabolic effects we consider negative. (Keep in mind that Ogg probably thought putting on a few pounds was a *good* thing.)

With this in mind, I used, in some of these recipes, ingredients that have minimal quantities of nonpaleo stuff, on the theory that a teaspoon of hot sauce that has a little sugar in it is not going to mess me up. I also used coconut milk that is organic, but contained guar gum, technically not "paleo kosher." (I thank That Nice Boy I Married for this useful term.) I did not use all grass-fed meat.

However, I avoided even tiny quantities of gluten, substituted for grain-derived ingredients like rice or malt vinegar, and made quite a few of my own condiments, especially ketchup—the commercial stuff is loaded with sugar. Ketchup is often used in quantity in recipes, potentially contributing a lot of sugar to the diet, so I've been making my own for years, anyway.

It's up to you how pure you want to be. My only worry is that if you get really obsessive and make this too difficult, you may get fed up and quit. Don't let the perfect become the enemy of the good.

The exception here is gluten. If you are gluten sensitive, you must avoid even traces of the stuff.

About the Word Natural

The cultural meme is that "natural" equals "healthful." Over and over, I hear, "But it's *natural*! It must be good for me!" People say this about whole grains, honey, all sorts of things.

Wake-up call: Many of the most toxic things on the planet are natural: rattlesnake venom, death angel mushrooms, tobacco. Natural stuff can ruin your health at least as quickly as artificial stuff. I whole-grained-and-beaned my way up to a size 20.

So don't get sucked into "But this sprouted whole grain bread is *natural*!" All sorts of natural things can and will hurt you. The gluten and opioids in that whole-grain bread are among them.

Meat is natural, but it's not part of the diet of a rabbit. Grass is natural, but it's not part of the diet of a tiger. The question for paleo peeps is, "Is this food natural *for human beings*?"

Is This a Low-Carb Cookbook?

Lower carb than your average cookbook, certainly, but not as low carb as my previous cookbooks. You'll find very-low-carb meat and egg recipes here, absolutely, and recipes for nonstarchy vegetables, nuts and seeds, and other low-carb favorites. But you'll also find recipes for sweet potatoes, winter squash, and other starchy vegetables. You'll find more fruit than I have hitherto used, and recipes including honey (see my notes about sweeteners), which is pure sugar.

Just as many low-carb folks don't eat paleo, many paleo folks are not strictly low carb. Most low carbers were drawn to their diet because of obesity, blood sugar problems, or a combination of the two. Many paleo folks, though, have always been slim and athletic, with robust metabolisms that can tolerate a little more carbohydrate.

As always, you need to pay attention to your body. If you have blood sugar problems, your glucometer is your friend. Pay attention to your body and pick and choose the recipes that work for you.

How Are Nutrition Counts in These Recipes Calculated?

The nutrition counts have been calculated using MasterCook software, a very useful program that allows the user to enter the ingredients of a recipe, and the number of servings it makes, and then spits out the nutritional breakdown for each serving. MasterCook does not, however, calculate for such things as skimming the fat off a soup or draining and discarding a marinade.

The nutrition counts for these recipes are as accurate as we can make them. However, they are not, and cannot be, 100 percent accurate. MasterCook gets its nutritional information from the USDA Nutrient Database. MasterCook also lets the user enter new ingredients in the database, and I have done this with ingredients such as coconut aminos and unsweetened coconut milk. In these cases, I have taken the nutritional information from the labels.

Every stalk of celery, every onion, every head of broccoli is going to have a slightly different level of vitamins, minerals, and carbohydrate in it, because it grew in a specific patch of soil, in specific weather, with a particular kind of fertilizer. You may use slightly meatier chicken than I do You may be a little more or less generous with how many bits of chopped green pepper you fit into a measuring cup.

Don't sweat it. These counts are, as the old joke goes, near enough for government work.

In this spirit, you'll find that many of these recipes call for "1 large rib of celery," "half a green pepper," "a clove of garlic." This is how most of us cook, after all. These things do not come in standardized sizes; they're analyzed for the average. Don't sweat it. The important thing here is eating appropriate foods for your body, and skipping the toxic modern interlopers.

Ingredients

Most of the ingredients here are familiar and need no explanation, but there are a few that bear elaboration.

ALMOND MEAL AND COCONUT FLOUR
These are the flour substitutes I have used. Both are widely available in health food stores, and often in regular grocery stores as well. The widely distributed Bob's Red Mill brand includes both.

I often make my own almond meal, simply by running shelled almonds through my food processor until it reaches cornmeal texture. This can be subbed for the commercial version, but it takes a decent food processor. (If you don't have a really good food processor, consider buying one. I've had a $30 Black and Decker, and a $125 Cuisinart, and there's no question which is the better, more powerful, more versatile machine.)

Coconut flour is milled from coconut that has first been pressed for its oil. Putting shredded coconut through your food processor will not give you coconut flour. You'll have to purchase it.

COCONUT AMINOS
Brewed from coconut sap, coconut aminos are a soy- and wheat-free substitute for soy sauce. They are interchangeable with soy sauce in cooking, giving substantially similar results. All my local health food stores carry these, but if you can't find coconut aminos locally, like everything else, you can order them online. They're pricier than soy sauce.

I'll say here, though, that of all the forms soy takes, I consider soy sauce to be the most benign. The fermentation process breaks down the soy estrogens, and the mineral-binding phytates are filtered out. In fact, for me the most questionable parts of most commercial soy sauces are the wheat and sugar most of them contain. When I do use soy sauce, I use San-J brand wheat-free soy sauce. Depending on how strictly paleo you want to be, you could substitute this for the coconut aminos.

COCOA POWDER AND BITTER BAKING CHOCOLATE
Obviously sugary chocolate candy is not paleo, but what about chocolate itself? It seems to me that the antichocolate sentiment comes from chocolate's sugary reputation, and perhaps from the conviction that since people love and crave it so much, it must be bad. The

cacao fruit and bean (not a legume, but the seed of a fruit) are eaten not only by humans but by wild animals as well. That strikes me as paleo.

Better, chocolate is a tremendously rich source of antioxidants. It also is surprisingly high in fiber, if that concerns you.

Accordingly, I've used unsweetened cocoa powder and bitter baking chocolate in a few recipes here. Enjoy.

EGGS

If you have a source of pastured eggs—eggs from chickens who are actually allowed to run free, eating grass and clover and worms and bugs—pony up the extra buck or two a carton. They're so totally worth it. Be aware that "free-range eggs" come from chickens who have a door to a pen outside, but may very well never actually venture into the sun, much less have access to the grass, bugs, and other stuff that are the natural diet of a chicken. If you're getting proper eggs, the yolks won't be lemon yellow, they'll be golden-orange. I know, because I have thirty chickens running around my backyard as I write this, eating grass and bugs (and ticks, bless them). The yolks in their eggs are so brilliant it's practically blinding.

Ever see those eggs that say "From chickens fed vegetarian feed?" That phrase never fails to make me sad. Chickens are not vegetarians. Not even a little bit. My birds will eat almost anything, but they fight over meat scraps, and heaven help any bug or salamander or baby snake that gets in their way. Living with chickens, I'm pretty sure I know what dinosaurs were like. Among the eggs from chickens forced into vegetarianism are those from Eggland's Best, which are advertised as being rich in omega-3 fatty acids. This, apparently, is from being fed flaxseed. Nothing wrong with that, but be aware that eggs from pastured hens are extraordinarily rich in omega-3s, plus all kinds of vitamins and antioxidants.

You will find many recipes in this book calling for raw eggs. This runs directly counter to the food safety information we've had drummed into our heads for the past couple of decades. However, it has been stated that only one out of every 16,000 uncracked, properly refrigerated eggs is actually contaminated. I had a conversation with a public health and food scientist who said, "The risk is less than the risk of breaking your leg on any given trip down the stairs." And that's with factory-farmed eggs; I consider small-farm eggs—or the eggs from my backyard—even safer.

It's not that there's no risk; there's a risk to everything. But I'm increasingly convinced that people worry about the wrong things, getting panicky about raw eggs or raw milk while consuming Coca-Cola, Lucky Charms, and Wonder Bread. For what it's worth, I've never gotten sick from a raw egg. But your risks are your own to take.

If you're really unhappy about raw eggs, you can pasteurize them. You'll need a digital thermometer. Put your eggs in a saucepan and cover with water. Put them on a high burner and bring the water to 140°F (60°C). Hold them at that temperature—and no hotter—for 3 minutes. Then immediately pour off the hot water, and flush the eggs with several changes of cold water. Store in the refrigerator until needed or use right away.

FATS

Fat has been reviled for so long that it can take a while to wrap our heads around the idea that proper, traditional fats are one of the most valuable foods we can eat. Most of the vegetable oils we've been told are "healthy" are anything but. I have used only a few, carefully chosen fats in this book:

Lard. For a very long time, lard was the most widely used cooking fat in America. It was only in the twentieth century that the marketing of vegetable oils moved lard out of its central position. It deserves a place in your kitchen.

Proper lard, that is: unprocessed lard from pastured pigs. Even if you're eating grocery store meat, seek out a source of proper lard. Don't even consider the stuff in the grocery store. Not only does the grocery store junk have a less favorable fatty acid balance, but it's been bleached, and usually hydrogenated—you know, the process that creates trans fats.

Proper lard, on the other hand, is a lovely blend of mono-unsaturated and saturated fats, as healthful as can be. It's also one of the best dietary sources of vitamin D. Turns out pigs make vitamin D in their skin on sun exposure, just like we do, and that vitamin D is stored in the fat.

I buy lard in five-pound buckets from a local small farmer. At this writing, I'm paying $14, or just under $3/pound. Absolutely worth it. Any time I want a bland fat—for sautéing, pan-broiling, basting, or what-have-you—I reach for my lard. I keep the main bucket in my deep freeze, to keep it fresh, scooping out enough for about a week at a time into a smaller jar that I keep by the stove.

Bacon grease. If you've spent the money for nitrate-free bacon from pasture-raised pigs, do not, for the love of all that's holy, throw away the grease. That's manna from heaven, as delicious as it is good for you. Similar fatty acid profile to lard, of course.

Coconut oil. Coconut oil is one of the most saturated fats available. Despite propaganda, that's a good thing. Why? Because saturated fats are extremely stable. Unlike polyunsaturates, they don't go rancid easily—coconut oil will keep a year without refrigeration, even when open—and do not cause inflammation in the body. Interestingly, they also help remove fat from your liver—this, according to Drs. Michael and Mary Dan Eades, of *Protein Power* fame, and I have no reason to doubt them.

Coconut oil has other benefits. It's loaded with lauric acid, a fatty acid that kills yeasts and fungi. Indeed, coconut oil is used to treat systemic yeast infection. It stimulates the thyroid, which can help with weight loss. It also has a very high content of medium-chain triglycerides, or MCTs. These fats can be used directly as fuel by the muscles, and so can be used for quick energy, without the letdown sugar brings.

There are two kinds of coconut oil: extra-virgin coconut oil and just plain coconut oil. The extra virgin is simply pressed from coconut meat, with no processing. It is extremely healthful, but it also has a distinct coconut aroma, which may or may not work with the recipe you're planning. There is also just plain "coconut oil," widely used in Indian cuisine. It's more processed, but still resists rancidity, will clear fat out of your liver, and provides quick energy to your muscles. It's also quite bland, which makes it suitable for a wider range of cooking purposes. It's up to you how strict you want to be. Personally, I think both are useful to keep on hand. (Of course, I write cookbooks for a living and have a remarkable variety of ingredients in the house.)

Olive oil. Olive oil is not authentically paleo, but it has a very long history of use and appears to be pretty benign. The paleo community has, for the very most part, embraced it. It is useful because more-saturated fats are not liquid at room temperature, making them unsuitable for salad dressings and the like. Too, if you're looking for a Mediterranean flavor, olive oil is essential.

I have called for two grades of olive oil in this book: Extra-virgin olive oil and "light" olive oil. Extra virgin is more nutritious, but it does have a pronounced flavor. This is wonderful in many uses, but occasionally I wanted a blander liquid fat. In these cases, I used "light" olive oil. The fatty acid balance, which I consider essential, is not substantially affected by the refining process used to make light olive oil. However, it is up to you whether you wish to use this more refined oil, and to decide if the stronger flavor of the extra-virgin olive oil will suit you in, say, mayonnaise.

There are other paleo fats. Indeed, the fat of any grass-fed or pastured meat is healthful and valuable for cooking. Tallow (beef dripping), chicken fat, fat from roasted marrow—it's all worth keeping and using as cooking fat. I didn't use them in these recipes because, for the most part, they can't be purchased, but rather have to be rendered in your kitchen. I'm guessing most of you don't want the hassle.

MEAT, POULTRY, AND FISH

It doesn't come any more paleo than game. If you have a hunter or fisherman in the house, thank him or her, and enjoy. However, I have only one game recipe in this book, a very nice venison chili. Why? Because neither my husband nor I hunt, and selling game is illegal in Indiana.

Most of us will be buying our meat. You can buy elk, venison, etc., at the specialty butcher, but it's sky-high, and around here it's farm raised, which makes it less than wild. So I've been cooking beef, pork, lamb, chicken, and turkey, and chances are you will, too.

Whenever possible, choose grass-fed or pasture-raised meat and poultry and wild-caught fish. Why?

For the past couple of decades, we've been given to believe that fish is better for us than red meat. This, we're told, is because fish is rich in omega-3 fatty acids, while red meat has less omega-3 and more omega-6. Not to mention those "dangerous" saturated fats. (Nice, stable, noninflammatory saturated fats. Saturated fats such as stearic acid, abundant in beef, which lowers LDL and raises HDL, just like olive oil.)

Turns out that this is only sort of true. *Wild-caught* fish is higher in omega-3 fatty acids than *feedlot* beef or pork. This is because fish, in the wild, eat their proper evolutionary diet—fish paleo, if you like. In the meanwhile, the steers and pigs are being crammed full of grains, soybeans, and other things nature never intended them to eat. They are, of course, fed grains and beans because those foods make them fat. Cows are natural grass-eaters. Their proper place in the food chain is turning grass into more concentrated foods—and, I might add, in the process fertilizing the grass. Pigs in the wild are omnivores, but certainly never evolved in tandem with huge fields of Roundup-soaked corn and soy. Acorns, beechnuts, windfall fruit, eggs, any small animal that gets in their way, and any carrion they can scavenge, but not corn and soybeans.

It turns out that if you feed cows and pigs their proper diets, they're leaner than feedlot animals, but what fat there is has a high concentration of omega-3 fatty acids. Conversely, if you farm fish and feed them corn and soybeans, they're fatter than their wild-caught counterparts, but far less of that fat is omega-3.

It's not mammal versus fish. It's a question of animals eating the diet they evolved for, versus the same grains and beans the agricultural industry is trying to shovel into us.

Grass-fed beef and lamb and pastured pork and chickens are pricier than meat raised in controlled animal feedlot operations (CAFOs). After all, CAFOs exist because they can raise a whole lot of meat, very quickly, with minimum work. They're bad for the animals, the environment, and your health, all three, but they do produce cheap meat.

And, frankly, I think that cheap meat is more healthful than grains. A lot of people have made a lot of mileage, health-wise, simply by dropping grains and beans for meat, even the cheap stuff. I would sooner eat CAFO beef or pork than organic whole wheat bread and pasta.

That said, grass-fed and pastured meats and wild-caught fish are dramatically better for your health and the planet than the cheap stuff at the grocery store. If you can possibly afford them, buy them. Many people find that the most economical way to do this is to buy a deep freezer—an investment, to be sure—and then purchase grass-fed beef by the half or quarter steer. I live in farm country, and many local small farms only sell their meat this way, direct to the consumer. All of their animals are spoken for before slaughter, then they have the meat processed and wrapped for the freezer. At this writing, prices hover somewhere between $4 and $5/pound. That sounds high for ground chuck, but it's cheap for prime rib and porterhouse, so these things balance out.

Buying pork in bulk is not a winning a proposition. Pork simply doesn't freeze as well as beef. After about six months in the freezer it develops an off-taste all the spices in the world can't disguise. Still, it's worth negotiating bulk prices for as much pork as you're likely to eat in 6 months.

Chicken freezes well, but a side of chicken isn't going to last you long. See if a local small farm will cut you a deal if you buy, say, a dozen chickens at a time. They'll be cheaper if you buy them whole than if you get them cut up. Consider investing in a poultry shears—cutting a chicken into quarters isn't hard.

Lamb is virtually all grass-fed, so the grocery store stuff is comparable to the small-farm stuff. Still, you may be able to get a deal if you buy a whole lamb, processed for the freezer.

Where do you find these small farmers? Around here, we have an excellent farmer's market on Saturdays, almost an embarrassment of riches. As with everything else, you can also find small farms online. Google "grass-fed meat" or "pastured pork" and your region, and see what you find.

A wonderful option is community supported agriculture, or CSAs. These are popping up around the country. You buy a share in a farm's annual yield in advance, then receive regular "shares" of whatever they produce, with the cost averaging out to lower than retail. Many CSAs specialize in produce—nothing wrong with that—but others also offer grass-fed meats or pastured eggs. Take a look at www.localharvest.org/csa to see if there is such a farm near you.

About bacon. Processed meats are not particularly paleo, and most of them are injected with solutions that contain sugar and nitrates. Accordingly, I have left out most cured meats, including ham and commercial sausages. The exception is bacon. Why? Because everybody loves it, of course, and because a modest quantity of bacon can elevate a run-of-the-mill dish to superstar status. Anyway, all the paleo folks I know eat bacon.

If all you've ever had is grocery store bacon, you're in for a treat. Get yourself some small-farm bacon from pastured pigs. Expensive, but insanely good, and free of the usual chemical additives.

Nuts and Seeds

Kurt Harris, of the *Archevore* blog, feels that nuts should be eaten sparingly, because many of them are rich sources of omega-6 fatty acids. He has a point, but I respectfully disagree.

I suspect our hunter-gatherer ancestors ate all the nuts they could gather. After all, they're a rich source of calories, and they naturally keep well. Gather all the nuts you can find in the autumn, and on winter days when it's too nasty to go hunting you can sit around the fire, cracking nuts and telling stories. Too, nuts neither run nor fight back, qualities I suspect our ancestors greatly appreciated.

So you will find nuts used throughout this book, particularly almonds, pecans, walnuts, pine nuts, and pistachios. Generally I started with raw, shelled nuts that I purchased in bulk at the health food store. The exception is pistachios, which I could only purchase locally already roasted and salted. If you can find raw pistachios, grab them! You can easily toast them in the oven.

I have also used coconut quite a lot. Coconut is one of the ultimate hunter-gatherer foods: They don't run or fight back, they're big, they contain a lot of food for the effort, they provide both food and drink, they're loaded with calories, and they keep well. Add to that the notable benefits of coconut oil, and the exceptional fiber content, and coconut has to be considered a superfood. Youcan, if you like, buy whole fresh coconuts, crack them, and shred the meat, but I confess to taking the easy route: I buy shredded, unsweetened coconut in bulk at a local health food store. At this writing, it costs me $3/pound. Look for a place that sells coconut in bulk and has a good turnover for the best deals and the freshest product.

The "nuts" you will not find in this book are peanuts and cashews. I love them both, but neither are true nuts, and neither is edible raw. In fact, raw cashews contain the same chemical irritant found in poison ivy! (The "raw" cashews you see at the health food store have actually been steamed to destroy the toxin.) Peanuts are a legume, not a nut.

The seeds I've used most in this book are sunflower and pumpkin. Both of these are New World foods and were used by Native Americans. I've used flaxseed meal in a few recipes, but feel that it's actually unlikely hunter-gatherers ate much flax. The seeds are too small to make them worth gathering, and the hulls so tough that, unground, they pass whole through the digestive tract. I've used a few sesame seeds here and there, and the occasional splash of dark sesame oil for flavor, but again, sesame seeds are so tiny it seems unlikely that hunter-gatherers would have bothered with them very often.

NUT MILKS

Almond milk. Some paleo cookbooks call for almond milk, but all the packaged almond milk I have found is replete with additives. I did not use it for this book. I have, however, occasionally used Silk and Blue Diamond brands of unsweetened almond milk in the past, and can tell you they are good-tasting products. If the additives are acceptable to you, have at it.

Coconut milk. It is entirely possible to make coconut milk at home; I did it a few times while writing this book. If you want to be seriously paleo kosher, you certainly may do this; you'll find instructions on page 28. You can use this homemade coconut milk for any recipe in the book that calls for it, though you'll find it's a bit thinner than canned.

I overwhelmingly used canned coconut milk. Indeed, it was the only canned product I used regularly, and I went through several cans per week. That's why I bought it—I used a *lot* of coconut milk, enough that making my own was a hassle. So I bought organic coconut milk a half-a-dozen cans at a time—mostly Thai Kitchen brand, but any organic coconut milk should be fine. Confession: Thai Kitchen Organic Coconut Milk contains guar gum, which is not "paleo kosher." There are a few brands of canned coconut milk that contain nothing but coconut and water; if it matters to you, read labels.

All of these recipes were developed using full-fat coconut milk. Coconut oil is very healthful stuff, and my body is happiest on a high-fat diet, so low-fat coconut milk simply made no sense. You can try it if you prefer, but I can't vouch for the results.

Some coconut milk comes in 13.5-ounce (400 ml) cans, and some in 14-ounce (425 ml) cans. A half ounce more or less is not going to make a difference in any of these recipes, so don't sweat it.

Just recently I have seen thinner, more pourable coconut milks, meant for drinking These are packaged in cartons, like dairy milk. So Delicious company makes one, and so does Silk. These do have additives, though the So Delicious sugar-free coconut milk doesn't have anything that strikes me as really obnoxious. Silk coconut milk has added evaporated cane juice, a.k.a. Sucanat, which explains why it has 7 grams of carbohydrate per cup. Of the two, I'd take the So Delicious brand. But be aware that these are substantially thinner than canned coconut milk, and not what these recipes were standardized on.

SALT

As I mentioned in the "Paleo or Not Paleo" section, I'm not in favor of eliminating salt. I am, however, in favor of eliminating standard grocery store table salt, which bears little resemblance to the salt available to our ancestors. Grocery store salt is refined to eliminate all minerals except for sodium and chlorine, often with iodine added as well. Other stuff is added, largely to keep the salt from caking in damp weather. One popular brand of table salt includes sodium silicoaluminate, dextrose, potassium iodide, sodium bicarbonate. Yep, dextrose, as in sugar. Yuck.

Sea salt, on the other hand, contains a wide variety of trace minerals. It shouldn't contain any noxious additives, either. Just one problem: Our seas and oceans are sadly polluted. There is, however, a way around this: mined sea salt. All around the world, there are deposits of salt that

are remnants of ancient seas. This salt was deposited long before mankind was around, much less had a chance to dump chemicals in the oceans. This is the finest and most nutritious—and most paleo—salt you can use.

I use a brand called Real Salt, mined in Utah, while friends of mine favor salt from deposits in the Himalayas. (And how long ago does an ocean have to have dried up to have left salt in the Himalayas?!) Any salt from ancient deposits should be fine, so long as nothing is added. Your ancient sea bed salt will not be pure white—the stuff I get is pale pink, as is a lot of Himalayan salt. Pure white salt is suspect.

Good salt is more expensive than table salt; at this writing I pay $7 for 26 ounces of Real Salt. I pay it gladly; I consider good salt a very important part of my nutritional plan, and I have been using it for many years.

Be aware that unadulterated salt will clump in damp weather. The only solution I have is the old tradition of the salt dish, in place of the saltshaker—just put a small dish of salt on the table, pinch up a bit, and sprinkle as needed.

SWEETENERS

There aren't a lot of paleo sweeteners. Our paleo ancestors simply didn't sweeten things much. The most paleo thing you can do is to stop expecting to eat sweet stuff with any regularity.

That said, there are a very few sweeteners that at least some paleo folks would have been acquainted with, and that I have used in this book.

Honey. I mention honey with trepidation, because it has a good reputation it does not deserve. It's sugar. Yes, raw organic honey has some enzymes and a little pollen in it, but it's more than 99 percent sugar. It will spike blood sugar and cause an insulin release just like table sugar will.

That said, there's little doubt that those cavemen who shared their environment with honeybees did, indeed, eat honey when they found it. (Honeybees are not native to the New World. They were brought by European settlers.) However, the discovery of a bee tree would have been an occasional thing, and getting to the honey would have involved some risk. It would have taken some sophistication to create vessels for carrying and storing honey. I suspect that the discovery of a bee tree would have occasioned a party, but that day-to-day consumption of honey was virtually nil.

I cannot caution you strongly enough: Do not seize on "Honey is paleo!" as an excuse to eat honey-sweetened cookies, cakes, and other desserts on a regular basis. I have, however, used some honey in this book, both in desserts and in some sauces, condiments, and the like.

Maple syrup. This one is iffier. Forty gallons of maple sap boil down to just one gallon of maple syrup. Surely that calls for as much technology as cooking grains and beans. Still, you can drink maple sap raw, and again, maple syrup has a reputation as being "natural," so some paleo folks use it. I've included maple syrup in just a few recipes, largely for its incomparable flavor.

Like honey, maple syrup has a few nutrients in it, but derives 99 percent of its calories from sugar. Govern yourself accordingly.

Sucanat. This is unrefined sugar cane juice that has been dried and ground to a coarse powder. It tastes a lot like brown sugar, though the texture is different. I don't think it's strictly paleo, but it seems as paleo as maple syrup to me. Folks who live where sugarcane is grown have long chewed on the cane itself as a sweet treat. I've only used Sucanat in a couple of recipes. Buy Sucanat at health food stores.

Stevia. For the uninitiated, stevia is a South American shrub with very sweet leaves. That sweetness comes not from sugar, but from *steviosides*, naturally occurring super-sweet compounds exclusive to the stevia plant. This means that stevia is virtually carb free, with no effect on blood sugar.

I have no doubt at all that South American hunter-gatherers figured out that the stevia plant's leaves were a tasty addition to their diet. Unlike honey, the stevia shrub isn't guarded by bees, and unlike maple syrup it doesn't require fire, huge vats, and long, tedious boiling to yield a useful sweetener. Nor did you need jugs to store it.

You can buy dried stevia leaves, and this would be the most authentically paleo form. The leaves are also hard to use, with a flavor some compare to licorice, and a bitter undertaste. I have used the whole herb in only one recipe in this book, for iced tea.

Extracted steviosides are available as a fine white powder. The stuff is unbelievably sweet, and again, can have a bitter undertaste. Again, I find it hard to use.

There are stevia blends on the market, some of which are good, but I'm not sure the various things they're blended with can be considered paleo—Stevia in the Raw is blended with maltodextrin, while Truvia is blended with erythritol.

The form of stevia I have found easiest to use, and consider acceptably paleo, is liquid stevia extract. This comes in dropper bottles and is generally blended either with water, glycerin (a fraction of fat, so hardly a stranger to the human diet), or alcohol—so little alcohol per drop that it should have virtually no impact on your body. Liquid stevia comes both plain and in flavors. In particular, I have used both French vanilla and chocolate liquid stevia in this book. My plain liquid stevia is from NuNaturals, while the flavored stuff is the NOW Better Stevia brand, but I see no reason why other brands shouldn't work fine. I buy mine at local health food stores. If you don't have a good health food store in town, you can, of course, order your liquid stevia online.

In many recipes I have combined honey with liquid stevia, the honey for texture, and the stevia to bring the recipe up to the desired sweetness without additional sugar.

Fruit. Fruit can lend sweetness to dishes, and I've used various fruits for that purpose in this book. Again, the sweetness in fruit comes from sugar, though of course fruit is not the concentrated source of sugar that honey or maple syrup are. (see note, right) If you've got blood sugar trouble, you'll want to keep an eye on even this source of sugar.

The big exception here is dates. Dates are candy that grows on trees, and very likely were eaten by preagricultural man. They derive 96 percent of their calories from sugar. If you have never been obese, and have no blood sugar trouble, dates, eaten occasionally, are an acceptable paleo treat. And you could consider using tiny quantities of date sugar—dried dates ground to a coarse powder—as a sweetener. But, like honey and maple syrup, it's still basically sugar. I haven't used it in any recipes, because, quite honestly, my blood sugar doesn't like it.

That's pretty much it for paleo sweeteners.

If you've never been obese, never had blood sugar problems or any of the associated health problems, and have always been athletic, you may ignore the following message.

Note for those of you who, like me, are profoundly carbohydrate intolerant: My body doesn't care how paleo honey is. It says honey is sugar, and it doesn't like sugar. Same for maple syrup.

There are substitutes available for these ingredients. They are not paleo; they are made from sugar alcohol (polyol) syrup, generally maltitol, xylitol, sorbitol, or a combination. They do sometimes contain artificial flavors. There is no chance any caveman even conceived of them.

I use them anyway. I have a lot of experience with these sweeteners, enough to know that they function the same as their natural counterparts in recipes. I have never had a recipe fail because of a honey-for-imitation-honey swap, or sugar-free-pancake-syrup-for-maple-syrup. And I am convinced that given my medical history, they are a better choice for me than honey and maple syrup.

Decide for yourself which is more important, paleo authenticity or keeping your blood sugar down, and make your choices accordingly. If you do have blood sugar problems, your glucometer is your friend. Let it guide you.

THICKENERS

What to do when you want to thicken a gravy, a sauce, a soup? Cornstarch is not paleo, and wheat flour is right out. The low-carb thickeners I've used all along, guar and xanthan, are not strictly paleo kosher—guar comes from a legume, while xanthan is created by growing a particular bacteria in glucose. (Okay, that's kinda-sorta paleo, since cavemen were, no doubt, exposed to both bacteria and glucose. Still . . .)

There are two paleo thickeners I'm aware of:

Arrowroot. Arrowroot is a starch derived from the root of a tropical plant. It is, indeed, edible raw. Arrowroot is used similarly to cornstarch. Like cornstarch, it is pure starch—a carbohydrate, and a highly refined one at that. Because of this, I prefer not to use it, and have not used it in this book. However, if your blood sugar and waistline are more impressive than mine, you might try it.

If you do, be aware that arrowroot only thickens with heating. This means it works for gravies, sauces, and the like, but not for smoothies, or other cold applications. Remove arrowroot-thickened dishes from the heat as soon as they thicken, as arrowroot loses its thickening power with prolonged heat. Arrowroot is a more powerful thickener than cornstarch or wheat flour—substitute 2 teaspoons of arrowroot for 1 tablespoon (8 g) of cornstarch, or 1 teaspoon (3 g) of arrowroot for 2 tablespoons (10 g) of wheat flour.

Glucomannan. My paleo thickener of choice is glucomannan. Like guar or xanthan, it is a finely milled soluble fiber powder that thickens without heat. However, glucomannan comes from a Japanese root called *konyaku*, or *konjac*, a traditional food, and one that does not require cooking to be edible. Because konjac is edible raw, this seems acceptably paleo to me, especially since the quantity used in any dish will be very small.

Glucomannan is a much more powerful thickener even than arrowroot, and it is easy to overdo it. I find the easiest way to use fiber-based thickeners of this sort is to keep them in an old salt or spice shaker. When you have a gravy or soup to thicken, start whisking it before you sprinkle in the glucomannan, or you will get lumps. Sprinkle the glucomannan *lightly* over the surface of your dish, whisking constantly, then wait a minute or two to see how thick it becomes before adding more. Glucomannan takes a few minutes to reach its full thickening power.

Unlike arrowroot, glucomannan will thicken without heat, so you can use it to thicken cold foods such as smoothies and salad dressings. Again, do not sprinkle

in the glucomannan and then stir or blend—instead, start whisking, or turn on the blender, then sprinkle in glucomannan sparingly.

Many health food stores carry glucomannan. Some even sell it in capsules, as a weight loss supplement. (The idea is that the swelling fiber will make you feel full, and whisk some of your calories through your body before they can be absorbed.) It also appears to help stabilize blood sugar. Again, if you can't find glucomannan locally, you can order it online. A pound of glucomannan should last you the better part of a year, at least, and very likely longer. So long as you keep glucomannan dry, it will not spoil.

Regarding Organic Produce

Your best option is fresh, locally grown organic produce in season. Many paleo folks turn to gardening, a wonderful idea. Others, though, may have neither the space nor the time. Most of us do buy quite a lot of our produce.

But for so many of us, the budget is perpetually a little tight, and occasionally downright vise-like. Too, some of you may not live where there's a farmers' market, and your local grocery store may have a limited selection of organic produce. Where best to put your money?

The Environmental Working Group (EWG) has compounded lists of the varieties of produce most likely and least likely to be contaminated with pesticides and other noxious chemicals. These were originally called the Dirty Dozen and the Clean Fifteen, but both lists have since been expanded. If the food budget is tight, it makes sense to buy organic when purchasing items from the first list, and save money by purchasing conventionally grown produce when buying foods on the second list.

First, the ones to watch out for. These are the foods that are most likely to be heavily contaminated, ranked in order, from dirtiest to least objectionable. If you're trying to leverage your organic food dollar, these are the items where it will most serve you to pony up the bucks:

1. Peaches
2. Apples
3. Sweet bell peppers
4. Celery
5. Nectarines
6. Strawberries
7. Cherries
8. Pears
9. Grapes (imported)
10. Spinach
11. Lettuce
12. Potatoes
13. Carrots
14. Green beans
15. Hot peppers
16. Cucumbers
17. Raspberries
18. Plums
19. Grapes (domestic)
20. Oranges

I am happy to report that the list of fruits and vegetables least likely to be badly contaminated has expanded to twenty-one items. According to the EWG, the following produce has the lowest pesticide load, ranked in order with the produce with the absolute lowest pesticides first.

1. Onion
2. Avocado
3. Sweet corn (frozen)
4. Pineapples
5. Mango
6. Asparagus
7. Sweet peas (frozen)
8. Kiwi
9. Bananas
10. Cabbage
11. Broccoli
12. Papaya
13. Blueberries
14. Cauliflower
15. Winter squash
16. Watermelon
17. Sweet potatoes
18. Tomatoes
19. Honeydew melon
20. Cantaloupe
21. Mushrooms

Because of these lists, I buy organic berries, lettuce, celery, and apples, but will buy the cheap onions in the net sack, conventional cabbage (always dirt cheap), and the big, pretty heads of cauliflower, a vegetable that, as you will see in this book, I use in a wide variety of ways.

Paleo Preservation?

Surely our hunter-gatherer ancestors ate quite a lot of their food fresh. Did they have any means of preservation?

I suspect they did. Finding wild fruit that had dried on the bush, and seeing that it didn't readily spoil, surely paleolithic folks figured out that they could gather berries when they were abundant and spread them in the sun, no doubt assigning a couple of kids to chase off marauding birds. They can't have failed to notice that the antelope they killed in cold weather stayed fresh considerably longer than meat killed in the summer. (I have a mental image of Ogg and Grok ducking out of the cave, into the snow, just long enough to hack another roast off of the mammoth carcass outside. I do not doubt this happened.)

Accordingly, most paleo plans allow dried fruit. I have used dried fruit as an ingredient in some of these recipes, but I would caution you to be careful with the stuff. It's a very concentrated source of sugar—natural sugar, but sugar nonetheless. A 1.5-ounce (43 g) snack-size box of raisins contains 34 grams of sugar. That's just five grams less than a 12-ounce (355 ml) can of soda. Yet because dried fruit is so compact, it doesn't feel like you're eating a lot. If you have no blood sugar problems, are not prone to obesity, and get a great deal of exercise, treat dried fruit as paleo candy. If you have to keep a constant eye on your blood sugar and your waistline, dried fruit must be considered a fringe food, an occasional ingredient, not a staple.

Other things can be dried, of course. Dehydrators are sold with the idea of homemade jerky, and surely this is better for you than the stuff at the mini-mart. If you garden, you can make your own dried tomatoes, much cheaper than the sundried ones I buy in a jar. Mushrooms dry beautifully. Herbs can be dried, though some hold their flavor better than others. Oregano and other members of the mint family, rosemary, and sage all hold a lot of aroma and flavor, but dried parsley and cilantro aren't worth the shelf space.

If you have dogs, there is no better or more nutritious dog treat than thin slices of organic liver, dried till they're brittle. Doesn't your best friend deserve healthful food, too?

As for freezing, I feel that there is no reason to scorn plain, unadulterated frozen food, particularly meat. If you're serious about this, the day will come when you want to invest in a quarter or a side of grass-fed beef, and a deep freezer is the only sensible way to store it. Surely you don't want to make 200 pounds (91 kg) of jerky? (That said, I have a great jerky recipe in here.)

Similarly, I see no reason not to freeze your garden surplus. I also think that plain frozen fruits and vegetables (as opposed to the ones with pasta or sauce or other unpaleo additives) are an acceptable stand-in for fresh.

With both these kinds of preserved foods, you will want to keep an eye on those clean-versus-dirty produce lists. If you're buying frozen strawberries, buy frozen organic strawberries.

Canning is distinctly unpaleo, having been invented just two hundred years ago, as a way of preserving food for Napoleon's armies. I have used canned tomato paste and tomato sauce in just a few recipes in this book, because cooking down tomatoes for paste is a job that I quite honestly do not want, and I suspect that few of you do, either. Again, it is recommended that you use organic products. Because tomatoes are acidic, and leach chemicals, look for products packed in glass jars, or in cans labeled "BPA-free."

Regarding Microwave Ovens

I use my microwave all the time, not just for reheating leftovers, but for cooking, especially for steaming vegetables. I know of no simpler nor more satisfactory method, and my Tupperware microwave steamer is out of the cabinet more often than in it. Further, I have seen some fairly convincing arguments for microwave steaming of vegetables retaining more nutrients than most other cooking methods.

However, I suspect that at least some of the people who buy this book will be appalled that I would even consider using a microwave. There is a faction that considers them, and all food cooked in them, to be horribly dangerous.

I'm not going to argue the point here. Just take it as read that anything I steam in my microwave, you are welcome to steam on your stovetop.

And remember that, technically speaking, all cooking is nonpaleo.

Chapter 1

FOUNDATIONAL RECIPES

In this chapter you will find a few recipes not for dishes, but rather for ingredients, things that are called for in other recipes throughout the book. Because so many commercially packaged ingredients we have long relied on contain sugar, dairy, bad fats, or other objectionable ingredients, making some of these staples becomes a part of creating a lively, varied low-carb cuisine. Just like the commercially produced versions we're turning away from, once you have these in your kitchen, you will reach for them over and over again. And once you get used to making them, you'll realize they're really no big deal.

Broth Concentrate

For years I have used bouillon concentrate as a flavoring, especially for Cauli-Rice dishes. (See page 87 for the lowdown on Cauli-Rice.) But even the best bouillon concentrate has sugar and other unpaleo ingredients. This takes time, but almost no hands-on work, and a batch lasts me for a couple of months.

6 cups (1.4 L) chicken or beef broth

This, of course, is best with homemade bone broth or stock. (See page 255.) Just put your broth in a heavy saucepan and put it over a very low burner. Let it simmer till it's reduced to ½ cup (120 ml). Put it in a snap-top container and stash it in the freezer.

YIELD: ½ cup (120 ml), 8 servings

Nutritional Analysis
Per serving: 29 calories; 1 g fat; 4 g protein; 1 g carbohydrate; 0 g dietary fiber; 1 g net carbs

A step up from simple concentrated broth is:

Slow-Cooker Demi-Glace

Don't even attempt this with anything less than good, homemade beef stock! After all, the point is concentrating the flavor—you want to concentrate great flavor!

8 cups (2 L) beef stock
2 shallots, minced
1 cup (235 ml) dry red wine

So easy! Just combine everything in your slow cooker. Cover and set on high for an hour or two, to bring it up to heat fairly quickly. Once it's hot, uncover the pot and turn it down to low. Now leave it alone. For a long time. Leave it alone until you've got about 1 cup (320 g) of syrupy liquid left. Scrape it into a snap-top container and stash it in the freezer.

To use, thaw it just enough so you can scoop out a spoonful or two. Use to give a quick hit of flavor to sauces, gravies, Cauli-Rice dishes, all sorts of things.

YIELD: 1 cup, (325 g), 16 servings

Nutritional Analysis
Per serving: 22 calories; trace fat; trace protein; 1 g carbohydrate; 0 g dietary fiber; 1g net carbs

NOTE

This is based on a classical French recipe, except that the French usually make demi-glace with veal stock. I find beef bones easier to find and cheaper to buy than veal bones, and this tastes fantastic.

Coconut Milk

The canned stuff is ubiquitous anymore, but if you'd like to make your own, here's how. It's simple, and cheaper than canned, too. That said, I confess I mostly use organic canned coconut milk.

2 cups (60 g) shredded coconut meat
4 cups (950 ml) water

Have a strainer lined with a double layer of cheesecloth in a big bowl standing by.

Combine the coconut meat and water in a saucepan and bring to a simmer. Let it cook for 5 minutes.

Now transfer the whole thing to your blender and run the blender for 5 minutes, scraping down the sides as necessary.

Pour the whole kaboodle into the cheesecloth-lined strainer. Let it cool a while, then press good and hard with the back of a spoon. When it's cool enough, gather up the edges of the cheesecloth into a bag, twist it closed, and squeeze the whole thing dry. You can now dry out the coconut and use it for baking, if you like—I just feed mine to my chickens.

Store your coconut milk in a tightly lidded jar or snap-top container in the fridge and use it up within a few days. You can also use it to make Cocoyo (recipe follows).

YIELD: About 3 cups (700 ml)

Nutritional Analysis
Total for the whole batch—well, MasterCook says: 566 calories; 54 g fat; 5 g protein; 24 g carbohydrate; 14 g dietary fiber; 10 g net carbs. But MasterCook can't calculate the value of the coconut you strain out. Sorry.

NOTE
If you decide you want to go the homemade coconut milk route, you might buy a fine-mesh strainer to use instead of the cheesecloth. Simpler, and you can throw it in the dishwasher.

Cocoyo (Coconut Milk Yogurt)

This was the recipe that took the most work and experimentation, and I confess the results were variable. Let me explain to you how I went about it, and what I learned:

The basic idea is the same as making dairy yogurt: Add yogurt bacteria to coconut milk, then incubate at a low temperature for about 10 to 12 hours. (I use an old electric heating pad set on low, tucked down into a bowl to hold it up around the yogurt container.) For the most part, the results are thinner than dairy yogurt—even pourable—but do have a "yogurty" flavor. I have found that the canned organic coconut milk with guar thickener added makes a somewhat thicker, more consistent yogurt than homemade coconut milk, but guar is not paleo kosher.

Linda Vander Voort, who tested recipes for me, figured out that adding 1 tablespoon (14 g) unflavored gelatin to 2 cans' worth of coconut milk—that's 28 fluid ounces (825 ml), a little over 3 cups—creates a thicker, spoonable

Cocoyo. I tried it, and it works nicely. If you'd like to do this, pour your coconut milk into a saucepan and sprinkle the gelatin powder on top. Slowly heat to hottest-tap-water temperature, and whisk the gelatin in till there are no lumps. Let it cool before you add your yogurt culture.

While canned coconut milk is sterile, homemade coconut milk must be heated before culturing, to kill any less-than-friendly germs. You don't want to culture them along with the good ones. Again, getting your coconut milk to about the same temperature as the hottest possible tap water should do fine. Add the gelatin as you do this. Again, cool before adding culture.

I tried several cultures for making Cocoyo. Originally, I used Yogourmet yogurt culture, purchased at my local health food store. This worked well and yielded the tartest, most yogurty results. However, Yogourmet contains milk powder and a little sugar, making it, too, not paleo kosher. I tried culturing a second batch using the first (sometimes called "serial yogurting") and it worked very well, yielding a similar result. The quantity of milk and sugar in the second-generation Cocoyo would be small indeed.

It is my experience that you can only take serial yogurting so far. After four or five iterations, you start to get weird results, and the only solution is to start again with fresh culture. If you initially used Yogourmet or a similar product, you would have to accept that every now and then you'd have a batch that included a little milk and sugar.

I tried a dairy-free yogurt culture I ordered online, called GI ProStart. I was unimpressed with the results, which barely tasted any different from plain coconut milk. I prefer a tarter Cocoyo.

I also tried using dairy- and sugar-free probiotic capsules from the health food store, pulling them apart and adding the contents to my coconut milk. It did not work; I noticed no change after culturing. It may be that I got a dead batch of probiotics, I suppose; I have had success in the past making dairy yogurt by this method.

Finally, I tried using So Delicious brand coconut yogurt as a starter. This worked pretty well and eliminated the dairy found in the Yogourmet. Why not just use the So Delicious coconut milk yogurt? It, too, has ingredients that are not paleo kosher, including tapioca maltodextrin and rice starch. Again, using a tablespoon (15 g) or two (30 g) as culture for your own Cocoyo will yield a product with near-homeopathic levels of nonpaleo-kosher ingredients, especially by the second iteration.

I should warn you that often I have made Cocoyo that was uninspiring when first incubated, sort of gray and watery, but that improved vastly with a few days' chilling. Knowing this will keep you from throwing away a perfectly good batch of Cocoyo in disgust because it looks sort of funny. Chill it, then see.

Despite all this futzing around, I find Cocoyo to be a very useful ingredient to have around the kitchen, especially for sauces, salad dressings, and the like. I urge you to find a coconut milk and a culture you like. Once you've discovered this, making Cocoyo is very simple and takes almost no hands-on time.

Coconut Sour Cream

I was so happy when I figured out how to do this!

14 fluid ounces (425 ml) unsweetened coconut milk
Yogurt culture (see Cocoyo recipe, page 28)

Refrigerate your coconut milk and let it sit for at least a few days—you want all of the cream to rise to the top and separate from the watery part.

(continued)

Now spoon the thick, creamy part off of your coconut milk and put it in a snap-top container. Add yogurt culture and whisk it up.

Incubate just like yogurt—I did mine overnight, using an electric heating pad set on low.

My coconut sour cream was uninspiring at first—kind of gray and not as thick as I'd hoped. But after refrigerating overnight, it was gorgeous. There was a thin layer of hardened coconut oil on top; you can stir that in or simply spoon it off, whichever you prefer.

Be aware: Sometimes a batch of Cocoyo will separate into a thick top layer with watery liquid underneath—very much like dairy yogurt sometimes does. You can whisk it up, if you like, and use it as Cocoyo, but you can also spoon the thick part into another container to use for sour cream, discarding the liquid.

YIELD: 1 cup (28 g), 8 servings

Nutritional Analysis
Per serving: 97 calories; 10 g fat; 1 g protein; 1 g carbohydrate; 0 g dietary fiber; 1 g net carbs

NOTE

I've read of people draining coconut milk yogurt in a coffee-filter-lined sieve, the way dairy yogurt is drained to create Greek yogurt. I tried this and was unimpressed by the results. I think it's far easier to scoop off the coconut cream and culture it alone, and when you have a batch of Cocoyo that naturally separates, all you have to do is pour off the liquid. No coffee filter needed.

Pork Rind Crumbs

This is almost not a recipe, but I've found that often folks don't think of this themselves, so here it is. By the way, the only reason this recipe calls for 3 ounces (85 g) is that this made an even 1 cup (50 g) of crumbs. Make more if you like. Great as a filler for meat loaves and the like, or for "breading" fish, chicken, or chops.

3 ounces (85 g) pork rinds

Put 'em in the food processor and run till you have fine crumbs. Use in meat loaves, to "bread" fish or chops, all sorts of ways. Store in an airtight container in the refrigerator.

NOTES

Pork rinds, far from being the nutritional anathema many folks assume, are the most nutritious thing in the snack aisle. Among other things, pork rinds are a terrific source of gelatin, which is wonderful for your joints, will do good things for your nails and hair, and is anti-inflammatory. So much for pork rinds being bad for you. Read the label; you want them to contain nothing but "pork skins" or "pork rinds." Especially avoid any rinds fried in soy or canola oils, or other vegetable oils.

To make Italian Seasoned Crumbs, add to each cup (50 g) of Pork Rind Crumbs:

½ teaspoon dried parsley
½ teaspoon dried oregano
¼ teaspoon garlic powder
¼ teaspoon onion powder

YIELD: 2 tablespoons (57 g), 8 servings

Nutritional Analysis
Per serving: 58 calories; 3 g fat; 7 g protein; 0 g carbohydrate; 0 g dietary fiber

Coconut Butter

Coconut butter is deservedly popular among paleo folks, but it's also very pricey—$12 a pound at this writing. Fortunately, it's dead simple to make yourself, and shredded coconut is cheap!

3 cups (240 g) shredded coconut meat

You'll need a good food processor for this, but if you eat a lot of coconut butter, this recipe alone will pay for a Cuisinart pretty quickly. Just put your coconut in the food processor with the S blade in place and run the sucker for 12 to 15 minutes. Stop once or twice during that time to scrape down the sides, just to make sure everything gets ground up evenly. That's it. Sum total of the effort involved in making coconut butter.

YIELD: 1 cup (224 g)

Nutritional Analysis
Per batch: 850 calories; 80 g fat; 8 g protein; 37 g carbohydrate; 22 g dietary fiber; 15 g net carb

NOTE

I used 3 cups (240 g) in this recipe because that's the quantity of shredded coconut that I found made exactly 1 cup (224 g) of coconut butter. But actually, my big, professional-model Cuisinart will handle more than that, and the stuff keeps well, because coconut oil doesn't go rancid easily. (Just another benefit of it being so saturated!) So if you have a good, big food processor, feel free to make a bigger batch.

If you're feeling particularly hard core, you can buy a fresh coconut, crack it, pry out the meat, and so on. I don't bother. I just scoop lovely unsweetened, shredded coconut out of a bin. By the way, 3 cups (240 g) of shredded coconut weigh about 9 ounces (255 g), so 4 cups should equal a 1-pound (450 g) jar of coconut butter. At this writing, I pay $3/pound for bulk shredded coconut at Sahara Mart, my local health food store; that's a lot cheaper than $12/pound! However, the other health food store in town doesn't have coconut in bulk and charges $4 for a 7-ounce (200 g) packet. The moral of the story is find a store that carries shredded coconut in bulk!

Chapter 2

APPETIZERS, SNACKS, AND PARTY FOOD

I find the question, "What can I have for a snack?" funny. The answer, of course, is, "A smaller portion of anything you might eat at a meal." To our grandparents (or, for you young 'uns, great-grandparents), a snack was an apple, or a half a sandwich, or the leftover drumstick from last night's chicken.

The processed-food industry has brainwashed us into equating "snack" with "salty, crunchy, starchy substance eaten out of a Mylar bag." I hope this chapter gives you some better and more appealing ideas.

Then there's the question of party food. So much of the typical party food is junk. Happily, many of the best party foods, the ones that people oh and ah over, are fine for us. Who wouldn't rather have chicken wings and deviled eggs than tortilla chips and jarred salsa? You'll find here an array of finger foods that will do any party proud. I promise you, your friends will not be thinking, "Oh. Health food." They'll be thinking, "YUM!"

So let's talk good pick-up nibbles!

Mixed Nuts

Everyone loves mixed nuts, but peanuts and cashews are definitely not paleo, nor is the oil they're fried in. Plus here you can control the salt. And they taste better to boot! Look for bulk nuts at your health food store.

3 tablespoons (39 g) coconut oil
1 cup (135 g) Brazil nuts
1 cup (100 g) pecans
1 cup (135 g) hazelnuts
1 cup (145 g) almonds
Salt (optional)

Preheat your oven to 350°F (180°C, or or gas mark 4). While the oven is heating, put the coconut oil in a roasting pan and put it in the oven to melt.

When the oil is melted, add the nuts and stir it up till the nuts are all evenly coated. Roast for 12 to 15 minutes, stirring a couple of times in the process.
Add a little salt if you like. Then cool and store in an airtight container.

YIELD: 16 servings

Nutritional Analysis
Per serving: 232 calories; 23 g fat; 5 g protein; 5 g carbohydrate; 2 g dietary fiber; 3 g net carbs

Spiced Pecans

So good! Little containers of these would make nice holiday gifts for your paleo friends. Or anyone else, actually.

1 tablespoon (13 g) coconut oil
2½ teaspoons (6 g) ground cumin
2½ teaspoons (5 g) ground coriander
1½ teaspoons honey
½ teaspoon hot sauce
½ teaspoon black pepper
2 cups (200 g) pecan halves
Salt

Preheat oven to 300°F (150°C, or or gas mark 2).

In a small saucepan, melt the coconut oil and add everything else but the pecans and salt. Stir it all together very well.

Put your pecans in a roasting pan—line it with nonstick foil first, if you want easy cleanup. Pour the seasoning mixture over the pecan halves and stir it all up, till the nuts are evenly coated.

Slide your pecans into the oven and set your timer for 5 minutes. When it beeps, stir them, put them back in, and give 'em another 5. Stir one more time, give them another 3 to 5 minutes, and pull them out. Cool, salt them lightly if you wish, and store in a snap-top container—for the roughly 36 hours before you've devoured them all.

YIELD: 8 servings

Nutritional Analysis
Per serving: 203 calories; 20 g fat; 2 g protein; 7 g carbohydrate; 2 g dietary fiber; 5 g net carbs

Spiced Almonds

These will erase all thought of cocktail peanuts from your mind.

2 cups (290 g) shelled almonds
2 tablespoons (28 ml) olive oil
½ teaspoon paprika
½ teaspoon ground cumin
Salt (optional)

I blanched my almonds (removed the brown skins) to make this, though you don't have to. If you'd like to, put them in a bowl and cover them with boiling water. Let them sit until they're just cool enough to handle, and you'll find that the skins are loosened and pop off—most of them should come off with a squeeze. Drain your almonds well and if you have the time, let them dry for several hours or even overnight.

Now preheat your oven to 350°F (180°C, or or gas mark 4). Put the oil in a roasting pan and add the almonds, blanched or not. Stir them around till they're all coated with the oil, then spread them out in a single layer.

Roast for 20 to 30 minutes, stirring them a couple of times in the process—spread them out in a single layer again after stirring. If you blanched them, you're looking for a pretty golden color all over. If you didn't, you'll just have to bite one and see if it's crunchy enough.

When they're done and crunchy, stir in the spices and the salt, if using. Fabulous warm or cold.

YIELD: 8 servings

Nutritional Analysis
Per serving: 240 calories; 22 g fat; 7 g protein; 7 g carbohydrate; 4 g dietary fiber; 3 g net carbs

Rosemary Walnuts

Subtle but dazzling.

2½ tablespoons (33 g) coconut oil
2 teaspoons ground rosemary
¼ teaspoon cayenne
2 cups (200 g) walnuts
Salt (optional)

Preheat oven to 300°F (150°C, or gas mark 2).

While the oven's heating, put the coconut oil in a roasting pan and put it in the oven. Give it a few minutes to melt the oil.

When the oil is melted, pull out the pan and measure the rosemary and cayenne into the pan. Stir them into the coconut oil until they're evenly distributed.

Now add the walnuts to the pan. Stir very well, making sure they're all evenly coated with the seasoned oil, then spread them in an even layer. Put the pan back in the oven and set your timer for 5 minutes.

When the timer beeps, stir your walnuts well—I used a rubber scraper and scraped the seasoned oil up off the bottom of the pan as I stirred, to work it into the walnuts better. Again, spread in an even layer and put them back in the oven. Set your timer for another 5 minutes.

Repeat the stirring and put them back for 5 more minutes. Then cool, salt if desired, and store in a snap-top container.

YIELD: 8 servings

Nutritional Analysis
Per serving: 227 calories; 22 g fat; 8 g protein; 4 g carbohydrate; 2 g dietary fiber; 0 mg cholesterol; trace sodium.

Cajun Pecans

Super-easy, super-addictive.

2 tablespoons (26 g) coconut oil
2 cups (200 g) pecans
1 tablespoon (7 g) Cajun Seasoning (page 286)

Preheat oven to 350°F (180°C, or gas mark 4). While it's heating, put the coconut oil in a roasting pan and stick it in the oven for a few minutes to melt.

When the oil has melted, dump your pecans into the pan and stir till they're all coated. Now spread evenly and put them back in the oven. Give them 10 minutes.

Pull them out of the oven, stir in the Cajun Seasoning, and let them cool. Store in a snap-top container.

YIELD: 8 servings

Nutritional Analysis
Per serving: 213 calories; 22 g fat; 2 g protein; 6 g carbohydrate; 2 g dietary fiber; 4 g net carbs

Wasabi Almonds

I loved canned wasabi almonds until I read the label. Between the soy oil and the wheat, I gave 'em up. Here's my version!

1 tablespoon (13 g) coconut oil
2 cups (290 g) almonds
2 tablespoons (28 ml) coconut aminos
2 teaspoons wasabi powder
2 teaspoons garlic powder
Salt (optional)

Preheat oven to 350°F (180°C, or gas mark 4). Put the coconut oil on a shallow baking pan—I used a jelly roll pan—and put it in the oven while it heats, to melt the oil.

When the oil is melted, add the almonds to the tray and stir until the almonds are all evenly coated with the oil. Put them in the oven and set your timer for 5 minutes.

When the timer beeps, stir your almonds, then put them back in for another 5 minutes.

Timer beeped again! Pull your almonds out of the oven and add the coconut aminos, stirring very well. A lot of the coconut aminos will puddle on the baking tin. Do not panic. Put your almonds back in the oven.

Keep roasting your almonds for another 5 minutes, then stir them well. Keep roasting, now stirring every 2 or 3 minutes, until the coconut aminos have mostly dried and the surface of the almonds is just a little tacky. Pull 'em out.

Stir together the wasabi and garlic powders and sprinkle evenly over the almonds, stirring as you add it. Keep stirring till the seasonings are evenly distributed. Taste one, decide whether you want a little salt, and add it if you do. Store in an airtight container.

YIELD: 8 servings

Nutritional Analysis
Per serving: 230 calories; 20 g fat; 7 g protein; 9 g carbohydrate; 4 g dietary fiber; 5 g net carbs

NOTE

These are not as nose-twisting as the commercial variety. Feel free to up the wasabi and garlic if you want them stronger

Addictive Pumpkin Seeds

I love pumpkin seeds, and they're full of minerals. If you can't find shelled pumpkin seeds at your health food store, try a Hispanic grocery, or even the Mexican section of the international aisle at your big grocery store.

1 tablespoon (13 g) coconut oil

2 tablespoons (28 ml) coconut aminos

¼ teaspoon anchovy paste

½ teaspoon hot sauce, such as Tabasco

1 teaspoon onion powder

⅔ teaspoon garlic powder

1 teaspoon seasoned salt

2 cups (280 g) pumpkin seeds, shelled

Set oven to 250°F (120°C, or gas mark ½). Put the coconut oil in a roasting pan and put it in the oven to melt as the oven heats.

In the meanwhile, in a small dish, mix together the coconut aminos, anchovy paste, and hot sauce, stirring till the anchovy paste dissolves.

In another small dish, mix together the onion powder, garlic powder, and seasoned salt.

When the coconut oil is melted, pull the pan out and dump the pumpkin seeds into the pan. Stir till they're all coated with the oil. Now pour the coconut amino mixture over them and stir again. Finally, sprinkle the seasoning blend over the whole thing and stir to coat.

Slide 'em into the oven and set the timer for 20 minutes. When it beeps, stir 'em up, put 'em back, and set the timer for another 20. When it beeps again, check that they're dry. If not, give them another 10 minutes. Assuming they are, pull them out. Either way, when they're dry and golden, let them cool and put them in a snap-top container to store. Hide them in an obscure, hard-to-reach place if you hope for them to last longer than a day or two!

YIELD: 8 servings

Nutritional Analysis
Per serving: 299 calories; 24 g fat; 19 g protein; 8 g carbohydrate; 2 g dietary fiber; 6 g net carbs

Paprika Pumpkin Seeds

1 tablespoon (13 g) coconut oil

2 teaspoons hot smoked paprika

¼ teaspoon ground cumin

1 teaspoon garlic powder

2 cups (280 g) pumpkin seeds, shelled

Salt (optional)

Preheat your oven to 300°F (150°C, or gas mark 2). Line a roasting pan with foil (just for easy cleanup; you can skip this if you want) and put the coconut oil in it. Slide the pan into the oven for a big 2 to 3 minutes, until the oil melts. In the meanwhile, mix together the seasonings.

Pull the pan out of the oven and dump the pumpkin seeds into it. Stir to coat with the oil. Sprinkle the seasoning mixture evenly over the seeds, and stir to coat again, then spread 'em in an even layer. Slide your pan back into the oven and set a timer for 5 minutes.

When the timer beeps, stir your seeds again and return them to the oven for another 10 minutes. If they're a little puffed with a touch of gold when the timer beeps again, they're done. If not, give them just a few more minutes. Then cool and store them in a tightly lidded container—for as long as you can, which won't be long.

YIELD: 8 servings

Nutritional Analysis

Per serving: 314 calories; 26 g fat; 19 g protein; 8 g carbohydrate; 2 g dietary fiber; 6 g net carbs

Beef Jerky

So much better than that nasty stuff in plastic at the mini-mart. Better tasting, better for you. If you're a hiker or camper, in particular, you'll find this a great choice for take-along food. Or keep a Baggie of this in your desk for an afternoon snack at work.

1½ pounds (710 g) beef round, trimmed
½ cup (120 ml) Paleo Worcestershire (page 293)
½ cup (120 ml) coconut aminos
2 teaspoons honey
1 ½ teaspoons black pepper
2 tablespoons (20 g) chopped onion
1 teaspoon red-pepper flakes
1 teaspoon liquid smoke flavoring (optional;
   Read the label—some have sugar, some don't.)

Slice your beef as thinly as possible, parallel to the grain. This is far easier if the meat is partially frozen. Put your meat slices in a big zipper-lock bag.

Put everything else in your blender or food processor and run until the onion is pulverized. Pour into the bag with the meat. Seal the bag, pressing out the air as you go. Turn and knead the bag to make sure all the slices are completely coated in the marinade. Now throw the bag in the fridge. Let your meat marinate for about 4 to 6 hours.

Drain the meat slices and lay them flat in a dehydrator. Run it for at least 12 hours, then check the jerky for dryness. It should be dry enough that at the thinnest points it will snap when bent.

Store in a zipper-lock bag.

YIELD: 24 servings

Nutritional Analysis

Per serving: 69 calories; 4 g fat; 6 g protein; 3 g carbohydrate; trace dietary fiber; 3 g net carbs

NOTES

Obviously, this requires a dehydrator. You can buy one new, of course, but you might first look for a used one at Goodwill, on Craigslist, or on Freecycle. Mine cost me $7 on half-price day at Goodwill, and it works perfectly.

For the best way to boil your eggs, see page 55.

Good Ol' Deviled Eggs

A surefire crowd-pleaser. Go ahead and double or triple this recipe—you know you'll eat them all!

6 eggs, hard-boiled
3 tablespoons (42 g) Mayonnaise in the Jar (page 278)
2 teaspoons brown mustard
2 dashes Louisiana-style hot sauce
Salt (optional)
Paprika

Peel the eggs and halve them. Turn the yolks out into a mixing bowl and reserve the whites on a plate for later.

(*continued*)

Use a fork to smash up the yolks pretty good. Now add the mayonnaise, mustard, and hot sauce. Taste to see whether you think it needs a little salt.

Now stuff the yolks back into the whites. Sprinkle lightly with paprika and serve.

YIELD: 12 servings

Nutritional Analysis
Per serving: 64 calories; 6 g fat; 3 g protein; trace carbohydrate; trace dietary fiber; trace net carbs

Horseradish-Dill Eggs

Just an easy twist on classic deviled eggs.

6 eggs, hard-boiled
4 tablespoons (56 g) Mayonnaise in the Jar (page 278)
2 teaspoons brown mustard
2 teaspoons Prepared Horseradish (page 288)
1 teaspoon minced fresh dill weed (or ¼ teaspoon dried)
Salt (optional)

NOTES

In this book, the eggs come before the chicken. I love stuffed eggs and have learned that they're a surefire crowd pleaser. They're also a wonderful thing to find in the fridge when you open the door, looking for something easy to eat.

Peel your eggs. Halve 'em and turn the yolks out into a mixing bowl, while putting the whites on a plate. Set the whites aside, while you . . .

Mash up the yolks with a fork. Now add the mayonnaise, mustard, horseradish, and dill, and keep mashing and stirring till your yolks are smooth. Salt to taste and stuff back into the whites. If you've got a little extra dill weed, you could put a teeny sprig on each one for garnish. Or you could just stuff them in your face.

YIELD: 12 servings

Nutritional Analysis
Per serving: 73 calories; 7 g fat; 3 g protein; trace carbohydrate; trace dietary fiber; trace net carbs

Wasabi Eggs

I like wasabi in almost anything. Read the labels on your wasabi paste to get the cleanest one you can find.

6 eggs, hard-boiled
¼ cup (60 g) Mayonnaise in the Jar (page 278)
1 teaspoon wasabi paste
½ teaspoon coconut aminos
3 scallions, minced
1 pinch salt (optional)

Peel your eggs. Halve them, turning the yolks out into a mixing bowl and arranging the whites on a plate. Use a fork to mash up the yolks.

Now add the mayonnaise, wasabi paste, and coconut aminos, and keep mashing and mixing till the yolks are smooth and creamy.

Stir in the minced scallions and the salt, if using, and stuff the yolks back into the whites. That's it!

YIELD: 12 servings

Nutritional Analysis
Per serving: 73 calories; 7 g fat; 3 g protein; 1 g carbohydrate; trace dietary fiber; 1g net carbs

Green Eggs, No Ham

Don't make these in advance! You know how avocado discolors. Well worth making for immediate devouring, though. How about making these for family movie night? Throw in some vegetables and dip, and there's supper.

6 eggs, hard-boiled
½ avocado
¼ cup (60 g) Mayonnaise in the Jar (page 278)
1 teaspoon brown mustard
½ teaspoon Celery Salt (page 285, or use store-bought)
1 scallion, minced
2 dashes hot sauce, such as Tabasco
Paprika (for garnish)

Slice your eggs in half and turn the yolks out into a deep, narrow mixing bowl. (If you only have a short, wide one, that's okay, but the deeper, narrower one is easier here.) Use a fork to mash 'em up a bit.

Use a spoon to scoop the avocado out of its shell, into the bowl. Add the rest of the stuff, too.

Now use your stick blender to blend it all until it's super-creamy.

Stuff this lovely pale-green stuff back into the whites. Because you added that avocado, you'll have plenty of filling, so pile it high. Arrange 'em on a plate as you go.

Sprinkle lightly with paprika for a nice contrast—I used hot smoked paprika, and it was great, but regular paprika will do.

Whistle for the troops and stuff them in your faces!

YIELD: 12 servings

Nutritional Analysis
Per serving: 86 calories; 8 g fat; 3 g protein; 1 g carbohydrate; trace dietary fiber; 1 g net carbs

Anchovy Eggs

I mention in the recipe note for Anchovy Dip/Sauce (page 283) that That Nice Boy I Married is, er, very fond of anchovies. So these eggs were for him.

6 eggs, hard-boiled
¼ cup (60 g) Mayonnaise in the Jar (page 278)
1½ tablespoons Anchovy Dip/Sauce (page 283)

So simple! Peel the eggs and halve 'em, turning the yolks out into a bowl. Add the mayo and Anchovy Dip and mash the yolks up with a fork, mixing until they're creamy. Spoon or pipe back into the whites and you're done.

YIELD: 12 servings

Nutritional Analysis
Per serving: 70 calories; 6 g fat; 3 g protein; trace carbohydrate; trace dietary fiber; trace net carbs

Bacon Balsamic Eggs

Made these for a Christmas party, and people raved!

6 eggs, hard-boiled
3 tablespoons (42 g) Mayonnaise in the Jar (page 278)
½ teaspoon Celery Salt (page 285, or store-bought)
2 slices cooked bacon, crumbled fine
2 tablespoons (20 g) minced red onion
¼ teaspoon black pepper
½ teaspoon balsamic vinegar
½ teaspoon brown mustard
Minced fresh parsley (for garnish)

Peel your eggs, halve them, and turn the yolks out into a mixing bowl.

Add the mayo to the yolks and mash them up till they're smooth. Now add celery salt, bacon, red onion, pepper, balsamic vinegar, and mustard and mash them all in as well.

Stuff the seasoned yolks back into the whites. Sprinkle with minced parsley to make them look pretty, and serve.

YIELD: 12 servings

Nutritional Analysis
Per serving: 71 calories; 6 g fat; 4 g protein; 1 g carbohydrate; trace dietary fiber; 1 g net carbs

After the eggs, the chicken! I think we need to breed chickens that look like Shiva, with six wings apiece. I love wings. Not only are they great party food, but they're also quicker to cook than larger bits of chicken, so I often make simple wings for a quick supper. On a nutritional note, wings are high in gelatin, which is why they're so juicy and flavorful. The gelatin makes them good for your joints, skin, hair, intestinal tract—all of you, really.

Addictive Wings

This is based on Heroin Wings from 500 Low-Carb Recipes. *They're hugely popular, but the Parmesan and butter in them aren't paleo.*

4 pounds (1.75 kg) chicken wings
¾ cup (90 g) Pork Rind Crumbs (page 30)
¾ cup (90 g) almond meal
2 tablespoons (2.5 g) dried parsley
1 tablespoon (3 g) dried oregano
2 teaspoons paprika
½ teaspoon salt
½ teaspoon black pepper
½ cup (104 g) lard (or bacon grease or other
  fat of choice)

Preheat oven to 350ºF (180ºC, or gas mark 4). Line a roasting pan with foil—the nonstick kind is great.

If your wings aren't cut up, cut them at the joints, saving the pointy wing tips for broth. (Those wing tips make insanely good broth.)

Mix the pork rind crumbs and almond meal with the seasonings.

Melt the lard. Now dip each wing in the lard, then roll in the seasoned crumbs. Arrange in the foil-lined pan. Bake for an hour, then serve hot.

YIELD: 50 servings

Nutritional Analysis
Per serving: 78 calories; 6 g fat; 5 g protein; 1 g carbohydrate; trace dietary fiber; 1 g net carbs

Prehistoric Buffalo Wings

Everyone loves buffalo wings, but they're generally coated with wheat flour, fried in vegetable oil, and coated—if you're lucky—in a mixture of butter and hot sauce. If you're not lucky, the sauce will have vegetable oil and who knows what else? Here you've got all the flavor, none of the junk.

10 chicken wings
⅓ cup (38 g) coconut flour
¼ teaspoon paprika
¼ teaspoon cayenne
¼ teaspoon salt (optional)
Lard, for frying (or try half lard, half bacon grease)
2 tablespoons (25 g) lard (or 1 tablespoon each lard and bacon grease)
1 garlic clove, crushed
¼ cup (60 ml) hot sauce (Frank's, or other Louisiana-style)

Cut the wings at the joints, saving the pointy tips for broth.

Mix the coconut flour with the paprika, cayenne, and salt, if using. Now toss the wings in this mixture, to coat. Let the wings sit for 30 minutes or so.

Now put your big, heavy skillet over medium heat and add lard or lard and bacon grease to a depth of about ¼ inch (6 mm). When it's good and hot, throw in the wings and fry 'em till they're brown and crunchy all over—fry them in batches, since crowding stuff too much makes for soggy fried food.

In the meanwhile, put the 2 tablespoons (25 g) of additional lard or lard and bacon grease in a small saucepan over medium-low heat and sauté the garlic in it for a minute or so. Now stir in the hot sauce and let the whole thing cook, stirring often, until the wings are done.

Using a tongs, remove the wings to a big bowl. Pour the sauce over them, toss, and devour!

YIELD: 20 servings

Nutritional Analysis
Per serving: 84 calories; 6 g fat; 5 g protein; 3 g carbohydrate; 2 g dietary fiber; 1 g net carbs

Mustard Wings

2 pounds (900 g) chicken wings
¼ cup (60 ml) olive oil
1 lemon
2 tablespoons (30 g) brown mustard
2 garlic cloves, crushed
¼ teaspoon black pepper
¼ teaspoon hot sauce

Cut the wings at the joints, saving the pointy tips for broth.

Put your wings in a big zipper-lock bag. Mix together everything else and pour it over the wings. Seal the bag, pressing out the air as you go. Turn the bag to coat the wings, then toss in the fridge for an hour or two.

(continued)

When the time comes, you can cook these one of two ways: You can roast 'em at 375°F (190°C, or gas mark 5) for about 45 minutes, basting once or twice with the marinade from the bag, or you can broil them about 4 inches (10 cm) from the heat, turning often till they're done through—again, basting with the marinade from the bag. Either way, quit basting them a good 5 to 10 minutes before they're done, so the heat has time to kill any raw chicken germs you've basted 'em with!

Serve with plenty of napkins.

YIELD: 20 servings

Nutritional Analysis
Per serving: 81 calories; 7 g fat; 5 g protein; 1 g carbohydrate; trace dietary fiber; 1 g net carbs

Grapefruit Wings

10 chicken wings
Salt and black pepper
Paprika
¼ batch Grapefruit Balsamic Vinegar (page 283)
1 clove garlic, crushed

So simple! Preheat your oven to 350°F (180°C, or gas mark 4). If your wings are whole, cut them at the joints, making two "drummettes" from each wing. Keep the pointy bones from the ends for broth.

Sprinkle your wings lightly with salt and pepper and paprika and arrange them in a roasting pan—you might line it with foil first, for easy cleanup. Put your wings in the oven. Set a timer for 30 minutes.

In the meanwhile, measure the Grapefruit Balsamic Vinegar and crush the garlic into it. Stir it and let it sit.

When the timer beeps, baste the wings with the vinegar-garlic mixture, turning to coat both sides. Let them roast another 15 minutes and baste again. Give them another 10 to 15 minutes, then serve with any remaining vinegar poured over them.

YIELD: 20 servings

Nutritional Analysis
Per serving: 56 calories; 4 g fat; 5 g protein; 1 g carbohydrate; trace dietary fiber; 4 g net carbs

Duck Liver Pâté

When you buy a duck, it will generally come with giblets inside. Here's how you can turn the liver into a rich and elegant appetizer for two.

2 tablespoons (26 g) duck fat
½ large shallot, minced
1 duck liver
¼ teaspoon dried marjoram
¼ teaspoon dried thyme
¼ teaspoon dried savory
1 pinch ground rosemary
2 teaspoons cognac
1 pinch black pepper
1 pinch salt (optional)

In a small, heavy skillet, over medium-low heat, melt the duck fat and start sautéing the shallot.

In the meanwhile, cut your duck liver into 1-inch (2.5 cm) chunks. When the shallot is soft—about 5 minutes—add the liver and sauté till the red juice stops running and the surface changes color. Your liver chunks should still be pink in the middle. Stir in the herbs and sauté just another 30 seconds or so.

Transfer everything from the skillet to your food processor (a small processor is good here) and add the cognac, pepper, and salt, if using. Run till you have a paste. Scoop into a ramekin and chill for several hours before serving.

Since we won't be having toast to eat the pâté on, consider stuffing it into celery stalks. Good eaten plain, though!

YIELD: 2 servings

Nutritional Analysis
Per serving: 159 calories; 14 g fat ; 4 g protein; 2 g carbohydrate; trace dietary fiber; 1 g net carbs

Seriously WASPy Girl Chopped Chicken Liver

5 ounces (140 g) chicken livers
1 cup (160 g) onion, chopped fine
3 tablespoons (39 g) lard or schmaltz (rendered chicken fat) if you have some—the traditional fat for this dish, since lard is not kosher. Olive oil would work, too.
Salt and black pepper
2 eggs, hard-boiled
1 tablespoon (14 g) Mayonnaise in the Jar (page 278)
2 scallions—sliced thin

Bring a small saucepan of water to a boil. Add the livers, turn it down to a bare simmer, and set a timer for 5 minutes. When the timer goes off, turn off the heat but leave the livers in the water for at least 10 to 15 minutes more.

Sauté the onion in the lard or schmaltz over medium-low heat. Sprinkle it with a little salt and pepper while it's cooking. Continue sautéing the onion, stirring often, until it's well browned and starting to get a bit crispy. While the livers are sitting in the hot water and the onions are browning, you may as well peel your eggs. Then chop them, using a knife and cutting board—you don't want to use a food processor, because you want actual little pieces of white and yolk in your finished dish.

Put your onions in your food processor, with the S blade in place. Pulse a few times. Now drain the livers well and add them to the food processor, along with the mayonnaise. Pulse till you have something just a little coarser than a completely smooth paste—a little texture is nice. Scoop this out into a bowl.

Stir in the chopped egg and scallion and add some more salt and pepper if you think it needs it. Serve stuffed into celery stalks, wrapped in lettuce leaves, or on the sunflower crackers in chapter 4. For that matter, you could just eat this with a fork.

YIELD: 4 servings

Nutritional Analysis
Per serving: 125 calories; 7 g fat; 10 g protein; 5 g carbohydrate; 1 g dietary fiber; 4 g net carbs

Kwee's Appetizer

My erstwhile friend Kwee Hong Ong, a native of Singapore, brought this to a dinner party one evening, though she used soy sauce, of course. An amazingly good combination.

2 cups (370 g) fresh pineapple chunks
¼ cup (60 ml) coconut aminos
Red pepper flakes

(continued)

So simple! Put out the pineapple chunks on a plate, with toothpicks. Put the coconut aminos in a little dish and scatter some red-pepper flakes on a plate. Guests spear a pineapple chunk, dip it in coconut aminos, then in red-pepper flakes—more flakes for the chili-heads, fewer for the timid. That's it!

YIELD: 4 servings

Nutritional Analysis
Per serving: 38 calories; trace fat; trace protein; 10 g carbohydrate; 1 g dietary fiber, 9 g net carbs

Anticuchos

This is my loose translation of a popular Peruvian appetizer. The marinade tenderizes the heart nicely. Please don't be scared. These are just beef muscle meat, you know?

2 chipotle peppers, dried
Boiling water
1 pound (455 g) beef heart
¼ cup (60 ml) apple cider vinegar
¼ cup (60 ml) olive oil
1 tablespoon (7 g) ground cumin
¼ teaspoon black pepper
2 cloves garlic, crushed
1 tablespoon (4 g) minced fresh parsley
1 tablespoon (1 g) minced fresh cilantro

First, put your chipotles in a small, heat-proof dish (a custard cup is ideal) and pour just enough boiling water over them to cover. Let those sit while you . . .

Trim any veiny bits off the beef heart, also thick layers of fat. Cut the heart into cubes about 1-inch (2.5 cm) square—you want 20 cubes.

Mix together everything left on the list. By now your chipotles should be softened, so purée 'em—use your stick blender or run them through your regular blender—and add them, too.

Put your heart cubes in a big zipper-lock bag and dump in the oil and vinegar mixture. Seal the bag, pressing out the air as you go. Now stash the bag in the fridge and leave the heart chunks to marinate—at least 10 to 12 hours, and 24 works great, as I have reason to know.

When cooking time rolls around, either have your grill ready or turn on your broiler with the rack about 4 to 5 inches (10 to 13 cm) below it.

Either way, drain your heart cubes and reserve the marinade. String the cubes on skewers, 5 per skewer. Now put 'em on the grill or on a broiler rack under the broiler. Give them 5 to 7 minutes per side, basting with the reserved marinade a couple of times during cooking. Do not overcook! Your cubes should be pink inside. Serve hot.

YIELD: 4 servings

Nutritional Analysis
Per serving: 247 calories; 17 g fat; 17 g protein; 7 g carbohydrate; 1 g dietary fiber; 6 g net carbs

Bacon, Walnut, and Sundried-Tomato-Stuffed Mushrooms

¼ pound (115 g) bacon
1 pound (455 g) fresh mushrooms
1 cup (100 g) walnuts
1 medium onion

½ cup (55 g) oil-packed sundried tomatoes

1 clove garlic, crushed

½ teaspoon salt

½ teaspoon black pepper

2 tablespoons (8 g) minced fresh parsley

Preheat oven to 350°F (180°C, or gas mark 4).

In your big, heavy skillet, over medium-low heat, start cooking the bacon.

While that's happening, wipe your mushrooms clean with a damp paper towel and remove the stems, but keep 'em—they're going in the stuffing. Turn your bacon!

Oven's hot by now! Put your walnuts in a shallow baking pan, put them in the oven, and set your timer for 8 minutes.

Peel your onion and whack it into eighths. Throw it in your food processor with the *S* blade in place and pulse a few times. Throw in those mushroom stems and pulse a few more times, until your mushrooms and onion are chopped fairly fine.

By now your bacon should be about half-done, which is how you want it. Remove it from the pan, set it on a plate, and put it by your food processor.

Throw the onions and mushroom stems in the bacon grease and start sautéing them.

Put the food processor bowl and blade back on the base. Your walnuts should be done by now, so dump 'em in there. Throw in the bacon, too. Now measure your sundried tomatoes (lift them out of the jar with a fork,

to let some of the oil drain off, but getting some in the stuffing is nice). Pulse till it's all chopped together, but don't go too fine; you want the nuts to have a little texture.

Add the walnut mixture to the onions and mushrooms and stir it all up. Stir in the crushed garlic, the salt, and the pepper, and sauté it all together for a minute or two. Then stir in the parsley.

Film the bottom of a 9 x 13-inch (23 x 33 cm) baking pan with olive oil. Now stuff the walnut-bacon-tomato mixture into the mushroom caps and arrange them in the pan. Cover with foil and bake for 30 minutes. Take the foil off and give 'em another 10, then serve hot.

YIELD: 36 servings

Nutritional Analysis
Per serving: 47 calories; 4 g fat; 2 g protein; 2 g carbohydrate; trace dietary fiber; 2 g net carbs

Bacon-Wrapped Enoki

This traditional Japanese savory is quite picturesque! Look for enoki at Asian markets.

1 pound (455 g) enoki mushrooms

6 slices bacon

½ lemon

Put 12 toothpicks in water to soak.

Enoki are little teeny mushrooms with skinny stems, joined together in clumps. We're going to make bacon bundles with them. First trim the root, but do it without separating the stems. Divide your little clumps of mushrooms into 12 roughly equal bunches.

(continued)

Cut your bacon slices in two, crossways, so you have 12 bacon strips.

Now gently wrap a bacon slice around each bunch of enoki, an inch to an inch and a half (2.5 to 3.5 cm) above the bottom. Tuck any stray stems in there. Now use one of those soaked toothpicks to skewer the bacon in place. Repeat with the rest of the enoki and bacon slices. You can do up to this point ahead of time, if you like, and refrigerate until you're ready to cook and serve them.

Preheat your broiler. Oil your broiler rack and lay your enoki bundles on it. Grill, turning carefully at least once, until the bacon is crisp and the enoki are starting to brown—about 10 to 12 minutes.

Remove your enoki from the broiler and use a tongs to transfer them to your cutting board. Using a very sharp, thin-bladed knife, cut each bundle in two, crossways, so you have a bundle of stems and a bundle with cute little mushroom tops standing up. For each serving, arrange three of each kind of bundle on a little plate, the stem parts lying down and the little tufts of mushrooms standing on end. (I told you this was picturesque! The Japanese are very into presentation.)

Cut your half lemon into thin wedges, add one to each plate, then serve.

YIELD: 4 servings

Nutritional Analysis
Per serving: 89 calories; 5 g fat; 5 g protein; 7 g carbohydrate; 2 g dietary fiber; 5 g net carbs

NOTE

For a less-exalted version of this idea, you can wrap good ol' button mushrooms in bacon, again, holding them with soaked toothpicks. Throw them on the grill till the bacon is crisp and serve to a delighted cookout crowd.

Chicken-Chutney Stuffed Mushrooms

16 medium mushroom caps
2 tablespoons (26 g) coconut oil, melted
Chicken-Chutney Spread/Stuffing (page 189)
1 tablespoon (1 g) minced fresh cilantro (very fine)

Preheat oven to 350ºF (180ºC, or gas mark 4). Brush the mushrooms lightly with the oil and arrange in a baking pan—an 8 x 8 inch (20 x 20 cm) should be about right. Put 'em in the oven and let them bake for 5 minutes or so.

Pull the mushrooms out of the oven and stuff them with the Chicken-Chutney Spread/Stuffing. Bake for 12 to 15 minutes.

Sprinkle with the cilantro (if you hate cilantro, use parsley) and serve hot.

YIELD: 16 servings

Nutritional Analysis
Per serving: 97 calories; 5 g fat; 4 g protein; 10 g carbohydrate; 2 g dietary fiber; 8 g net carbs

Crab-and-Almond-Stuffed Cuke Slices

You wouldn't go to this kind of trouble for a casual get-together, but for a fancier party, this impresses.

¼ cup (28 g) chopped almonds
¼ cup (60 ml) extra-virgin olive oil
6 ounces (170 g) crabmeat, preferably fresh; steamed, drained, and cooled
2 scallions, trimmed and chunked
2 tablespoons (8 g) minced fresh parsley
2 tablespoons (28 ml) dry white wine
2 tablespoons (28 g) Mayonnaise in the Jar (page 278) or to bind
1 dash hot sauce, such as Tabasco
Salt (optional)
2 large cucumbers, whole

In a small, heavy skillet, over medium heat, sauté the almonds in the olive oil until golden. Let cool.

Pick over the crab to make sure there are no shell bits. Put in your food processor.

Add the almonds, scallions, parsley, and wine. Run the processor till the mixture is smooth.

Now add the mayonnaise, 1 tablespoon (14 g) at a time—you want to bind the mixture, but you don't want it too soft. Add the hot sauce and salt to taste.

Cut the ends off your cucumbers and use an apple corer or a knife to remove the seeds, leaving a nice cucumber tunnel. Pack the crab mixture into the hollow, filling completely. Put them in a plastic bag and chill for several hours.

Just before serving, remove the cucumbers from the refrigerator and cut in ½-inch (1 cm) slices. Sprinkle with a little more salt, if desired, and serve.

YIELD: about 40 slices

Nutritional Analysis
Per slice: 30 calories; 2 g fat; 1 g protein; 1 g carbohydrate; trace dietary fiber; 1 g net carbs

Clams on the Half Shell

My mother told the story of her college boyfriend, Harvey, visiting her family down at the Jersey Shore. One evening, as was their custom, the family was eating freshly dug clams on the half shell. Harvey was dubious but tried one or two. Then he squeezed lemon on one, and it wiggled . . . Hard to think of anything more paleo than that. Be very sure of the source of your clams and pick them up right before you plan to eat them.

24 clams, shucked
Florida Cocktail Sauce (page 274)
Lemon wedges

Do yourself a favor and ask the nice fish guys to shuck your clams for you. Then set them out on a bed of crushed ice, the clam in the deeper half of the shell. Put out wedges of fresh lemon and cocktail sauce to season them.

YIELD: 4 servings

Nutritional Analysis
Per serving: 64 calories; 1 g fat; 11 g protein; 2 g carbohydrate; 0 g dietary fiber; 2 g net carbs

Oysters on the Half Shell

Again, raw oysters are as paleo as it gets. Again, be very, very sure of the source of your oysters.

24 oysters, shucked
Florida Cocktail Sauce (page 274)
Lemon Wedges

Do yourself a favor and ask the nice fish guys to shuck your oysters for you. Then set them out on a bed of crushed ice, in the deeper half of the shells. Put out wedges of fresh lemon and cocktail sauce to season them.

YIELD: 4 servings

Nutritional Analysis
Per serving: 34 calories; 1 g fat; 4 g protein; 2 g carbohydrate; 0 g dietary fiber; 2 g net carbs

Chicken Chips

This is a ringer, brought in from 500 Low-Carb Recipes. I repeat it here because every time I mention chicken chips on my Facebook fan page (Dana Carpender's Hold The Toast Press), someone will ask how to make them— and everybody who makes them loves them. I buy extra chicken skin to make these with!

Chicken skin (however much you've got)
Salt or other seasonings

Heat oven to 350°F (180°C, or gas mark 4). While that's happening, spread your chicken skin flat on your broiler rack. Include any lumps of fat you might have pulled off the chicken, too. Now bake for 15 minutes or so, until it's brown and crunchy. Sprinkle it with the seasoning of your choice, or just eat it plain.

I don't have a nutritional breakdown for this, because I couldn't find the information. 0 g carbs, though.

NOTES

I invented this because I had a bunch of recipes that called for skinning the chicken before cooking. It broke my heart to throw the skin away. So I started doing this, and it's one of my most popular ideas.

Look in that broiler pan. See that golden fat? That's schmaltz, or chicken fat, one of the most popular of traditional cooking fats. Especially if you're paying the price for pasture-raised chickens, do not throw it away! Pour it into a clean old jar with a lid, stash it in the fridge, and use it for sautéing and such. (I've even used it to make mayonnaise, which I called "Schmaltzonnaise." Not bad, though it did have a slight chicken-y flavor.)

Avocado Dip or Pâté

2 avocados
½ cup (112 g) Coconut Butter (page 31)
1 large shallot
½ lemon
3 garlic cloves, crushed
½ teaspoon chili powder
Salt to taste
2 tablespoons (8 g) minced fresh parsley
¼ cup pistachio nuts, chopped

Halve and seed your avocados and scoop them into your food processor, with the *S* blade in place. Add the coconut butter and process till they're well combined and smooth, scraping down the sides of the processor a couple of times in the process.

Peel your shallot, cut it in chunks, and add to the processor. Pulse till it's finely minced, but there are still little bits of visible shallot.

Add the juice from your half lemon, the garlic, chili powder, and salt, and process to blend, again, scraping the side of the processor at least once.

Add the parsley and pistachios and process just long enough to mix them in, but not long enough to pulverize the pistachios!

You can serve this at room temperature as a dip. Or, if you prefer, you can mold it, chill it well, then unmold and serve in slices, on a bed of lettuce.

If you're feeling particularly energetic, you could put this in a pastry bag and use the star tip to pipe it into hollowed-out cherry tomatoes. But who has that kind of time?

YIELD: 6 servings

Nutritional Analysis
Per serving: 216 calories; 20 g fat; 3 g protein; 11 g carbohydrate; 4 g dietary fiber; 7 g net carbs

NOTE

Our tester Saskia says that you shouldn't make your own coconut butter unless you have a good food processor. I concur; if you don't have a good processor, go buy some coconut butter instead.

Guacamole

Of course you're not eating tortilla chips, you caveperson, you. But there's no reason you can't dip it with pork rinds, you know. Or stuff it in tomatoes. Or spoon it over a steak. Or eat it with a spoon.

2 tablespoons (20 g) minced red onion
1 garlic clove, crushed
2 avocados (little black ones, good and ripe)
½ lime
4 dashes hot sauce or to taste
2 pinches salt
1 tablespoon (1 g) minced fresh cilantro (optional)

Have your onion minced and your garlic crushed and in a bowl first.

Halve your avocados and use a spoon to scoop the flesh out into the bowl.

Use a fork to mash up the avocado. Don't go for a super-smooth texture; leave some little lumps of avocado.

Now squeeze in the juice of the half lime and add the hot sauce and salt and cilantro if using. Stir it up and serve immediately! Guacamole just doesn't hold very well.

YIELD: 4 servings

Nutritional Analysis
Per serving: 167 calories; 15 g fat; 2 g protein; 9 g carbohydrate; 3 g dietary fiber; 6 g net carbs

Salmon Dip

8 ounces (225 g) salmon fillet
Water
3 scallions
1½ tablespoons (25 ml) lemon juice
¼ cup (60 ml) unsweetened coconut milk
2 tablespoons (8 g) minced fresh dill weed
½ teaspoon salt
¼ teaspoon black pepper
1 dash hot sauce, such as Tabasco

Lay your salmon in a skillet and add water to about half the depth of the fish. Bring to a simmer, cover the pan, turn off the burner, and let the whole thing cool.

Drain your cooled salmon. Remove the skin (well, you don't really have to, but you can) and break it up into your food processor. Add everything else and pulse till you have a dip consistency.

Spoon into the bowl you plan to serve it with and chill for a few hours. Then serve with crudités.

YIELD: 4 servings

Nutritional Analysis
Per serving: 99 calories; 5 g fat; 12 g protein; 2 g carbohydrate; trace dietary fiber; 2 g net carbs

Shrimp Dip

Our tester, Kim, called this "very easy and delicious."

10 ounces (280 g) shrimp, peeled
½ cup (120 ml) coconut milk
½ cup (115 g) Mayonnaise in the Jar (page 278)
3 tablespoons (45 ml) lemon juice
1 tablespoon (4 g) minced fresh parsley
1 tablespoon (4 g) minced fresh dill weed
½ garlic clove, crushed (Oh, heck, throw in the whole thing if you really want to!)
1 to 3 tablespoons Sriracha (page 276)
Salt (optional)

First you need to cook your shrimp—just poach them briefly in simmering water, just till they're pink and firm, maybe 5 minutes. Drain them very well—indeed, it's a good idea to do this a bit ahead of time and set them on a couple of layers of paper toweling for 30 minutes or so.

Combine the shrimp with the coconut milk, mayo, lemon juice, parsley, dill, garlic, and sriracha in your food processor. Pulse till the shrimp is chopped up, but not puréed—you want a dippable consistency but with discernible bits of shrimp in it. Salt to taste.

Chill well, then serve with cut-up vegetables.

YIELD: 8 servings

Nutritional Analysis
Per serving: 172 calories; 16 g fat; 8 g protein; 2 g carbohydrate; trace dietary fiber; 2 g net carbs

Not-Really-Peruvian Dipping Sauce

Okay, this was supposed to be made with peanuts, but peanuts aren't paleo.

1 tablespoon (13 g) coconut oil
1 large onion, chopped
3 cloves garlic, crushed
1 ½ cups (355 ml) chicken broth
¾ cup (195 g) almond butter
1 tablespoon (15 ml) unsweetened coconut milk
1 tablespoon (15 ml) lime juice
2 jalapeños, seeded and minced

Put your big, heavy skillet over medium heat and melt the coconut oil. Throw in the onion and sauté it, stirring frequently, until it's soft and browned—maybe 10 to 15 minutes. Crush the garlic and stir it up. Let the whole thing sauté another minute or two.

Now turn down the heat and stir in the chicken broth, almond butter, coconut milk, lime juice, and jalapeño. Now wash your hands well with soap and water! Don't leave the hot pepper on your hands, or you'll be sorry the next time you rub your eye.

Bring this mixture to a simmer and let it cook slowly for 10 minutes or so.

Now transfer to your food processor and purée the whole thing smooth. Then scrape it into a serving dish, cover with plastic wrap, and chill for several hours.

Serve with grape tomatoes, slices of jicama, blanched asparagus spears, and other crudités.

YIELD: 10 servings

Nutritional Analysis
Per serving: 141 calories; 12 g fat; 5 g protein; 5 g carbohydrate; 3 g dietary fiber; 2 g net carbs

Prehistoric Dill Dip

I've always loved dill dip with crudités. Here is a version with good mayonnaise and no dairy.

1 cup (225 g) Mayonnaise in the Jar (page 278)
1 cup (230 g) Coconut Sour Cream (page 29)
2 pinches paprika
1 clove garlic, crushed
1 tablespoon (10 g) minced red onion
½ teaspoon salt
1 tablespoon (4 g) minced fresh dill weed

Just assemble everything in your food processor and run it for 30 seconds or so—if you've already crushed your garlic and minced your onion and dill, it shouldn't take long. (If you put those things in the processor in bigger bits, you'll want to run it longer.)

Refrigerate for 24 hours, to let the flavors blend. Serve with vegetables.

YIELD: 8 servings

Nutritional Analysis
Per serving: 295 calories; 34 g fat; 1 g protein; 2 g carbohydrate; trace dietary fiber; 2 g net carbs

Onion Dip

When I was a kid, every party required onion dip, made with sour cream and onion soup mix. It's out of fashion now, but I always liked it. Here's my paleo version.

1 onion
2 tablespoons (26 g) lard
1 cup (230 g) Coconut Sour Cream (page 29)
2 teaspoons coconut aminos
2 tablespoons (28 ml) Slow-Cooker Demi-Glace (page 27)
½ teaspoon black pepper
Salt

Mince the onion. Melt the lard in your big, heavy skillet over medium heat and sauté the onion slowly until caramelized.

Mix with everything else, then refrigerate for several hours for the flavors to blend.

Serve with crudités or pork rinds or both.

YIELD: 8 servings

Nutritional Analysis
Per serving: 234 calories; 23 g fat; 2 g protein; 4 g carbohydrate; trace dietary fiber; 4 g net carbs

Mushroom Caviar

Our tester Kim calls this "Good, quick, and easy!"

8 ounces (225 g) mushrooms
4 shallots
3 tablespoons (29 g) bacon grease
2 tablespoons (18 g) pine nuts
1 tablespoon (15 ml) dry red wine
1 clove garlic, crushed
2 tablespoons (28 ml) coconut milk
1½ teaspoons red wine vinegar
Salt and black pepper to taste

Wipe your mushrooms clean and put them in your food processor with the *S* blade in place. Pulse till chopped fine. Remove from the food processor and reserve, while you . . .

Peel the shallots and repeat the process with them—put 'em in the food processor and chop them fine. Why not do them together? Because they're different textures and will chop at different rates, that's why.

In your big, heavy skillet, over medium-high heat, melt the bacon grease and start sautéing the mushrooms and shallots. Cook till the mushrooms have changed color, about 5 to 7 minutes.

In the meanwhile, put your pine nuts in a little bitty skillet, put 'em over medium heat, and toast them, stirring now and then, until they're just touched with gold.

Okay, stir the wine and garlic into the mushroom mixture and let the whole thing cook another minute or two. Then scrape it all into a bowl.

Stir in the coconut milk and the vinegar. Salt and pepper to taste. Now gently stir in the pine nuts. Cover and chill well.

Scoop in pretty mounds on lettuce leaves to serve, or use to stuff celery.

YIELD: 4 servings

Nutritional Analysis
Per serving: 155 calories; 14 g fat; 3 g protein; 6 g carbohydrate; 1 g dietary fiber; 5 g net carbs

Eggplant Spread

Kim says to tell you this is especially good with sweet red peppers as dippers.

1 eggplant
1 bunch scallions, minced
2 teaspoons Caveman Ketchup (page 273)
1 tablespoon (15 ml) extra-virgin olive oil
3 cloves garlic, crushed
1 teaspoon lemon juice
1 teaspoon red wine vinegar
Salt and black pepper to taste

Preheat oven to 375°F (190°C, or gas mark 5). Ruthlessly stab your eggplant all over, put it on a rack in a roasting pan, and bake it for an hour, or until soft.

When it's done, let it cool till you can handle it. Then split it, scoop the innards into a bowl, and mash 'em up with everything else. Chill well, then serve with cucumbers, peppers, and celery for dipping.

YIELD: 3 to 4 servings

Nutritional Analysis
Per serving (assuming 3): 90 calories; 5 g fat; 2 g protein; 12 g carbohydrate; 4 g dietary fiber, 8 g net carbs

Avocado-Cocoyo Dip

Lisa C., who tested this, says the lemon-shallot-tarragon combo is a winner and called this "an awesome dip."

1 cup (230 g) Cocoyo (page 28)
1 large, ripe avocado
2 shallots
3 scallions
2 teaspoons fresh tarragon
3 tablespoons (45 ml) lemon juice
2 teaspoons fresh oregano
1 teaspoon hot sauce, such as Tabasco, or to taste
Salt and black pepper to taste

Simply assemble everything in your food processor and run till it's smooth. Scrape into a serving dish and cover with plastic wrap smoothed directly on the surface—this prevents the avocado from browning. Chill for a few hours before serving with veggies.

YIELD: 6 servings

Nutritional Analysis
Per serving: 61 calories; 5 g fat; 1 g protein; 4 g carbohydrate; 1 g dietary fiber; 3 g net carbs

Chapter 3

EGGS

Ogg ate all kinds of eggs—bird eggs, insect eggs, turtle eggs, whatever he could find. After all, they fall into the "Doesn't run, doesn't fight" category. If you can find duck eggs, quail eggs, or any other kind of eggs, go for it. Caviar, too. However, this chapter deals with the familiar chicken egg.

This is a mighty big chapter. There are a few reasons for this:

- I adore eggs, and so does my husband.
- Eggs are among the most nutritious foods, and good pastured eggs are more affordable than grass-fed meat.
- Eggs are quick and easy to cook, making them a great choice for busy lives.
- If I start thinking about new recipes before breakfast, I tend to cook eggs.
- We have, as I write this, 28 chickens in the backyard. Unsurprisingly, I find myself drawn to egg recipes.

So let's get to it!

The Best Way to Hard Boil Eggs

Hard-boiled eggs are one of the most useful things you can keep in your refrigerator. Make them a staple!

12 eggs
2 tablespoons (36 g) salt

Useful Piece of Information: Fresh eggs are not good for hard boiling. They will stick to their shells tenaciously. If you're buying local pastured eggs, they are likely to be quite fresh. So buy eggs ahead of time for hard boiling and age them for at least two weeks. (Do not be afraid of this. Grocery store eggs are generally at least 45 days old. Aging your eggs for a couple of weeks will not result in spoiled eggs.)

In a saucepan big enough to hold your eggs in a single layer, put enough cold water to just cover them. Add the salt and stir to dissolve. Add the eggs and put them over a medium-high burner. Bring the water to a boil.

As soon as the water reaches a boil, turn off the burner and cover the pan. Set your stove timer for 15 to 20 minutes, depending on how well done you like your hard-boiled eggs—I do 17 minutes.

When the timer beeps, pour off the hot water and immediately run several changes of cold water over your eggs. That's it! Put them in an old egg carton, write "BOILED" on it with a Sharpie, and stash them in the fridge. Egg salad for lunch tomorrow!

YIELD: 12 servings

Nutritional Analysis
Per serving: 65 calories; 5 g fat; 6 g protein; 0.5 g carbohydrate; 0 g dietary fiber; 0.5 g net carbs

NOTE

I ran across the idea of adding baking soda to the water for hard-boiling eggs which reduces the sticking of the shell when peeling them. I haven't tried it yet, but some people I greatly respect (such as Drs. Michael and Mary Dan Eades) swear by this, so I'll be trying it soon. Baking soda's cheap, so give it a shot—a half teaspoon is about right.

Now for another basic egg-cooking skill. This will be familiar to those of you who have used my previous books.

Dana's Easy Omelet Method

If I had to choose just one skill to teach to everyone trying to improve his or her diet, it would be how to make an omelet. They're fast, they're easy, and they make a wide variety of simple ingredients seem like a meal!

First, have your filling ready. If you're using vegetables, you'll want to sauté them first. If you're making an omelet to use up leftovers—a great idea, by the way—warm them through in the microwave and have them standing by.

The pan matters here. For omelets, I recommend a 8- to 9-inch (20 to 23 cm) nonstick skillet with sloping sides. Put it over medium-high heat. While the skillet's heating, grab your eggs—two is the perfect number for this size

(continued)

pan, but one or three will work—and a bowl, crack the eggs, and beat them with a fork. Don't add anything; just mix them up.

The pan is hot enough when a drop of water thrown in sizzles right away. Add a little fat, whatever works with the ingredients of your omelet, and slosh it around to cover the bottom. Now pour in the eggs, all at once. They should sizzle and immediately start to set. When the bottom layer of egg is set around the edges—this should happen quite quickly—lift the edge using a spatula or fork and tip the pan to let the raw egg flow underneath. Do this all around the edges, until there's not enough raw egg to run.

Now, turn your burner to the lowest heat if you have a gas stove. If you have an electric stove, you'll have to have a "warm" burner standing by; electric elements don't cool off fast enough for this job. Put your filling on one half of the omelet, cover it, and let it sit over very low heat for a minute or two, no more. Peek and see if the raw, shiny egg is gone from the top surface. (Although you can serve it that way if you like. That's how the French prefer their omelets.)

When your omelet is done, slip a spatula under the half without the filling, and fold it over, then lift the whole thing onto a plate.

This makes a single-serving omelet. I think it's a lot easier to make several individual omelets than to make one big one, and omelets are so fast to make that it's not that big a deal. Anyway, that way you can customize your omelets to each individual's taste. If you're making more than two or three omelets, just keep them warm in your oven, set to its very lowest heat.

Now for some things to put in your omelets! I am famous for wrapping any and everything in an eggy envelope. Start looking at foods, especially bits of leftovers, with omelet potential in mind!

Spinach-Mushroom Omelet

This is a little complicated for a workday breakfast, but what a great light supper!

2 teaspoons pine nuts (pignolia)
½ shallot, minced
½ cup (35 g) sliced mushrooms
1 tablespoon (7 g) oil-packed sundried tomatoes
2 tablespoons (28 ml) olive oil, divided
1 cup (30 g) fresh baby spinach, loosely packed
2 eggs

Over medium heat, stir your pine nuts in your omelet pan until they're golden. Remove and reserve.

Mince your half shallot and slice your mushrooms if you didn't buy them already sliced. Drain and coarsely chop your sundried tomatoes.

With the omelet pan still over medium heat, heat 1 tablespoon (14 ml) of the olive oil and sauté the mushrooms and shallot until the mushrooms have softened and changed color. Stir in the sundried tomatoes and sauté for just another minute. Stir in the baby spinach and continue cooking just till it wilts. Remove from the pan and reserve.

Wipe the pan and whisk your eggs. Put the pan back over the heat and turn the burner up to medium high. Add the rest of the olive oil and make your omelet according to Dana's Easy Omelet Method (page 55). Fill with the mushroom-tomato-spinach mixture sprinkled with the pine nuts. Serve!

YIELD: 1 serving

Nutritional Analysis
Per serving: 436 calories; 40 g fat; 14 g protein; 7 g carbohydrate; 2 g dietary fiber; 5 g net carbs

Curried Lamb Omelet

½ tablespoon (6.5 g) coconut oil

2 ounces (55 g) leftover roast lamb

1 small shallot or a chunk of a big one

1 tablespoon (14 g) Mayonnaise in the Jar (page 278)

1 tablespoon (15 g) Cocoyo (page 28) (If you don't have any in the house, use another tablespoon [14 g] of mayonnaise.)

½ teaspoon curry powder

1 tablespoon (1 g) chopped fresh cilantro

⅛ teaspoon black pepper

Salt to taste

2 eggs

Whack your leftover lamb into chunks and throw 'em into the food processor with the shallot. Pulse until they're ground up. Now add the mayo, Cocoyo, curry powder, cilantro, pepper, and salt if using.

Whisk your eggs. Make your omelet according to Dana's Easy Omelet Method (page 55), adding the coconut oil first. When time comes to add the filling, spoon the lamb mixture evenly over half the omelet, cover, turn the heat down, and cook till done to your liking. Fold and serve as usual. I put a little mango hot sauce on mine, and thought it complemented it well, but that's up to you.

YIELD: 1 serving

Nutritional Analysis

Per serving: 403 calories; 35 g fat; 20 g protein; 4 g carbohydrate; trace dietary fiber; 4 g net carbs

Creamed Mushroom Omelet

1 shallot, minced

½ cup (35 g) chopped mushrooms

1 tablespoon (13 g) lard or other fat, divided

1 tablespoon (4 g) minced fresh parsley

Salt and black pepper

¼ teaspoon paprika

2 tablespoons (30 g) Coconut Sour Cream (page 29)

2 eggs

In your omelet pan, sauté the shallot and mushrooms in half the lard (reserve remaining to cook the omelet) till the mushrooms soften and change color.

Stir in the parsley, salt and pepper, paprika, and the Coconut Sour Cream. Remove the mushroom mixture to a plate and reserve. Wipe the pan.

Now make your omelet according to Dana's Easy Omelet Method (page 55), using the mushrooms for filling.

YIELD: 1 serving

Nutritional Analysis

Per serving: 364 calories; 32 g fat; 13 g protein; 7 g carbohydrate; 1 g dietary fiber; 6 g net carbs

Tomato and Avocado Omelet

A great summery breakfast. Or lunch. Or supper. Or all three.

½ tablespoon fat
¼ medium tomato, ¼-inch (6 mm) dice
½ avocado, ¼-inch (6 mm) dice
1 tablespoon (10 g) minced red onion
½ garlic clove, crushed
½ teaspoon lime juice
1 tablespoon (1 g) minced fresh cilantro
½ teaspoon minced jalapeño (optional)
2 eggs

Mix the tomato, avocado, and onion gently—so as not to smoosh the avocado—with the garlic, lime, cilantro, and jalapeño if using.

Make your omelet by Dana's Easy Omelet Method (page 55), adding the fat first. Fill with the tomato-avocado mixture and serve with hot sauce, coconut sour cream, or both, if desired.

YIELD: 1 serving

Nutritional Analysis
Per serving: 364 calories; 31 g fat; 13 g protein; 12 g carbohydrate; 3 g dietary fiber; 9 g net carbs

Chicken and Guacamole Omelet

If you have leftover guacamole in the house, this gets even easier. Though I rarely have leftover guacamole.

2 tablespoons (26 g) coconut oil, or fat of choice
1 avocado
2 tablespoons (20 g) minced red onion
1 garlic clove, or half a big one, crushed
2 teaspoons lime juice
Salt (optional)
2 ounces (55 g) cooked chicken
¼ cup (4 g) chopped fresh cilantro, divided
4 eggs
2 pinches ground cumin
2 pinches oregano

First make your guac. Cut your avocado in half and remove the seed by whacking it with the blade of a sharp knife and twisting. Use a spoon to scoop the avocado into a bowl. Add the onion, the garlic, and the lime juice, and mash it up with a fork, leaving some texture. Taste and decide if you want salt—I added a little.

Now dice your chicken—you could use leftover turkey, for that matter. Chop the cilantro, too.

Make your omelet according to Dana's Easy Omelet Method (page 55), adding the fat first. Add a pinch of cumin and oregano to each pair of eggs as you whisk them. When your eggs are ready for the filling, put in the chicken first, then spoon/spread guac on top. Sprinkle in a tablespoon (1 g) of cilantro and cover till done to taste. Fold, plate, top with another tablespoon (1 g) of cilantro, and cover to keep warm while you make the second omelet.

Serve with your favorite hot sauce.

YIELD: 2 servings

Nutritional Analysis
Per serving: 468 calories; 39 g fat; 22 g protein; 10 g carbohydrate; 3 g dietary fiber; 7 g net carbs

Avocado-Bacon Omelets

Why, yes, I am crazy about avocados. Why do you ask?

4 bacon slices
1 avocado
2 tablespoons (20 g) minced red onion
1 tablespoon (1 g) minced fresh cilantro
1 dash hot sauce
4 eggs

Cook your bacon till crisp—I microwave mine, but cook it as you like.

While the bacon is cooking, whack your avocado in half, remove the pit, and scoop the flesh into a bowl. Mash it up, but not too fine—a little texture is nice.

Add the onion and cilantro to the avocado. When the bacon is done, drain it and crumble or snip it in, too. Stir it all up.

Now make your omelets, one at a time, following Dana's Easy Omelet Method (page 55). Use half the avocado mixture in each. I like a little more hot sauce on top, but that's up to you.

YIELD: 2 servings

Nutritional Analysis
Per serving: 370 calories; 30 g fat; 17 g protein; 9 g carbohydrate; 3 g dietary fiber; 6 g net carbs

Simple Avocado Omelet

Simple is good.

½ avocado, sliced
2 teaspoons minced red onion
1 quarter lime
2 teaspoons minced fresh cilantro (optional)
2 eggs
Hot sauce (to serve)

(continued)

Have your avocado sliced, your onion and cilantro minced, and your lime quarter cut. Set it all by the stove.

Now make your omelet according to Dana's Easy Omelet Method (page 55), covering one half with the avocado slices and onion, and squeezing in just a few drops of lime juice—a half teaspoon or so across the avocado slices.

Serve your omelet with your favorite hot sauce on the side—I like chipotle sauce.

YIELD: 1 serving

Nutritional Analysis
Per serving: 316 calories; 24 g fat; 14 g protein; 16 g carbohydrate; 3 g dietary fiber; 13 g net carbs

Chicken Liver and Tomato Omelet

I love chicken livers and eggs together in any form! And this is about as nutritious as a meal can get.

2 chicken livers
⅛ small red onion, sliced paper thin
¼ cup (45 g) diced tomato, ¼-inch (6 mm) dice
2 tablespoons (26 g) bacon grease or other fat, divided
1 pinch dried thyme
1 pinch ground rosemary
2 eggs

Snip your chicken livers into ½-inch (1-cm) bits. Slice your onion and dice your tomato and have them on hand.

Put your omelet pan over medium-high heat and add 1 tablespoon (13 g) of the bacon grease. When it's hot, add the chicken liver. Sauté quickly, stirring near constantly, until the liver has "seized" on the outside—the surface has sealed over and the red juice has stopped running.

Stir in the thyme and rosemary, and remove from the heat. Do not overcook your liver! It should be pink in the middle.

Remove the liver from the pan and give it a quick wipe. Put it back on the burner and get it good and hot again. Add the rest of the bacon grease, whisk your eggs, and make your omelet according to Dana's Easy Omelet Method (page 55), layering the liver, then onion, then tomato.

YIELD: 1 serving

Nutritional Analysis
Per serving: 465 calories; 38 g fat; 23 g protein; 7 g carbohydrate; 1 g dietary fiber; 6 g net carbs

Another Leftover Lamblet

I can't resist—all sorts of leftovers wind up in omelets, and it takes a while for the two of us to eat up a whole leg of lamb. This was delicious and kept me full for a good five or six hours.

1 tablespoon (13 g) lard or other fat
3 ounces (85 g) leftover roast lamb
2 scallions, trimmed and chunked
1 tablespoon (7 g) oil-packed sundried tomatoes
2 tablespoons (28 g) mayonnaise
1 teaspoon Paleo Worcestershire (page 293)
½ teaspoon lemon juice
1 small garlic clove, crushed
2 dashes hot sauce, such as Tabasco
4 eggs

Cut your leftover lamb into 1-inch (2.5 cm) chunks and throw 'em in the food processor with the *S* blade in place. Pulse till the meat is coarsely chopped. Add everything from the scallions through the hot sauce and run the processor till you have a coarse paste or spread.

Now make your omelet according to Dana's Easy Omelet Method (page 55), adding the fat first. Use half of the lamb spread in each.

YIELD: 2 servings

Nutritional Analysis
Per serving: 392 calories; 34 g fat; 17 g protein; 4 g carbohydrate; 1 g dietary fiber; 3 g net carbs

NOTE

This filling was good right off a spoon! It would be good stuffed into celery, or wrapped in lettuce leaves, or stuffed into tomatoes.

How about adding tasty things to scrambled eggs?

Eggs with Green Beans and Tomatoes

This makes a quick, easy, inexpensive supper.

1 cup (100 g) green beans, snipped in ½-inch (1 cm) pieces
2 tablespoons (26 g) bacon grease or coconut oil
2 medium tomatoes, diced
4 scallions, sliced
10 eggs

Steam your green beans till just tender—maybe 5 to 6 minutes on high in the microwave.

Put your big, heavy skillet over medium heat and add the bacon grease. Throw in the beans and sauté for a minute or two while you dice up your tomato. Add to the skillet and keep sautéing till the tomato softens and becomes easy to mash with a fork—not that you need to mash it all up, you just want it soft. You can slice up your scallions while the tomatoes are cooking—include the crisp part of the green.

When the tomatoes are soft, add the scallions, stir them in, and sauté for another minute or two.

Whisk the eggs and add to the skillet. Scramble till set and serve.

YIELD: 4 servings

Nutritional Analysis
Per serving: 249 calories; 18 g fat; 15 g protein; 7 g carbohydrate; 2 g dietary fiber; 5 g net carbs

Horseradish Scrambled Eggs

A little twist on an old favorite.

4 slices bacon, raw
6 eggs
1 teaspoon horseradish

Put your big, heavy skillet over medium heat. Use your kitchen shears to snip the bacon into the skillet. Fry it crisp, separating the bits as it cooks. While that's happening, whisk your eggs with the horseradish.

(continued)

When the bacon bits are crisp, scoop them out of the skillet to a plate and reserve.

Pour off all but a tablespoon (15 ml) or so of the grease. Now pour in the eggs and scramble till they're almost set. Then add the bacon bits and scramble them in. Serve!

YIELD: 2 servings

Nutritional Analysis
Per serving: 450 calories; 39 g fat; 20 g protein; 2 g carbohydrate; trace dietary fiber; 2 g net carbs

Menemen

I read about this dish in a Middle Eastern cookbook. It's apparently the ultimate Turkish comfort food, and infinitely variable. The basics are tomatoes, peppers, onions, and eggs; feel free to play with it.

¼ cup (40 g) diced red onion
1 medium tomato, ¼-inch (6 mm) dice
½ cup (75 g) green bell pepper, diced
1 tablespoon (15 ml) olive oil
1 garlic clove, crushed
¼ teaspoon ground cumin
¼ teaspoon black pepper
¼ teaspoon turmeric
¼ teaspoon red-pepper flakes
¼ teaspoon salt
3 eggs
1 tablespoon (4 g) minced fresh parsley

In your big, heavy skillet, over medium-low heat, start sautéing the onion, tomato, and pepper in the olive oil. Crush the garlic and throw it in, and stir in the spices, too. Keep cooking, stirring often, till the vegetables have softened and exuded juice into the mix—you want a coarse sauce.

While your veggies are cooking, crack your eggs into a dish and whisk them.

When you've got a nice sauce going in the skillet, pour in the eggs and scramble till they're softly set. It should be creamy.

Scoop onto a plate, sprinkle with the parsley, and devour. May well be the best breakfast ever.

YIELD: 1 serving

Nutritional Analysis
Per serving: 388 calories; 28 g fat; 19 g protein; 18 g carbohydrate; 4 g dietary fiber; 14 g net carbs

NOTES

Recipes for menemen vary a lot. Some call for grating the tomatoes into a pulp before adding them to the skillet, but that seemed like a lot of work for little payoff. Some use regular yellow onion instead of the sweet red onion, others use scallions. One said that if you can get 'em, hot banana peppers are the best, instead of the green bell pepper. I've made this with yellow bell pepper, and it was awesome.

I've also seen variation in the spices; you could add ground coriander, ginger, cinnamon, and not be off the track. I included turmeric not only because it's tasty, but also because it's seriously healthful stuff.

Just play with this. I'm pretty sure it would be hard to really screw it up.

Spinach and Mushroom Eggs

½ cup (80 g) minced onion
1 cup (70 g) chopped mushrooms
2 tablespoons (26 g) bacon grease or other fat
2 cups (60 g) fresh spinach, chopped
6 eggs

Put your big, heavy skillet over medium heat, and start sautéing the onion and mushrooms in the bacon grease. While that's happening, chop your spinach and whisk your eggs.

When the onions are translucent and the mushrooms have softened and changed color, add the spinach. Sauté, mixing it up with the mushrooms and onions, until the spinach is just barely wilted.

Pour in the eggs, scramble till set, and serve.

YIELD: 2 servings

Nutritional Analysis
Per serving: 346 calories; 27 g fat; 19 g protein; 8 g carbohydrate; 2 g dietary fiber; 6 g net carbs

Sweet and Smoky Eggs

I confess, most chipotle hot sauce has at least a little sugar in it. Read the labels to find the one with the least sugar. You won't get more than a gram or two of sugar per serving. If you prefer, you could mince a tablespoon (14 g) of the Chipotles in Adobo (page 294) to use in place of the hot sauce.

½ cup (80 g) diced onion
½ cup (75 g) diced red bell pepper
½ medium tomato, ¼-inch (6 mm) dice
2 tablespoons (26 g) lard or coconut oil
6 eggs
2 teaspoons chipotle hot sauce
1 teaspoon oregano
½ teaspoon ground cumin
2 cloves garlic

Dice up your veggies. Put your big, heavy skillet over medium heat and start sautéing your vegetables in the lard. In the meanwhile, whisk your eggs with the chipotle hot sauce, oregano, cumin, and garlic.

When the vegetables are soft, pour in the eggs, and scramble till set. Personally, I'd like a little cilantro on this, but it's not essential.

YIELD: 2 servings

Nutritional Analysis
Per serving: 353 calories; 26 g fat; 18 g protein; 11 g carbohydrate; 2 g dietary fiber; 9 g net carbs

Wake-Up Eggs

Bright color, bright flavor, should wake you right up!

4 whole mushrooms, chopped
½ red bell pepper, diced
2 scallions, sliced thin
1 tablespoon (13 g) fat (I used lard.)
6 eggs
6 tablespoons (90 ml) unsweetened coconut milk
1 tablespoon (15 g) brown mustard

Reduce your veggies to bits and start them sautéing in the fat, over medium heat.

While that's happening, whisk the eggs with the coconut milk and mustard.

(continued)

When the vegetables are soft, pour in the eggs and scramble till set. Done!

YIELD: 2 servings

Nutritional Analysis
Per serving: 367 calories; 29 g fat; 19 g protein; 8 g carbohydrate; 1 g dietary fiber; 7 g net carbs

Busy Day Breakfast

Why is a breakfast that takes this much work called Busy Day Breakfast? Because if you take 15 minutes to make and eat this in the morning, you won't even think about lunch, and your energy will be high all day long. But if you prefer, make this for supper.

6 slices bacon
1 medium turnip, ¼-inch (6 mm) dice
½ cup (80 g) diced onion
½ green or red bell pepper
6 eggs

Put your big, heavy skillet over low-medium heat and snip the bacon into it with your kitchen shears. Let the bacon bits brown.

Peel and dice your turnip. Put in a microwaveable dish, add just a teaspoon or two of water, and cover with a saucer. Nuke on high for 3 minutes.

Go back and stir your bacon! Use your pancake turner to separate the little pieces of bacon as you stir.

Dice your onion and pepper while the bacon finishes browning.

When the bacon is crisp, remove to a plate. Add the onion and pepper to the skillet, along with the turnip, which should be reasonably tender by now, and turn the burner up a little, to medium. Sauté until the onion and pepper are soft and everything's getting a few brown spots.

Whisk your eggs. Now add the bacon back to the skillet, pour in the eggs, and scramble the whole thing together till the eggs are set. Plate and serve!

YIELD: 2 servings

Nutritional Analysis
Per serving: 346 calories; 23 g fat; 23 g protein; 11 g carbohydrate; 2 g dietary fiber; 9 g net carbs

NOTE

If you can't face dicing things before breakfast, go ahead and chop the veggies in your food processor. I just like little, even dice.

Scrambled Eggs with Shrimp and Leeks

½ leek (white part; thinly sliced)
2 tablespoons (28 ml) olive oil
5 ounces (140 g) shrimp, shelled
2 eggs
2 tablespoons (28 ml) unsweetened coconut milk
1 small garlic clove, minced

1 dash hot sauce (I used Frank's, but any Louisiana-style hot sauce will be fine.)
1 dash Liquid Umami (page 288)

Put a medium-size, heavy-bottomed skillet over a medium-low burner and start sautéing the leeks in the olive oil. If you're using raw shrimp, throw them in as the leeks start to soften. If you're using precooked shrimp, hold off.

In the meanwhile, whisk the eggs with the coconut milk, garlic, hot sauce, and Liquid Umami if you have it.

If you are using those aforementioned cooked shrimp, put them in when the leeks are soft, and just let them warm through. If you started with raw ones, you'll want to wait till they're pink and firm.

Then pour in your eggs and scramble the whole thing very slowly, keeping the heat low. When the eggs are set but still moist, plate and serve.

YIELD: 1 serving

Nutritional Analysis
Per serving: 607 calories; 44 g fat; 41 g protein; 10 g carbohydrate; 1 g dietary fiber; 9 g net carbs

Creamy Coconut Eggs

Creamy and fluffy! The coconut flavor is subtle.

3 eggs
¼ cup (60 ml) unsweetened coconut milk
2 teaspoons fat of choice

Put your skillet—I use a heavy-bottomed nonstick skillet—over medium-low heat.

Break your eggs into a mixing bowl, add the coconut milk, and whisk them for at least 30 to 40 seconds. A full minute is great.

Melt your fat in the hot pan and slosh it around, then pour in the eggs. Scramble them slowly, till just set—they should still be moist. Plate and serve!

YIELD: 1 serving

Nutritional Analysis
Per serving: 385 calories; 34 g fat; 18 g protein; 3 g carbohydrate; 0 g dietary fiber; 3 g net carbs

Dilled Eggs

If you eat 'em, I think a few green peas would be good in this, too, or some snipped sugar-pea pods.

2 scallions, sliced thin
½ tablespoon (6.5 g) coconut oil or lard
½ teaspoon minced fresh dill weed
3 eggs
3 tablespoons (45 ml) unsweetened coconut milk

Slice your scallions first, including the crisp part of the green shoot. Put a medium-size, heavy skillet over low heat and start the scallions sautéing in the oil, while you mince your dill weed.

Crack the eggs into a bowl, add the coconut milk and dill, and whisk.

Now pour the eggs over the scallions and scramble slowly until the eggs are set but still moist. Plate and serve.

YIELD: 1 serving

Nutritional Analysis
Per serving: 348 calories; 29 g fat; 18 g protein; 5 g carbohydrate; 1 g dietary fiber; 4 g net carbs

End-of-the-Summer, Down-by-the-Border Eggs

Think eggs scrambled with salsa—not on top, but scrambled right in.

½ cup (80 g) diced onion
1 tablespoon (12.5 g) fat
1 medium tomato
½ green pepper, diced
1 small hot pepper, minced
6 eggs
1 clove garlic, crushed
1 teaspoon ground cumin
½ teaspoon ground coriander
1 teaspoon dried oregano

This is very straightforward: Start sautéing the onion in the fat in your big, heavy skillet, over medium-low heat.

In the meanwhile, cut the tomato through the equator and gently squeeze/scoop out the seeds. Now dice the flesh and cut up your peppers, too. Throw these all in the pan with the onion. Now wash your hands really well with soap and water! If you don't, you'll be sorry the next time you touch your eyes or nose.

While the veggies are cooking, whisk the eggs with the garlic and seasonings. When the veggies are tender but not limp, pour in the eggs and scramble till set. Serve and pass the hot sauce for the chile-heads.

YIELD: 2 servings

Nutritional Analysis
Per serving: 309 calories; 20 g fat; 19 g protein; 14 g carbohydrate; 3 g dietary fiber; 11 g net carbs

NOTE

Adjust the heat of this by what sort of hot pepper you use. This would also be good with a couple of hot banana peppers in place of the green pepper and the hot pepper. Oh, and a little minced fresh cilantro would be lovely on top, should you happen to have some kicking around the fridge.

Exotic, Vegetable-y Eggs

½ medium red onion, sliced
1 small tomato, ¼-inch (6 mm) dice
2 tablespoons (26 g) coconut oil
½ teaspoon cumin
½ teaspoon ground coriander
2 pinches cayenne (optional)
2 cloves garlic, crushed
½ teaspoon turmeric
2 teaspoons curry powder
6 eggs
6 tablespoons (90 ml) unsweetened coconut milk

In your big, heavy skillet, over medium heat, start sautéing the onion and tomato in the coconut oil.

When the onion and tomato are soft, stir in the cumin, coriander, cayenne (if using), garlic, turmeric, and curry powder.

Turn the burner very low and let the whole thing cook while you quickly whisk the eggs with the coconut milk. Pour into the skillet and scramble until set, then serve.

YIELD: 2 servings

Nutritional Analysis

Per serving: 441 calories; 36 g fat; 19 g protein; 12 g carbohydrate; 2 g dietary fiber; 10 g net carbs

Not-Machaca Eggs

Huevos con machaca, *a.k.a.* Machaca Eggs, *is a traditional Mexican dish made with dried beef boiled until it shreds. I didn't feel like drying the beef first, and the Crispy Shredded Beef is traditionally Mexican, too. This is just as good as machaca!*

1 medium tomato, ¼-inch (6 mm) dice

½ medium onion, ¼-inch (6 mm) dice

1 medium jalapeño, seeded and minced

1 tablespoon (13 g) lard

6 eggs

½ cup (112 g) Crispy Shredded Beef (page 220)

1 avocado

2 tablespoons (2 g) minced fresh cilantro

In your big, heavy skillet, over medium heat, start the tomato, onion, and jalapeño all sautéing in the lard. Now wash your hands really well with soap and water!

While the vegetables are cooking, whisk the eggs and measure your Crispy Shredded Beef. You might as well slice your avocado now, too.

When the vegetables are soft, add the eggs and beef to the skillet and scramble till set.

Plate the eggs and top with the cilantro and avocado slices before serving.

YIELD: 3 servings

Nutritional Analysis

Per serving: 529 calories; 42 g fat; 28 g protein; 11 g carbohydrate; 3 g dietary fiber; 8 g net carbs

Eggs Fu Yong

If you have any leftover meat in the house, dice it up, throw it in, and call this supper. This is for one serving—25 grams of protein seems about right to me—but you can easily increase this. And if you add meat, you'll serve more folks.

4 eggs

2 teaspoons coconut aminos

½ teaspoon grated gingerroot

1 teaspoon dry sherry

½ cup (35 g) shredded cabbage (napa or green)

3 scallions, sliced

¼ cup (17.5 g) chopped mushrooms

½ cup (25 g) bean sprouts

1 tablespoon (13 g) coconut oil

Break the eggs into a bowl and add the coconut aminos, ginger, and sherry. Whisk 'em up and sit 'em by the stove.

Shred the cabbage and slice the scallions, chop your mushrooms, and measure out your bean sprouts. Have them all on a plate, while you . . .

Put your big skillet or wok over highest heat. Add the coconut oil. When it's good and hot, dump in the veggies and stir-fry till they're just tender-crisp.

If you're using a wok, you may want to do this the traditional way: Mix the stir-fried veggies with the eggs in a big bowl, then add the mixture back to the wok and cook, a ladleful at a time. If you're using a skillet, it's easier to spread the veggies evenly over the bottom of the skillet,

(continued)

pour in the eggs, and let them cook for a minute or so. Start pulling back the edge of the egg mixture to let the raw egg run underneath. When there's not enough raw egg left to run, use your pancake turner to lift big sections of the mixture and flip them to cook the other side. Either way, when the eggs are done, plate and eat.

YIELD: 1 serving

Nutritional Analysis
Per serving: 439 calories; 32 g fat; 25 g protein; 13 g carbohydrate; 3 g dietary fiber; 10 g net carbs

Asparagus and Shiitake Frittata

Why, yes, this is yet another spin-off of the Asparagus and Shiitake Sauté recipe. Why do you ask?

Asparagus, Shiitake, and Chicken Skillet (page 188)
9 eggs
1 teaspoon dried thyme

Make your Asparagus, Shiitake, and Chicken Skillet, omitting the coconut aminos. While it's sautéing, whisk the eggs with the thyme.

When the asparagus is tender-crisp and the pink is gone from the chicken, spread it all evenly in your skillet. Pour in the eggs, and stir it about some until the bottom part is set. Smooth it all out with your spatula, turn the burner to low, and cover the skillet.

Give it 5 minutes and check. If the top is set, it's done. If it's still too liquid on top, run it under the broiler for a minute or two. Then serve!

YIELD: 4 servings

Nutritional Analysis
Per serving: 355 calories; 15 g fat; 29 g protein; 29 g carbohydrate; 5 g dietary fiber; 24 g net carbs

NOTE

As mentioned in the recipe notes for Asparagus and Shiitake Sauté (page 98), shiitake are higher in carbs than most mushrooms. Feel free to substitute crimini or portobellos, either of which will be far lower carb.

Cajun Eggs

Eggs simmered in a quick-and-easy sauce.

1 tablespoon (15 ml) olive oil
2 tablespoons (20 g) minced onion
½ garlic clove, crushed, or 1 little one
1 small tomato, ¼-inch (6 mm) dice
¼ green bell pepper, diced
1 teaspoon Cajun seasoning
1 teaspoon dried basil
1 teaspoon Tabasco sauce or other Louisiana
   hot sauce, to taste
3 eggs

In a smallish skillet, over low heat, heat the olive oil and start sautéing the onion and garlic slowly while you dice up the tomato and pepper. Throw them in, too, and stir in the Cajun seasoning, basil, and hot sauce. Let the whole thing cook for 5 minutes or so, till the vegetables have softened a bit.

Now crack in the eggs, cover the pan, and let it cook till the eggs are done to your liking—about 5 minutes is right for me, so the whites are set, but the yolks are still runny. Tilt the pan over a plate to slip the whole thing out together and serve.

YIELD: 1 serving

Nutritional Analysis
Per serving: 373 calories; 27 g fat; 19 g protein; 15 g carbohydrate; 3 g dietary fiber; 12 g net carbs

Eggs in Creamy Mustard Sauce

This is a random invention, and one of the best things I came up with for this book. I want to have this for breakfast every day.

2 tablespoons (20 g) diced onion
1 clove garlic, crushed
1 small tomato, diced (about ⅓ to ½ cup [60 to 90 g])
1 tablespoon (9 g) minced green chile or a few dashes of hot sauce
½ tablespoon (6.5 g) coconut oil
¼ cup (60 ml) unsweetened coconut milk
1 tablespoon (15 g) brown mustard
3 eggs

In a medium skillet, over medium-low heat, start the onion, garlic, tomato, and chile, if you have one on hand, sautéing in the coconut oil.

When the vegetables are soft, stir in the coconut milk and the mustard. Add the hot sauce if you didn't have a chile on hand. Bring the sauce to a simmer and let it cook for a minute or two to thicken up a tad.

Now break the eggs into the sauce, turn the burner to low, cover the pan, and let the eggs poach to your liking, probably about 5 minutes, but how do I know? Scoop 'em out with a big spoon onto a plate, scrape any remaining sauce in the pan over the eggs, and devour.

YIELD: 1 serving

Nutritional Analysis
Per serving: 422 calories; 34 g fat; 20 g protein; 13 g carbohydrate; 2 g dietary fiber; 11 g net carbs

Eggs Baked in Portobellos

This would make a nice company brunch dish. Easy to expand or contract.

¼ cup (60 ml) olive oil
2 cloves garlic, crushed
4 portobello mushroom caps
4 scallions, thinly sliced
4 eggs

Preheat oven to 350°F (180°C, or gas mark 4).

Pour the olive oil into a small dish and crush the garlic into it. Reserve.

(*continued*)

Remove the stem from your portobellos and use your fingers, a paring knife, or the tip of a spoon to remove the gills (that ribbed stuff). Trim off any fringy bits around the edge of the cap, too.

Use a basting brush to coat your portobellos all over with the garlicky olive oil. Place them in a roasting pan concave side up, and put 'em in the oven. Set your timer for 10 minutes.

While your portobellos are baking, slice your scallions.

Okay, the timer beeped. Pull out the pan of portobellos. Sprinkle one of the sliced scallions into each mushroom. Now use a spoon to fish up some of the crushed garlic from the dish of olive oil, and spoon that into the mushrooms, too.

Break an egg into each mushroom—I've tried using two, and they just slide over the side of the mushroom. If you want 2 eggs for breakfast, you get 2 mushrooms, too. Put them back in the oven and bake for 10 to 15 minutes, till set to your liking—I like my whites firm but my yolks still runny.

Use a big spoon to transfer to plates and serve.

YIELD: 4 servings

Nutritional Analysis
Per serving: 223 calories; 18 g fat; 8 g protein; 8 g carbohydrate; 2 g dietary fiber; 6 g net carbs

Eggs Ogg

Vaguely inspired by Eggs Benedict. Quite different, really, but very good.

4 portobello mushroom caps
2 tablespoons (26 g) bacon grease
4 slices bacon
4 eggs
1 batch Hollandaise for Sissy Cavemen (page 279)

Preheat oven to 350°F (180°C, or gas mark 4).

Remove the stems from your mushroom caps. Use your fingers, the tip of a spoon, or a paring knife to remove the gills (the ribby stuff). Remove any fringy bits around the edge of the cap, too.

Melt the bacon grease, and brush each cap all over with it. Arrange them, concave side up, in a roasting pan.

Use your kitchen shears to snip a slice of bacon into each cap. Spread the bits out evenly in the hollows.

Now bake your mushroom caps for 10 to 15 minutes. Halfway through, pour off the liquid that accumulates to help the bacon cook. (The liquid will absorb back into the caps through the side that's down.)

When your bacon is done through—it will probably not get crisp—break an egg into each mushroom cap. Put the mushrooms back in the oven and bake for another 10 to 15 minutes, till the eggs are set to your liking.

If you haven't got Hollandaise for Sissy Cavemen on hand, this would be a good time to make some!

When the eggs are done—I like mine with the whites firm but the yolks still runny—plate 'em. Then put a couple of tablespoons (30 g) of the Hollandaise for Sissy Cavemen over each serving. If you really want to, you could snip a little parsley over your eggs for presentation value, but they're awfully good just as-is.

YIELD: 4 servings

Nutritional Analysis
Per serving: 238 calories; 18 g fat; 12 g protein; 7 g carbohydrate; 2 g dietary fiber; 5 g net carbs

Portobellos with Guacamole and Eggs

6 portobello mushroom caps, about 4 inches (10 cm) across
3 tablespoons (39 g) bacon grease or fat of your choice, melted
2 tablespoons (28 ml) vinegar
1 batch Guacamole (page 50)
1 medium tomato, ¼-inch (6 mm) dice
6 fresh eggs
2 tablespoons (2 g) minced fresh cilantro (optional)

Preheat oven to 350°F (180°C, or gas mark 4). Brush the portobellos all over with the bacon grease and place them, concave side up, in a roasting pan. Put 'em in the oven and set the timer for 10 minutes.

Put about 2 inches (5 cm) of water in a big saucepan, add a couple of tablespoons of vinegar (any kind), and put it on a medium-high burner. You're bringing it to a bare simmer.

In the meanwhile, make your guac—it's easy! Dice your tomato, too.

Somewhere in here the oven timer will beep. Pull your portobellos out of the oven and set them somewhere to wait while you . . .

Break your eggs, one by one, into a custard cup, then slip them carefully into the simmering water. (Not only does breaking them into a cup first make it easier to slip the eggs gently into the water, it also lets you catch any with broken yolks.)

While the eggs are poaching, plate your portobellos and spread the insides of each one with guacamole, making sure it hollows a bit in the center, to hold the eggs.

When your eggs are done to your liking, carefully lift them out, one by one, with a slotted spoon, and place each one in the center of a mushroom. Sprinkle a little diced tomato over each one and add a little cilantro if you like it. Serve immediately!

YIELD: 6 servings

Nutritional Analysis
Per serving: 272 calories; 22 g fat; 10 g protein; 13 g carbohydrate; 4 g dietary fiber; 9 g net carbs

Eggs on a Bed of Mediterranean Vegetables

2 tablespoons (20 g) diced onion
2 tablespoons (18.5 g) minced green bell pepper
2 tablespoons (7 g) dry-packed sundried tomatoes
1 jarred artichoke heart, drained
2 tablespoons (28 ml) olive oil, divided
1 clove garlic, crushed
1 teaspoon dried oregano
3 eggs

Dice up your onion, mince your pepper (if you have a hot banana pepper on hand, that would be good here, too—different, but good), and chop your sundried tomatoes. Slice your artichoke heart.

(continued)

In a medium-size skillet over medium-low heat, heat 1 tablespoon (14 ml) of the oil and start the veggies sautéing. While they cook, crush in the garlic and crumble in the oregano.

When the onion is translucent and the pepper soft, scoop the veggies out onto a serving plate. Put the pan back on the burner, add the rest of the oil, and crack in the eggs. Cover the skillet and let the eggs cook till the whites are set but the yolks are still soft—about 5 minutes, but you'll have to peek to be sure. (The lid holds in and reflects heat, so you don't have to flip your eggs to get the tops of the whites set.)

Place the eggs on the bed of veggies and serve.

YIELD: 1 serving

Nutritional Analysis
Per serving: 513 calories; 41 g fat; 21 g protein; 19 g carbohydrate; 7 g dietary fiber; 12 g net carbs

Eggs with Curry Sauce

Exotic and wonderful. And with hard-boiled eggs in the fridge, it's quick and easy, too.

6 eggs, hard-boiled, peeled, and halved
2 tablespoons (14 g) slivered almonds
1 tablespoon (13 g) coconut oil
1 teaspoon turmeric
2 garlic cloves, crushed
1 teaspoon chili powder
¼ lime
½ cup (115 g) Cocoyo (page 28)
1 tablespoon (15 ml) chicken Broth Concentrate (page 27)
1 tablespoon (1 g) minced fresh cilantro

Peel your eggs and halve them. If they're chilled, give them a very gentle warming—I gave mine about 90 seconds on power 3 in my microwave. Arrange six half eggs, spoke fashion, on each of two plates.

Put a medium-size skillet over medium heat and stir the slivered almonds in it until they're touched with gold. Remove to a small plate or dish and reserve.

Turn the heat down to low. Melt the coconut oil and add the turmeric, crushed garlic, and chili powder and sauté them together for just a minute.

Squeeze in the juice from your lime and stir in the Cocoyo and concentrated chicken broth. Keep the heat very low and let the whole thing cook, stirring, for a couple of minutes.

Now spoon the sauce—which will be a lovely golden-brown color—over the eggs. Sprinkle the almonds and cilantro on top and serve.

YIELD: 2 servings

Nutritional Analysis
Per serving: 734 calories; 68 g fat; 25 g protein; 12 g carbohydrate; 1 g dietary fiber; 11 g net carbs

Mushroom Stroganoff with Eggs

I originally made this in a single-serving size, and it worked fine. This is a great way to use up leftover Cauli-Rice and hard-boiled eggs.

½ head cauliflower
4 slices bacon
16 ounces (455 g) sliced mushrooms

1 cup (160 g) diced onion

Coconut oil or bacon grease, as needed

4 garlic cloves, minced

8 teaspoons (40 ml) Paleo Worcestershire (page 293)

1 cup (230 g) Cocoyo (page 28)

4 tablespoons (16 g) minced fresh parsley

Salt and black pepper

8 eggs, hard-boiled

First make Cauli-Rice (page 87). Run your cauliflower through the shredding blade of your food processor, then steam lightly—I gave mine 6 minutes on high in the microwave.

Put your skillet over medium heat and snip the bacon into it. Fry it out into nice, crispy little bacon bits. While that's happening, slice your mushrooms (if you didn't buy 'em sliced as I did) and dice your onion.

Scoop your bacon bits out of the skillet and hold them on a plate. Add the mushrooms and onion to the skillet and sauté them in the bacon grease. Add more coconut oil or bacon grease if needed.

When the mushrooms have changed color and the onion is translucent, stir in the garlic, Worcestershire, and Cocoyo. Cook over very low heat until it thickens up a bit. Now stir in the parsley and salt and pepper to taste. You might peel your eggs while this is happening.

Okay, here goes: Put a bed of Cauli-Rice on each of 4 plates. Slice 2 hard-boiled eggs over each serving of Cauli-Rice. Now spoon the mushroom mixture over that and top with bacon bits. That's it!

YIELD: 4 servings

Nutritional Analysis

Per serving: 495 calories; 40 g fat; 20 g protein; 18 g carbohydrate; 4 g dietary fiber; 14 g net carbs

Microwaved Egg

I don't have instructions for doing two eggs and doubling the mushrooms in one dish. I just used two dishes.

3 tablespoons (13 g) chopped mushrooms

1 tablespoon (10 g) minced onion

1 teaspoon fat of choice

Salt and black pepper (optional)

1 egg

1 teaspoon unsweetened coconut milk

Put the mushrooms, onions, and fat in a small, microwaveable dish—a custard cup or individual ramekin is perfect. Sprinkle lightly with pepper and salt if you like. Microwave on high for 1 minute. Stir and give it another 30 seconds.

Now break in the egg and use a toothpick or a sharp-pointed knife to poke a tiny hole in the membrane on the yolk. Spoon the coconut milk over the white.

Cover the dish loosely with a paper towel. Microwave on high for 1 minute and check for doneness. Give it another 20 to 30 seconds if it needs it, but remember that if you're going to let it sit for a minute or two—say, while you pour another cup of coffee or find your kid's missing sneaker—it'll continue cooking a bit. Eat right out of the dish, of course!

YIELD: 1 serving

Nutritional Analysis

Per serving: 120 calories; 10 g fat; 6 g protein; 2 g carbohydrate; trace dietary fiber; 2 g net carbs

Pink-and-Green Eggs

Keith the Organic Gardening God brought me some chard, so I turned it into breakfast. So good.

2 cups (110 g) chopped Swiss chard
¼ small onion, ¼-inch (6 mm) dice
1 tablespoon (15 ml) olive oil
1 clove garlic, crushed
1 pinch red-pepper flakes
¼ lemon
3 eggs

Trim the stems from your chard and slice across the leaves about ¼-inch (6 mm) wide. You need 2 cups (110 g) per serving.

Put your big, heavy skillet over medium-high heat and add the olive oil. Start sautéing the chard and onion, stirring frequently.

When the chard is tender and the onion translucent—about 5 minutes—stir in the crushed garlic and red-pepper flakes and squeeze in the juice from the lemon. (Flick the pits out first with the tip of a knife, so you don't have to retrieve them from your chard.) Stir it all up well, then spread evenly in the bottom of the skillet.

Break the eggs into the skillet, on top of the chard. Cover the skillet, turn the burner to low, and let the whole thing cook until the whites are set but the yolks are still soft in the middle. Plate and serve.

YIELD: 1 serving

Nutritional Analysis
Per serving: 343 calories; 27 g fat; 18 g protein; 8 g carbohydrate; 2 g dietary fiber; 6 g net carbs

Poached Eggs on Mushrooms, Onions, and Chicken Livers

1 bacon slice
¼ small onion
2 ounces (55 g) sliced mushrooms
2 eggs
1 chicken liver
Salt and pepper

First, put 1½ inches (3.5 cm) of water in a small saucepan and place it over medium-high heat. At the same time, put a medium, heavy-bottomed skillet (nonstick is nice) over medium heat. Crack your eggs—they should be super-fresh—into a custard cup and have 'em by the stove.

Using your kitchen shears, snip the bacon into the skillet. Let your bacon bits cook, remembering to stir now and then, while you . . .

Slice the onion thinly. If you didn't buy your mushrooms sliced, this is a good time to slice them, too.

When your bacon bits are crisp, scoop 'em out and reserve them on a plate. Throw the onions and mushrooms into the bacon fat. Sauté until they're softened, the onion's gone translucent, and the mushrooms have darkened.

Somewhere in here your water should start boiling. Turn it down to just below simmering—you don't want the water moving, but you want it to stay good and hot. Slip your eggs into the water.

Snip the chicken liver into the skillet, into bite-size bits. Continue sautéing, stirring frequently, until the liver is just barely done—it should have stopped running red, but should still be pink in the middle of each bit. Stir the bacon bits in, salt and pepper to taste, then transfer the whole thing to a plate, and keep it warm while your eggs finish poaching to your liking.

When your eggs are done—the yolks should still be runny—use a slotted spoon to lift them out and place them on top of the onion-mushroom-liver mixture and serve.

YIELD: 1 serving

Nutritional Analysis
Per serving: 232 calories; 13 g fat; 20 g protein; 7 g carbohydrate; 1 g dietary fiber; 6 g net carbs

Skillet Mushroom-Artichoke Eggs

Confession: I used canned artichoke hearts for this. Cooking enough artichokes to get half a cup of artichoke hearts was right out. If you can get them, use frozen artichoke hearts, steamed tender.

¼ cup (45 g) diced tomato
½ cup (35 g) chopped mushrooms
1 tablespoon (10 g) minced onion
½ cup (150 g) artichoke hearts, chopped
1 clove garlic, minced
½ tablespoon (7.5 ml) olive oil
3 eggs

Chop up all the veggies. Put a smallish (about 9-inch [23 cm]) skillet over medium heat. Add the olive oil and throw in the tomatoes, mushrooms, and onion. Sauté till the mushrooms soften and change color, then add the artichokes and garlic. Sauté another couple of minutes, just to blend the flavors.

Spread the vegetables evenly over the bottom of the skillet and break in the eggs. Cover the pan, turn the burner to low, and let it cook till the eggs are done to your liking— whites firm but yolks still runny in the middle is perfect for me. Slide the whole thing out onto a plate and serve.

YIELD: 1 serving

Nutritional Analysis
Per serving: 325 calories; 20 g fat; 21 g protein; 17 g carbohydrate; 6 g dietary fiber; 11 g net carbs

Chapter 4

GRANOLA, PANCAKES, CRACKERS, AND THE LIKE

This is a short chapter. Why? Because you really should be focusing your paleo diet on animal foods and vegetables, not coming up with ways to keep eating muffins and cereal and stuff. Still, these recipes are delicious and way better for you than anything at the grocery store.

Simple Sunflower Crackers

Sunflower crackers are amazingly, well . . . crackery. Delicious, crunchy—and near-addictive, so be careful, you hear?

1 cup (145 g) sunflower seeds
½ teaspoon salt
1 pinch baking powder
3 tablespoons (45 ml) water
Salt for sprinkling

Preheat oven to 350°F (180°C, or gas mark 4).

Put your sunflower seeds, salt, and baking powder in your food processor with the *S* blade in place. Run until the seeds are finely ground.

Leave the processor on while you pour in the water. You'll get a soft, sticky dough.

Line a cookie sheet with baking parchment. (DO NOT SKIP THE BAKING PARCHMENT. YOU WILL REGRET IT.) Take half your dough ball and put it in the middle of the cookie sheet. Put another sheet of parchment on top and use a rolling pin to roll the dough out very thin—the thinner the better, so long as it's pretty even and has no holes.

Peel off the top sheet of parchment and use a thin, sharp, straight-bladed (not serrated) knife to score the dough into squares or diamonds—I make mine about the size of Wheat Thins crackers.

Repeat this maneuver with a second cookie sheet and the other half of the dough. You can use the same sheet of parchment on top, for rolling.

Bake your crackers for 12 to 13 minutes, then check. Give them another 4 to 5 minutes if needed—you want them to be turning lightly golden all over.

Remove from the oven, re-score, break the crackers apart, and transfer to a wire rack for cooling. Sprinkle with salt. Store in an airtight container.

YIELD: 30 servings

Nutritional Analysis
Per serving: 27 calories; 2 g fat; 1 g protein; 1 g carbohydrate; 1 g dietary fiber; 0 g net carbs

Umami Crackers

As expected, the Paleo Umami Seasoning gives an extra kick in the pants to these crackers.

1 cup (145 g) sunflower seeds
2 teaspoons Paleo Umami Seasoning (page 288)
¼ teaspoon salt
3 tablespoons (45 ml) water
1 pinch baking powder
Salt for sprinkling

Mix, roll, and bake according to the directions for Simple Sunflower Crackers, adding the Paleo Umami Seasoning while you're grinding the seeds. That's all!

YIELD: 30 servings

Nutritional Analysis
Per serving: 31 calories; 2 g fat; 1 g protein; 2 g carbohydrate; 1 g dietary fiber; 1 g net carbs

Sundried Tomato Crackers

My favorite paleo crackers!

2 dry-packed sundried tomato halves
3 tablespoons (45 ml) boiling water
1 cup (145 g) sunflower seeds
¼ teaspoon salt
1 pinch baking powder
Salt for sprinkling

Put your sundried tomato halves in a small dish and add the boiling water. Let them soak for 15 minutes or so, till they soften up.

Now make your crackers according to the directions for Simple Sunflower Crackers (page 77), adding the rehydrated tomatoes along with the soaking water. Run the processor until they're well ground into the dough.

Roll and bake like the rest of the sunflower crackers.

YIELD: 30 servings

Nutritional Analysis
Per serving: 28 calories; 2 g fat; 1 g protein; 1 g carbohydrate; 1 g dietary fiber; 0 g net carbs

Eggy Wraps

Thin pancakes of mostly egg that you can use like you would tortillas.

5 eggs
2 tablespoons (14 g) almond meal
1 tablespoon (7 g) coconut flour
¼ teaspoon salt

Combine ingredients in your blender and run till it's smooth.

Put a big, heavy-bottomed nonstick skillet over medium-high heat. Let it get hot before you . . .

Pour in enough batter to make a circle about 4 inches (10 cm) across. Now use your spatula to draw the batter out a little thinner, into a circle 6 to 7 inches (15 to 18 cm) across, roughly the size of a standard tortilla.

Cover and let it cook for about 3 minutes, then check. You're looking for the edges to start lifting a little from the surface of the skillet.

When the edges detach from the skillet, carefully slide your spatula underneath, loosening it. Flip gently, and give it another couple of minutes. Then remove to a plate and repeat until you run out of batter. I got 6 wraps.

Store in a plastic bag in the fridge and use as you would any flat bread—wrap tuna or egg salad in them, make burritos or soft tacos, use your imagination!

YIELD: 6 servings

Nutritional Analysis
Per serving: 77 calories; 4 g fat; 6 g protein; 3 g carbohydrate; 1 g dietary fiber; 2 g net carbs

NOTE

These really do call for a nonstick skillet, unless you're far more delicate with a spatula than I.

Cinnamon-Honey Paleonola

You can serve this with coconut milk or almond milk, or any other way you might serve granola.

1 cup (104 g) flaxseed meal
2 cups (160 g) shredded coconut meat
¼ cup (32 g) sesame seeds (optional)
½ teaspoon salt
1 teaspoon ground cinnamon
½ cup (120 ml) water
½ cup (104 g) coconut oil, melted
⅓ cup (115 g) honey (or more or less, to taste)
2 cups (220 g) chopped pecans
½ cup (72 g) sunflower seeds
½ cup (60 g) chopped walnuts
½ cup (70 g) shelled pumpkin seeds
½ cup (55 g) sliced almonds

Preheat oven to 250°F (120°C, or gas mark ½).

In a big mixing bowl, combine the flax meal, coconut, sesame seeds if using, salt if using, and cinnamon. Stir them together so everything is evenly distributed.

In a 2-cup (475 ml) measure, measure the water, oil, and honey and stir them together. Pour this over the dry ingredients and use a whisk to stir it till everything is evenly damp.

Turn this mixture into an 11 x 13-inch (28 x 33 cm) roasting pan—you might want to line it with nonstick foil first. Press it into an even layer in the bottom of the pan and put it in the oven. Set your timer for 1 hour.

When the hour is up, pull out your pan. Use the edge of a spatula to cut the whole thing into 1-inch (2 cm) squares, and then to scoop up those chunks and stir them around in the pan. They'll crumble somewhat, and I like to cut mine into somewhat smaller pieces—maybe ½ inch (1 cm).

Now measure and stir in the nuts and seeds. Put the pan back in the oven and set your timer for 20 minutes. When time's up, stir and turn everything and put the pan back in the oven. Repeat two or three more times, till the nuts and seeds are toasted to your liking, then remove from oven, cool, and store in a tightly lidded container.

YIELD: 16 servings

Nutritional Analysis
Per serving: 396 calories; 35 g fat; 10 g protein; 18 g carbohydrate; 8 g dietary fiber; 10 g net carbs

Vanilla-Maple Paleonola

A good recipe deserves a variation!

1 cup (104 g) flaxseed meal
2 cups (160 g) shredded coconut meat
¼ cup (32 g) sesame seeds (optional)
½ teaspoon salt (optional)
1 teaspoon ground cinnamon
½ cup (120 ml) water
½ cup (104 g) coconut oil, melted
2 teaspoons vanilla
⅓ cup (115 g) maple syrup (or more or less, to taste)
2 cups (220 g) chopped pecans
½ cup (72 g) sunflower seeds
½ cup (60 g) chopped walnuts
½ cup (70 g) shelled pumpkin seeds
½ cup (55 g) sliced almonds

(continued)

Preheat oven to 250°F (120°C, or gas mark ½).

In a big mixing bowl, combine the flax meal, coconut, sesame seeds if using, salt if using, and cinnamon. Stir them together so everything is evenly distributed.

In a 2-cup (475 ml) measure, measure the water, oil, vanilla, and maple syrup and stir them together. Pour this over the dry ingredients and use a whisk to stir it till everything is evenly damp.

Turn this mixture into an 11 x 13-inch (28 x 33 cm) roasting pan—you might want to line it with nonstick foil first. Press it into an even layer in the bottom of the pan and put it in the oven. Set your timer for 1 hour.

When the hour is up, pull out your pan. Use the edge of a spatula to cut the whole thing into 1-inch (2.5 cm) squares and then to scoop up those chunks and stir them around in the pan. They'll crumble somewhat, and I like to cut mine into somewhat smaller pieces—maybe ½ inch (1 cm).

Now measure and stir in the nuts and seeds. Put the pan back in the oven and set your timer for 20 minutes. When time's up, stir and turn everything and put the pan back in the oven. Repeat this two or three more times, till the nuts and seeds are toasted to your liking, then remove from oven, cool, and store in a tightly lidded container.

YIELD: 16 servings

Nutritional Analysis
Per serving: 394 calories; 35 g fat; 10 g protein; 17 g carbohydrate; 8 g dietary fiber; 9 g net carbs

Paleo Hot Cereal

There's something soothing about hot cereal, isn't there?

1½ tablespoons (10.5 g) almond meal
1½ tablespoons (7.5 g) shredded coconut meat
1 tablespoon (6.5 g) flaxseed meal
1 teaspoon chia seeds
¼ teaspoon glucomannan
1 pinch salt
½ cup (120 ml) boiling water
½ teaspoon vanilla extract

Simply stir together everything from the almond meal through the salt (if using) in a cereal bowl.

Now stir in the water and vanilla extract and cover the bowl—a saucer works well. Let it sit for about 5 minutes. Then add a little honey, stevia, mashed fruit, maple syrup, whatever you like—but only a little! I find ½ teaspoon honey is about right for 1 serving of cereal.

YIELD: 1 serving

Nutritional Analysis
Per serving: 177 calories; 11 g fat; 10 g protein; 12 g carbohydrate; 5 g dietary fiber; 7 g net carbs

TO MAKE THE PALEO HOT CEREAL IN BULK, COMBINE:
⅓ cup (38 g) almond meal
⅓ cup (27 g) shredded coconut meat
⅓ cup (35 g) flaxseed meal
¼ cup (48 g) chia seeds
3 teaspoons (8 g) glucomannan

Mix it all together and store in a snap-top container in the fridge.

When it's breakfast time, put between ¼ and ⅓ cup of the mixture in a bowl and proceed as above.

Flax and Coconut Muffin-in-a-Mug

The muffin-in-a-mug is a popular low-carb recipe. This is my version, using stevia instead of Splenda and swapping coconut for part of the flax. Feel free to play with this— add a little nutmeg or maybe some ginger. Add a couple of teaspoons of maple syrup if you can tolerate the carbs.

1 teaspoon coconut oil
1 egg
20 drops French vanilla liquid stevia
2 tablespoons (13 g) flaxseed meal
2 tablespoons (10 g) shredded coconut meat
½ teaspoon baking powder
Scant ⅛ teaspoon salt
1 teaspoon ground cinnamon

Use a little extra coconut oil to grease a coffee mug thoroughly. Put the teaspoon of coconut oil in it and microwave for just 10 seconds, to melt.

Add the egg and the stevia to the coconut oil and use a fork to stir them up very well. Measure everything else into a bowl and stir it together, breaking up any clumps of baking powder. I realize this dirties up another dish, but I got better results this way. Add the dry mixture to the mug and stir with the fork till it's all blended, no pockets of dry stuff, but don't overmix.

Microwave on high for 1 minute, then check to see if it's done. If it's pulling away from the sides of the mug, it is.

Tip it out onto a plate, split, and eat. Instead of butter, consider putting a little sugar-free berry purée on your muffin, or honey if you can afford the carbs.

YIELD: 1 serving

Nutritional Analysis

Per serving: 296 calories; 23 g fat; 13 g protein; 17 g carbohydrate; 14 g dietary fiber; 3 g net carbs

Blueberry Pancakes

What a great Sunday breakfast! If you can afford the carbs, you could serve these with real maple syrup, but my blood sugar wouldn't like it. They're good as-is, though.

¾ cup (90 g) almond meal
2 tablespoons (13 g) flaxseed meal
2 tablespoons (14 g) coconut flour
¼ teaspoon salt, scant
½ teaspoon baking soda
¼ cup (20 g) shredded coconut meat
½ cup (115 g) Cocoyo (page 28)
2 tablespoons (26 g) coconut oil, melted
2 tablespoons (28 ml) water
10 drops French vanilla liquid stevia
3 eggs
1 cup (145 g) blueberries
Coconut oil, as needed

Measure all the dry ingredients into a mixing bowl and stir them till they're evenly distributed.

Now put your big, heavy skillet or a griddle over a medium-high flame and start it heating.

Measure the Cocoyo, melted coconut oil, water, and stevia together and break the eggs into them. Whisk the wet ingredients together. Now pour them into the dry ingredients and whisk till there are no pockets of dry stuff. Stir in the blueberries.

(continued)

By now the skillet or griddle should be hot! Add just enough coconut oil to film it lightly and scoop your batter by the quarter cup. Cook like any pancakes, cooking the first side until the edges of the pancake start to pull away from the pan and the bubbles that burst leave little holes. Flip, cook the second side, and serve.

YIELD: 10 servings

Nutritional Analysis

Per serving: 127 calories; 8 g fat; 7 g protein; 8.5 g carbohydrate; 3 g dietary fiber; 5.5 g net carbs

Pork Rind Pancakes

Sounds crazy, I know, but these are remarkably good. If you didn't know they were made from pork rinds, you would never guess.

2 ounces (55 g) pork rinds (There are bags this size that hold just this.)
3 eggs
¼ cup (60 ml) unsweetened coconut milk
½ teaspoon baking powder
½ teaspoon vanilla liquid stevia
½ teaspoon ground cinnamon
Coconut oil or lard

Dump your pork rinds in the food processor with the *S* blade in place and run until they're reduced to fine crumbs.

In a mixing bowl, whisk together the eggs, coconut milk, baking powder, stevia, and cinnamon. Now add the pork rind crumbs and whisk them in.

Let the batter sit for 10 minutes or so. During this time it will "gloppify"—thicken up and become gloppy. That's okay!

While you're waiting for the gloppification to occur, put your oiled skillet or griddle over medium-high heat. You'll want it hot for frying your pancakes.

Back to your gloppy batter. Thin it with water if you like—just depends on how thick a pancake you want. Then fry like any other pancake batter. I scoop my batter with a cookie scoop—like an ice cream scoop, only smaller—so they all come out the same size.

Serve with a tiny bit of honey or maple syrup, if you like, or with berries you've simmered in a little water, sweetened with stevia, and mashed a bit. That last is, of course, the lowest-sugar and most nutritious choice. Yummy, too.

YIELD: 8 servings

Nutritional Analysis

Per serving: 78 calories; 5 g fat; 7 g protein; 1 g carbohydrate; trace dietary fiber; 1 g net carbs

NOTE

The brand of pork rinds matters here. You want a brand that's quite fluffy, rather than super-crunchy, and you want them to not be too heavily salted.

Banana Fritters

Somewhere between Pork Rind Pancakes and banana nut bread!

1 ripe banana
2 eggs
¼ cup (60 ml) unsweetened coconut milk
½ teaspoon ground cinnamon
¼ teaspoon ground nutmeg
½ teaspoon baking powder
¾ cup (90 g) Pork Rind Crumbs (page 30)
2 tablespoons (28 ml) water
5 drops liquid stevia extract (optional), or to taste
¼ cup (30 g) chopped walnuts
Coconut oil or lard

Peel your banana and put it in a mixing bowl. Mash it up with a fork—you don't need to get it lumpless; that's okay. Just mash it up.

Add the eggs and coconut milk and whisk 'em up with the banana—it'll mash up more as you whisk.

Now whisk in the cinnamon, nutmeg, and baking powder. Then add the pork rind crumbs and stir till it's all blended.

Let the batter sit for 5 minutes, during which time it will thicken and become gloppy. While the batter's sitting, put your big, heavy skillet over medium-high heat, so it's ready when you are.

Thin out the batter with a little water. I used 2 tablespoons (28 ml). You still want your batter pretty thick. Taste and see whether you want your batter a little sweeter—this is the time to add a few drops of liquid stevia extract if you want them.

Stir in the walnuts.

Now melt a tablespoon (13 g) or so of coconut oil in your skillet and fry your batter like pancakes—I scooped mine with a cookie scoop (like an ice cream scoop, only smaller). It holds 2 tablespoons (30 g). I get nice, even-size fritters that way.

If you must, you can serve these with a smidgen of maple syrup or honey, or with Coconut Whipped Cream (page 296). But try them ungilded before you add anything.

YIELD: 3 servings

Nutritional Analysis
Per serving: 298 calories; 20 g fat; 20 g protein; 12 g carbohydrate; 2 g dietary fiber; 10 g net carbs

NOTE

I got exactly 12 fritters and figured on 4 per serving.

Chapter 5

SIDE DISHES

One of the issues we deal with when we give up grains and potatoes is "What goes on that third of the plate?!" The answer is vegetables—wonderful, wonderful vegetables. Here is an amazing variety of cool and interesting things to do with your vegetables!

Fauxtatoes

Low carbers know this, but recipes usually calling for butter and often cream cheese are good without.

½ large head cauliflower

Trim the leaves and the very bottom of the stem off your cauliflower and whack it into chunks. Steam it tender—mine gets 12 to 15 minutes on high in the microwave.

Now purée your cauliflower. I put my cauliflower in a deep, narrow mixing bowl and use my stick blender to purée it, but you could use your food processor instead.

If you're using a good gravy, just pour the gravy over the purée. If you're not making gravy—say, you've broiled a steak—pour the drippings in with the cauliflower, especially the browned juices. Purée them in, and add salt and pepper to taste. Or add a big dollop of Coconut Sour Cream (page 29) and maybe a few chopped chives!

YIELD: 4 servings

Nutritional Analysis
Per serving: 18 calories; trace fat; 1 g protein; 4 g carbohydrate; 2 g dietary fiber; 2 g net carbs

Horseradish Fauxtatoes

½ head cauliflower
¼ cup (60 g) Coconut Sour Cream (page 29)
2 tablespoons (30 g) horseradish
1 teaspoon walnut oil (optional, but it adds a certain something.)
Salt and black pepper to taste

Trim the leaves and the very bottom of the stem off your cauliflower and whack it into chunks. Steam it tender—mine gets 12 to 15 minutes on high in the microwave.

Now purée your cauliflower. I put my cauliflower in a deep, narrow mixing bowl and use my stick blender to purée it, but you could use your food processor instead.

Purée the cauliflower, then add the Coconut Sour Cream, horseradish, and walnut oil if using and process until they're blended in. Salt and pepper to taste, and serve.

YIELD: 4 servings

Nutritional Analysis
Per serving: 80 calories; 6 g fat; 2 g protein; 5 g carbohydrate; 2 g dietary fiber; 3 g net carbs

UnSour Cream Fauxtatoes

Miss potatoes with sour cream and chives? Try this.

1 head cauliflower
¼ cup (60 g) Coconut Sour Cream (page 29)
2 scallions, minced
Salt and black pepper

Trim the leaves and the bottom of the stem off your cauliflower, then cut it into chunks. Steam them till tender—I give mine 12 to 15 minutes or so on high in the microwave, but do them on the stovetop if you prefer.

Use a deep, narrow mixing bowl and a stick blender to mash/purée it, or you can put it in your food processor. Either way, purée the cauliflower, then add the Coconut Sour Cream, minced scallions, and process until they're blended. Salt and pepper to taste, and serve.

YIELD: 6 servings

Nutritional Analysis
Per serving: 58 calories; 4 g fat; 2 g protein; 6 g carbohydrate; 3 g dietary fiber; 3 g net carbs

Fauxtatoes with Caramelized Onions and Mushrooms

½ **head cauliflower**
½ **medium onion, diced fine**
1 tablespoon (13 g) lard or fat of choice, divided
½ **cup (35 g) chopped mushrooms**
¼ **cup (60 g) Coconut Sour Cream (page 29)**
1 tablespoon (15 ml) beef Broth Concentrate (page 27)
¼ **tablespoon black pepper**
Salt (optional)

Trim the leaves and the bottom of the stem off your cauliflower and whack it into chunks. Steam 'em tender—I give mine 12 minutes on high in the microwave.

In the meanwhile, dice your onion. Put a heavy skillet over low heat and melt half the fat. Add the onion and start slowly sautéing it—you want to brown it well. While the onion's cooking, chop your mushrooms.

When the onions are good and brown, scoop them out and reserve. Melt the rest of the fat and sauté the mushrooms until they soften and change color.

Somewhere in here, your cauliflower will be done. Drain it and put it in a deep mixing bowl. Use your stick blender to purée it well. Now blend in the Coconut Sour Cream and the beef Broth Concentrate.

When the mushrooms are done, stir them in along with the onions and the pepper. Salt if desired and serve.

YIELD: 4 servings

Nutritional Analysis
Per serving: 55 calories; 3 g fat; 2 g protein; 6 g carbohydrate; 2 g dietary fiber; 4 g net carbs

Fauxtato Pancakes

Worth making extra Fauxtatoes to make these the next night. Potato pancakes are traditionally served with applesauce; you could try that here. But they're darned good as-is.

1 cup (225 g) leftover fauxtatoes (I used Horseradish Fauxtatoes, but leftover Fauxtatoes will work.)
2 eggs
1 tablespoon (7 g) coconut flour
1 tablespoon (12.5 g) fat (or as needed)

Darned simple: Put your fauxtatoes in a mixing bowl, add the eggs and coconut flour, and whisk it up.

Put your big, heavy skillet over medium heat and add the fat—I used lard. When the skillet's hot, add the batter by the quarter cup. Fry till nicely browned on the bottom, flip, and brown the other side. Serve hot!

YIELD: 5 servings

Nutritional Analysis
Per serving: 62 calories; 5 g fat; 3 g protein; 2 g carbohydrate; 1 g dietary fiber; 1 g net carbs

Jerusalem Artichoke Fritters

These are similar to potato pancakes.

½ pound (225 g) Jerusalem artichokes
½ small onion
¼ teaspoon salt
¼ teaspoon black pepper
1 egg
2 tablespoons (14 g) coconut flour
Coconut oil

Scrub your Jerusalem artichokes well—a green scrubby pad works well for this—but do not peel. Run 'em through the shredding blade of your food processor, or you could grate them on your box grater. Dump your shreds onto a double thickness of paper towels and pat 'em dry. Then throw them in a mixing bowl.

Mince your onion quite fine—running through the same shredding blade of your food processor is a fine idea. Add it to the shredded Jerusalem artichokes. Add the salt and pepper, tossing all the while.

Now mix in the egg, then the coconut flour. Let the batter sit for a minute or two, while you . . .

Put your big, heavy skillet over medium heat, and melt some coconut oil—I started with about 2 tablespoons (26 g). When the pan is hot, drop in the batter in rounded tablespoonfuls (15 g). Flatten them slightly with the back of your spoon.

Let them fry till the bottoms are well browned. Now flip them carefully—they're pretty apt to fall apart, especially if you flip them too soon. Add more coconut oil to the skillet if it needs it and fry the other side brown, too. Remove to a plate and keep warm while you fry the rest of the batter, adding oil as needed, then serve.

YIELD: 4 servings

Nutritional Analysis
Per serving: 97 calories; 2 g fat; 4 g protein; 17 g carbohydrate; 4 g dietary fiber; 13 g net carbs

Cauli-Rice

This will be familiar to those of you who have seen my low-carb cookbooks, but it's such an important concept that it's essential to present it here. This is one of the basic ideas I use several times a week.

½ head cauliflower

Trim the leaves and bottom of the stem off your cauliflower. Now whack the rest into chunks and run 'em through the shredding blade of your food processor.

Steam your shreds lightly—I put mine in a microwave steamer, add a tablespoon (15 ml) or so of water, cover, and give it 6 minutes on high. You can do the same thing with any microwaveable casserole. If you're seriously antimicrowave, you can steam it on the stovetop, but it will take a little longer, because you have to bring the water to a boil first. Anyway, you want your cauliflower just tender but definitely not mushy. It's all about the texture here. When it's done, uncover it immediately or it will continue to cook, and be ruined.

Now you can do all sorts of things with it! You can use it in pilafs and "Rice-a-Phony," you can use it in place of rice, couscous, or bulgur wheat in salads, you can top it with stir-fry, or you can use it as a great way to sop up a great gravy.

YIELD: 4 servings

Nutritional Analysis
Per serving: 3 calories; trace fat; trace protein; 1 g carbohydrate; trace dietary fiber; 1 g net carbs

Paleo Chicken-Almond Rice-a-Phony

Thank my brother for the name. He sampled this dish and said, "I know a lot of this is cauliflower, but how much is cauliflower and how much is actually rice?" When I told him there was no rice in it at all, he registered amazement and dubbed it "Rice-a-Phony."

½ head cauliflower
¼ cup (28 g) slivered almonds
2 teaspoons coconut oil
1 bunch scallions, sliced
¼ cup (15 g) chopped fresh parsley
1 tablespoon (15 ml) chicken Broth Concentrate (page 27)

Do the cauliflower "rice" thing—trim your cauliflower, chunk it, run it through the shredding blade of your food processor, and microwave-steam the resulting cauliflower "rice" for 6 minutes.

In the meanwhile, put your big, heavy skillet over medium heat and start sautéing the almonds in it.

While the almonds and the cauliflower are cooking, slice your scallions, including the crisp part of the green. Chop your parsley, too. Don't forget to stir your almonds!

Okay, the almonds are golden, and the microwave has beeped. Drain the cauliflower and dump it into the skillet with the almonds. Stir in everything else, mixing till the chicken broth concentrate is dissolved and everything is well-distributed. You're done!

YIELD: 3 servings

Nutritional Analysis
Per serving: 130 calories; 9 g fat; 6 g protein; 8 g carbohydrate; 3 g dietary fiber; 5 g net carbs

Roasted Garlic-Bacon "Rice"

You'll need to start ahead of time to roast and cool the garlic. Our recipe tester, Yvonne, said, "I think it was very easy. It took me a little longer than I think you might have expected. But that's me. But I LOVED it!"

1 head garlic
2 tablespoons (28 ml) olive oil
½ large head cauliflower (If you've got a little head, you might use ¾ head. You need about 6 to 8 cups of Cauli-Rice, page 87.)
5 bacon slices
1 small onion, diced
¼ cup (60 ml) coconut aminos
4 scallions, sliced thin
Salt and black pepper to taste

Ahead of time, preheat the oven to 350°F (180°C, or gas mark 4). In the meanwhile, put your whole head of garlic on a piece of foil, drizzle it with olive oil, and wrap it tightly. Now roast it for an hour or until soft. Let it cool.

Time to cook! Trim the bottom of the stem and the leaves off your cauliflower. Whack the rest into chunks and run 'em through the shredding blade of your food processor. Steam your Cauli-Rice lightly—I'd give it 6 minutes on high in the microwave.

While your cauliflower is cooking, lay your bacon in your big, heavy skillet over medium heat and fry it crisp.

While the bacon is cooking, you might as well dice your onion, too.

When your bacon is crisp, remove it to a plate and reserve. Pour off all but a couple of tablespoons (30 ml) of the bacon grease. Add the onion to the skillet and sauté till soft.

When your onion is soft and your Cauli-Rice is tender-crisp, drain the "rice" and add it to the skillet. Toss it with the onions till combined.

Grab your roasted garlic! Slice off the top of the head and press out the softened, caramelized garlic. Mix it into the Cauli-Rice, stirring till it's well distributed. Now stir in the coconut aminos.

Slice the scallions, including the crisp part of the green, and stir into everything else. Crumble in the bacon, pepper to taste and salt if you think it needs it, and serve.

YIELD: 5 servings

Nutritional Analysis
Per serving: 112 calories; 9 g fat; 4 g protein; 6 g carbohydrate; 2 g dietary fiber; 4 g net carbs

Pecan, Sundried Tomato, and Bacon Rice-a-Phony

Unreal. Just unreal. And yet remarkably really like rice.

½ head cauliflower
½ tablespoon (6.5 g) bacon grease or lard or other fat
¼ cup (28 g) chopped pecans
3 bacon slices
1 small onion
¼ cup (28 g) oil-packed sundried tomatoes, chopped
¼ cup (15 g) chopped fresh parsley
1 tablespoon (15 ml) Slow-Cooker Demi-Glace (page 27) or beef Broth Concentrate (page 27)
1 tablespoon (15 ml) Paleo Worcestershire (page 293)
½ teaspoon black pepper

First, trim the leaves and the very bottom of the stem off the half head of cauliflower and whack it into chunks that'll fit in your food processor feed tube. Run it through the shredding blade and put the resulting Cauli-Rice in a microwave-able casserole with a lid, or even better, in a microwave steamer. Add a few tablespoons (45 ml) water, cover, and nuke on high for 6 to 8 minutes. (You want it tender-crisp, not mushy.)

In the meanwhile, in a small skillet, over medium-low heat, melt the bacon grease and start sautéing the chopped pecans. Put your big, heavy skillet over medium heat and use your kitchen shears to snip the bacon into it—you want it to be bacon bits when it's crisp.

Go chop your onion and sundried tomatoes! (I actually had julienned sundried tomatoes in oil; didn't even have to chop 'em.) You could chop the parsley, too, but don't forget to go give your 2 skillets a stir. You don't want your pecans or bacon burning.

(continued)

Sometime soon, your microwave will beep. Uncover your cauliflower right away, so it won't continue cooking and go mushy on you.

Okay, we're going to assume your bacon bits are crisp now. Scoop 'em out with a slotted spoon and reserve 'em on a plate. Pour off about half the grease (save it for cooking). Throw the onion in the remaining grease and sauté it till it's translucent.

Now drain the Cauli-Rice and add it to the skillet, along with the Demi-Glace, Paleo Worcestershire, and pepper. Stir carefully—your skillet will be very full—until the seasonings and onion are evenly distributed.

Stir in the pecans, tomatoes, parsley, and bacon bits, and serve.

YIELD: 6 servings

Nutritional Analysis
Per serving: 97 calories; 7 g fat; 3 g protein; 7 g carbohydrate; 2 g dietary fiber; 5 g net carbs

Orange-Pecan "Rice"

½ **large head cauliflower**
1½ **tablespoons (19.5 g) coconut oil, divided**
¼ **cup (28 g) chopped pecans**
½ **medium onion, chopped**
2 **tablespoons (18.6 g) minced red bell pepper**
½ **navel orange**
2 **tablespoons (28 ml) chicken Broth Concentrate**
   (page 27)
¼ **cup (15 g) chopped fresh parsley**
Salt and black pepper

Trim the leaves and the bottom of the stem off your cauliflower. Whack the remainder into chunks and run them through the shredding blade of your food processor. Put the resulting Cauli-Rice in a microwaveable casserole with a lid, add a few tablespoons (45 ml) of water, cover, and nuke on high for 6 minutes.

While that's happening, put your big, heavy skillet over medium-low heat and melt ½ tablespoon (6.5 g) of the oil. Add the chopped pecans and sauté them, stirring often, till they're fragrant. I'd be chopping the onion and mincing the pepper during this process, too, but then I'm a serious kitchen multitasker. Just don't scorch the pecans.

Okay, the pecans are done. Remove them from the skillet and reserve them on a little plate or dish. Turn up the heat to medium high and throw in the rest of the coconut oil. When it's melted, add the onion and red pepper and start them sautéing.

Somewhere in here your microwave is going to beep. Remove the cauliflower from the microwave and uncover immediately, to stop the cooking. You don't want mush. Now would be a good time to grate ½ teaspoon of zest from your orange.

Go stir your onion and pepper again! When the onion's translucent, drain the cauliflower and add it to the skillet. Stir it all up.

Stir in the orange zest and squeeze in the juice from that half orange. Stir that in, along with the parsley. (The easiest way to do the parsley is to just snip it into your skillet with your kitchen shears. Eyeball the quantity.)

Stir in the pecans, salt and pepper to taste, and serve.

YIELD: 4 servings

Nutritional Analysis
Per serving: 141 calories; 11 g fat; 4 g protein; 9 g carbohydrate; 3 g dietary fiber; 6 g net carbs

Jerusalem Fries

½ pound (225 g) Jerusalem artichokes
Coconut oil
Salt

Pick fairly straight, long, not-too-knobby Jerusalem artichokes for this. Scrub them well, then cut them lengthwise into strips about the size of a French fry.

Put your big, heavy skillet over medium heat and melt enough coconut oil in it to get it about ¼-inch (6 mm) deep. When it's good and hot, throw in your 'choke strips and fry, turning often, till they're a good golden brown all over. Drain, salt, and serve.

YIELD: 4 servings

Nutritional Analysis
Per serving: 43 calories; trace fat; 1 g protein; 10 g carbohydrate; 1 g dietary fiber; 9 g net carbs

Lemon-Garlic Broccoli

1 pound (455 g) broccoli
3 garlic cloves, crushed
2 tablespoons (28 ml) olive oil (or a little more,
  as desired)
1 lemon, cut in wedges

Cut your broccoli into florets. Peel the stems—if you've been tossing broccoli stems because of the tough skin on the stems, you'll be astonished—once you peel them, they're the best part! Cut the stems into bits about the same size as the florets, so they'll steam evenly. While it's cooking, crush the garlic.

Steam your broccoli till it's just brilliantly green, maybe 6 to 8 minutes on high in the microwave. Uncover immediately and drain any water.

Put your big, heavy skillet over medium-high heat and add the olive oil. When it's hot, add the broccoli. Stir-fry it for a minute or two. Add the garlic and stir-fry another minute, making sure the garlic is evenly distributed.

Serve immediately, with a lemon wedge to squeeze over each serving.

YIELD: 5 servings

Nutritional Analysis
Per serving: 68 calories; 6 g fat; 2 g protein; 5 g carbohydrate; 2 g dietary fiber; 3 g net carbs

Lemon-Glazed Broccoli

1 pound (455 g) broccoli
1 small shallot or half a big one
3 tablespoons (45 ml) olive oil
2 tablespoons (28 ml) lemon juice
½ teaspoon honey

Cut the broccoli into spears and peel the stems. Steam lightly—until just brilliantly green—about 6 to 8 minutes in the microwave, on high.

In the meanwhile, mince the shallot as fine as you can. Then throw it in your big skillet along with the olive oil and sauté over medium heat for just a few minutes.

When the broccoli is done steaming, add the lemon juice and honey to the skillet and stir them up. Add the broccoli and toss till it's coated. Then plate, scraping any lingering glaze and shallot bits over the broccoli using a rubber scraper. Serve!

YIELD: 4 servings

Nutritional Analysis
Per serving: 115 calories; 10 g fat; 2 g protein; 5 g carbohydrate; 2 g dietary fiber; 3 g net carbs

Braised Greens with Tomatoes

Make this with chard, mustard greens, collards, kale—or a combo thereof.

¼ cup (52 g) bacon grease or lard or other fat
1 medium onion, diced
3 garlic cloves, crushed
2 jalapeños, seeded and minced
2 pounds (900 g) greens, stems and heavy ribs
  removed, coarsely chopped
3 medium tomatoes, diced
2 tablespoons (28 ml) cider vinegar
½ cup (120 ml) water
Salt and black pepper

In a large pot, over medium heat, melt the bacon grease. Start sautéing the onion, garlic, and jalapeños, stirring till the onion is translucent. (Don't forget to wash your hands thoroughly after handling the jalapeños!)

Add the greens and toss till they wilt. Stir in the diced tomatoes, vinegar, and water. Turn the burner to low, cover the pot, and let it cook, stirring now and then, until the greens are tender—this will depend some on what sort of greens you're using. Salt, pepper, and serve.

YIELD: 6 servings

Nutritional Analysis
Per serving: 142 calories; 9 g fat; 5 g protein; 13 g carbohydrate; 6 g dietary fiber; 7 g net carbs

Kale Chips with Lemon Dip

Our tester, Lisa, said that rather than dipping, you should drizzle the lemon dip over the leaves, then pick 'em up by the uncoated corners.

¼ cup (60 ml) extra-virgin olive oil
2 garlic cloves, crushed
1 pound (455 g) kale
1 cup (230 g) Cocoyo (page 28)
1 lemon
2 scallions
Salt and black pepper

Preheat oven to 375ºF (190ºC, or gas mark 5).

Measure the oil into a small dish and crush the garlic into it.

Separate your kale and tear it into bits roughly 3-inches (7.5 cm) square. Put it in a big mixing bowl. (Depending on the size of your biggest mixing bowl, you may have to do this in 2 batches.)

Remove 1 tablespoon (15 ml) of the garlicky olive oil from the little dish—scoop up some of the crushed garlic, too—and put this in a cereal bowl–size bowl. Now pour the rest of the oil over the kale and toss with abandon till the leaves are all coated. Heck, plunge in and massage it into the leaves.

Spread the kale on a couple of baking sheets and roast it about 20 to 30 minutes, or until crisp. If you need to move the pans around in the oven to toast it evenly, go ahead and do that.

While that's happening, measure the Cocoyo into the cereal bowl with the remaining garlicky olive oil. Grate in about a teaspoon of the zest of your lemon, then whack the lemon in half, pick out the pits, and squeeze the juice into the Cocoyo. Mince the scallions and mix them in. Salt and pepper the dip to taste. When the kale is crisp, sprinkle it with a little salt, too, and serve with the dip.

YIELD: 5 servings

Nutritional Analysis
Per serving: 147 calories; 11 g fat; 3 g protein; 11 g carbohydrate; 2 g dietary fiber; 0 mg cholesterol; 41 mg sodium

Simple Roasted Brussels Sprouts

So good. Just so, so good.

1 pound (455 g) brussels sprouts
2 tablespoons (26 g) bacon grease (or lard or olive oil; take your pick)
Salt and black pepper

Preheat your oven to 400°F (200°C, or gas mark 6).

Trim the bottoms of the stems and any wilted leaves off your brussels and halve each one.

Put the fat in a roasting pan, and if you're using the bacon grease or lard, put it in the oven for a few minutes to melt.

Add the brussels sprouts to the pan and toss till they're coated with the fat. Salt and pepper and stir again, then put 'em in the oven.

Roast for 35 to 40 minutes, stirring now and then. When they're evenly browned, they're done! Add a little more salt if they need it and serve.

YIELD: 4 servings

Nutritional Analysis
Per serving: 103 calories; 7 g fat; 3 g protein; 9 g carbohydrate; 4 g dietary fiber; 5 g net carbs

Hot and Garlicky Brussels Sprouts

1 pound (455 g) brussels sprouts
2 tablespoons (26 g) bacon grease or lard
2 garlic cloves, minced
¼ teaspoon red-pepper flakes (or more, if you like)
Salt to taste (optional)

Trim your brussels sprouts and halve them. Steam them for just a couple of minutes in the microwave or on the stovetop. Drain and pat dry.

Put your big, heavy skillet over high heat. Add the bacon grease and let it get good and hot. Add your brussels, watching out for spitting oil! (The better you dry your brussels, the less spitting there will be.)

Let them sauté without stirring for a minute, then turn and repeat—keep going until they're browned and tender.

Now stir in the garlic and red pepper, and give them just another minute or two, stirring constantly. Salt, if desired.

YIELD: 4 servings

Nutritional Analysis
Per serving: 105 calories; 7 g fat; 4 g protein; 10 g carbohydrate; 4 g dietary fiber; 6 g net carbs

NOTE

If you'd rather, trim and halve the brussels, put them in a roasting pan with the bacon grease, and roast at 450°F (230°C, or gas mark 8) for 20 to 25 minutes, stirring now and then. When they're caramelized (have brown spots all over), stir in the garlic and red-pepper flakes, let 'em go just another minute, then remove from the oven. Salt, if you like, and serve.

Garlic Sautéed Mushrooms

A great side dish with a simple broiled steak or chop.

½ pound (225 g) mushrooms (Look for a package with fairly small ones.)
3 tablespoons (45 ml) olive oil (more as needed)
2 cloves garlic, crushed
½ lemon
2 tablespoons (8 g) chopped fresh parsley
Salt and black pepper to taste

Wipe the mushrooms clean with a damp cloth or paper towel and trim the bottoms of the stems.

In your big, heavy skillet, over medium-low heat, sauté the mushrooms in the olive oil until they're softened. Add more oil if needed, but you want them to have absorbed most of it when they're done.

Stir in the crushed garlic and sauté a few more minutes, stirring all the while. Squeeze in the juice from the lemon half and the parsley and season to taste.

YIELD: 4 servings

Nutritional Analysis
Per serving: 108 calories; 10 g fat; 1 g protein; 4 g carbohydrate; 1 g dietary fiber; 3 g net carbs

Creamy Garlic Mushrooms

Our tester Michelle says, "This was the best way I have ever had mushrooms. The sauce was to die for!" She rates this a "10 plus." She also says that despite our calling this four servings, her husband wanted to eat the whole thing all by himself.

4 tablespoons (52 g) coconut oil
8 ounces (225 g) sliced button mushrooms
8 ounces (225 g) sliced crimini mushrooms
8 ounces (225 g) sliced small portobello mushrooms
¼ cup (60 ml) dry white wine
4 garlic cloves, crushed
¼ cup (60 ml) unsweetened coconut milk
2 tablespoons (8 g) minced fresh parsley
Salt and black pepper

In your big, heavy skillet, over medium-high heat, melt the coconut oil and add the mushrooms. Sauté till they've softened and changed color.

Stir in the wine and the garlic and let it simmer till the wine is about half cooked away. Stir in the coconut milk and the parsley. Salt and pepper to taste, then serve.

YIELD: 4 servings

Nutritional Analysis
Per serving: 189 calories; 17 g fat; 3 g protein; 7 g carbohydrate; 1 g dietary fiber; 6 g net carbs

Savory Mushrooms

I originally made these for an omelet, but they'd be great on a steak or over a chicken breast. For that matter, you could add some cooked, crumbled ground beef and serve the whole thing over Cauli-Rice or Fauxtatoes.

1 large shallot, minced
8 ounces (225 g) sliced mushrooms (I used portobellos, but button or crimini would work, too. Buy 'em sliced!)
2 tablespoons (26 g) lard or as needed
2 teaspoons Spanish smoked paprika
2 tablespoons (14 g) oil-packed sundried tomatoes, minced

2 tablespoons (28 ml) Slow-Cooker Demi-Glace
  (page 27)

¼ cup (60 g) Coconut Sour Cream (page 29)

¼ teaspoon black pepper

2 tablespoons (8 g) minced fresh parsley

Mince your shallot and start sautéing it and the mushrooms in the lard. Use the edge of your spatula to break your sliced mushrooms up into smaller bits. (If you want to. I like them that way. But if you prefer whole slices of mushrooms, who am I to object?)

When the mushrooms soften, stir in the paprika and let it cook another minute or two.

Now stir in everything else, turn your burner down to low, and let everything simmer for 5 minutes. That's it!

YIELD: 3 servings

Nutritional Analysis
Per serving: 183 calories; 17 g fat; 3 g protein; 7 g carbohydrate; 2 g dietary fiber; 5 g net carbs

Grilled Portobellos

Bonus idea—marinate and grill the mushrooms, skip the dipping sauce, and place a grilled filet mignon on each. Tastes great and makes those little steaks seem bigger.

4 portobello mushroom caps (big ones,
  at least 4 inches [10 cm] across)

5 cloves garlic, crushed

2 tablespoons (28 ml) coconut aminos

2 drops liquid stevia extract

¼ teaspoon black pepper

6 tablespoons (90 ml) white balsamic vinegar

½ teaspoon salt

1 small red chile pepper

¼ cup (4 g) minced fresh cilantro

Put your portobellos in a zipper-lock bag. Mix together 4 cloves crushed garlic, coconut aminos, liquid stevia, and pepper. Pour over the portobellos and seal the bag, pressing out the air as you go. Let them marinate for an hour or so.

May as well make your dipping sauce in the meanwhile! Put the white balsamic, the remaining garlic clove, and salt in your blender or food processor. Stem and seed the chile and add. Now run the blender or food processor until the garlic and chile are pulverized.

When dinnertime rolls around, fire up the grill or heat your electric tabletop grill, whichever works for you. Pour off the marinade into a small dish. Now grill your mushrooms 3 minutes or so per side on your charcoal grill or about 4 minutes total if you're using the electric tabletop grill. Baste once or twice with the reserved marinade.

Sprinkle with cilantro and serve with the dipping sauce.

YIELD: 4 servings

Nutritional Analysis
Per serving: 54 calories; 1 g fat; 3 g protein; 12 g carbohydrate; 2 g dietary fiber; 10 g net carbs

Golden Roasted Cauliflower

Our tester Lisa says, "This was hands down our favorite so far! TOTALLY A KEEPER!"

½ teaspoon ground coriander

¼ teaspoon black pepper

½ teaspoon red-pepper flakes

½ teaspoon turmeric

6 cloves garlic, crushed

¼ cup (52 g) coconut oil, melted

1 large head cauliflower

(continued)

1 medium shallot, minced
¼ cup (4 g) minced fresh cilantro
Salt to taste

Preheat oven to 400°F (200°C, or gas mark 6).

In a small dish, combine the spices, garlic, and coconut oil and stir them up well. Let them sit while you . . .

Trim your cauliflower and separate it into 1-inch (2.5 cm) florets. Cut up the stem, too—why waste it? Put them in a roasting pan.

Pour the seasoned oil over the cauliflower and toss till the cauliflower is completely coated. Roast the cauliflower for 30 to 35 minutes, stirring a couple of times in the process.

In the meanwhile, mince your shallot and cilantro.

When the cauliflower is tender, toss with the shallot and cilantro, salt to taste, and serve.

YIELD: 5 servings

Nutritional Analysis
Per serving: 134 calories; 11 g fat; 3 g protein; 8 g carbohydrate; 3 g dietary fiber; 5 g net carbs

Skillet Fennel and Peppers

Try this with roast pork or chicken.

2 fennel bulbs
1 red bell pepper
1 small onion
¼ cup (60 ml) olive oil
2 garlic cloves
½ lime

1 teaspoon whole grain mustard
1 tablespoon (2.4 g) fresh thyme leaves
Salt and black pepper

Trim your fennel bulb, then cut it in quarters vertically, then slice thin. Seed your pepper and cut into thin lengthwise strips, then halve them. Halve your onion vertically, peel, and slice lengthwise.

Put your big, heavy skillet over medium-high heat and add the olive oil. When it's hot, add your vegetables. Sauté till everything is tender-crisp. Crush in the garlic and continue stir-frying for a couple more minutes.

Squeeze in the juice from the lime and add the mustard. Stir to coat everything. Stir in the thyme leaves.

Salt and pepper lightly and serve. The feathery leaves from the fennel make a beautiful, edible garnish.

YIELD: 4 servings

Nutritional Analysis
Per serving: 180 calories; 14 g fat; 2 g protein; 14 g carbohydrate; 5 g dietary fiber; 9 g net carbs

The Simplest Eggplant

That Nice Boy I Married was not a fan of eggplant, until I did this with it, and then he loved it. LOVED it.

1 eggplant
Olive oil—a lot of olive oil. I mean a whole lot
    of olive oil.

Slice your eggplant crosswise into rounds about ⅓-inch (8 mm) thick.

Put your big, heavy skillet over medium-high heat, and add about ¼ inch (6 mm) of olive oil. Get it good and hot.

Now fry your eggplant slices, three or four at a time, (or however many your skillet will hold without crowding) until they're golden brown on both sides. They will suck up olive oil like college students on spring break suck down beer, so be ready to add more as needed.

When your eggplant is beautifully golden on both sides, serve hot, with salt and pepper. That is all.

I served the first slices while subsequent batches were still frying, because the hot-and-crisp thing is part of the appeal, here.

YIELD: 5 servings

Nutritional Analysis
It's hard to get a calorie count on these, because you'd have to know how much oil it absorbs. Suffice it to say this is not a low-calorie dish. If 5 people share this, each will get 6 g carbohydrate; 2 g dietary fiber; 4 g net carbs.

Rebecca's Roasted Asparagus with Lemon-Anchovy Sauce

1 pound (455 g) asparagus
2 tablespoons (28 ml) olive oil
Salt and black pepper
¼ cup (60 g) Lemon-Anchovy Sauce (page 280)

Preheat oven to 400°F (200°C, or gas mark 6).

Snap the ends off your asparagus spears where they want to break naturally. Put them in a roasting pan, drizzle with the olive oil, and toss to coat.

Roast for 10 to 15 minutes, or until the asparagus is speckled with brown spots.

Now you have a choice: You can toss the asparagus with the lemon-anchovy sauce. Or you can give each diner a little dish of lemon-anchovy sauce to dip the asparagus in.

YIELD: 3 to 4 servings

Nutritional Analysis
Per serving: Assuming 3, each will have 221 calories; 22 g fat; 3 g protein; 4 g carbohydrate; 2 g dietary fiber; 2 g net carbs

NOTE
Rebecca says that she thinks this would also be good if you stirred in the lemon-anchovy sauce a few minutes before the asparagus was done and let it finish roasting with the sauce on it.

Asparagus Pecandine

I called this three servings because that seemed like what most people would consider it. But That Nice Boy I Married and I ate the whole thing ourselves.

1 pound (455 g) asparagus
1 tablespoon (13 g) bacon grease
1 tablespoon (15 ml) olive oil
¼ cup (28 g) pecans, finely chopped
1 teaspoon fresh tarragon, minced
2 tablespoons (28 ml) white wine vinegar
Salt and black pepper

(continued)

Snap the ends off the asparagus where it wants to break naturally. (Feed the ends to any pugs who might be hanging around.) Steam till just tender—I give mine 5 minutes in the microwave.

While that's happening, put a medium-size skillet over medium heat and melt the bacon grease with the olive oil. Swirl them together, then add the pecans and sauté till they smell all toasty.

DO NOT OVERCOOK ASPARAGUS! When the microwave beeps, pull it out and uncover it immediately, to stop the cooking. Mushy asparagus is a crime against nature.

Okay, your pecans are toasty. Stir in the minced tarragon and cook another 20 seconds or so. Now hiss in the vinegar, all at once, and let the mixture cook, stirring, for about another minute. Salt and pepper lightly.

Plate your asparagus. Divide the sauce between them, and serve!

YIELD: 3 servings

Nutritional Analysis
Per serving: 165 calories; 16 g fat; 3 g protein; 6 g carbohydrate; 2 g dietary fiber; 4 g net carbs

NOTE

The trick to this recipe is chopping your pecans very finely—not flour-fine, but pretty darn fine. You want the bits to stick to the asparagus.

Asparagus and Shiitake Sauté

Warning: Shiitake, though delicious and nutritious, are one of the carbiest mushrooms. If you need to keep your carbs rock bottom, substitute crimini or portobellos instead.

1 pound (455 g) asparagus
4 ounces (115 g) shiitake mushrooms
1 tablespoon (13 g) fat (I used lard, but use what you like; something fairly bland.)
½ orange

Snap the ends off your asparagus where they want to break naturally, then cut the stalks into 2-inch (5 cm) lengths. Chop your shiitake into medium-size bits.

Put your big, heavy skillet over medium-high heat. Add the fat and let it melt, then throw in the asparagus and shiitakes. Sauté, stirring frequently, until the asparagus is tender-crisp and brilliantly green.

Grate in about ½ teaspoon of zest from your orange half, then squeeze in the juice. Keep sautéing for just another minute, then serve.

YIELD: 3 servings

Nutritional Analysis
Per serving: 179 calories; 5 g fat; 6 g protein; 35 g carbohydrate; 6 g dietary fiber; 29 g net carbs

Asparagus with Balsamic Dressing and Almonds

You know it's polite to eat asparagus with your fingers, right? This makes it even more fun. By the way, this calls for a half-batch of dressing. Do you have another pound of asparagus on hand?

½ batch White Balsamic Vinaigrette (page 140)
1 pound (455 g) asparagus
½ cup (60 g) almond meal

We're going to assume you have your dressing made. If you don't, that's the first step. Don't hold back, though; it's quick and easy to make.

Snap the ends off your asparagus where it wants to break naturally. Put the stalks in a microwaveable container—a Pyrex pie plate works well, though I use my trusty microwave steamer. (If you do use the pie plate, lay the asparagus spoke fashion, with the tips in the center.) Add just a teeny bit of water—maybe a tablespoon (15 ml)—and cover. (You can cover a pie plate with a regular dinner plate that fits, so long as it's microwaveable.) Nuke it on high for just 3 to 4 minutes.

In the meanwhile, put the almond meal in a dry skillet over medium heat and stir it till it smells toasty. Remove from the heat.

When the asparagus is just barely tender and brilliant green, divide it between plates. Give everyone a puddle or dish of dressing to drag their asparagus through and a heap of almond meal to dip it in.

YIELD: 3 servings

Nutritional Analysis
Per serving: 193 calories; 13 g fat; 11 g protein; 11 g carbohydrate; 2 g dietary fiber; 9 g net carbs

Asparagus Pie

It was a toss-up whether to put this with side dishes or egg dishes, but it's got more asparagus than eggs, so here it is.

1 pound (455 g) asparagus
2 tablespoons (20 g) minced onion
2 tablespoons (28 ml) olive oil
1 garlic clove, minced
4 eggs
¼ cup (60 ml) unsweetened coconut milk
¼ teaspoon black pepper
¼ teaspoon salt
¼ lemon
2 dashes hot sauce, such as Tabasco

Preheat your oven to 350°F (180°C, or gas mark 4). Grease a 9-inch (23 cm) pie plate.

Snap the ends off the asparagus where it wants to break naturally. Cut into 1-inch (2.5 cm) lengths. Mince your onion, too.

Put your big, heavy skillet over medium heat and add the olive oil. Sauté the asparagus and onion until the asparagus is brilliantly green. Add the garlic, sauté just another minute, and turn off the pan. Transfer the asparagus mixture to the pie plate.

Break the eggs into your blender. Add the coconut milk, pepper, and salt. Grate in the zest of the quarter lemon and squeeze in the juice, too. Add the hot sauce. Run the blender for 30 seconds or so.

Pour the egg mixture over the asparagus. Bake for 45 minutes. Remove from the oven, let cool for 15 minutes, then slice and serve.

YIELD: 6 servings

Nutritional Analysis
Per serving: 114 calories; 9 g fat; 5 g protein; 3 g carbohydrate; 2 g net carbs

Stir-Fried Cabbage

Quick, easy, cheap, tasty. What's not to like?

2 tablespoons (26 g) coconut oil
4 cups (280 g) shredded cabbage
½ small onion, diced
2 cloves garlic, crushed
½ teaspoon red-pepper flakes

Put your big, heavy skillet over high heat. Add the coconut oil, and when it's hot, add the cabbage and onion. Stir-fry till the cabbage is just starting to soften. Stir in the garlic and red pepper and stir-fry for another minute or two, then serve.

YIELD: 4 servings

Nutritional Analysis
Per serving: 84 calories; 7 g fat; 1 g protein; 5 g carbohydrate; 2 g dietary fiber; 3 g net carbs

Bacon-Mustard Brussels Sprouts

2 strips bacon, raw, medium slice
1 pound (455 g) brussels sprouts
1 tablespoon (13 g) fat (bacon grease or coconut oil)
1 ½ tablespoons (22.5 g) brown mustard
1 teaspoon cider vinegar
½ teaspoon honey

Put your big, heavy skillet over medium heat. Chop or snip up your bacon and throw it in. Start that cooking to crispy bits while you . . .

Trim the stems of the brussels sprouts and remove any wilted or bruised leaves. Don't forget to stir your bacon!

When the brussels are all trimmed, run 'em through the slicing blade of your food processor.

By now your bacon is crisp. Scoop it out, leaving the grease in the skillet. Hold your bacon bits on a plate while you're cooking the brussels.

Add the extra fat to the skillet and throw in the sliced brussels sprouts. Sauté them, stirring often, till they've got plenty of brown spots and are tender-crisp.

Stir together the mustard, vinegar, and honey. Now scrape this mixture into the skillet and stir to mix it in well. Stir in the bacon bits and serve.

YIELD: 4 servings

Nutritional Analysis
Per serving: 144 calories; 10 g fat; 5 g protein; 10 g carbohydrate; 4 g dietary fiber; 6 g net carbs

Balsamic Chard

2 quarts (440 g) chard
½ cup (80 g) chopped onion
1 clove garlic, crushed
2 tablespoons (26 g) lard
2 tablespoons (28 ml) balsamic vinegar
Salt and black pepper

Lay your chard on a cutting board and cut in ½-inch (1 cm) strips, and then cut across the strips once or twice. Chop your onion and crush your garlic.

Put your big, heavy skillet over medium heat. Melt the lard and add the onion and garlic. Sauté for a couple of minutes, then add the chard. It will overwhelm your skillet!! Cover the skillet for a couple of minutes, then uncover and stir it up, turning everything over. Repeat this—cover, let it cook, uncover, and stir—until the greens have cooked down enough that they're not threatening to escape. Cook a few more minutes, stirring often, until tender. Sprinkle in the balsamic and stir it up, then salt and pepper to taste, and serve.

YIELD: 4 servings

Nutritional Analysis
Per serving: 82 calories; 7 g fat; 2 g protein; 5 g carbohydrate; 2 g dietary fiber; 3 g net carbs

Garlic Ginger Chard

2 pounds (900 g) chard
2 tablespoons (12 g) finely minced gingerroot
4 garlic cloves, finely minced
¼ cup (52 g) coconut oil
Hot sauce to taste (I'd use Sriracha, page 276)

Make sure your chard is clean and dry. Lay the leaves in a stack on your cutting board, fold in half lengthwise, and slice out the stems. Cut them into 1-inch (2.5 cm) lengths. Now cut the leaves into ½-inch (1 cm) strips. Cut the strips crossways a couple of times, too. Mince your ginger and garlic, too, and have them ready.

Heat a big ol' pot with a heavy bottom over high heat. Melt the coconut oil. Add the chard stems and sauté them till tender, 5 to 10 minutes. Add the leaves, then the ginger and garlic on top. Sauté/stir-fry the chard quickly, tossing the whole time. When it's wilted, sprinkle with hot sauce to taste and serve.

YIELD: 6 servings

Nutritional Analysis
Per serving: 109 calories; 9 g fat; 3 g protein; 6 g carbohydrate; 2 g dietary fiber; 4 g net carbs

NOTE

Our recipe tester Lisa emphasizes the importance of thoroughly drying your chard. She suggests wiping each leaf. I might bundle it in a towel, gather the corners, and whirl it around fast, though that splatters a bit of water around the kitchen. Tidiness has never been my long suit.

Mustard Greens

Rebecca says, "It's a real good side dish that could go with anything." She also reminds you to wash your greens well to remove any sand or dirt that might be lurking in their folds.

3 pounds (1.3 kg) mustard greens, stems removed
4 garlic cloves, peeled and thinly sliced
2 tablespoons (28 ml) extra-virgin olive oil
¾ teaspoon red pepper
Salt and black pepper
2 tablespoons (28 ml) red wine vinegar

Bring a large pot of water to a boil. Add the greens and blanch them for 3 minutes, stirring a couple of times. Scoop 'em out with a slotted spoon into a colander and drain them very well, pressing with a spoon.

Transfer your blanched greens to a cutting board and chop them coarsely. While you're at it, peel your garlic and slice it as thinly as you can.

(continued)

Put the olive oil in a big, heavy skillet over medium-high heat and let it heat. Add the garlic, salt, black and red pepper, and sauté them for a minute or so. Then add your chopped greens and stir it all up, making sure the seasonings are completely incorporated. Cover the skillet and let your greens cook for 3 minutes. Stir 'em up, re-cover, and repeat. Do it one more time, for a total of about 9 minutes.

Sprinkle in the vinegar and toss. Serve hot or cold.

YIELD: 4 servings

Nutritional Analysis
Per serving: 154 calories; 7 g fat; 9 g protein; 18 g carbohydrate; 7 g dietary fiber; 11 g net carbs

Brussels Sprouts with Onions and Red Pepper

1 pound (455 g) brussels sprouts
6 tablespoons (78 g) coconut oil
½ small onion, diced fine
½ teaspoon red-pepper flakes

Trim the bottoms of the stems and any wilted or bruised leaves off the brussels sprouts and cut them in half.

Put your big, heavy skillet over medium heat and melt the coconut oil. Throw in the brussels sprouts and sauté them, turning them over from time to time, for about 10 minutes, or until just tender and covered with brown spots. (The whole flat surface may well be browned. This is great!)

Stir in the onion and cook for another few minutes, until the onion is translucent. Stir in the red-pepper flakes and serve.

YIELD: 4 servings

Nutritional Analysis
Per serving: 225 calories; 21 g fat; 4 g protein; 10 g carbohydrate; 4 g dietary fiber; 6 g net carbs

Chipotle Beef "Rice"

A great side dish with a simple broiled steak.

½ head cauliflower
1 chipotle pepper in adobo, dried
½ onion
½ green bell pepper
2 tablespoons fat
1 tomato
1 large garlic clove, crushed
2 tablespoons (28 ml) beef Broth Concentrate (page 27)
2 teaspoons dried oregano
2 teaspoons ground cumin
Salt and black pepper
¼ cup (4 g) minced fresh cilantro

Turn your cauliflower into Cauli-Rice (see page 87).

Chop your chipotle, onion, and pepper. Put your big, heavy skillet over medium heat and start sautéing the veggies in the fat. While they're softening, dice the tomato. When the onion's softened, add the tomato and sauté it with the other vegetables for a minute or two. Now crush in the garlic.

By now your Cauli-Rice is steamed, yes? Add it to the skillet and stir it all up. Now stir in the beef Broth Concentrate, oregano, and cumin. Turn the burner down and let the mixture cook for just a couple of minutes.

Salt and pepper to taste, stir in cilantro, and serve.

YIELD: 6 servings

Nutritional Analysis
Per serving: 56 calories; 5 g fat; 1 g protein; 4 g carbohydrate; 1 g dietary fiber; 3 g net carbs

Broccoli with Lemon-Balsamic Mayo

Lemon-Balsamic Mayonnaise (page 278)
1 bunch broccoli

Make the Lemon-Balsamic Mayonnaise first, which is super-quick and easy to do. (See Note below)

Cut your broccoli into spears. Don't discard the stems—peel them! Once you peel off the tough skin, the stems are the best part.

Steam for 5 to 7 minutes, or until brilliantly green and tender-crisp. Serve with little dishes of the Lemon-Balsamic Mayonnaise to dip it in.

YIELD: 4 servings

Nutritional Analysis
Per serving: 512 calories; 53 g fat; 6 g protein; 9 g carbohydrate; 5 g dietary fiber; 4 g net carbs

NOTE

You won't need all the Lemon-Balsamic Mayonnaise for this. You can make a half batch or savor the rest—it's nice to have Lemon-Balsamic Mayonnaise in the fridge.

Celeriac Purée

The texture of this purée is so like mashed potatoes it's uncanny. My husband is not a fan of celery, but he is a fan of mashed potatoes, and he really liked these.

2 large celery roots
Coconut Sour Cream (page 29)
Salt and black pepper

Halve your celery roots—this will take a good-size knife. Grab a paring knife and cut away the skin and the tough layer just under it. If your celery roots have a pithy bit at the center, cut that out, too.

Grab the big knife again and cut your celery roots into cubes—about an inch (2.5 cm) is right. Now steam them till soft—mine took about 15 minutes on high in the microwave.

Transfer your celery root to a deep, narrow bowl and use your stick blender to purée it. Alternatively, you could put it in your food processor to purée.

Now mix in the coconut sour cream. How much will depend a bit on how big your roots were and how much needed to be trimmed, but I used ¼ cup (60 g), and it was perfect.

Salt and pepper to taste, and serve.

YIELD: 4 servings

Nutritional Analysis
Per serving: 10 calories; trace fat; trace protein; 2 g carbohydrate; 1 g dietary fiber; 1 g net carbs

Chipotle Onions

Smoky-sweet, these are great with burgers, steaks, or even on grilled salmon.

1 large Vidalia onion, sliced
1 tablespoon (13 g) bacon grease or lard
2 tablespoons (28 ml) chipotle chile canned in adobo, minced
Salt (optional)

Slice your onion fairly thin. Melt the fat in your big, heavy skillet, over medium heat, and start sautéing the onions. Don't let it get too hot—you don't want them to scorch before they turn limp and yummy-brown-caramelized. Stir often.

While the onions are sautéing, quickly mince up your chipotle. When the onions are limp, stir it in. Keep sautéing till the onions are quite soft and getting brown. Salt if desired, and serve.

YIELD: 3 servings

Nutritional Analysis
Per serving: 53 calories; 4 g fat; 1 g protein; 3 g carbohydrate; 1 g dietary fiber; 2 g net carbs

Creamed Spinach

I found the most beautiful spinach at the farmers' market! This is what I did with it.

¼ cup (40 g) minced onion
8 ounces (225 g) spinach
1 tablespoon (13 g) coconut oil
1 garlic clove, crushed
½ cup (120 ml) unsweetened coconut milk
¼ teaspoon black pepper
¼ teaspoon ground nutmeg
Salt to taste
Glucomannan (optional)

Mince your onion, first, while you've got room on your cutting board. Set aside. Make sure your spinach is good and clean—mine came from the farmer's market absolutely pristine. Lay it on your cutting board and chop, slicing across the leaves at ¼-inch (6 mm) intervals.

Put your big, heavy skillet over medium heat and melt the coconut oil. Sauté the onion for a minute or two first, then add the spinach and stir it all together. Crush in the garlic. Keep sautéing, stirring frequently, until the spinach wilts.

Stir in the coconut milk, pepper, and nutmeg, and salt to taste—I added about ¼ teaspoon. Let the spinach simmer in the coconut milk for a few minutes.

Thicken up with a teeny sprinkle of glucomannan, if you like, then serve.

YIELD: 2 servings

Nutritional Analysis
Per serving: 207 calories; 19 g fat; 5 g protein; 8 g carbohydrate; 4 g dietary fiber; 4 g net carbs

Sautéed Sesame Spinach

1 tablespoon (8 g) sesame seeds
3 tablespoons (45 ml) olive oil
1 garlic clove, crushed
8 ounces (225 g) spinach leaves (I used baby spinach, but full-grown would be fine.)
1 teaspoon coconut aminos

Put a small skillet over a medium-low burner and add the sesame seeds. Stir or shake them over the heat until they're lightly golden. Remove from heat and keep 'em nearby while you . . .

Put a big skillet over a medium-high burner. Add the olive oil, slosh it around, and add the garlic. Now throw in the spinach—unless your skillet is bigger than mine, it will be very full. Sauté quickly, stirring often—carefully, so as to keep the spinach in the pan while turning it over to make sure that all of it comes in contact with the heat—until it's barely wilted. Stir in the coconut aminos.

Plate it, top with the sesame seeds, and serve.

YIELD: 4 servings

Nutritional Analysis
Per serving: 114 calories; 11 g fat; 2 g protein; 2 g carbohydrate; 1 g dietary fiber; 1 g net carbs

Fennel with Pine Nuts and Raisins

1 tablespoon (9 g) pine nuts
1½ tablespoons (13.5 g) raisins
½ fennel bulb
½ medium onion
2 teaspoons (26 g) lard or coconut oil
¼ teaspoon ground cinnamon
¼ teaspoon anchovy paste

In a dry skillet, over medium heat, stir the pine nuts until they're touched with gold. Remove from the skillet and set aside.

Put the raisins in a little dish and just barely cover them with boiling water. Let them sit while you . . .
Cut the top off the fennel, whack it in half, and cut out the core. Now slice it as paper-thin as you possibly can. Slice the onion just as thin.

Turn the heat under the skillet to medium high and melt the fat. Add the fennel and onion and sauté, stirring fairly often, till tender-crisp, 10 to 15 minutes.

When the fennel is tender-crisp, use a fork to lift the raisins out of the water and put them in the skillet. Stir the cinnamon and anchovy paste into the water left in the dish till the anchovy paste is dissolved. Dump into the skillet and stir it in. Keep sautéing for another minute or two until the liquid has evaporated.

Stir in the pine nuts and serve.

YIELD: 3 servings

Nutritional Analysis
Per serving: 76 calories; 4 g fat; 2 g protein; 9 g carbohydrate; 2 g dietary fiber; 7 g net carbs

Ginger-Walnut Sweet Potato

2 large sweet potatoes
8 teaspoons (40 ml) walnut oil
1 teaspoon ground ginger

Scrub the potatoes and throw 'em in a 350°F (180°C, or gas mark 4) oven. Bake them till soft, about an hour.

Cut into 4 servings and use a fork mash up the innards right there in the shell. Add 2 teaspoons (10 ml) of walnut oil and ¼ teaspoon of ginger to each, mash it in, and serve.

YIELD: 4 servings

Nutritional Analysis
Per serving: 150 calories; 9 g fat; 1 g protein; 16 g carbohydrate; 2 g dietary fiber; 14 g net carbs

Orange-Sweet Potato Casserole

1 pound (455 g) sweet potatoes
1 orange
Salt and black pepper
½ teaspoon ground rosemary
2 tablespoons (26 g) coconut oil

Preheat oven to 350ºF (180ºC, or gas mark 4). Grease an 8 x 8-inch (20 x 20 cm) baking dish. Peel your sweet potatoes and cut in ¼-inch (6 mm) slices. Without peeling it, slice your orange paper-thin.

Arrange a single layer of sweet potato slices in your prepared casserole dish. Sprinkle with salt and pepper and a little of the rosemary. Cover with a layer of orange slices.

Repeat your layers. Melt the coconut oil and mix it with any remaining rosemary. Drizzle over the whole casserole.

Cover your dish with foil and bake for 1 hour. Uncover and bake 15 minutes more, then serve.

YIELD: 5 servings

Nutritional Analysis
Per serving: 128 calories; 6 g fat; 1 g protein; 19 g carbohydrate; 3 g dietary fiber; 16 g net carbs

Sweet Potatoes with Caramelized Onions and Bacon

Down-home flavor at its best

4 medium sweet potatoes
4 slices bacon
1 cup (160 g) diced onion
1 teaspoon Cajun seasoning or to taste

Scrub the sweet potatoes, stab them all over with a fork, and put them into the microwave. I gave mine 7 minutes on full power, which turned out to be exactly right, but your time may vary a bit according to the size of your sweet potatoes and the power of your oven.

Put a heavy-bottomed skillet over low heat and start cooking the bacon. In the meanwhile, dice your onion—you want it fairly fine.

When the bacon is crisp, remove from the skillet and reserve. Throw the onion in the bacon grease and sauté slowly until it's not simply translucent, but browned.

While the onion's browning, peel your sweet potatoes. This will be very easy—you can just pull the skin off with your fingers.

When the onion is well browned, slice the sweet potatoes into the skillet in big chunks. Use a fork to mash the sweet potatoes till all the onion and bacon grease are worked in. Now crumble in the bacon, add the Cajun seasoning, and mash that in, too. Serve!

YIELD: 6 servings

Nutritional Analysis
Per serving: 127 calories; 2 g fat; 3 g protein; 24 g carbohydrate; 3 g dietary fiber; 21 g net carbs

Oven-Baked Sweet Potato Chunks with Curry

4 tablespoons (52 g) coconut oil
2 sweet potatoes
2 teaspoons salt
1 teaspoon curry powder

Preheat oven to 375°F (190°C, or gas mark 5). Put coconut oil on a shallow baking tin and put it in the preheating oven.

Scrub your potatoes (it's super-easy to double or treble this) and slice 'em about 1-inch (2.5 cm) thick or a little less. Halve each round, and if they are pretty big in diameter, quarter 'em.

Mix together the salt and the curry powder.

Pull the baking tin out of the oven and spread your sweet potato chunks on it. Use a pancake turner to turn them over and coat them completely with the oil.

Now sprinkle them with the curry and salt mixture, again, turning and making sure you get all the cut sides. Slide the baking tin back into the oven. Set the timer for 10 minutes.

NOTE

A dark metal baking tin works best here, because it browns the sweet potato chunks. I used my thoroughly ancient jelly roll pan.

When the timer beeps, use that pancake turner to turn your sweet potato chunks over. Put them back in and give 'em another 10 minutes.

They should be soft and golden by now, but if they're not, you could turn them and give them another 5. Serve hot as a side with a steak.

YIELD: 4 servings

Nutritional Analysis
Per serving: 187 calories; 14 g fat; 1 g protein; 16 g carbohydrate; 2 g dietary fiber; 14 g net carbs

Grilled Tomatoes

Super-simple, and good with a steak or omelet. I wouldn't do this in the electric tabletop grill; it'll squish 'em too much. But you could do it with the grill open, using it like a griddle, I suppose. If you do, set it to high.

4 medium tomatoes
2 tablespoons (28 ml) olive oil
Salt and black pepper
1 tablespoon (15 ml) balsamic vinegar
2 teaspoons minced fresh rosemary

Heat your grill or a ridged grill pan. Slice the tomatoes about ½-inch (1 cm) thick and brush with the olive oil. Grill for 5 minutes or so, turning once—you want them to have nice brown grill lines.

Plate the tomato slices, sprinkle lightly with salt and pepper, and drizzle with balsamic vinegar. Sprinkle with rosemary and serve. That's it!

YIELD: 4 servings

Nutritional Analysis
Per serving: 86 calories; 7 g fat; 1 g protein; 6 g carbohydrate; 1 g dietary fiber; 5 g net carbs

Green Beans with Caramelized Onions and Mushrooms

1 pound (455 g) green beans (the smaller and more tender, the better)

¼ cup (40 g) minced onion

2 tablespoons (26 g) lard or coconut oil, divided

½ cup (35 g) chopped mushrooms

Snip the ends off your green beans and put them in your steamer—I use a microwave steamer, but you can use a stovetop one if you like. Start 'em cooking; you want them just barely tender.

In the meanwhile, mince your onion. Put your big, heavy skillet over medium-low heat and melt half the lard. Throw in the onion and sauté it slowly, stirring now and then, till it's browned all over.

While the onion is browning, chop your mushrooms.

Okay, your onion is caramelized. Remove it to a plate and reserve. Add the rest of the lard to the skillet and throw in your mushrooms. Now check your green beans! They're getting close to done.

Sauté the mushrooms until they've softened and changed color.

When the beans are tender-crisp, drain them. Now add them to the skillet and add the onions back to the mix. Stir it all up together, then serve.

YIELD: 4 servings

Nutritional Analysis
Per serving: 95 calories; 7 g fat; 2 g protein; 8 g carbohydrate; 4 g dietary fiber; 4 g net carbs

Green Beans with Criminis and Caramelized Onion

Consider this a fancier version of the previous recipe. This would be a great substitute for that gooey green bean casserole at your next holiday meal.

½ medium onion, diced

2 tablespoons (26 g) coconut oil or fat of your choice, divided

4 ounces (115 g) crimini mushrooms

1 pound (455 g) green beans

½ cup (120 ml) chicken broth

Salt and black pepper to taste

Put your big, heavy skillet over low heat and let it heat while you dice your onions. Melt a tablespoon of the coconut oil and throw in the onion. You're going to sauté it, stirring fairly often (but not standing over the stove) until it's pretty well browned—that is, caramelized—but you don't want to burn it, so keep the heat low.

While the onions start cooking, wipe your criminis clean and slice them. If your onions aren't brown yet (or if you bought presliced mushrooms), you might start processing your green beans.

You want to rinse them, snip off the ends, and perhaps snip them in two; I did. I think a kitchen shears is the easiest tool for this task.

Okay, your onions are a pretty brown. Add the rest of the fat and throw in your criminis. If you like, you can break those slices up further with the edge of your spatula—I did. Or you can keep them in picturesque slices; up to you. Sauté with the onion until the mushrooms have softened and changed color.

Add the green beans to the skillet and stir everything up. Now pour in the chicken broth, cover the skillet, and set the stove timer for 20 minutes. Your beans should be just tender by then, but give them another 5 if they need it. Then serve.

YIELD: 4 servings

Nutritional Analysis
Per serving: 107 calories; 7 g fat; 3 g protein; 10 g carbohydrate; 4 g dietary fiber; 6 g net carbs

NOTE

This recipe can be made dramatically quicker and easier by using frozen green beans. They generally don't have anything added to them, so I'd consider them okay, but many paleo folks prefer all fresh ingredients. Up to you.

Green Beans with Shallots and Celery

1 pound (455 g) green beans (as skinny and young as you can get 'em)
3 shallots
2 celery ribs (pale, tender ones)
3 tablespoons (45 ml) extra-virgin olive oil
¼ lemon
2 tablespoons (8 g) minced fresh parsley
Salt and black pepper

Trim your beans and slice your shallots paper thin. Slice your celery about ¼-inch (6 mm) thick, leaves included.

Put your big, heavy skillet over medium-high heat and add the olive oil. Add the green beans and sauté for 5 minutes. Add the shallots and celery and keep sautéing till the beans are just tender.

Squeeze in the juice of the quarter lemon and stir in the parsley. Salt and pepper to taste. Serve hot or cold.

YIELD: 4 servings

Nutritional Analysis
Per serving: 130 calories; 10 g fat; 2 g protein; 10 g carbohydrate; 4 g dietary fiber; 6 g net carbs

Green Beans and Carrots with Orange and Rosemary

Our tester, Lynda VV, says of this dish, "It was a nice ratio of carrots to beans and the color combo was a sight to behold!"

2 medium carrots, peeled and sliced
¾ pound (340 g) green beans, trimmed and cut in halves or thirds
2 tablespoons (28 ml) olive oil
½ orange
2 teaspoons minced fresh rosemary
Salt (optional)

Peel your carrots and slice them on the diagonal. Put them in a microwaveable dish, add a teaspoon of water, cover, and microwave on high for 3 to 4 minutes. Use that time to trim and cut up your beans.

(continued)

Put your big, heavy skillet over medium-high heat, add the olive oil, and start sautéing the green beans. When the microwave beeps, drain the carrots and add them to the skillet, too. Sauté till everything's just tender—probably 10 to 12 minutes.

While the beans and carrots are sautéing, grate ¼ teaspoon orange zest. When the veggies are tender, add this to the skillet, squeeze in the juice from your half orange, and add your rosemary, too. Sauté, stirring frequently, for another minute or two, just till the juice reduces to a glaze, then serve.

YIELD: 4 servings

Nutritional Analysis

Per serving: 106 calories; 7 g fat; 2 g protein; 11 g carbohydrate; 4 g dietary fiber;7 g net carb

Savory Green Beans

Our tester Lisa says, "I plan to make this a regular staple!"

4 ounces (115 g) sliced bacon (roughly 4 slices)
1 pound (455 g) fresh green beans, trimmed (about 1¼ pounds before trimming)
8 ounces (225 g) chopped mushrooms
3 scallions, minced
2 tablespoons (8 g) fresh savory, stripped from the stems
2 tablespoons (8 g) minced fresh parsley
1 tablespoon (15 ml) lemon juice
1 tablespoon (15 ml) white cider vinegar
2 drops liquid stevia
¼ teaspoon black pepper

In your big, heavy skillet, start frying the bacon.

In the meanwhile, steam your green beans tender-crisp. I would probably give mine 9 to 10 minutes on high in the microwave, but do 'em on the stove top if you prefer.

When your bacon is done, remove it from the skillet and reserve. Drain off all but about 2 tablespoons (30 ml) of the grease and start sautéing the mushrooms and scallions in it.

While the mushrooms are sautéing, mince your herbs.

Okay, your green beans are done. Uncover them immediately, to prevent overcooking.

When your mushrooms have softened and changed color, stir in the green beans, the savory, and the parsley. Stir together the lemon juice, cider vinegar, liquid stevia, and pepper, then pour into the skillet and stir to coat.

Crumble in the bacon, stir it in, and serve.

YIELD: 4 servings

Nutritional Analysis

Per serving: 216 calories; 14 g fat; 12 g protein; 13 g carbohydrate; 5 g dietary fiber; 8 g net carbs

Grilled Artichokes

¼ cup (60 ml) extra-virgin olive oil
3 garlic cloves, crushed
2 artichokes
1 lemon

Put a large saucepan of water over a high burner; you're bringing it to a boil.

Put your olive oil in a small dish or cup and crush the garlic into it. Let that sit while you . . .

Whack your artichokes in half. If you want to do the whole fussy bit of trimming the leaves, go ahead, but I rarely bother. Do, however, take the tip of a spoon and scrape out the fuzzy "choke." Rinse them well under the tap to get rid of any clinging hairs.

When the water comes to a boil, add your artichokes, turn the burner down to keep the water at a simmer, and cover the pot. Set a timer for 20 minutes.

About 5 minutes before the timer goes off, turn on your broiler and put the rack up close to it.

Now pull your artichokes out of the water with a tongs, holding each cut side down over the pot until it stops dripping. Arrange them, cut side up, on your broiler rack. Make a nice tight formation, so you can get them all under the flame.

Use a spoon to drizzle garlicky olive oil into the hollows and down between the leaves of the artichokes. Use about half of it. Spoon some of the crushed garlic onto the artichokes, too.

Slide your artichokes under the broiler, very close to the flame. Set your timer for 5 minutes. In the meanwhile, quarter your lemon.

When the timer beeps, pull out the broiler pan and squeeze lemon over them; use 2 of your lemon quarters—one per whole artichoke. Use a tongs to rearrange the artichokes so they'll char evenly—outer edges to the inside—and give them another 2 to 3 minutes under the broiler.

When they're done, plate your artichokes and drizzle the rest of the garlicky olive oil over them, once again getting it down between the leaves. Serve with the remaining lemon wedges, lots of napkins, and a spare plate for the leaves.

YIELD: 2 servings

Nutritional Analysis
Per serving: 311 calories; 27 g fat; 5 g protein; 18 g carbohydrate; 7 g dietary fiber; 11 g net carbs

Gingered Carrots

If you can get real baby carrots—not the "baby-cut carrots" in bags at the grocery stores, but actual, little, tiny, fresh carrots, use 'em! If not, regular carrots cut in strips.

1 pound (455 g) carrots (the freshest and smallest you can get)
½ tablespoon (6.5 g) lard
½ tablespoon (7.5 g) olive oil
1 teaspoon walnut oil
1 tablespoon (20 g) honey
½ lemon
2 teaspoons grated gingerroot
½ teaspoon ground cumin

If you can get true baby carrots, just trim off the tops and scrub them. If you're working with bigger carrots, still pick the littlest, then peel them and cut them in strips—about the length of the baby-cut carrots and about ¼-inch (6 mm) thick.

Steam these till just tender—maybe 5 to 6 minutes in the microwave.

(continued)

When the carrots are almost done steaming, put your skillet over medium-high heat. Add the lard and olive oil and combine. Drain the carrots and throw them in the skillet. Sauté for just a couple of minutes. Now add the walnut oil and honey and squeeze in the juice from the half lemon (pick out the seeds first, of course). Stir in the ginger and cumin, too.

Keep sautéing for just a couple of minutes, till the carrots are glazed, then serve.

YIELD: 5 servings

Nutritional Analysis
Per serving: 81 calories; 4 g fat; 1 g protein; 13 g carbohydrate; 3 g dietary fiber; 10 g net carbs

Maple-Glazed Carrots

Yvonne, who tested these, asked if she'd make them again, said "100 percent YES" and added that her husband ate "a huge pile."

Again, if you can get real baby carrots—not the "baby-cut carrots" in bags at the grocery stores, but actual, little, tiny, fresh carrots, use 'em! If not, use regular carrots cut in strips.

1 pound (455 g) carrots (the freshest and smallest you can find)
½ tablespoon (6.5 g) lard
½ tablespoon (7.5 ml) olive oil
1 teaspoon walnut oil
1 tablespoon (20 g) maple syrup
½ lemon

If you can get true baby carrots, just trim off the tops and scrub them. If you're working with bigger carrots, still pick the littlest, then peel them and cut them in strips—about the length of the baby-cut carrots and about ¼-inch (6 mm) thick.

Steam these till just tender—maybe 5 to 6 minutes in the microwave.

When the carrots are almost done steaming, put your skillet over medium-high heat. Add the lard and olive oil and combine. Drain the carrots and throw them in the skillet. Sauté for just a couple of minutes. Now add the walnut oil and maple syrup and squeeze in the juice from the half lemon (pick out the seeds first, of course).

Keep sautéing for just a couple of minutes, till the carrots are glazed, then serve.

YIELD: 4 servings

Nutritional Analysis
Per serving: 97 calories; 5 g fat; 1 g protein; 14 g carbohydrate; 3 g dietary fiber; 11 g net carbs

Plantanos Fritos

Puerto Rican French fries! Really good, too. Please note, however, that these are not any lower carb than potatoes.

1 large plantain
Lard or coconut oil

Start your lard heating in your big, heavy skillet over a medium-high burner. You want about ¼ inch (6 mm) of fat or a little more.

In the meanwhile, peel and slice your plantain somewhere between ¼- and ½-inch (6 mm and 1 cm) thick.

When the fat is hot, add your plantain slices and fry them golden brown on both sides. While that's happening, lay a brown paper bag out on the counter or kitchen table. When your plantain slices are nicely brown on both sides, use a pancake turner to transfer them to the bag, arranging them all at one end. When they're all on the bag, fold the other end over the plantain slices and squash 'em a bit. Don't flatten them like cornflakes, but do squish them some.

Now transfer them back to the hot fat and fry them till they're browned a bit more, and crispy. Drain again and serve with salt, if you use it, and Caveman Ketchup (page 273).

YIELD: 2 servings

Nutritional Analysis
Per serving: 109 calories; trace fat; 1 g protein; 29 g carbohydrate; 2 g dietary fiber; 27 g net carbs

Roasted Pumpkin and "Rice"—and Seeds! And Bacon! And Orange!

This dish is hard to define or describe, but it's awfully good. Try it as a side with roast pork for a perfect autumn supper. If you have any left over, try cubing the leftover pork and mixing it in, to reheat for supper the next night.

2 tablespoons (26 g) coconut oil
1 pound (455 g) pumpkin or other winter squash (about ½ small pumpkin)
¼ cup (36 g) sunflower seeds
¼ cup (35 g) squash kernels (pepitas)
4 slices bacon
½ head cauliflower
1 medium onion
1½ tablespoons (3 g) dried sage or 3 tablespoons (7.5 g) fresh, minced
2 tablespoons (28 ml) coconut aminos
2 tablespoons (28 ml) chicken Broth Concentrate (page 27)
½ orange
½ teaspoon black pepper
Salt (optional)

Preheat your oven to 350°F (180°C, or gas mark 4). Put the coconut oil in a roasting pan and put it in the oven while it heats, to melt the oil.

Scrape the seeds and pulp out of your pumpkin or squash, cut it in slices, and peel them. (I just find it easier to peel the slices than to peel the whole thing.) Now cut it into cubes somewhere in the ½-inch (1 cm) neighborhood. Pull the pan out of the oven, throw your pumpkin or squash chunks in there, and toss them with the coconut oil. Spread them in a single layer, slide back into the oven, and set your timer for 10 minutes.

Spread your seeds—both kinds—in another pan and put them in the oven, too.

Put your big, heavy skillet over medium-low heat and lay the bacon in it. You're frying it crisp.

Do the whole Cauli-Rice thing (page 87), with the cauliflower—trim off the leaves and the bottom of the stem, whack it in chunks, run them through the shredding blade of your food processor, and steam lightly. I've said this before.

Go back to the bacon—it probably needs turning by now. Go back and chop your onion.

Your oven timer beeped! Pull out your seeds and check your squash chunks. Are they good and soft? If so, pull them out. If not, turn them, and put them back in for another 5 minutes.

Don't forget to uncover the Cauli-Rice when it's done steaming! You don't want mush.

Now check your bacon. When it's crisp, remove it from the skillet and save it on a plate. Drain off all but about 2 tablespoons (26 g) of fat and add the onion to the skillet. Sauté till it's translucent.

(continued)

Okay! We're getting to assembly time! Add the Cauli-Rice and roast squash to the skillet. Stir it up well with the onion. Now add the sage, the coconut aminos, and the chicken Broth Concentrate. Grate in the zest of your half orange and squeeze the juice in, too. Stir it all up really well, while trying not to completely mash the squash chunks.

Stir in the toasted seeds. Now grab your kitchen shears and snip the bacon into the skillet. Sprinkle in the pepper. Stir it up again, check to see whether you want to salt it, and serve.

YIELD: 6 servings

Nutritional Analysis
Per serving: 198 calories; 14 g fat; 8 g protein; 14 g carbohydrate; 3 g dietary fiber; 9 g net carbs

Simple Pan-Roasted Turnips

My mother used to roast cut-up potatoes in the pan around a roast, browning in the drippings. I long since gave up potatoes, but the same cooking method works wonderfully for turnips.

4 medium turnips
Pan drippings

This assumes you're making a roast—roast beef, leg of lamb, roast pork, something simple like that.

Peel your turnips, and cut them into wedges about 1-inch (2.5 cm) thick at the base.

Forty-five minutes or so before the end of the roast's cooking time, pull it out of the oven and put the turnip wedges around it, on the bottom of the pan, in the drippings. Try to get them with a flat side against the pan, for maximum browning. Use a basting brush to coat the rest of the surfaces with drippings. Put your roast back in the oven.

About 20 to 25 minutes later, pull your roast out again and turn the turnip wedges over so the other side of each wedge will brown. Assuming your roast is on a rack—mine always is—it's probably easier to lift out the rack with the roast on it and put it in a convenient place (like in your sink) for the minute or two it takes to do this. Put the rack and roast back in the pan and once again put the whole thing back in the oven. This time roast until your meat is done. Serve the turnips with the roast and any gravy.

YIELD: 4 servings

Nutritional Analysis
Per serving: 33 calories; trace fat; 1 g protein; 8 g carbohydrate; 2 g dietary fiber; 6 g net carbs. This, however, doesn't include the fat the turnips will absorb from the drippings. It's impossible to know the numbers for that.

NOTE

This is based on one turnip per customer, assuming the turnips are a tad bigger than a tennis ball. If you have little baby turnips—and very nice they are— go with three per person.

Hash Browns

These are killer! But unfortunately, if you want more servings, you'll need a bigger skillet. By the way, this works great with leftover chunks of rutabaga, too. Just chop 'em up—and remember you won't have to cook them as long.

2 medium turnips
½ medium onion
¼ cup (52 g) bacon grease or lard, and more as needed

Peel your turnips and run them through the shredding blade of your food processor. Dump 'em out of your food processor and swap the shredding blade for the *S* blade. Chunk your half onion, put it in the processor, and pulse till it's chopped fairly fine.

Put your big, heavy skillet over medium heat and add a couple of tablespoons (30 ml) of bacon grease. Add the turnips and onion and stir it all up, then spread in an even layer. Cover the skillet and let it cook for 5 minutes. Uncover, stir it up, re-cover, and let it cook for 5 more minutes. Repeat this maneuver till the turnips are tender. Add more bacon grease by the tablespoon (15 ml) as you think it needs it.

When the turnips are tender, start "tilting" the lid between stirrings—leave a crack for the steam to escape. Your hash browns should start browning on the bottom. When you stir them, use your spatula to lift the crust forming on the bottom and turn the whole thing over.

After you've done this 3 or 4 times, your turnips should be pretty browned. Mix 'em up again, spread them evenly, and this time leave the lid off altogether. Give them 5 minutes undisturbed, then serve.

YIELD: 2 servings

Nutritional Analysis
Per serving: 280 calories; 26 g fat; 1 g protein; 10 g carbohydrate; 3 g dietary fiber; 7 g net carbs. Fat will vary according to how much you add.

Chapter 6

SIDE DISH SALADS

Ah, salad. Wonderful, wonderful salad. I just love salad in every possible form—tossed green salads, coleslaw, deli-type make-ahead salads, you name it. If it involves bits of vegetables in a tasty dressing, count me in.

All fruits and vegetables are paleo, of course, but virtually all dressings on the market are not, because they contain objectionable oils. They also often include dairy products—think Ranch dressing and Parmesan Peppercorn. And sugar? I've seen salad dressings that have more corn syrup in them than anything else.

Here you will find a broad variety of salads. You will also find an assortment of salad dressings to appeal to every taste and to complement every salad combination.

Avocado-Grapefruit Tossed Salad

This will vary with the lettuces you use but will always be good! This salad should be made right before eating; it won't hold well.

1 batch White Balsamic Vinaigrette (page 140)
1 avocado
1 ruby red grapefruit
2 quarts (440 g) lettuce

Assemble your dressing in the blender first. Before you run the blender . . .

Split your avocado in half, remove the pit, and slice the flesh.

Cut your grapefruit in half and use a thin-bladed, sharp knife to cut around each section to loosen it, putting them in a bowl as you go. When all your segments are out of the rinds, squeeze the juice out of the empty grapefruit rinds into the dressing. Now run the blender to emulsify the dressing.

Put your lettuce in a big salad bowl and pour on the dressing. Toss till it's all well coated, then pile it on 4 plates. Arrange the grapefruit sections and avocado slices artistically on the salads and serve.

YIELD: 4 servings

Nutritional Analysis
Per serving: 364 calories; 35 g fat; 3 g protein; 14 g carbohydrate; 4 g dietary fiber; 10 g net carbs

Herb Garden Salad

If you grow your own herbs, you'll love this salad! Our tester, Rebecca, says, "I used to trade meals with a neighbor woman from Switzerland. She would bring over these wondrous green salads, and I could never figure out why they tasted so good, or how to reproduce them myself. I'd ask her how she made them and she would say, 'I added some herbs from the garden.'"

24 fresh snow pea pods
2 quarts (440 g) lettuce, half spring mix, half romaine
4 scallions
¼ cup (15 g) minced fresh parsley
¼ cup (9.6 g) thyme leaves, stems removed
¼ cup (16 g) minced fresh marjoram
2 tablespoons (8 g) minced fresh tarragon
½ cup (120 ml) Dilly Dressing (page 145)
4 tablespoons (36 g) toasted sunflower seeds (salted or unsalted, your choice)

Pinch the ends off your snow peas and pull off the strings. Put them in a microwaveable bowl, cover with a saucer, and give them just 45 seconds on high. Uncover immediately! Let 'em cool. You can do this in advance and refrigerate them.

When it's salad time, combine the lettuces in a salad bowl. Slice your scallions thin, separating the white part and the green shoot. Add the white parts to the lettuce.

Have all your herbs minced, including the green scallion shoots. In a separate bowl, toss them all together and have them standing by. Now pour the dressing over the lettuce and toss till every last millimeter is coated with dressing.

(continued)

Pile the lettuce on 4 salad plates. Sprinkle a good handful of the herbs over each salad. Make a pretty pinwheel of 6 snow peas on top of that, then sprinkle each salad with a tablespoon (9 g) of sunflower seeds and serve.

YIELD: 4 servings

Nutritional Analysis
Per serving: 233 calories; 19 g fat; 6 g protein; 14 g carbohydrate; 7 g dietary fiber; 7 g net carbs

Far Afield Salad

This started with a recipe in an Indiana cookbook. The original called for candied walnuts, meaning sugar. The dressing was super-sugary, too. It also called for blue cheese, not paleo. So this is what I came up with.

¼ cup (30 g) chopped walnuts
4 slices bacon
2 quarts (440 g) leaf lettuce or mixed baby greens
6 strawberries, sliced
2 scallions, sliced
½ batch Horseradish-Vanilla Vinaigrette (page 141)

Set your oven to 350°F (180°C, or gas mark 4). Spread your chopped walnuts on a shallow baking tin and slide 'em in. Set your oven for 8 minutes, though they may take 10. Better to give them an extra couple of minutes than to burn them.

Start your bacon cooking by your preferred method.

(We're assuming for the purposes of this recipe that your dressing is already made. But if it isn't, this would be a good time to make it. It's easy.)

Wash and dry your lettuce (do dry it, or the dressing won't stick) and tear it up into a big salad bowl.

Slice your strawberries and scallions, both pretty thin, and have them waiting.

Okay, your walnuts and bacon should be getting close to done. You want your walnuts crisp and toasty-tasting, and your bacon crisp.

Everything ready? Okay. Pour the dressing over the lettuce and toss like mad, till it's all evenly coated. Pile it in 4 bowls or on 4 salad plates.

Snip a strip of bacon over each serving. Scatter sliced scallions over the bacon. Arrange strawberry slices prettily on top of that. Now scatter a tablespoon of walnuts over each salad and serve immediately.

YIELD: 4 servings

Nutritional Analysis
Per serving: 287 calories; 28 g fat; 5 g protein; 6 g carbohydrate; 3 g dietary fiber; 3 g net carbs

Spinach Salad

This serves three as a starter but also makes a great main dish for one. A traditional addition to this salad is sliced mushrooms; a cup or so would go well, though I prefer it without.

2 slices bacon
3 cups (90 g) fresh spinach
¼ cup (40 g) thinly sliced red onion
2 eggs, hard-boiled
Kinda '60s Dressing (page 144)

Start your bacon cooking however you like to cook it; you want it crisp.

While that's cooking, put your spinach in a big salad bowl. Slice your onion paper-thin and peel and slice your eggs. Make your dressing, too.

Okay, bacon's crisp; drain and crumble it. Pour your dressing over the spinach and toss till it's evenly coated. Pile the spinach in three bowls and top each one with a third of the bacon, sliced onion, and egg. That's all!

YIELD: 3 servings

Nutritional Analysis
Per serving: 171 calories; 15 g fat; 7 g protein; 4 g carbohydrate; 1 g dietary fiber; 3 g net carbs

Spinach-Plum Salad

Light and exquisite, try this with grilled fish or seafood for a summer dinner party.

3 quarts (360 g) baby spinach
2 red plums, diced
2 scallions, sliced
2 tablespoons (28 ml) olive oil
2 tablespoons (28 ml) white balsamic vinegar
1 teaspoon coconut aminos
½ teaspoon grated gingerroot

Dump your baby spinach in your big salad bowl.

Whack the plums in half, remove the pits, and cut into ½-inch (1 cm) dice. Slice your scallions, including the crisp part of the green shoot.

In a small bowl whisk together the olive oil, white balsamic, coconut aminos, and ginger. Pour this over the spinach and toss till it's coated with the dressing. Pile the spinach on 6 salad plates, top each serving with plum cubes and scallions, and serve.

YIELD: 6 servings

Nutritional Analysis
Per serving: 68 calories; 5 g fat; 2 g protein; 6 g carbohydrate; 2 g dietary fiber, 4 g net carbs

Wilted Spinach Salad

Our tester Ashley said, "Very easy and fast to make . . . the end result looked gourmet!" She also called this "yummo."

To be seriously paleo, see if you can find fresh water chestnuts—Asian groceries generally carry them.

4 tablespoons (60 ml) extra-virgin olive oil
1 large garlic clove, minced
2 tablespoons (28 ml) coconut aminos
½ cup (70 g) water chestnuts (slice 'em thin, then into strips)
½ lemon
18 ounces (510 g) bagged baby spinach
2 eggs, hard-boiled and peeled

Put your biggest skillet over medium heat, add the olive oil, and sauté the garlic in it for a minute or so. Add the coconut aminos and water chestnuts and squeeze in the juice of the half lemon.

Now add the spinach—it will overwhelm your skillet!—and toss until it just barely wilts.

(continued)

Transfer to a salad bowl and use your box grater to shred the eggs over the top. Serve immediately.

YIELD: 5 servings

Nutritional Analysis

Per serving: 170 calories; 13 g fat; 6 g protein; 9 g carbohydrate; 3 g dietary fiber; 6 g net carbs

Fruity Spinach Salad

How summery is this? Our tester Deb says her husband called this "refreshing" and that it's going into her "regular salad rotation." She also suggested a little avocado would be a nice addition, so if you happen to have one on hand, throw it in.

6 ounces (170 g) bagged baby spinach
1 cup (155 g) watermelon balls or chunks
1 cup (170 g) sliced strawberries
1 cup (177 g) thinly sliced kiwifruit
½ cup (60 g) cucumber, quartered lengthwise, then thinly sliced
¼ cup (40 g) red onion, sliced paper-thin
⅓ cup (80 ml) White Balsamic Vinaigrette (page 140)

Not complicated! Just combine the spinach, fruit, and veggies in your salad bowl. Drizzle on the dressing, toss, and serve immediately.

YIELD: 6 servings

Nutritional Analysis

Per serving: 206 calories; 19 g fat; 2 g protein; 11 g carbohydrate; 3 g dietary fiber; 8 g net carbs

Valentine's Salad

I really did make this for Valentine's Day dinner with That Nice Boy I Married. It helped turn a simple steak into a romantic dinner-for-two.

3 tablespoons (21 g) slivered almonds
4 cups (120 g) baby spinach
1 scallion sliced thin, including the crisp part of the green shoot
5 strawberries, hulled and sliced
¼ cup (60 ml) Poppy Seed Dressing (page 143)

First, put a small skillet over medium-low heat and stir the almonds in it till they're lightly golden. Remove from the heat and reserve.

Put the spinach in your salad bowl. Have the scallion and strawberries sliced and your dressing made before assembling your salad.

Now pour the dressing on the spinach, and toss-toss-toss. Scatter the scallion, strawberries, and almonds on top and serve immediately.

YIELD: 2 servings

Nutritional Analysis

Per serving: 274 calories; 26 g fat; 5 g protein; 9 g carbohydrate; 4 g dietary fiber; 5 g net carbs

Grapefruit and Avocado Salad

Our tester Burma called this "unusual and delightful" and said both she and her husband enjoyed it very much.

2 ruby red grapefruit
1 tablespoon (15 ml) lime juice
2 tablespoons (28 ml) extra-virgin olive oil
1 tablespoon (15 ml) white balsamic vinegar
3 drops liquid stevia
1 medium shallot (about ½ cup [80 g])
2 avocados
Salt and black pepper
Leaf lettuce (to serve)
2 tablespoons (2 g) minced fresh cilantro

Holding a grapefruit over a nonreactive bowl to catch the juice, use a sharp knife to cut the skin and all the white pith off your grapefruit, then cut out each section. Put the sections in a second bowl and squeeze the remaining juice out of the membranes into the first bowl. (Are you getting this? You have a bowl with the juice and another with the sections.) Repeat with the second grapefruit.

Pour the grapefruit juice into your blender with the lime juice, olive oil, white balsamic vinegar, and liquid stevia. Peel the shallot, cut it into a few chunks, and throw it in, too. Now run the blender until the shallot is pulverized.

Everything up to here can be done a few hours early, if you like, but leave preperation of the avocados until right before serving.

Line 4 salad plates with lettuce. Now peel and slice your avocados—an avocado slicer is a huge help here—and arrange the slices spoke-fashion on the lettuce. Now arrange the grapefruit sections between them, making pretty pink-and-green pinwheels.

Whir up your dressing again and drizzle it over the salads. Sprinkle the cilantro on top and serve immediately

YIELD: 4 servings

Nutritional Analysis
Per serving: 266 calories; 22 g fat; 3 g protein; 19 g carbohydrate; 4 g dietary fiber; 15 g net carbs

Mango and Avocado Salad with Lime Vinaigrette

2 avocados
2 ripe mangos
¼ teaspoon salt
¼ teaspoon cayenne
1 lime
2 tablespoons (28 ml) Habanero-Lime Balsamic (page 284)
⅓ cup (80 ml) extra-virgin olive oil

Peel and slice the avocados and mangos and arrange slices in alternating spokes on 4 plates. Stir together the salt and cayenne and sprinkle evenly over the avocados and mangos.

Grate a couple of teaspoons of lime zest and reserve. Now squeeze the juice from the lime into your blender. Add the Habanero-Lime Balsamic and olive oil and run for 30 seconds or so.

Drizzle the dressing over the salads. Sprinkle with the lime zest and serve.

YIELD: 4 servings

Nutritional Analysis
Per serving: 398 calories; 34 g fat; 3 g protein; 28 g carbohydrate; 5 g dietary fiber; 23 g net carbs

Classic Coleslaw

This makes a vat of classic creamy coleslaw. I just love the stuff. And cheap? Oh, yes. Leave the onion out if you like, but I think it really lights up the flavor.

1 medium head cabbage, shredded
2 medium carrots, shredded
⅓ cup (55 g) minced red onion
1 batch Coleslaw Dressing (page 144)

Shred the vegetables, put them in a very big mixing bowl, pour on the dressing, and stir to coat. That's it. This keeps for a few days in the fridge and goes with any simple meat or poultry dish.

YIELD: Serving count will depend on your head of cabbage, of course, but this makes a lot. Call it 12 servings—the size you get in a restaurant.

Nutritional Analysis
Per serving: 155 calories; 15 g fat; 2 g protein; 7 g carbohydrate; 2 g dietary fiber; 5 g net carbs

Apple-Walnut Coleslaw

A perfect autumn salad!

½ cup (60 g) chopped walnuts
4 cups (280 g) shredded cabbage
1 apple
3 tablespoons (45 ml) walnut oil
2 tablespoons (28 ml) apple cider vinegar
¼ teaspoon Dijon mustard
2 tablespoons (28 g) Mayonnaise in the Jar (page 278)
¼ teaspoon black pepper
Salt to taste

Turn on your oven to 350°F (180°C, or gas mark 4). Spread your walnuts on a shallow baking tin and put them in the oven. Set your oven timer for 8 minutes.

In the meanwhile, shred the cabbage. Cut your apple in quarters, core, and cut it into bits roughly the size and shape of your cabbage bits—I cut mine in matchstick strips. Put the cabbage and apple in a big mixing bowl.

Measure the rest of the ingredients into a bowl and whisk 'em together.

When the timer beeps, taste one teeny walnut bit and see if they're toasty. If so, add them to the mixing bowl. If not, give them another 2 minutes, then add to the salad.

Now pour on the dressing and toss to coat. You can chill this for a few hours, but it's awfully good freshly made.

YIELD: 6 servings

Nutritional Analysis
Per serving: 183 calories; 17 g fat; 3 g protein; 8 g carbohydrate; 2 g dietary fiber; 6 g net carbs

Asian-Tex-Mex-Fusion Slaw

5 cups (350 g) thinly sliced napa cabbage
¼ pound (115 g) fresh snow pea pods or sugar snap peas
1 bunch scallions, sliced
½ red bell pepper, diced
1 navel orange, peeled and sectioned
⅓ cup (80 ml) Lime-Habanero Balsamic Dressing (page 143)

Make your dressing first.

Slice the cabbage. Pinch the stems off the pea pods, pulling off any strings, and snip them in thirds. Slice your scallions, including the crisp part of the green shoot. Dice your pepper fairly fine. Peel your orange and snip the sections into thirds as you go. Throw everything into a big mixing bowl as you go.

Pour on the dressing and toss. Let this chill an hour or so before serving.

YIELD: 4 servings

Nutritional Analysis
Per serving: 304 calories; 25 g fat; 1 g protein; 7 g carbohydrate; 1 g dietary fiber; 6 g net carbs

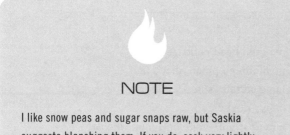

NOTE

I like snow peas and sugar snaps raw, but Saskia suggests blanching them. If you do, cook very lightly—maybe 45 seconds to 1 minute in a covered dish in the microwave. (Add a teaspoon of water to make steam.)

Sweet 'n' Tangy Slaw

Try this with grilled chicken!

½ head cabbage, shredded
1 medium apple, diced fine
1 cup (150 g) grapes, quartered
½ cup (80 g) diced red onion
½ cup (60 g) chopped walnuts
1 cup (225 g) Mayonnaise in the Jar (page 278)
3 dashes hot sauce or to taste
1 tablespoon (15 g) spicy brown mustard

Cut up your cabbage, apple, grapes, and onion and throw 'em in a big bowl. Chop the walnuts and add them, too.

Measure and whisk together the mayo, hot sauce, and mustard. Pour over the salad and toss till everything's well coated, then serve.

YIELD: 8 servings

Nutritional Analysis
Per serving: 269 calories; 28 g fat; 3 g protein; 7 g carbohydrate; 1 g dietary fiber; 6 g net carbs

Balsamic-Mustard Coleslaw

To me, the Cocoyo and white balsamic vinegar lend enough sweetness to this. But if you want it sweeter, add a few drops of liquid stevia extract, or a teaspoon or so of honey, to the dressing.

(continued)

½ cup (115 g) Mayonnaise in the Jar (page 278)

¼ cup (60 g) Cocoyo (page 28)

1 tablespoon (15 g) horseradish

1 tablespoon (15 g) spicy brown mustard

2 tablespoons (28 ml) white balsamic vinegar

1½ teaspoons black pepper

½ head cabbage, shredded

2 tablespoons (20 g) minced red onion

Mix together everything but the cabbage and onion. Let that sit while you . . .

Shred the cabbage and mince the onion—do go quite fine on the onion, so it carries its flavor throughout the slaw. Put these in a big mixing bowl, dump in the dressing, and stir to coat.

This is fine right away, but much better if you let it age awhile—overnight is best.

YIELD: 5 servings

Nutritional Analysis

Per serving: 189 calories; 19 g fat; 2 g protein; 7 g carbohydrate; 2 g dietary fiber; 5 g net carbs

Southwestern Slaw

Our tester Lisa M.M. calls this "super-tasty and really satisfying."

1 head cabbage, shredded

1 large carrot, shredded

⅓ cup (55 g) finely minced red onion

1 cup (225 g) Lime-Chipotle Mayonnaise (page 141)

¼ cup (60 ml) cider vinegar

1 teaspoon ground cumin

½ small chipotle chile, canned in adobo (or see Chipotles in Adobo, page 294)

¼ teaspoon dry mustard

3 drops liquid stevia or to taste

In a big, big mixing bowl, combine the veggies.

Put the rest of the ingredients in your blender or food processor and run for a minute, until the chipotle is completely pulverized.

Pour the dressing over the salad and toss to coat. Chill for several hours for flavors to blend.

YIELD: At least 8 servings

Nutritional Analysis

Per serving: 235 calories; 24 g fat; 2 g protein; 9 g carbohydrate; 3 g dietary fiber; 6 g net carbs

On-Tap Vinegar Slaw

This is fine fresh but notably improves with a couple of days in the fridge. That makes it a great salad to make in quantity and have on hand for a quick meal.

1 medium head cabbage

1 medium red onion, diced fine

2 large carrots, shredded

2 celery ribs, diced

1 cup (235 ml) white balsamic vinegar

¾ cup (175 ml) olive oil

1 teaspoon dry mustard

¼ teaspoon black pepper

4 drops liquid stevia

Salt to taste

Pretty simple: Cut up the vegetables and put them in a big, nonreactive bowl. Mix together everything else, pour over the veggies, and stir it up well. Store in a snap-top container in the fridge; this will continue to get better for several days.

YIELD: 10 servings

Nutritional Analysis

Per serving: 184 calories; 17 g fat; 2 g protein; 10 g carbohydrate; 3 g dietary fiber; 7 g net carbs

Shaved Asparagus with Balsamic Dressing

Lisa C. says, "You could pour the dressing over a paper towel and it would be good."

⅓ cup (27 g) chopped pecans
2 tablespoons (28 ml) balsamic vinegar
¼ cup (60 ml) extra-virgin olive oil
½ teaspoon Dijon mustard or spicy brown
½ tablespoon (7 g) Mayonnaise in the Jar (page 278)
1 clove garlic, crushed
2 pounds (900 g) asparagus
Salt and black pepper

First, turn on your oven to 350°F (180°C, or gas mark 4). Spread your pecans on a shallow baking tin, put 'em in the oven, and set a timer for 8 minutes.

Make your dressing first: Put the vinegar, olive oil, mustard, mayonnaise, and garlic in your blender and run till the garlic is pulverized and the dressing is emulsified. Leave it there in the blender while you . . .

Snap the ends off your asparagus where it wants to break naturally. Now use a vegetable peeler to shave the asparagus into long, thin strips. Shred them right into a salad bowl. Don't forget to take your pecans out of the oven when it beeps!

Whiz the blender just another second. Now pour the dressing over the asparagus and toss. Salt and pepper to taste, toss again, and serve, topped with pecans.

YIELD: 6 servings

Nutritional Analysis
Per serving: 152 calories; 15 g fat; 2 g protein; 5 g carbohydrate; 2 g dietary fiber; 3 g net carbs

NOTES

Our tester Lisa C. says: Notes on shaving asparagus:

It's freaking impossible and took forever trying to shave over the salad bowl. While the asparagus was crisp and my peeler sharp, I kept taking breaks because of the tediousness and hand exhaustion.

Here's the method that (finally) worked most expeditiously: Use a Y-shaped peeler instead of a swivel type. Line up four asparagus spears on a cutting board and hold them by the tough ends (don't snap off). Apply firm pressure with the peeler to shave the asparagus in long, thin strips.

So here's the alternative: Steam your asparagus till it's just brilliantly green, maybe 3 to 4 minutes. Chill, then serve with the dressing and little piles of pecans for dipping. Chop your pecans really fine—whizzing them in the food processor is good—so that they're fine enough to stick to the dressing.

Celery and Radish Salad

Our tester Burma says she and her husband both loved this. The leftovers are great the next day with grilled chicken or shrimp added.

¼ cup (34 g) hazelnuts
1 tablespoon (15 ml) cider vinegar
3 tablespoons (45 ml) light olive oil
1 tablespoon (15 ml) walnut oil
6 celery ribs (pale inner ribs)
3 radishes
¼ cup (15 g) chopped fresh parsley
Salt and black pepper

Preheat oven to 350°F (180°C, or gas mark 4). Spread your hazelnuts on a baking sheet, put 'em in the oven, and set your timer for 8 minutes.

In the meanwhile, mix together the vinegar and oils. Reserve.

Slice your celery very thinly and put it in a salad bowl. Slice up any unwilted leaves and add them, too. Slice your radishes as thinly as possible and add them to the celery. Chop and add the parsley, too.

Somewhere in here the timer will beep. Pull out your hazelnuts and let them cool a few minutes. When you can handle them, rub them between your palms to flake off most of the brown skin. (Don't panic if a little clings. It's no big deal.) Chop them and add them to the salad.

Pour on the dressing and toss well. Salt and pepper to taste. You can serve this immediately or make it in advance and stash it in the fridge—it'll hold overnight, no problem. Indeed, it may improve on standing.

YIELD: 4 servings

Nutritional Analysis

Per serving: 187 calories; 19 g fat; 2 g protein; 4 g carbohydrate; 2 g dietary fiber; 2 g net carbs

NOTE

For this you want pale, tender inner celery ribs, but not the little teeny ones in the heart—and not the big, strong-flavored outer ribs. And do buy organic celery. The conventionally raised stuff is likely to be contaminated with pesticides.

Apple-Fennel Salad

Yummy! I used a good, hot Madras curry powder for this, but you can use a mild one, if you prefer. This salad is as pretty as it is tasty.

½ fennel bulb
1 apple (I used a Gala)
¼ red bell pepper
¼ cup (60 g) Mayonnaise in the Jar (page 278)
½ lime
1 teaspoon spicy brown mustard
3 drops liquid stevia or ½ teaspoon honey
1 teaspoon curry powder

Dice up your fennel bulb, your apple, and your red pepper into roughly ¼-inch (6 mm) cubes and throw 'em in a mixing bowl. In a small bowl, stir together the mayo, grated zest, and the juice of the half lime, the mustard, liquid stevia or honey, and the curry powder. Blend well, then pour over the salad and toss to coat.

YIELD: 4 servings

Nutritional Analysis
Per serving: 135 calories; 12 g fat; 1 g protein; 9 g carbohydrate; 2 g dietary fiber; 7 g net carbs

About Cauli-Rice in Salads

Back when I was working on my very first cookbook, I saw a recipe for a salad combining rice with tomatoes, scallions, crumbled bacon, and mayonnaise. I tried it with Cauli-Rice instead of real rice and loved it so much I ate it all up that day and made it again the next day. I never looked back.

Cauli-Rice doesn't just stand in for rice in salads. It stands in beautifully for orzo, bulgur wheat, couscous, you name it. If a salad calls for a little bitty grain product, try it with the Cauli-Rice. You'll be shocked how great it is.

To start with is a recipe I lifted, whole and unaltered, from my *Every Calorie Counts Cookbook*. Why? Because tabouli is hugely popular, and this recipe is, if anything, better than the version made with cracked wheat. Next time you're going to a potluck, take this. You'll impress the heck out of everybody.

Cauli-Bouli

This happened because a friend posted his family's favorite tabouli recipe online. I had to try it with Cauli-Rice! Fabulous. Just fabulous. Double this for a party and make a lot of friends.

½ **large head cauliflower**
1 **medium tomato, diced small**
½ **medium cucumber, diced small**
¼ **small red onion, diced small**
½ **green bell pepper, diced small**
1 **cup (96 g) fresh mint leaves, minced**
¼ **cup (60 ml) extra-virgin olive oil**
¼ **cup (60 ml) lemon juice**
1 **clove garlic, minced very fine**
Salt and black pepper to taste

Run the cauliflower through the shredding blade of your food processor. Put it in a microwaveable casserole with a lid, add a couple of tablespoons (28 ml) of water, and cover. Nuke it on high for 6 minutes. Uncover it as soon as it's done, drain it, and let it cool a bit before continuing—stirring it from time to time helps release the steam.

Okay, your cauliflower's cool. Put it in a big darned mixing bowl. Dice up all your other veggies, and chop your mint, and throw all of that in with the cauliflower. Stir it all up.

Mix the olive oil, lemon juice, and garlic together. Pour over the salad, and toss very well to coat everything. Salt and pepper to taste, and chill before serving.

YIELD: 5 servings

Nutritional Analysis
Per serving: 137 calories; 11 g fat; 2 g protein; 9 g carbohydrate; 3 g dietary fiber; 6 g net carbs

Avocado, Tomato, and "Rice" Salad

This, a grilled steak, and a glass of red wine. What else could you need?

¼ **head cauliflower**
1 **cup (180 g) diced tomato**
1 **avocado**
2 **scallions, sliced, including the crisp part of the green**
¼ **cup (60 ml) olive oil**
2 **tablespoons (28 ml) cider vinegar**
¼ **teaspoon dried oregano**
¼ **teaspoon ground cumin**
¼ **teaspoon hot sauce, such as Tabasco**
¼ **teaspoon salt**
¼ **cup (15 g) minced fresh parsley**

First, turn your cauliflower into Cauli-Rice—see page 87.

In the meanwhile, dice your tomato, and halve, pit, peel, and dice your avocado. (An avocado slicer is a very handy gadget and makes this a snap. If you're fond of avocados, you might pick one up.) Slice your scallions, too. Put all this stuff in a big salad bowl.

By now your microwave has beeped. Pull out your cauliflower and uncover it immediately. Drain it and let it cool for a few minutes, stirring now and then to let the heat out.

While the cauliflower is cooling, measure everything else except the parsley and whisk it together. Pour the dressing over the tomatoes, avocado, and scallions and stir gently, to not break up the avocado.

When the cauliflower has cooled to just warm, rather than hot-hot, stir it into the salad, too. Now stir in the parsley and serve pretty promptly. You know how avocados are.

YIELD: 4 servings

Nutritional Analysis
Per serving: 217 calories; 21 g fat; 2 g protein; 7 g carbohydrate; 2 g dietary fiber; 5 g net carbs

"Rice" and Basil Salad

¼ **head cauliflower**
¼ **cup (10 g) chopped fresh basil, sliced very thin**
3 **tablespoons (30 g) diced red onion, diced small**
2 **tablespoons (8 g) minced fresh parsley**
1 **medium tomato, ¼-inch (6 mm) dice**
3 **tablespoons (42 g) Mayonnaise in the Jar (page 278)**
3 **tablespoons (45 g) Coconut Sour Cream (page 29)**
⅛ **teaspoon black pepper**
Salt to taste

First, turn your cauliflower into Cauli-Rice—see page 87.

While the cauliflower is cooking, chop the basil, dice the onion, and mince the parsley. Dice your tomato but keep that separate from the herbs and onion.

Measure and stir together the mayo and coconut sour cream. Add the pepper, too.

When the microwave beeps, or the cauliflower is otherwise just barely tender, uncover it to let the steam out, drain it if needed, and dump it in a big mixing bowl. Let it cool for a few minutes before you add the herbs, onion, and dressing, and stir it all up. Taste and salt if you like. Now stir in the diced tomato. You can serve this immediately, but it's really nice chilled for a while, or even overnight.

YIELD: 6 servings

Nutritional Analysis
Per serving: 87 calories; 9 g fat; 1 g protein; 3 g carbohydrate; 1 g dietary fiber; 2 g net carbs

NOTE

My quarter cauliflower yielded about 3 cups (495 g) of Cauli-Rice. If yours is considerably smaller, go ahead and use a half head if you need to.

Potluck "Rice" Salad

I really did make this for a potluck supper, and everyone loved it.

1 head cauliflower
1 small red onion
1 red bell pepper
1 bunch scallions
½ cup (30 g) minced fresh parsley
2 tablespoons (8 g) minced fresh oregano
½ cup (115 g) Mayonnaise in the Jar (page 278)
½ cup (115 g) Cocoyo (page 28)
½ cup (120 ml) olive oil
1 tablespoon (15 ml) white wine vinegar
2 tablespoons (28 ml) lemon juice
Salt and black pepper

First, turn your cauliflower into Cauli-Rice (see page 87).

While that's cooking, dice your red onion and your pepper and slice your scallions, including the crisp part of the green shoot. Throw all this in a huge mixing bowl. (I'm lucky enough to have one made by Tupperware that has a lid.) Mince your parsley and oregano, and throw that in, too.

Somewhere during all that chopping, your microwave will beep. Pull out the cauliflower and uncover it, to let out the steam and stop the cooking. Stir it up to let out more steam, then let it sit and cool a bit while you proceed with the rest of the recipe. Stirring it again every now and then will speed cooling.

Whisk together the mayonnaise, Cocoyo, olive oil, vinegar, and lemon juice, until the whole thing is smooth and nice. This, of course, is your dressing.

When your cauliflower is cool enough that it's not going to cook all your other veggies (it can still be warm), drain it well and add it to the mixing bowl. Stir the whole thing up. Now add the dressing and stir till everything is evenly coated.

Salt and pepper to taste. You can eat it right away if you like, but it's better if it's refrigerated for a few hours first.

YIELD: 12 servings

Nutritional Analysis
Per serving: 292 calories; 30 g fat; 3 g protein; 7 g carbohydrate; 2 g dietary fiber; 5 g net carbs

NOTE

This makes a huge vat of salad, enough for a crowd—depends somewhat on how big your head of cauliflower is; I used a real whopper.

Ensalada de Muchos Colores

You don't have to use all three colors of peppers, but they do make this salad gorgeous. But if you only have, say, two colors, just increase the quantity of each.

½ head cauliflower
½ cup (120 ml) olive oil
1 jalapeño (or 2, if you like it hot!)
1 lime
½ teaspoon ground cumin
¼ cup (4 g) minced fresh cilantro
⅓ green bell pepper
⅓ red bell pepper
⅓ yellow bell pepper
1 medium tomato
1 carrot
1 bunch scallions
Salt and black pepper

First, trim the leaves and very bottom of the stem off your cauliflower. Whack the rest into chunks and run 'em through the shredding blade of your food processor. Steam lightly—I give mine 6 minutes in my microwave steamer, on high.

While the cauliflower's steaming, make your dressing: Measure your olive oil—I used a 1-cup (235 ml) Pyrex measuring cup. Seed your jalapeño and mince it very fine. Add to the oil and then immediately wash your hands very well! Halve the lime and squeeze every last drop of juice in; you want about 3 tablespoonful (45 ml). Stir in the cumin, then mince your cilantro and stir it in, too. Set this aside to let the flavors blend while you . . .

Uncover your cauliflower as soon as it's barely tender! Leave it covered and it will continue steaming, and you'll wind up with mush. Not what you want. Dump your Cauli-Rice in a big salad bowl and let it cool a bit while you . . .

Dice your three colors of peppers and your tomato, shred your carrot, and slice your scallions thinly, including the crisp part of the green shoot. When your Cauli-Rice is cool enough to not cook the other veggies, add them to the bowl.

Stir in the dressing, salt and pepper to taste, and either serve or chill for later. Good either way, but it really is great the next day.

YIELD: 6 servings

Nutritional Analysis
Per serving: 195 calories; 18 g fat; 2 g protein; 8 g carbohydrate; 2 g dietary fiber; 6 g net carbs

NOTE

Embarrassing admission: I was originally planning to add toasted pepitas (pumpkin seeds) to this, but I totally spaced. The salad was fantastic without them, but if you'd like a little crunch, go for it.

Confetti "Rice" Salad

So pretty! So good! And easy to double.

¼ head cauliflower
2 celery ribs, diced
½ green bell pepper, diced
½ red bell pepper, diced
1 bunch scallions, sliced thin, including the crisp part
  of the green
½ cup (150 g) chopped artichoke hearts
½ cup (70 g) pine nuts, toasted
¼ cup (60 ml) extra-virgin olive oil
2 tablespoons (28 g) Mayonnaise in the Jar (page 278)
2 tablespoons (28 ml) white balsamic vinegar
½ teaspoon curry powder
1 teaspoon dried thyme
¼ teaspoon black pepper
Salt (optional)
½ clove garlic, crushed

First, trim the bottom of the stem and any leaves from your cauliflower. Whack the remainder into chunks and run 'em through the shredding blade of your food processor. Throw the resulting Cauli-Rice (page 87) into a microwaveable casserole with a lid, or a microwave steamer, add a tablespoon or two (15 to 28 ml) of water, cover, and nuke on high for 5 minutes.

In the meanwhile, dice and slice up all your other veggies and put 'em in your salad bowl.

Somewhere in here your microwave will beep. Pull out your cauliflower and uncover it immediately, to stop the cooking and let it start to cool. While it's cooling a bit . . .

In a dry skillet, over medium heat, stir pine nuts until they have a touch of gold. Throw those in the salad bowl, too.

Measure all the remaining ingredients and whisk 'em together. I mix mine up in the Pyrex measuring cup.

Okay, the Cauli-Rice is a tad cooler by now. Drain it and add it to the salad bowl. Now pour on the dressing and stir till everything's coated evenly. Stash in the fridge until dinnertime—unless you're a big pig, like me, at which point you'll immediately eat a good third of the stuff in the name of "sampling."

YIELD: 5 servings

Nutritional Analysis
Per serving: 241 calories; 23 g fat; 5 g protein; 8 g carbohydrate; 3 g dietary fiber; 5 g net carbs

NOTE

I confess I used canned artichoke hearts. I just wasn't going to cook and process enough fresh artichokes to get a half cup, chopped, though you certainly may if you like. If your grocery store carries frozen artichoke hearts, they might be a nice compromise.

Tomato Platter

The better your tomatoes, the better this will be.

1 medium red onion
4 medium tomatoes
Celery Salt (page 285, or use purchased celery salt)
Black pepper
2 tablespoons (6 g) minced fresh chives
2 tablespoons (8 g) minced dill weed
¼ cup (10 g) minced fresh basil

Have a platter standing by.

Peel your onion whole and slice it into rings about ¼-inch (6 mm) thick. Separate the rings. Cover the platter completely with onion rings, touching but not overlapping. You're making a rack of onion to elevate the tomato slices.

Slice the tomatoes a little thicker, but not as much as ½-inch (1 cm). Cover the onion-rack with tomato slices, again, not overlapping.

Sprinkle lightly with celery salt and pepper. Now sprinkle the chives, dill weed, and basil evenly over the whole thing, too.

Cover the whole thing with foil and refrigerate for a couple of hours.

Before serving, peel back the foil just enough to make a little opening, but not enough to let the tomatoes slide. Pour off any water that has collected on the platter, then serve.

YIELD: 5 servings

Nutritional Analysis
Per serving: 37 calories; trace fat; 2 g protein; 8 g carbohydrate; 2 g dietary fiber; 6 g net carbs

Asparagus and Avocado Salad

I had fresh asparagus in the house, and I had an avocado in the house; this is what happened. Yummy!

1 pound (455 g) asparagus
1 avocado
2 tablespoons (20 g) minced red onion
2 tablespoons (28 ml) extra-virgin olive oil
2 tablespoons (28 ml) lemon juice
3 tablespoons (45 ml) white balsamic vinegar
⅛ teaspoon black pepper

Snap the ends off your asparagus where it wants to break naturally. Cut your spears into 2- to 3-inch (5 to 7.5 cm) lengths and steam them briefly, just till they become more brilliantly green—I give mine 4 minutes in the microwave.

Halve your avocado, remove the pit, scoop out the flesh, and dice. (This is made MUCH easier with an avocado slicer, one of the few single-use kitchen gadgets I'll give drawer space to.) Put your avocado in a salad bowl. When your asparagus is done, throw it in, too. Mince up your onion and throw it in.

Now measure everything else and whisk it together or throw it in the blender and run it for 5 seconds. Pour it over the asparagus and avocado, toss, and serve.

If you prefer, you can combine the steamed asparagus and onion with the dressing, then refrigerate till supper. Add the diced avocado just before serving.

YIELD: 4 servings

Nutritional Analysis
Per serving: 160 calories; 15 g fat; 2 g protein; 8 g carbohydrate; 3 g dietary fiber; 5 g net carbs

Avocado and Tomato Salad

Quick, simple, and perfect—and dependent on all the ingredients being right.

1 avocado, perfectly ripe
1 large tomato, perfectly ripe
¼ cup (40 g) diced red onion
¼ cup (4 g) chopped fresh cilantro
½ lime
2 dashes hot sauce or to taste

Halve your avocado and remove the pit. Slice it—I couldn't live without my avocado slicer—and cut those slices into dice. Put in a mixing bowl.

Dice your tomato and throw it in with the avocado. Dice the onion, chop the cilantro, and throw them in, too.

Squeeze the half lime over everything, add the hot sauce, and use a spoon to gently stir/toss till everything's friendly. Serve immediately.

YIELD: 4 servings

Nutritional Analysis
Per serving: 94 calories; 8 g fat; 1 g protein; 7 g carbohydrate; 2 g dietary fiber, 5 g net carbs

Avocado, Cucumber, and Tomato Salad

Yes, this sounds similar to the previous salad. Yes, the cucumber makes a difference.

1 small cucumber, sliced lengthwise then crosswise quite thin
½ avocado, peeled and diced
½ medium tomato, diced
¼ cup (40 g) finely diced red onion
2 tablespoons (28 ml) extra-virgin olive oil
¼ lemon
¼ lime
Salt
2 tablespoons (2 g) minced fresh cilantro

Slice and dice your veggies and toss 'em in a mixing bowl. Add the olive oil and stir gently—you don't want to squish all your avocado bits. Now squeeze in the juice from your lemon and lime and stir again. Add just a touch of salt if you like, and the cilantro, stir one more time, and serve immediately.

YIELD: 4 servings

Nutritional Analysis
Per serving: 119 calories; 11 g fat; 1 g protein; 6 g carbohydrate; 2 g dietary fiber; 4 g net carbs

Waldorf Salad

Somehow Waldorf Salad got tarted up over the years with marshmallows and Cool Whip, heaven forbid, and all sorts of other junk. This is what Waldorf Salad was originally, what it was meant to be, and it's wonderful.

1 apple
2 large celery ribs
⅓ cup (40 g) chopped walnuts
3 tablespoons (42 g) Mayonnaise in the Jar (page 278)
1 teaspoon walnut oil (not essential, but very nice)

Leave the skin on the apple—it adds both color and texture. Dice the apple and the celery and put 'em in a mixing bowl. Add the walnuts.

Whisk the mayo with the walnut oil, then add to the salad, stir to coat, and serve.

YIELD: 4 servings

Nutritional Analysis
Per serving: 171 calories; 16 g fat; 3 g protein; 7 g carbohydrate; 2 g dietary fiber; 5 g net carbs

Winter Salad

I love apples and fennel together. I think of this as the twenty-first-century version of Waldorf salad.

¼ cup (34 g) hazelnuts, shelled
2 large celery ribs
1 fennel bulb
1 apple (I used a Gala)
⅓ cup (80 ml) olive oil
2 tablespoons (30 g) brown mustard

2 tablespoons (28 ml) white vinegar
1 tablespoon (15 ml) lemon juice
¼ teaspoon salt
1 clove garlic, crushed

Put the hazelnuts in a Pyrex pie plate and microwave on high for 2 minutes, or until fragrant.

While your hazelnuts are toasting, run your celery and fennel through the slicing blade of your food processor. Cut your apple into matchstick strips; unless you have a julienne blade. (The easiest way I've found to do this is to quarter it and remove the core, then set each quarter, in turn, on your cutting board. Cut straight down through the quarter, lengthwise—in other words, don't cut it into thin wedges, just even-thickness slices. Then cut across those to make matchstick strips. Throw all your veggies in a big salad bowl.

By now the microwave has beeped. Pull your hazelnuts out and let them cool a few minutes while you . . .

Measure the olive oil, mustard, vinegar, lemon juice, and salt. Crush the garlic and throw it in, too. Whisk everything together well and pour it over the salad. Toss till everything's evenly coated.

Rub the hazelnuts between your hands, so most of the brown skin flakes off. Now chop them medium fine and throw them into the salad. Toss and serve.

YIELD: 5 servings

Nutritional Analysis
Per serving: 213 calories; 19 g fat; 2 g protein; 11 g carbohydrate; 3 g dietary fiber; 8 g net carbs

Classic UnPotato Salad Redux

This originated with a recipe by Hellmann's/Best Foods, designed to sell mayonnaise. Consequently, it called for a LOT of mayonnaise! This has a bit less, and I trust you're making your own. This is the classic picnic salad—except it's cauliflower instead of potatoes, of course. Don't be surprised if it takes people three or four bites to notice.

4 cups (400 g) cauliflower, in ½-inch (1 cm) chunks
1 cup (60 g) diced celery
½ cup (80 g) diced red onion
⅔ cup (150 g) Mayonnaise in the Jar (page 278)
1½ tablespoons (25 ml) cider vinegar
½ teaspoon salt (optional)
5 drops liquid stevia extract (optional)
¼ teaspoon black pepper
2 eggs, hard-boiled

Steam your cauliflower till it's tender but not mushy—try 8 to 10 minutes in the microwave. Uncover it as soon as it's done, to stop the cooking. Put it in a big mixing bowl and let it cool a bit while you . . .

Dice the celery and onion and add 'em to the cauliflower.

Mix the mayonnaise, vinegar, salt, liquid stevia, and pepper. Pour over the salad and mix to coat.

Peel and chop your eggs. Now stir them gently into the salad—you want to preserve some hunks of yolk. Chill for a few hours before serving.

YIELD: 6 servings

Nutritional Analysis
Per serving: 227 calories; 23 g fat; 4 g protein; 6 g carbohydrate; 2 g dietary fiber; 4 g net carbs

Dilled UnPotato Salad

Lisa C., who tested this, says, "The hardest part was waiting to eat it. Having the flavors mingle overnight made this extra special."

½ head large cauliflower
⅔ cup (150 g) Mayonnaise in the Jar (page 278)
3 tablespoons (45 g) Cocoyo (page 28)
1½ tablespoons (22.5 g) spicy brown mustard
¼ cup (16 g) minced fresh dill weed, loosely packed
¼ teaspoon black pepper or to taste
¾ cup (90 g) diced celery
½ cup (80 g) diced red onion
Salt to taste

Trim the leaves and the bottom of the stem off your cauliflower, then cut the rest into ½-inch (10 cm) chunks. Steam till tender but not mushy—I'd give mine 8 to 10 minutes on high in the microwave.

In the meanwhile, mix together the mayo, Cocoyo, mustard, dill, and pepper. This is your dressing. (As if you hadn't figured that out.)

Dice your celery and your onion while the cauliflower is steaming, too.

When the cauliflower is tender, drain it and throw it in a big mixing bowl. Let it cool till it's just lukewarm. Add everything else and stir till it's all coated. Refrigerate for several hours, or better yet, overnight.

YIELD: 6 servings

Nutritional Analysis
Per serving: 199 calories; 21 g fat ; 2 g protein; 5 g carbohydrate; 2 g dietary fiber; 3 g net carbs

Tex-Mex UnPotato Salad

If you've never tried making "potato" salad with cauliflower instead, you are in for a big ol' happy surprise.

1 smallish head cauliflower, about 6 to 7 cups (600 to 700 g)
⅓ cup (75 g) Mayonnaise in the Jar (page 278)
⅓ cup (77 g) Cocoyo (page 28)
2 tablespoons (28 ml) lime juice
1 tablespoon (15 ml) chipotle chile canned in adobo (or see Chipotles in Adobo, page 294)
2 cloves garlic, crushed
¼ teaspoon cayenne
1 medium tomato, ¼-inch (6 mm) dice
¼ cup (4 g) minced fresh cilantro
2 scallions, thinly sliced

Start by whacking your cauliflower in half, trimming off the leaves and the very bottom of the stem, and cutting it in ½-inch (1 cm) chunks. Steam it till tender but not mushy— I give mine 8 to 10 minutes on high in the microwave.

While that's happening, put everything from the mayo through the cayenne in your food processor or blender and run till it's all well blended.

When your cauliflower is done, uncover it immediately and dump it in a big mixing bowl. Let it cool a bit while you . . .

Cut up your tomato, cilantro, and scallions.

When the cauliflower has cooled enough not to cook them, add the tomato, cilantro, and scallions to the bowl. Now pour on the dressing and stir till everything's well coated. Chill for several hours before serving.

YIELD: 6 servings

Nutritional Analysis
Per serving: 370 calories; 37 g fat; 5 g protein; 10 g carbohydrate; 3 g dietary fiber; 7 g net carbs

Mustard-Tarragon UnPotato-and-Tomato Salad

This is great served warm, but try it chilled, too.

½ head cauliflower, about 1 pound (455 g)
⅓ cup (55 g) diced red onion, diced small
1 tablespoon (15 g) spicy brown mustard
1 tablespoon (15 ml) red wine vinegar
3 tablespoons (45 ml) extra-virgin olive oil
¼ teaspoon black pepper
½ teaspoon fresh tarragon, minced fine
1 medium tomato, ¼-inch (6 mm) dice

Trim the leaves and very bottom of the stem off your cauliflower, then cut the remainder into ½-inch (1 cm) chunks. Steam until just tender—I give mine about 8 to 10 minutes on high in the microwave.

Meanwhile, dice your onion and throw it in a salad bowl.

Measure the mustard, vinegar, olive oil, and pepper into a bowl. Mince the tarragon and throw it in, too. Whisk the dressing till it's a uniform consistency.

When the cauliflower is done, uncover immediately to stop the cooking. Let it cool for 10 minutes or so, then add it to the salad bowl.

While the cauliflower is cooling, dice your tomato. When your cauliflower has cooled enough to not cook the tomato, add it and the diced tomato to the salad bowl.

Pour on the dressing and stir it all up, till everything is evenly coated.

YIELD: 4 servings

Nutritional Analysis
Per serving: 109 calories; 11 g fat; 1 g protein; 4 g carbohydrate; 1 g dietary fiber; 3 g net carbs

Sweet Potato Salad

For the carb-tolerant only.

1 pound (455 g) sweet potatoes
1 small apple
1 tablespoon (15 ml) lemon juice, divided
3 celery ribs, sliced
3 scallions, sliced
⅓ cup (27 g) chopped pecans
2 heads Belgian endive
¼ cup (60 ml) extra-virgin olive oil
1 garlic clove
2 tablespoons (28 ml) white balsamic vinegar
2 teaspoons fresh thyme leaves

Peel your sweet potatoes and cut in 1-inch (2.5 cm) cubes. Steam for 5 minutes, or until tender. Let cool.

Meanwhile, dice your apple. Toss with 1 teaspoon of the lemon juice to prevent discoloring.

Slice the celery and the scallions, including the crisp part of the green shoot. Put all of this in a mixing bowl. Add the pecans, and the sweet potatoes when cool. Stir it up.

Separate your heads of endive and line 4 salad plates with the leaves, laying them in spoke fashion.

Put the olive oil, garlic, white balsamic, and the rest of the lemon juice in your blender and run till the garlic is pulverized. Pour over the sweet potato mixture and add the thyme leaves. Stir to coat.

Make a mound of the sweet potato mixture in the center of each "wheel" of endive and serve.

YIELD: 4 servings

Nutritional Analysis
Per serving: 347 calories; 21 g fat; 6 g protein; 39 g carbohydrate; 13 g dietary fiber; 26 g net carbs

Green Pea Salad

As one of the rare legumes that are edible raw, peas are paleo! I cheat and use frozen peas, because the fresh ones are nearly impossible to find around here.

1 pound (455 g) frozen peas, thawed
1 tablespoon (10 g) minced shallot
1 tablespoon (4 g) minced fresh parsley
1 teaspoon minced fresh tarragon
3 tablespoons (45 g) Simple Vinaigrette (page 139)
Lettuce leaves, to line plates

Put your thawed peas in a mixing bowl and add the shallot, parsley, and tarragon.

Make your vinaigrette and add 3 tablespoons (45 g) to the salad. Toss and let it marinate for an hour or two.

Line plates with a few pretty lettuce leaves and serve a scoop of the peas on each.

YIELD: 4 servings

Nutritional Analysis
Per serving: 334 calories; 28 g fat; 6 g protein; 17 g carbohydrate; 5 g dietary fiber; 12 g net carbs

NOTE

If you grow your own peas or have a very good local farmer's market, go ahead and use fresh peas. Just steam them till they're just tender, maybe 10 minutes.

Kaleidoscope Salad

All these colors!

4 slices bacon
1 red bell pepper
1 yellow bell pepper
8 radishes
1 medium celery rib
2 medium tomatoes, diced
3 tablespoons (45 ml) extra-virgin olive oil
1 tablespoon (15 ml) white wine vinegar
1 tablespoon (2.5 g) fresh thyme leaves
Salt and black pepper

Put a skillet over medium heat and snip the bacon into it. Fry your bacon bits till they're crispy. Remove, drain, and reserve.

Halve and seed your peppers. Cut them in long, thin strips. Cut the strips in two, across. Put 'em in a salad bowl.

Halve your radishes, then slice as thin as possible. Add to the pepper strips. Slice your celery thin, too, and add it to the salad. Dice up your tomatoes and add them, too.

Toss the salad with the olive oil, vinegar, and thyme leaves. Salt and pepper to taste.

Now serve, topping each serving with bacon bits.

YIELD: 4 servings

Nutritional Analysis
Per serving: 159 calories; 14 g fat; 3 g protein; 8 g carbohydrate; 2 g dietary fiber; 6 g net carbs

Green Mango Salad

I saw this recipe—with sugar, of course—in an article about Thai food. My curiosity was piqued, so I ran out to the Asian market and bought a green mango and altered the recipe to eliminate the sugar. It was wonderful! I served mine with a couple of poached eggs on top, but it would be good with almost anything—try chicken, shrimp, or crab.

Use this as a relish, as you would salsa or chutney.

1 mango, as green and hard as you can find
3 shallots, sliced very thinly
2 hot peppers, the little red super-hot Thai peppers
1 tablespoon (15 ml) fish sauce
1½ teaspoons lime juice
Honey or stevia (optional)
¼ cup (4 g) minced fresh cilantro

Peel and seed your mango and run it through the shredding blade of your food processor. Throw your shreds in a nonreactive bowl.

Peel your shallots and slice them paper thin, separating the layers. Put them in the bowl as well. Slice your peppers very thinly—you can remove the seeds first, if you like, but I didn't bother—and add them, too.

Now stir together the fish sauce, lime juice, and sweetener if using, and stir it in. Taste for balance—the flavor should be evenly poised between sweet, sour, salty, and hot. Adjust if necessary.

Stir in the cilantro and serve.

YIELD: 4 servings

Nutritional Analysis
Per serving: 54 calories; 1 g fat; 1 g protein; 13 g carbohydrate; 2 g dietary fiber; 11 g net carbs

Habanero-Lime Cucumber Salad

I was contemplating a cucumber, trying to come up with something new to do with it, when my gaze wandered to my container of Habanero-Lime Balsamic. See? Messy kitchens are inspiring.

1 large cucumber

⅓ cup (55 g) minced red onion

¼ cup (60 ml) Habanero-Lime Balsamic (page 284)

1 small garlic clove, crushed

Salt to taste

2 tablespoons (2 g) minced fresh cilantro (optional)

Quarter your cuke lengthwise, then slice it thin. Put it in a big mixing bowl. Mince up the onion and add that, too.

Measure the Habanero-Lime Balsamic and crush the garlic into it. Stir it up, then pour it over the salad. Taste and decide if you think it needs a suspicion of salt. (I added about ⅛ teaspoon.)

Mince and add the cilantro, if using. Refrigerate for a few hours before serving, if possible—but it's good right away.

YIELD: 4 servings

Nutritional Analysis

Per serving: 25 calories; trace fat; 1 g protein; 7 g carbohydrate; 1 g dietary fiber; 6 g net carbs

I was wondering if I had too many salad dressing recipes for this book, when a friend asked hopefully, "Are you going to have salad dressing recipes? You just can't find paleo salad dressings in the store." I realized she was right. Dressings are a big deal. I mean, you can figure out how to put some lettuce, tomatoes, maybe a little green pepper or shredded carrot or sliced cucumber in a bowl, right? But what to dress it with? You'll never ask again.

Simple Vinaigrette

Classic.

½ cup (120 ml) extra-virgin olive oil

¼ cup (60 ml) red wine vinegar

2 teaspoons Dijon mustard

1 garlic clove, crushed

¼ teaspoon black pepper

2 pinches salt

You can put everything in the blender and run it for a few seconds, or you can just whisk stuff together. Either way, this is almost classically French. The "almost" part is that they'd probably use a little more oil to a little less vinegar, but I like a fairly assertive acidic note in my dressing.

YIELD: 4 servings

Nutritional Analysis

Per serving: 244 calories; 27 g fat; trace protein; 1 g carbohydrate; trace dietary fiber; 1 g net carbs

White Balsamic Vinaigrette

Mild and a little sweet. Try this with delicate baby greens or butter lettuce.

½ cup (120 ml) extra-virgin olive oil
1 teaspoon spicy brown mustard
4 tablespoons (60 ml) white balsamic vinegar
¼ teaspoon black pepper

Just put everything in your blender and run till it's emulsified. That's all!

YIELD: 4 servings

Nutritional Analysis
Per serving: 243 calories; 27 g fat; trace protein; 1 g carbohydrate; trace dietary fiber; 1 g net carbs

Killer Italian Dressing

Similar to the Simple Vinaigrette, but with more seasonings thrown in. Good for green salads, sure, but try it tossed with chunked ripe tomatoes and cucumbers, or on a chicken salad in place of the usual mayo.

½ cup (120 ml) extra-virgin olive oil
½ cup (120 ml) red wine vinegar
3 cloves garlic
2 teaspoons dried oregano
2 teaspoons dried basil
2 teaspoons black pepper
¼ cup (40 g) chopped onion
2 teaspoons Dijon mustard or spicy brown mustard

Just throw everything in the blender and run it till the garlic and onion are completely pulverized.

YIELD: 8 servings

Nutritional Analysis
Per serving: 129 calories; 14 g fat; trace protein; 3 g carbohydrate; 1 g dietary fiber; 2 g net carbs

Creamy Italian Dressing

Great on a crisp green salad. Add a few tomatoes and a little red onion, and you're done!

1 egg
1 teaspoon Italian seasoning
1 clove garlic
¼ teaspoon dry mustard
¼ cup (60 ml) red wine vinegar
¼ teaspoon salt
⅛ teaspoon black pepper
⅔ cup (160 ml) extra-virgin olive oil

Put everything but the oil in your blender. Have your oil measured and ready, in a measuring cup with a pouring lip.

Turn on the blender. Now slowly pour in the oil, in a stream no thicker than a pencil lead. When all the oil is blended in, you're done! You can adjust the seasoning a bit if you like. Store in a snap-top container or screw-top jar in the fridge, of course, and use it up within a few days.

YIELD: 8 servings

Nutritional Analysis
Per serving: 170 calories; 19 g fat; 1 g protein; 1 g carbohydrate; trace dietary fiber; 1 g carbohydrate

Greek Vinaigrette

Romaine, tomatoes, green peppers, and cucumbers, tossed with this dressing—serve with Greek roasted chicken or a lamb chop.

⅛ quart (118 ml) extra-virgin olive oil
3 cloves garlic
1 tablespoon (3 g) dried oregano
1 tablespoon (2 g) dried basil
1 tablespoon (14 g) black pepper
1 tablespoon (14 g) salt
¼ cup (40 g) minced onion
1 tablespoon (15 g) Dijon mustard
½ cup (118 ml) red wine vinegar

Put all ingredients in the blender and run for 30 seconds or so. You're done!

YIELD: 10 servings

Nutritional Analysis
Per serving: 134 calories; 14 g fat; trace protein; 2 g carbohydrate; trace dietary fiber; 2 g net carbs

Horseradish-Vanilla Vinaigrette

I heard about this and had to try it. I eliminated the sugar, of course. The horseradish and vanilla are not obvious, but they add a real modern twist to the same old vinaigrette.

¼ cup (60 ml) white balsamic vinegar
⅛ teaspoon vanilla extract
¼ teaspoon black pepper
¾ cup (175 ml) olive oil
⅛ teaspoon dry mustard
2 tablespoons (30 g) Prepared Horseradish (page 288)

Just combine everything in your blender and run till it's emulsified.

YIELD: 8 servings

Nutritional Analysis
Per serving: 182 calories; 20 g fat; trace protein; 1 g carbohydrate; trace dietary fiber; 1 g net carbs

Lime-Chipotle Mayonnaise

Our tester Lisa M. M. says, "Looking forward to using this for chicken salad, egg salad, and of course the Southwestern Slaw."

2 egg yolks
2 tablespoons (28 ml) lime juice
2 teaspoons chipotle chile canned in adobo (or see Chipotles in Adobo, page 294), minced (or more to taste)
⅛ teaspoon ground cumin
1 pinch salt (optional)
1 cup (235 ml) extra-light olive oil

Easiest is to make this with your stick blender, right in the jar: Put your egg yolks, the lime juice, the chipotle, the cumin, and salt if using, in the bottom of an old, clean salsa or peanut butter jar. What originally came in the jar is unimportant. Measure the oil and have it standing by in a glass measuring cup with a pouring lip.

Put your stick blender down into the jar and turn it on, mixing the yolks with the juice and chipotle. After 5 seconds or so, start slowly pouring in the oil—the stream should be about the diameter of a pencil lead. Work the blender up and down in the jar as needed to emulsify the mayonnaise. When it's good and thick, and oil starts to puddle on the top, you're done—any leftover oil can go

(continued)

back in the bottle. Cap the jar and stash in the fridge.

YIELD: 1 cup (240 g), 16 servings

Nutritional Analysis

Per serving: 127 calories; 14 g fat; trace protein; trace carbohydrate; trace dietary fiber; trace net carbs

Free-Range Dressing

This is a ringer for standard ranch dressing, but it has no bad oils, no dairy, and fresh seasonings.

½ cup (115 g) **Mayonnaise in the Jar (page 278)**
3 tablespoons (45 g) **Cocoyo (page 28)**
2 **scallions**
½ tablespoon (2 g) **minced fresh parsley**
½ tablespoon (2 g) **minced fresh dill weed**
½ **garlic clove**
⅛ teaspoon **black pepper**
1 pinch **salt**

Assemble everything in your food processor or blender and run till the scallion and garlic are pulverized. Store in a container with a tight lid and use just as you would ranch dressing or dip.

YIELD: ⅔ cup (160 g), 6 servings

Nutritional Analysis

Per serving: 149 calories; 17 g fat; trace protein; 1 g carbohydrate; trace dietary fiber; 1 g net carbs

NOTE

Make this with Coconut Sour Cream (page 29) for a thicker, dip-like consistency.

Chipotle Free-Range Dressing

What's a good dressing without a variation?

½ cup (115 g) **Mayonnaise in the Jar (page 278)**
3 tablespoons (45 g) **Cocoyo (page 28)**
2 **scallions**
½ tablespoon (2 g) **minced fresh parsley**
½ tablespoon (2 g) **minced fresh dill weed**
½ **garlic clove**
⅛ teaspoon **black pepper**
1 pinch **salt (optional)**
1 tablespoon (15 ml) **lime juice**
1 tablespoon (15 ml) **chipotle chile canned in adobo, (or see Chipotles in Adobo, page 294), plus 1 teaspoon adobo sauce**
¼ teaspoon **ground cumin**
1 tablespoon (1 g) **minced fresh cilantro**

Assemble everything in your food processor or blender and run till the scallion, garlic, and chipotle are pulverized. Store in a container with a tight lid and use just as you would chipotle ranch dressing or dip.

YIELD: 1 cup (240 g), 16 servings

Nutritional Analysis

Per serving: 120 calories; 14 g fat; 1 g protein; 1 g carbohydrate; trace dietary fiber; 1 g net carbs

Raspberry Vinaigrette

Raspberry vinaigrette is a favorite, but it's usually quite sugary. This one isn't, and it's still sweet-tart and super-tasty.

2 tablespoons (28 ml) raspberry vinegar
2 tablespoons (28 ml) white balsamic vinegar,
½ cup (120 ml) extra-virgin olive oil
2 teaspoons Dijon mustard
⅛ teaspoon black pepper
1 pinch salt
6 drops liquid stevia extract or to taste

Just put everything in the blender and run it. That's it!

YIELD: 6 servings

Nutritional Analysis
Per serving: 162 calories; 18 g fat; trace protein; 1 g carbohydrate; trace dietary fiber; 1 g net carbs

NOTE

Some raspberry vinegars have sugar added. Read the labels!

Poppy Seed Dressing

Poppy seed dressing is often very sugary. This gets a mild sweetness from the white balsamic vinegar, and that's enough.

½ cup (120 ml) extra-virgin olive oil
¼ cup (60 ml) white balsamic vinegar
1 tablespoon (9.5 g) poppy seeds
¼ teaspoon paprika
¼ teaspoon Paleo Worcestershire (page 293)
1 tablespoon (10 g) minced onion

Just assemble everything in your blender and run it till the onion is pulverized. Refrigerate for an hour or two for the flavors to blend for best results.

YIELD: ¾ cup (6 servings)

Nutritional Analysis
Per serving: 170 calories; 19 g fat; trace protein; 1 g carbohydrate; trace dietary fiber; 1 g net carbs

Lime-Habanero Balsamic Dressing

This dressing is the reason I came up with the recipe to make your own Habanero-Lime Balsamic (see page 284). Great on a salad, but try it as a dip for seafood, too.

4 tablespoons (56 g) Mayonnaise in the Jar (page 278)
2 tablespoons (28 ml) Habanero-Lime Balsamic (page 284)
4 tablespoons (60 ml) olive oil
4 cloves garlic, crushed
2 teaspoons spicy brown mustard
4 teaspoons (20 ml) lemon juice

(continued)

Just whisk everything together. That's it!

YIELD: 4 servings

Nutritional Analysis
Per serving: 226 calories; 25 g fat; 1 g protein; 2 g carbohydrate; trace dietary fiber; 2 g net carbs

Lemon-Apple-Thyme Dressing

Sweet tart and mellow—Try this over a mix of lettuces and some paper-thin red onion and chunks of avocado.

½ cup (120 ml) extra-virgin olive oil
1 medium garlic clove
½ lemon
2 tablespoons (30 ml) apple cider vinegar
1 teaspoon fresh thyme leaves or ¼ to
** ½ teaspoon dried**
⅛ teaspoon pepper
⅛ teaspoon salt
10 drops liquid stevia

Put the olive oil in your blender along with the garlic.

Grate the zest of the half lemon and squeeze the juice. It should yield about 2 tablespoons (30 ml). Add to the blender, along with the rest of the ingredients.

Blend until the garlic is pulverized, and then toss with your salad!

YIELD: ¾ cup (180 g), 6 servings

Nutritional Analysis
Per serving:162 calories; 18 g fat; trace protein; 1 g carbohydrate; trace dietary fiber; 1 g net carbs

Coleslaw Dressing

The paleo version of my favorite coleslaw dressing. For me, this is enough for a whole head of cabbage, shredded, but it depends on how heavily dressed you like your slaw.

½ cup (115 g) Mayonnaise in the Jar (page 278)
½ batch Cocoyo (page 28)
2 tablespoons (28 ml) cider vinegar
2 teaspoons spicy brown mustard
6 drops liquid stevia extract

Just measure everything and mix together!

YIELD: 1 cup (240 g), 8 servings

Nutritional Analysis
Per serving: 194 calories; 22 g fat; 1 g protein; 2 g carbohydrate; trace dietary fiber; 2 g net carbs

Kinda '60s Dressing

This is a riff on the sweet, tomato-y "French" dressing of the 1960s—you know, the stuff no Frenchman would have recognized. Very popular here in the States, though.

8 tablespoons (120 ml) olive oil
4 tablespoons (60 g) Caveman Ketchup (page 273)
4 tablespoons (60 ml) cider vinegar
2 cloves garlic, crushed
1 teaspoon yellow mustard
½ teaspoon black pepper

Just throw everything in the blender and run till it's smooth, then use.

YIELD: 4 servings

Nutritional Analysis
Per serving: 251 calories; 27 g fat; trace protein; 3 g carbohydrate; trace dietary fiber; 3 g net carbs

Creamy White Balsamic and Mustard Dressing

Sorta mayonnaisey, but mine didn't emulsify. Still incredibly tasty, though, and very much worth shaking up before using! And who knows, if you make it on a sunny day, yours may hold together.

2 egg yolks
1 tablespoon (15 ml) white balsamic vinegar
2 garlic cloves, crushed
2 teaspoons spicy brown mustard
½ cup (120 ml) extra-virgin olive oil

Put everything but the oil in your blender and turn it on. Now very slowly drizzle in the oil, until it's all blended in. Turn off the blender; you're done!

YIELD: ⅔ cup (160 g), 3 servings

Nutritional Analysis
Per serving: 365 calories; 40 g fat; 2 g protein; 1 g carbohydrate; trace dietary fiber; 1 g net carbs

Dilly Dressing

⅓ cup (80 ml) white wine vinegar
⅓ cup (21 g) minced fresh dill weed
2 shallots, peeled and chopped
1 tablespoon (15 g) brown or Dijon mustard
¾ cup (175 ml) extra-virgin olive oil
¼ teaspoon pepper
⅛ teaspoon salt

In your food processor, with the *S* blade in place, combine the vinegar, dill weed, and mustard. Process till the shallots are minced fine. Now, with the processor running, pour in the olive oil. Add the salt and pepper and turn off the processor. Pour into a tightly lidded container for storage.

YIELD: 1½ cups (360 g), 12 servings

Nutritional Analysis
Per serving: 123 calories; 14 g fat; trace protein; 1 g carbohydrate; trace dietary fiber; 1 g net carbs

Avocado Mayonnaise

The white balsamic makes this dressing mild and sweet. Great on salads that include fruit.

1 Hass avocado
1 egg yolk
1 tablespoon (15 ml) lemon juice
1 tablespoon (15 ml) white balsamic vinegar
¼ teaspoon dry mustard
½ teaspoon salt

Whack your avocado in half, remove the pit, and scoop the flesh into your food processor. Add everything else and run the processor till it's all emulsified. Use it up fast!

YIELD: 1 cup (240 g), 8 servings

Nutritional Analysis
Per serving: 49 calories; 5 g fat; 1 g protein; 2 g carbohydrate; 1 g dietary fiber; 1 g net carbs

Green Prehistoric Goddess

Great over a salad, but consider this as a dip for crudité, too. For that matter, consider spooning this over a steak. Oh, c'mon, just eat it off a spoon.

1 avocado, good and ripe

3 scallions

1 garlic clove

2 anchovy fillets or ½ tablespoon anchovy paste

1 tablespoon (15 ml) red wine vinegar

1 tablespoon (15 ml) lemon juice

¼ cup (15 g) minced fresh parsley (I've omitted this, and it's still good.)

2 dashes hot sauce, such as Tabasco

Easy! But perishable. Have your salad already made and your main dish nearly ready to serve. Make this right before you're ready to take it to the table. If the kid is playing Wii or the husband is searching for his set of Allen wrenches, round them up first.

Halve the avocado and remove the pit—the easiest way is to whack a sharp blade into it and twist. Scoop the flesh into your food processor. Cut the root and the limp part of the green shoot off the scallions and throw the good part in the food processor. Add everything else and run until it's smooth and creamy.

Scrape the whole batch out of the food processor over a good big salad, and toss till everything's coated. Serve immediately!

YIELD: 4 servings

Nutritional Analysis

Per serving: 93 calories; 8 g fat; 2 g protein; 6 g carbohydrate; 2 g dietary fiber; 2 mg cholesterol; 4 g net carbs

NOTE

The seasonings in this were inspired by those of green goddess dressing, a 1960s favorite. These proportions assume you're using a California avocado—one of the little, black, bumpy ones. If you've got a big, smooth, green Florida avocado, you'll need to double or triple everything else—and have a much bigger salad, and a much bigger crowd to eat it.

Chapter 7

MAIN DISH SALADS

I love main dish salads! They're the ultimate in one-dish meals, delicious, nutritious, and endlessly variable. They're also a great way to use up leftover protein foods, to the point where I often deliberately cook more chicken or steak or whatever than we need so that I can make a salad for lunch the next day.

Here, accordingly, are many tasty and satisfying salads for your enjoyment.

Let's start, as all of us did, with the egg.

My Standard Egg Salad

I've been making this style of egg salad for at least twenty-five years, and I never get tired of it. The homemade mayo is a big upgrade!

½ green bell pepper, diced
2 large celery ribs, diced—include any crisp leaves
4 scallions, sliced thin—include the crisp
  part of the green
2 tablespoons (8 g) minced fresh parsley
6 eggs, hard-boiled, peeled, and chopped
6 tablespoons (84 g) Mayonnaise in the Jar (page 278)
1 tablespoon (15 g) brown mustard
Salt and black pepper to taste

Simple! Cut up your vegetables and your eggs and combine them in a mixing bowl. Stir together the mayonnaise and mustard, then add to the salad and stir it all up. Add salt and pepper to taste.

You can just eat this as-is, of course, but consider wrapping it in lettuce leaves or stuffing it into tomatoes.

YIELD: 2 to 3 servings

Nutritional Analysis
Assuming 3, each serving will have: 374 calories; 35 g fat; 14 g protein; 5 g carbohydrate; 1 g dietary fiber; 4 g net carbs

Sunday Morning Egg Salad

I really did make this up on a Sunday morning, when I had a craving for egg salad and "boilies"—and all the other ingredients—in the fridge. Worth making again!

6 eggs, hard-boiled
2 celery ribs
4 scallions
4 tablespoons (16 g) minced fresh parsley
¼ batch White Balsamic Vinaigrette (page 140)

Simple! Just peel the eggs and chop 'em up—I like mine in fairly big bits, but do it the way you like it. Cut up the celery, scallions, and parsley, too—don't forget to use all the crisp part of the green shoot on the scallions. Throw everything in a bowl. Add the dressing, mix to coat, and serve. You can wrap this in lettuce leaves if you like, though it's awfully good just eaten from a fork.

YIELD: 2 to 3 servings

Nutritional Analysis
Assuming 3 servings, each will have: 248 calories; 20 g fat; 13 g protein; 4 g carbohydrate; 1 g dietary fiber; 3 g net carbs

Artful Egg Salad

So pretty, with all those colors! Serve on a bed of lettuce or stuffed into a tomato. Or just eat it out of the mixing bowl. Did I say that out loud?

4 eggs, hard-boiled

¼ green bell pepper

¼ red bell pepper

4 scallions

2 tablespoons (8 g) minced fresh parsley

2 tablespoons (28 g) Mayonnaise in the Jar (page 278)

1 teaspoon brown mustard

½ teaspoon lemon juice

1 dash hot sauce, such as Tabasco

Black pepper to taste

Salt to taste

Peel your eggs and coarsely chop them—I like big hunks of egg in my salad, for the texture. Put 'em in a mixing bowl. Dice your peppers and slice your scallions thin, including the crisp part of the green shoot. Throw the veggies in with the eggs. Mince your parsley and add it too, or just use your kitchen shears to snip it into the bowl.

Whisk together the mayonnaise, mustard, lemon juice, and hot sauce. Pour over the salad and stir it up. Salt and pepper to taste, and serve.

YIELD: 2 servings

Nutritional Analysis

Per serving: 275 calories; 23 g fat; 14 g protein; 6 g carbohydrate; 1 g dietary fiber; 5 g net carbs

Bacon-and-Egg Salad

I was thinking wistfully of turkey club sandwiches, especially the bacon-and-tomato vector. I didn't have turkey on hand, but I did have hard-boiled eggs, so I tried this. Wonderful!

1 tomato, diced

4 scallions, sliced

4 slices cooked bacon, crumbled

6 eggs, hard-boiled, peeled, and chopped

4 tablespoons (56 g) Mayonnaise in the Jar (page 278)

Just combine everything and stir well. You can serve this with lettuce leaves to wrap it in, or be really revolutionary and eat it with a fork.

YIELD: 2 servings

Nutritional Analysis

Per serving: 452 calories; 40 g fat; 20 g protein; 7 g carbohydrate; 1 g dietary fiber; 6 g net carbs

Poached Egg and Chicken Liver Salad

This is a huge pile of food; I wasn't hungry again for hours. And do you have any idea how nutritious this is?

3 tablespoons (45 ml) Habanero-Lime Balsamic (page 284)

6 cups (330 g) mixed lettuce—I used red leaf, romaine, mâche, frisée, and a handful of baby spinach

⅛ small red onion, sliced paper-thin

½ avocado

½ small tomato

4 chicken livers

3 tablespoons (21 g) coconut flour

¼ teaspoon paprika

1 pinch cayenne

Salt and black pepper

3 tablespoons (39 g) coconut oil or fat of choice

2 eggs

(continued)

Make your dressing first. Have the lettuce in a big salad bowl and cut up the red onion, avocado, and tomato but don't add them to the salad yet. Just have them standing by.

Put a couple of inches (5 cm) of water in a small saucepan and bring to a simmer.

While the water's heating, cut your livers into bite-size pieces. On a rimmed plate, mix the coconut flour with the paprika, cayenne, and a pinch of salt and pepper. Toss the liver in the seasoned flour. Put your skillet over medium-high heat and add the coconut oil.

Okay, your water should be simmering. One at a time, break your eggs into a custard cup and slip them gently into the water. (Use the freshest eggs you can get for poaching.) Turn the water down to just below a simmer. Your oil is hot! Add the liver bits, sautéing quickly, just till browned. Do not overcook! Remove from the heat as soon as they're browned.

Pour the dressing on your lettuce and toss till it's evenly coated. Pile on 2 plates. Top each serving with half the onion, tomato, and avocado. Divide the liver between the 2 servings. As soon as the whites of your eggs are set, but the yolks are still soft, scoop them out one at a time with a slotted spoon and put one atop each salad, then serve.

YIELD: 2 servings

Nutritional Analysis
Per serving: 639 calories; 52 g fat; 22 g protein; 27 g carbohydrate; 11 g dietary fiber; 16 g net carbs

After the egg, comes the chicken! Here's a whole coopful of chicken salad recipes.

My Chicken Salad Declaration

My darling Southern-belle friend and recipe tester, Julie McIntosh, tells me that down south chicken salad absolutely must be made with chicken breast only. One chunk of dark meat, and you'll be a topic of discussion at the next Junior League meeting—"Did you see? She used dark meat in her chicken salad, bless her heart."

That's all well and good, but I'm a Yankee, and I prefer dark meat, even in my chicken salad. I find it moister and more flavorful than breast. So except where I've mentioned otherwise, I've used thigh meat for these chicken salads. Use what you like, of course. But if you, like me, prefer dark meat, I say to heck with the Junior League.

Bright and Beautiful Chicken Salad

Both the colors and the flavors of this chicken salad are bright and beautiful!

1 cup (140 g) diced cooked chicken
½ cup (75 g) diced red bell pepper
1 artichoke heart, cooked and chopped
2 scallions, sliced thin, including the crisp part of the green shoot
1 tablespoon (4 g) minced fresh parsley
⅓ cup (75 g) Lemon-Balsamic Mayonnaise (page 278), or to taste

Very straightforward—just cut up everything but the mayo and put in a mixing bowl. Then make the mayo (unless you've got some in the fridge—I often have two or three varieties of mayonnaise in the fridge), add to the other ingredients, and toss to coat.

Nutritional Analysis
Per serving: 698 calories; 64 g fat; 24 g protein; 9 g carbohydrate; 3 g dietary fiber; 6 g net carbs

Coleslaw with Chicken, Strawberries, and Almonds

What a nice summer luncheon dish this would make! If you don't have time for luncheons, you can make this ahead and eat it a few days in a row. Just save the strawberries to add at the last minute.

1 batch Poppy Seed Dressing (page 143)
½ cup (55 g) slivered almonds
8 cups (560 g) shredded cabbage
8 scallions
8 large strawberries (if they're little, use a dozen or more)
12 ounces (340 g) diced cooked chicken

We're going to assume your dressing is already made, but if it's not, take care of that first.

Put your almonds in a dry skillet and stir them over medium-low heat until they're lightly gold. Don't walk away! Just stand there and stir them, or those almonds will as soon burn as look at you.

Shred your cabbage and throw it in a big mixing bowl. Slice your scallions thin, including the crisp part of the green shoot, and add to the mixing bowl.

Slice your strawberries and add to the bowl. Now dice your chicken—I just snip it right into the mixing bowl with my kitchen shears.

Pour on the dressing and toss to coat.

Pile your salad on 4 plates, sprinkle the almonds on top, and serve.

YIELD: 4 servings

Nutritional Analysis
Per serving: 559 calories; 42 g fat; 33 g protein; 17 g carbohydrate; 6 g dietary fiber; 11 g net carbs

Lunch with Girlfriends!

My girlfriends, Virginia and Missy, came over for lunch, and took the opportunity to try a new recipe. So good!

½ head cauliflower
8 dried apricots or 16 dried apricot halves
3 large scallions
¼ cup (24 g) minced fresh mint,
¼ cup (4 g) minced fresh cilantro
¼ cup (15 g) minced fresh parsley
2 tablespoons (28 ml) lime juice
2 tablespoons (28 ml) Habanero-Lime Balsamic (page 284)
6 tablespoons (90 ml) extra-virgin olive oil
2 tablespoons (28 g) mayonnaise
½ teaspoon brown mustard
1 garlic clove, crushed
Salt and black pepper
1 pound (455 g) boneless, skinless chicken breast
¼ cup (35 g) pistachio nuts, shelled, roasted, and salted
½ head lettuce

Turn your half head of cauliflower into Cauli-Rice (see page 87).

(continued)

In the meanwhile, dice your dried apricots into ¼-inch (6 mm) pieces. Slice the scallions, including the crisp part of the green. (My scallions were really quite large. If yours are smallish, use 4 or 5.)

When the cauliflower is done, uncover it immediately and dump it into a big mixing bowl. Add the apricot bits to the bowl and stir them in—the heat and moisture will hydrate them.

Mince your herbs while the Cauli-Rice is cooling. Now make your dressing:

Put the lime juice, Habanero-Lime Balsamic, olive oil, mayonnaise, mustard, and garlic in your blender and run till the dressing is emulsified.

Time to cook your chicken! I use my electric tabletop grill. Salt and pepper the chicken lightly and throw it in the grill for 4 to 5 minutes, while you . . .

Pour the dressing over the Cauli-Rice. Add the herbs and the scallions and toss like a mad thing. Add the pistachios and toss again.

Your chicken should be done by now. (By the way, if you don't have an electric grill, you can give it 4 or 5 minutes per side in a skillet instead.) Throw it on your cutting board and cut in strips, across the grain.

Line 4 plates with lettuce. Pile the salad on the lettuce, then divide the chicken between the 4 salads and serve.

If you like, you can make the salad up to the point of adding the pistachios and stash it in the fridge—you can even do it the day before. Then all you have to do is grill your chicken, toss in the pistachios, and serve.

YIELD: 4 servings

Nutritional Analysis
Per serving: 475 calories; 33 g fat; 30 g protein; 19 g carbohydrate; 5 g dietary fiber;14 g net carbs

Summer Chicken Salad

Arleen clearly had fun testing this. She says, "Very easy. And can be a family thing. Your husband can grill while the kids prepare the salad. She rated this a solid 10.

¼ cup (28 g) slivered almonds
3 tablespoons (45 ml) olive oil
1½ tablespoons (25 ml) white balsamic vinegar
1½ tablespoons (25 ml) lemon juice
5 drops liquid stevia extract
1 tablespoon (8 g) grated gingerroot
¼ teaspoon ground cinnamon
1 pound (455 g) boneless, skinless chicken breast
Salt and black pepper
12 ounces (340 g) baby spinach
3 celery ribs, thinly sliced (Add any unwilted leaves, too.)
½ cucumber, thinly sliced
2 scallions, thinly sliced, including the crisp part of the green shoot
½ cup (30 g) minced fresh parsley

First, put a small, heavy skillet over medium-low heat and stir your slivered almonds in it until they're golden. Remove from the heat and reserve.

Next, make your dressing. Put the olive oil, white balsamic, lemon juice, liquid stevia, gingerroot, and cinnamon in your blender and run till it's emulsified.

Preheat your electric tabletop or outdoor grill. Pour a tablespoon (15 ml) of the dressing into a small dish (to prevent contamination) and use it to brush the chicken breasts all over. Salt and pepper them lightly. Throw them on the grill and give them 5 to 6 minutes, each side, or until they're cooked through. (Timing will, of course, depend on the thickness of your chicken breasts.)

In the meanwhile, assemble your baby spinach, celery, cucumber, scallions, and parsley in your salad bowl.

When the chicken is done, throw it on your cutting board and slice it thin, across the grain.

Pour the dressing on your salad and toss till everything is coated. Pile the salad on 4 plates. Top each salad with ¼ of the chicken and 1 tablespoon of toasted almonds and serve.

YIELD: 4 servings

Nutritional Analysis
Per serving: 314 calories; 18 g fat; 30 g protein; 9 g carbohydrate; 4 g dietary fiber; 5 g net carbs

Chicken Salad on a Bed of Avocado Slices

1 cup (140 g) diced cooked chicken
1 large celery rib, diced fine
2 scallions, sliced thin
¼ cup (60 g) mayonnaise
½ teaspoon brown mustard
½ teaspoon lemon juice
2 dashes chipotle hot sauce
3 cups (165 g) shredded iceberg or romaine lettuce
1 avocado

In a mixing bowl, combine the diced chicken, celery, and scallions. Stir together the mayonnaise, mustard, lemon juice, and hot sauce. Add to chicken mixture and toss well to coat.

Divide lettuce between 2 plates. Halve your avocado, remove the pit, and slice it, dividing the slices between the 2 plates. Mound chicken salad on top and serve.

YIELD: 2 servings

Nutritional Analysis
Per serving: 627 calories; 56 g fat; 25 g protein; 12 g carbohydrate; 5 g dietary fiber; 7 g net carbs

Throwback Chicken Salad

Regina, who tested this, says she and her husband both greatly preferred this warm, rather than chilled, but do as you like.

½ head cauliflower, in ½-inch (1 cm) chunks
8 ounces (225 g) boneless, skinless chicken breast
Salt and black pepper
1 celery rib, diced
½ red or yellow bell pepper
⅓ cup (55 g) red onion, diced fine
½ cup (65 g) frozen peas
⅓ cup (½ batch or 80 ml) Free-Range Dressing (page 142)
½ teaspoon black pepper
1 clove garlic, crushed

Trim the leaves and the very bottom of the stem from your cauliflower and whack it into ½-inch (1 cm) chunks. Steam them till tender but not mushy—I'd give mine about 10 minutes on high in the microwave.

(*continued*)

One at a time, put your chicken breasts in a big, heavy zipper-lock bag. Seal it, pressing out the air as you go. Now use a heavy blunt object—I use a 3-pound (1.3 kg) dumbbell—to pound your chicken to a nice, even thinness—you want it about ½-inch (1 cm) thick. Salt and pepper it lightly, then grill. I use my electric tabletop grill, myself. Takes just 4 to 5 minutes in there, especially if you preheat, but you can grill outdoors.

While the cauliflower and the chicken are doing their thing, dice your celery, pepper, and onion.

Okay, the chicken and cauliflower are done. Now you . . .

Throw the cauliflower in a big mixing bowl. Let it cool a few minutes while you throw the chicken on a cutting board and dice it about the same size as the cauliflower.

Add the peas to the cauliflower. Don't thaw them first—they'll cool your cauliflower down a bit for you. Now add your other veggies and your diced chicken.

Stir together the dressing, pepper, and garlic. Pour over the salad and toss till everything's well-combined.

YIELD: 3 servings

Nutritional Analysis
Per serving: 465 calories; 39 g fat; 22 g protein; 14 g carbohydrate; 5 g dietary fiber; 9 g net carbs

James Beard Memorial Chicken Salad

This started with a recipe for a chicken-potato-and-green-bean salad in a James Beard cookbook. Unsurprisingly, with that kind of pedigree, it came out wonderfully.

1 cup (100 g) green beans, in 1-inch (2.5 cm) lengths
2 cups (200 g) cauliflower, in ½-inch (1 cm) chunks
1¼ cups (175 g) diced cooked chicken (I used thigh meat.)
1 batch Simple Vinaigrette (page 139)
¼ teaspoon anchovy paste
3 tablespoons (30 g) capers, drained
1½ tablespoons (4 g) minced fresh basil

Steam your green beans and cauliflower. You want your beans tender-crisp and your cauliflower tender but not mushy. Combine 'em in a mixing bowl.

Cut your chicken into ½-inch (1 cm) bits—I just snip mine up with my kitchen shears. You can use chicken breast if you like, but I used roasted thighs, because they're wonderfully moist and flavorful. Add the chicken to the beans and cauliflower.

Make your vinaigrette, adding the anchovy paste. Pour it over the salad and toss.

Now add the capers and basil and toss again. You can chill this for a while if you like, but I ate it still warm, and it was fantastic.

YIELD: 3 servings

Nutritional Analysis
Per serving: 559 calories; 51 g fat; 20 g protein; 8 g carbohydrate; 3 g dietary fiber; 5 g net carbs

Spicy Citrus Chicken Salad

Bright citrus flavor and the toasty crunch of pumpkin seeds make this chicken salad something out of the ordinary.

4 tablespoons (35 g) pumpkin seeds (pepitas)
1 ½ cups (210 g) diced cooked chicken
6 tablespoons (60 g) diced red onion
½ cup (60 g) diced celery
½ navel orange
2 teaspoons fresh lime juice
1 teaspoon ground cumin
½ teaspoon cayenne or to taste
1 clove garlic, crushed
⅓ cup (75 g) Mayonnaise in the Jar (page 278)
Salt

First, over medium heat, stir your pumpkin seeds in a dry skillet until they puff and brown slightly. Let them cool while you . . .

Assemble your diced chicken, onion, and celery in a mixing bowl.

Squeeze the juice from your half orange into a small bowl and grate in ¼ teaspoon of the zest. Add the lime juice, cumin, cayenne, garlic, and mayonnaise. Whisk it up and pour it over the salad. Stir to coat.

Now mix in the toasted pumpkin seeds and serve immediately. If you'd like to, you can do everything up through tossing the salad with the dressing and add the pumpkin seeds just before serving.

YIELD: 3 servings

Nutritional Analysis
Per serving: 534 calories; 46 g fat ; 28 g protein; 6 g carbohydrate; 2 g dietary fiber; 4 g net carbs

Chicken-and-Pear Salad

Lisa C. says, "Easiest one yet!"

¾ pound (340 g) boneless, skinless chicken breast
6 tablespoons (90 ml) olive oil, divided
½ cup (60 g) coarsely chopped walnuts
2 scallions, thinly sliced
1 pear, cored and diced
8 cups (440 g) leaf lettuce
2 tablespoons (28 ml) cider vinegar
Salt and black pepper
2 tablespoons (17.2 g) capers, drained and chopped

Brush your chicken with a little of the olive oil and start it cooking in your electric tabletop grill. (If you don't have one, sauté it over medium-high heat in a bit more of the oil.)

While that's happening, turn your oven on to 350°F (180°C, or gas mark 4). Chop your walnuts, spread them on a shallow baking tin, and slide them into the oven. Set a timer for 8 minutes.

Slice your scallions, including the crisp part of the green shoot. Core and dice your pear.

Pile your lettuce into a big salad bowl and pour on the rest of the olive oil. Toss-toss-toss till everything's coated. Add the vinegar and toss again.

(continued)

Chicken done? Throw it on your cutting board and slice it up.

Now taste your lettuce and add a little salt and pepper. Toss-toss-toss again. Now pile it on 4 plates.

Top each salad with a quarter of the sliced chicken, a quarter of the pear, 2 tablespoons (15 g) of walnuts, ¼ of the scallions, and a half tablespoon of capers. Serve immediately!

YIELD: 4 servings

Nutritional Analysis
Per serving: 414 calories; 32 g fat; 24 g protein; 11 g carbohydrate; 3 g dietary fiber; 8 g net carbs

Strawberry Chicken Salad

How nice would this be for a luncheon with girlfriends?

¼ cup (30 g) chopped walnuts
¾ pound (340 g) boneless, skinless chicken breast
½ cup (120 ml) olive oil, divided
Salt and black pepper
⅓ cup (80 ml) balsamic vinegar
1 tablespoon (15 ml) coconut aminos
1 garlic clove
½ tablespoon grated gingerroot
2 quarts (440 g) romaine lettuce, broken up
12 strawberries, quartered
2 scallions, sliced thin

Turn your oven on to 350°F (180°C, or gas mark 4). Spread the chopped walnuts on a shallow baking tin and slide them into the oven. Set a timer for 8 minutes.

Brush your chicken with a little of the oil, salt and pepper it, and start it cooking in your electric tabletop grill or in a heavy skillet over medium heat. In the tabletop grill, figure 4 to 5 minutes, in the skillet, a little longer.

Now assemble the rest of the oil, the balsamic vinegar, the coconut aminos, the garlic, and the ginger in your blender. Run it till you have a smooth dressing, with no chunks of garlic in it.

Break up your lettuce into your big salad bowl. Quarter the strawberries and slice the scallions.

Okay, by now your chicken is done. Throw it on your cutting board and slice it up.

Pour your dressing over the lettuce and toss till everything's well-coated. Add the quartered strawberries and the scallions and toss again. Pile this on 4 plates.

Top each serving with a quarter of the chicken and a tablespoon (7.5 g) of walnuts, then serve immediately.

YIELD: 4 servings

Nutritional Analysis
Per serving: 420 calories; 34 g fat; 23 g protein; 8 g carbohydrate; 3 g dietary fiber; 5 g net carbs

Chicken Salad with Sundried Tomatoes, Basil, and Pine Nuts

And peas! And red onion! And Lemon-Balsamic Mayonnaise! Just how much fabulousness can you take in one dish?

2 cups (330 g) Cauli-Rice (page 87)

2 tablespoons (18 g) pine nuts (pignolia)

1 cup (140 g) diced cooked chicken

¼ cup (37.5 g) peas (I used frozen, thawed. If you have a good source of fresh, use them, steamed lightly.)

2 tablespoons (20 g) diced red onion

2 tablespoons (14 g) oil-packed sundried tomatoes, chopped

2 tablespoons (5 g) minced fresh basil

3 tablespoons (42 g) Lemon-Balsamic Mayonnaise (page 278)

Salt and black pepper

You've turned your cauliflower into Cauli-Rice, yes? A quarter-head will give you about 2 cups (330 g). Put it in a microwaveable bowl—I used a cereal bowl, since I'm not eating cereal anymore. Add just a teaspoon or so of water, cover it with a saucer, and microwave for 4 to 5 minutes.

While that's happening, put a small, heavy skillet over low heat and spread the pine nuts in it to toast.

Start cutting and measuring the chicken, veggies, and basil and throwing 'em in a mixing bowl. Don't forget to stir your pine nuts once or twice!

When the microwave beeps, add the Cauli-Rice to the salad. You can cool it first if you like, but I didn't bother.

Stir in the Lemon-Balsamic Mayonnaise and salt and pepper to taste. You can serve it still warm or chill it for a while to let the flavors blend—up to you.

YIELD: 2 servings

Nutritional Analysis
Per serving: 586 calories; 49 g fat; 27 g protein; 12 g carbohydrate; 4 g dietary fiber; 8 g net carbs

Duck and Raspberry Salad

I made the Unsightly but Delicious Duck (page 208) and had half a duck left over the next day. So this is what I made for lunch. Unbelievable. The crispy bits of skin really put the whole thing over the top.

3 tablespoons (45 ml) Raspberry Vinaigrette (page 143)

3 tablespoons (23 g) chopped walnuts

4 ounces (115 g) roasted, leftover duck meat

1 quart (220 g) mixed lettuce (I used red leaf, Boston, and leaf lettuces.)

1 cup (30 g) baby spinach

2 scallions, thinly sliced

12 raspberries

If you don't have Raspberry Vinaigrette on hand, make some first.

Preheat your oven to 350°F (180°C, or gas mark 4) while you chop your walnuts. Spread them on a baking sheet and put them in the oven. Set your timer for 8 minutes.

(continued)

Remove the skin from your leftover duck and lay it in a small skillet. Put it over medium-low heat to crisp. Use a fork to pierce any fatty places several times.

Tear or cut up your lettuce into your big salad bowl and add the baby spinach. Slice the scallions, including the crisp part of the green.

Warm your leftover duck, if you like—I did. Then dice it into bite-size bits.

Okay, your walnuts are toasted and the duck skin is crisp. Time to assemble your salad.

Pour your dressing on your lettuce and toss-toss-toss. Pile it on a plate. Scatter the raspberries artistically over it. Now add the duck. Scatter the walnuts over that. Use your kitchen shears to snip the crispy skin over that.

YIELD: 1 serving

Nutritional Analysis
Per serving: 871 calories; 85 g fat; 20 g protein; 10 g carbohydrate; 4 g dietary fiber; 6 g net carbs

NOTE

This is a big salad with a lot of lettuce, because I like my salads that way. You could reduce it, if you like.

Asian Duck Salad

If you don't have leftover duck in the house, you can make this lovely salad with chicken instead. I would very much recommend dark meat chicken for this, but it's up to you.

1 cup (140 g) leftover, diced duck meat
1 cup (75 g) snow peas or sugar snap peas
1 cup (50 g) mung bean sprouts
2 scallions
2 tablespoons (28 ml) coconut aminos
2 tablespoons (28 ml) white balsamic vinegar
1 small garlic clove, crushed
½ teaspoon dark sesame oil
Lettuce leaves (to serve)

Dice your leftover duck and put it in a bowl. Remove the tips from your sugar snap peas and snip each one in half; add to the bowl, along with the bean sprouts.

Slice the scallions thin, including the crisp part of the green shoot, and add to the bowl.

Now mix together everything else but the lettuce leaves, pour over the salad, and stir to coat. Serve on lettuce-lined plates.

YIELD: 2 servings

Nutritional Analysis
Per serving: 528 calories; 46 g fat; 16 g protein; 12 g carbohydrate; 3 g dietary fiber; 9 g net carbs

Gulfview Shrimp Salad

Delicious, but remember that all this fruit means this isn't for the carb-intolerant.

12 ounces (340 g) small, peeled shrimp
2 lemons
⅓ cup (75 g) Mayonnaise in the Jar (page 278)
2 tablespoons (28 ml) olive oil
2 tablespoons (30 g) Caveman Ketchup (page 273)
1 apple
2 large celery ribs
½ cucumber
¾ cup (124 g) fresh pineapple chunks
½ cup (75 g) red grapes, halved
1 avocado
6 cups (330 g) shredded romaine lettuce

First poach the shrimp: In a large saucepan, bring a quart (1 L) of water to a boil. Add ½ teaspoon salt and stir to dissolve. Add the shrimp, turn off the heat, and let the shrimp sit in the water for 4 to 5 minutes. Drain and chill. You can peel before or after cooking—up to you.

Okay, we're assuming you've got the chilled shrimp in the fridge. Make your dressing: Whisk together the juice of the lemons, mayonnaise, olive oil, and ketchup. Reserve while you . . .

Core and dice your apple and dice your celery and cucumber. Cut your pineapple chunks into ½-inch (1 cm) dice and halve your grapes. Put all of this in a mixing bowl.

Add the shrimp, then the dressing, and mix to coat.

Now peel and dice your avocado and stir it in gently.

On 3 plates, make beds of the lettuce. Mound the shrimp-and-fruit mixture in the center and serve.

YIELD: 3 servings

Nutritional Analysis
Per serving: 589 calories; 43 g fat; 27 g protein; 34 g carbohydrate; 7 g dietary fiber; 27 g net carbs

Fish Taco Salad 1

Fish tacos are usually wrapped in tortillas, of course, and garnished with shredded cabbage. So I figured, "Why not serve the fish right on the cabbage?"

1 pound (455 g) mahi mahi fillet
½ cup (120 ml) light-flavor olive oil
2 limes
2 tablespoons (15 g) ancho chile powder
1 jalapeño, seeded and chopped
½ cup (8 g) minced fresh cilantro
8 cups (560 g) shredded cabbage
¼ cup (40 g) minced red onion
2 medium tomatoes, diced
Salt and black pepper, to taste
½ cup (115 g) Coconut Sour Cream (page 29)
Salsa (page 281)

Cut your fish into 4 portions and lay it in a nonreactive dish or rimmed plate just big enough to hold it.

Measure and whisk together the olive oil, juice of the limes, chile powder, jalapeño, and minced cilantro. Pour half of the mixture over the fish, turning the fillets several times to coat. Let the fish marinate for a half hour or so.

(continued)

Shred your cabbage (or use bagged coleslaw mix, I won't tell) and dice your red onion and tomatoes. Combine them in a mixing bowl, pour the rest of the olive oil–lime juice mixture over it, and toss. Salt and pepper to taste. Pile the salad on 4 plates.

Have your grill medium hot—you can use your barbecue grill or your electric tabletop grill. Either way, grill your fish for about 5 minutes, basting once or twice with the marinade, until it's white and flaky. (Stop basting a good minute before you're done grilling. Germs, you know.)

Put a fish fillet on each salad, garnish with Coconut Sour Cream and Salsa, and serve.

YIELD: 4 servings

Nutritional Analysis
Per serving: 536 calories; 40 g fat; 26 g protein; 26 g carbohydrate; 7 g dietary fiber; 19 g net carbs

Fish Taco Salad 2

Okay, so I'd already come up with a fish taco salad. But I saw another recipe for fish tacos that I thought would adapt well, and thought, "Why not?" Just as well. Our tester Rebecca says, "This combination of flavors was so amazingly good."

1 pound (455 g) mahi mahi fillet
Taco Seasoning (page 290)
1 tablespoon (13 g) lard
½ batch Southwestern Slaw (page 124)
2 medium tomatoes, diced
¼ cup (8 g) minced fresh cilantro
1 lime
Hot sauce, if desired

Divide your fish into 4 portions and sprinkle well with Taco Seasoning. Let it sit for 5 minutes to absorb the flavor.

Now either sear your fish in the lard in a hot skillet or grill it quickly on your electric tabletop grill (skip the lard if you do this).

While it's cooking, divide your slaw between 4 plates, making nice beds. Dice your tomatoes, mince your cilantro, and divide between the salads.

When the fish is just done, place a portion on each bed of slaw. Serve with a lime wedge each, and hot sauce.

YIELD: 4 servings

Nutritional Analysis
Per serving: 404 calories; 29 g fat; 24 g protein; 18 g carbohydrate; 5 g dietary fiber; 13 g net carbs

NOTE

Rebecca says any firm white fish would do and suggests cod if you can't find mahi mahi.

Leftover Steak Salad

This is why you should always buy a bigger flank steak than you need for supper! Or you could grill one fresh, quadruple or quintuple this recipe, and there's dinner on a hot summer night.

½ cup (60 g) chopped walnuts

½ cup (120 ml) olive oil

4 tablespoons (60 ml) red wine vinegar

4 teaspoons (20 ml) Paleo Worcestershire (page 293)

¼ cup (60 g) brown mustard

2 cloves garlic, crushed

2 quarts (440 g) lettuce leaves (I use Romaine.)

4 tablespoons (16 g) minced fresh parsley

1 small cucumber, quartered lengthwise and sliced thin

½ green bell pepper, in small strips

½ cup (80 g) red onion, sliced paper-thin

6 ounces (170 g) cooked, leftover flank steak

Turn on your oven to 350°F (180°C, or gas mark 4). Spread your walnuts on a baking tin, put 'em in the oven, and set the timer for 8 minutes.

Assemble the olive oil, vinegar, Worcestershire, brown mustard, and garlic in your blender and run till it's emulsified.

In a big salad bowl, assemble your lettuce and parsley in a big salad bowl. Slice up your cucumber, green pepper, and red onion. Slice your steak thin, across the grain.

Pour the dressing over the lettuce and toss with barely controlled abandon. Pile the lettuce on 2 plates. Top each with half the cucumber, pepper, onion, and steak. Your walnuts are toasted! Sprinkle them over the salads and serve!

YIELD: 2 servings

Nutritional Analysis

Per serving: 933 calories; 84 g fat; 31 g protein; 25 g carbohydrate; 8 g dietary fiber; 17 g net carbs

Steak Cobb Salad

This happened because I was trying to figure out a way to use up some leftover steak and a single hard-boiled egg. Obviously, you can double or triple this, no sweat.

3 slices cooked bacon, crumbled

3 tablespoons (45 ml) Simple Vinaigrette (page 139)

1 quart (220 g) mixed greens (lettuce, watercress, radicchio, whatever you've got)

2 tablespoons (8 g) minced fresh parsley

3 ounces (85 g) leftover, diced flank steak

1 egg, hard-boiled, peeled, and diced

¼ avocado, peeled and diced

½ medium tomato, diced

2 tablespoons (20 g) finely diced red onion

Start your bacon cooking—I do mine in the microwave, but cook it by your preferred method.

If you don't have the dressing in the fridge, that's next, but we're going to assume for the purpose of this recipe that you've got some vinaigrette kicking around the fridge. Take your lettuces—try to have a balance of mild lettuce, like romaine, iceberg, butterhead, red leaf, etc., with a few sharper greens, like radicchio, frisée, or watercress, for contrast—and put them all on your cutting board. Cut across the leaves, into strips about ¼-inch (6 mm) wide. If the leaves are wide, chop those strips into shorter lengths, too. Throw it all into a big salad bowl. Use your kitchen shears to snip the parsley in, too. (Come to think of it, you could use your kitchen shears to snip right across heads of lettuce, too. Up to you.)

(continued)

Dice up the steak, peel and dice the egg and the avocado, and dice the tomato and onion. Drain and crumble your bacon, too. You want all your stuff in its requisite bits before you dress your lettuce.

Now pour the dressing over the lettuce and toss well, till it's all evenly coated. Pile it on a plate.

Now arrange your diced ingredients in pretty stripes or spokes on top of your lettuce. Serve and devour!

YIELD: 1 serving

Nutritional Analysis
Per serving: 743 calories; 59 g fat; 37 g protein; 22 g carbohydrate; 10 g dietary fiber; 12 g net carbs

NOTE

Part of the charm of a Cobb salad is all of the ingredients in similar little cubes. So try to get 'em about the same size—mine were between ¼ and ½ inch (6 mm and 1 cm). Except the onion, which should be a little finer.

Lobster Salad in Tomatoes

Simple. Classic. Expensive.

3 cups diced cooked lobster meat
¼ cup (15 g) minced fresh parsley
1 tablespoon (4 g) minced fresh tarragon
2 thinly sliced scallions, including the crisp part of the green
1 cup (225 g) Mayonnaise in the Jar (page 278)
Salt (optional)
4 medium tomatoes
8 lettuce leaves, for lining plates

Dice the lobster and combine it with the parsley, tarragon, and scallions in a mixing bowl. Add the mayonnaise and stir to coat. Salt to taste.

Cut the cores out of your tomatoes, then cut them vertically into 8 wedges (quarter, then cut each quarter in two) without cutting through the skin at the bottom.

Line 4 plates with lettuce. Put a tomato on each and open them up into flowers. Put a scoop of lobster salad in each tomato flower, letting any extra spill picturesquely around the tomato.

Snip up a little extra crisp, green scallion top and some parsley. Scatter on top, if desired, then serve.

YIELD: 4 servings

Nutritional Analysis
Per serving: 533 calories; 48 g fat; 24 g protein; 8 g carbohydrate; 2 g dietary fiber; 6 g net carbs

In the meanwhile, dice your celery, onion, and apple, all about ¼ inch (6 mm). Peel and chop the eggs, too. Throw everything in a mixing bowl

When your tuna's done, drain it, put it on your chopping board, and cut it in ¼-inch (6 mm) dice. Add it to everything else.

Add the mayo and stir it all up. Salt and pepper it if you like and serve. You can stuff this into a tomato or serve it on a bed of lettuce; I ate mine out of the mixing bowl.

YIELD: 2 servings

Nutritional Analysis
Per serving: 450 calories; 39 g fat; 20 g protein; 7 g carbohydrate; 2 g dietary fiber; 5 g net carbs.

NOTE

If you choose to use good-quality canned tuna in olive oil (not the stuff in soy oil or soy broth), I promise not to tell.

Good Ol' Tuna Salad

I have a very unsophisticated taste for tuna salad made from cheap canned tuna, but of course that's not paleo. Here's the fresh, no-junk-added version.

4 ounces (115 g) tuna steak
½ cup (60 g) diced celery, including tops
¼ cup (40 g) diced red onion
½ Granny Smith apple, diced
2 eggs, hard-boiled
⅓ cup (75 g) Mayonnaise in the Jar (page 278)
Salt and pepper (optional)

Put your tuna in a small, nonreactive pan and add water to about half the depth of the fish. Put on a low burner and bring to a simmer. Cover, turn off the burner, and let it sit for 10 minutes.

Chapter 8

FISH AND SEAFOOD

This is a big chapter, partly because my husband adores fish in every form, and partly because it's so quick and easy to cook.

Is some fish more paleo than other fish? I believe so. I suspect that shellfish is a very, very old component of the human diet. Why? Because you can simply dig clams out of the sand and pluck oysters and mussels off the sea bed near the shore. They neither run nor fight back. Crabs, lobsters, and crayfish may pinch, but they can still be picked up by hand with little effort or risk.

Fin fish are a little tougher to catch, but if animals can do it, so did Ogg. However, I think it likely that he caught smaller fish, closer to shore. How on Earth would he go deep-sea fishing, catching tuna and swordfish? Accordingly, you'll find a lot of recipes here for smaller fish. That smaller fish are less likely to be contaminated with mercury is a bonus.

My local markets all label their fish as either "wild caught" or "farm raised." Buy wild-caught fish as often as possible. If you have an angler in the house and access to reasonably unpolluted lakes, streams, or beachfront, better still.

Orange-Fennel Salmon

I invented this for my 50th birthday party, and it was a huge hit. It's an easy, yet impressive, way to feed a crowd. Your timing will, of course, depend a bit on the size of your fish, as will the number of servings you get.

8 pounds (3.6 kg) whole salmon (A little bigger or smaller is no big deal.)
¼ cup (60 ml) olive oil, or as needed
Salt and black pepper
1 bulb fennel
2 oranges, divided
1 bunch scallions

Preheat your oven to 350°F (180°C, or gas mark 4). Lay your big fishy in a roasting pan long enough to hold him. Now use a sharp, thin-bladed knife to slash him to the bone about 2 inches (5 cm) apart all down both sides. (Diagonal slashes look cooler than straight across.)

Give Mr. Salmon a nice little massage with all that olive oil, inside and out. Sprinkle with salt and pepper to taste. Set the roasting pan aside while you . . .

Trim the stalks off your fennel, then halve the bulb, trim the root, and slice the rest paper-thin. Slice one and a half of your oranges paper-thin, too. Trim the roots and any wilted greens off your scallions and slice them thinly lengthwise, into long ribbons.

Now stuff your fish! Lay the fennel slices inside the body cavity, topping them with a layer or two of orange slices and the scallions.

Arrange a pretty layer of overlapping orange slices on top of your salmon and heap any remaining fennel and orange around him in the pan. Squeeze the remaining half orange over everything.

Now roast your salmon for 30 to 45 minutes, until he's done through. Serve on a very long platter or right from the roasting pan.

YIELD: 8 servings

Nutritional Analysis
Per serving: 606 calories; 22 g fat; 91 g protein; 5 g carbohydrate; 1 g dietary fiber; 4 g net carbs

Orange-Glazed Salmon

24 ounces (680 g) salmon fillet
½ orange
½ teaspoon Celery Salt (page 285, or use store-bought)
1 teaspoon ground rosemary or ½ tablespoon minced fresh, if you have it
2 garlic cloves, minced
2 tablespoons (28 ml) olive oil
Black pepper

Lay your salmon on a plate with a rim. Grate ½ teaspoon of zest off the orange half and reserve. Squeeze the juice over the salmon fillets, turning to coat. Let them sit for 5 or 10 minutes.

While your fish is marinating, mix together the celery salt and rosemary. Mince up your garlic clove, too, and cover it with the olive oil.

Put a skillet over medium heat. When it's hot, add the oil and garlic. Throw in your salmon, and while the bottom is cooking, sprinkle half the celery salt/rosemary mixture over it. Shake a little pepper over it, too. Give it 3 to 5 minutes, depending on the thickness of your fish.

Flip the fish. Sprinkle the rest of the celery salt and rosemary over the cooked side and sprinkle it with a little pepper, too.

(continued)

When your fish looks done, pour in the orange juice you marinated the fish in. Turn the fish once or twice to coat and let it cook another minute to kill germs. Plate the fish and pour any liquid left in the bottom of the skillet over it before serving.

YIELD: 4 servings

Nutritional Analysis
Per serving: 275 calories; 13 g fat; 34 g protein; 4 g carbohydrate; 1 g dietary fiber; 3 g net carbs

Horseradish-Honey Glazed Salmon

Comments from my pal Julie McIntosh, who has been testing recipes for me for, what, four books now? Five? "As written, the glaze is not as much of a 'glaze' as it is a sauce-you-cook-with or thick marinade or whatever you would call that in cook-y terms. Now, it's freaking DELICIOUS just as written, but it's not 'glaze-y.' SO . . . I made this twice. The first time I made it as directed. It was fab. It was not glaze-y. The second time, I doubled the honey. NOW we're doing more glaze-y.

I would offer the choice so that people who aren't so worried about carbs/sugar can get glaze-y, and those of us who watch that kind of thing can still have a fabulous salmon without the extra sugar. Either way, it's exceptionally good. It's SO easy, SO fast, and tastes like it was a pain in the neck. This is going to become a staple of mine."

So, per Julie: If you want a really glazed surface texture, go ahead and add another tablespoon (20 g) of honey, remembering, of course, that you're also adding 4 grams of carb per serving. If you'd rather keep the carb count low, you'll just have to settle for "fab but not glaze-y."

24 ounces (680 g) salmon fillets
3 tablespoons (39 g) bacon grease, melted (or coconut oil, if you prefer)
Salt
1 teaspoon cracked pepper, divided
2 tablespoons (30 g) brown mustard
2 tablespoons (30 g) horseradish (I grated my own, to avoid sugar)
1 tablespoon (20 g) honey
¼ cup (15 g) minced fresh parsley

You can grill this or broil it. Either way, start your cooking device heating before you do anything else. If you're using a grill, make sure it's good and clean, so your fish won't stick.

Brush your fish on either side with bacon grease. Salt and pepper it lightly. (If you're using bacon grease, you may want to skip the salt.)

Mix together the mustard, horseradish, and honey and have it standing by.

Lay your fish on the broiler pan or grill and give it 3 minutes. Flip and grill the other side for 3 minutes. Now brush with the glaze, turn, and coat the other side, too. Give it another minute or so, then pull off the grill and plate. Sprinkle ¼ teaspoon cracked pepper and 1 tablespoon (4 g) minced parsley over each fillet. Serve with any remaining glaze. (Heat the glaze for a couple of minutes first, to kill any germs!)

YIELD: 4 servings

Nutritional Analysis
Per serving: 313 calories; 16 g fat; 35 g protein; 6 g carbohydrate; trace dietary fiber; 6 g net carbs.

Salmon Hash

You can make this with either glazed salmon recipe. Our tester, Julie, suggests that if you plan to do this, you make extra glaze for this purpose. You can serve this as-is, or you can top it with fried eggs. If you're going to serve it with the eggs, call this 7 to 8 servings.

1 pound (455 g) turnips, in ½-inch (1 cm) cubes
1 pound (455 g) cauliflower, in ½-inch (1 cm) cubes
6 slices bacon
1 medium onion, chopped
½ apple, diced
1 batch Orange-Glazed Salmon (page 165) or
Horseradish-Honey Glazed Salmon (page 166), plus any leftover glaze
Salt and black pepper to taste

Peel and dice your turnips. Dice your cauliflower, too. (Of course, cauliflower will not wind up in perfect cubes. Just go for about the same size pieces as the turnip.) Steam the two—I'd give them 10 to 12 minutes in my microwave steamer. You're looking for tender but not mushy.

In the meanwhile, put your big, heavy skillet over medium-high heat and snip the bacon into it with your kitchen shears. You're making crispy bacon bits.

While your bacon's cooking, chop your onion and dice your apple.

When the bacon's crisp, scoop it out with a slotted spoon and reserve. Pour off all but a few tablespoons (45 ml) of the bacon grease. Throw in the onion and apple and let them start sautéing over medium-low heat.
When the turnip and cauliflower are done, add them to the skillet and mix everything together. Keep sautéing until everything's soft. Now spread it all in an even layer in the bottom of the skillet and let it cook for 5 minutes. Turn everything over and repeat, then do it a third time—you're creating a nice golden crust.

While stuff is browning, dice up the glazed salmon.

When the vegetables are nicely browned, stir in the salmon and any leftover glaze. Let the salmon heat through, salt and pepper, then serve.

YIELD: 5 servings

Nutritional Analysis
Per serving: 353 calories; 17 g fat; 33 g protein; 18 g carbohydrate; 5 g dietary fiber; 13 g net carbs

Lemon-Basil Trout

These instructions are for one whole trout, which will serve one or two people. I trust you can see that you simply repeat as many times as necessary for the number of people you're serving?

1 garlic clove, crushed
2 tablespoons (28 ml) extra-virgin olive oil
½ lemon
12 ounces (340 g) trout, whole
Salt (optional) and black pepper
1 teaspoon dried basil or 1 tablespoon (2.5 g) minced fresh basil, divided

Preheat oven to 350°F (180°C, or gas mark 4).

Crush the garlic clove and put it in a small dish. Pour the olive oil over it and let it sit while you . . .

(continued)

Slice the lemon as thinly as possible, removing the seeds as you go. Don't peel the lemon before slicing.

Tear a piece of foil a good 8 to 10 inches (20 to 25 cm) longer than your trout. Lay it on your work surface and put the trout on it, lengthwise. Sprinkle it lightly inside and out with pepper, and salt if desired. Brush the inside with some of the garlicky olive oil. Now make a layer of lemon slices inside the trout, from one end to the other. Sprinkle half the basil over that.

Cover the top of the trout with the rest of the lemon slices. Sprinkle with the remaining basil. Now bend the edges up, pour the rest of the olive oil and garlic over Mr. Trout, and fold the foil over it, making a nice tight seam. Roll up the ends to make a nice tight packet.

Put your packet in the oven and bake for 20 to 25 minutes. To serve, simply put the packet on a plate and let the diner open it.

YIELD: This can make 1 large but picturesque serving, or you can cut it into servings and have 2 less-beautiful but more moderate servings.

Nutritional Analysis
Assuming 2 servings, each will have: 378 calories; 25 g fat; 36 g protein; 3 g carbohydrate; trace dietary fiber, 3 g net carbs

Snapper on the Gulf

¼ cup (60 ml) olive oil
1 bunch scallions, sliced thin, including the crisp part of the green shoot
3 medium tomatoes, ¼-inch (6 mm) dice
1 jalapeño pepper, seeded and minced
¼ cup (8 g) minced fresh cilantro, divided
2 cloves garlic, crushed
2 limes, quartered
1½ pounds (710 g) red snapper fillets
⅛ teaspoon black pepper
Salt (optional)

Put your big, heavy skillet over medium heat. Add the olive oil and sauté the scallions, tomatoes, jalapeño pepper, half the cilantro, and the garlic, until the vegetables are softened. (In the meanwhile, wash your hands! You handled a hot pepper!) Add the grated zest and juice of one of the lime quarters and let the mixture simmer for 5 minutes.

Sprinkle the fish with pepper, and salt if desired. Lay on top of the sauce, cover the skillet, and let the fish steam for 10 minutes, or until it flakes easily. Serve the fish with the sauce spooned over it, the remaining cilantro sprinkled over it, and lime wedges for squeezing.

YIELD: 6 servings

Nutritional Analysis
Per serving: 105 calories; 9 g fat; 1 g protein; 7 g carbohydrate; 1 g dietary fiber; 6 g net carbs

Pink Grapefruit Flounder

⅓ cup (38 g) coconut flour
Salt and black pepper
1 pinch cayenne
2 tablespoons (26 g) lard or coconut oil
1 pound (455 g) flounder fillet
2 shallots
1 ruby red grapefruit
1 tablespoon (15 ml) balsamic vinegar
⅛ teaspoon black pepper

Mix the coconut flour with the seasonings. I use about ⅛ teaspoon salt and pepper and a pinch of cayenne. Roll the fillets, so they have a nice dusting all over.

Put your big, heavy skillet over medium-high heat—make sure it's one that doesn't stick, since fish can be delicate. When the skillet's hot, melt the lard or coconut oil, slosh it around to cover the bottom of the skillet, and throw in your fillets.

While they're cooking, quickly mince up your shallots.

Go flip your fish! It shouldn't take more than about 4 minutes per side to get nice and golden, and the fillets are thin, so they cook through quickly.

Whack your grapefruit in half. Over a bowl (to catch the juice), use a sharp knife to cut out each section and cut each in half again, just to have more bits. Squeeze all the juice out of the remaining grapefruit shells, into the bowl.

When your fish is golden and flaky, plate it and put it in a warm place.

Throw the shallots into the skillet and sauté them—add just a touch more fat if you need it—just for a minute or two. Now stir in the grapefruit juice, the vinegar, and the pepper and boil the whole thing for a minute or so, till it gets a little syrupy. Stir in the grapefruit bits, just heat them through, and spoon the sauce over the fish. Serve immediately.

YIELD: 3 servings

Nutritional Analysis
Per serving: 360 calories; 13 g fat; 33 g protein; 27 g carbohydrate; 12 g dietary fiber; 15 g net carbs

Orange-Cumin Flounder

Fast, ultra-tasty, and no cleanup!

4 cups (120 g) fresh baby spinach
24 ounces (680 g) flounder fillet, cut into fourths
2 shallots, thinly sliced
2 oranges
1 teaspoon ground cumin
Salt (optional) and black pepper

Preheat oven to 350°F (180°C, or gas mark 4).

Tear squares of foil—I like to use nonstick foil—big enough to wrap each of your fillets. On each square, arrange the spinach into a bed about the size of each flounder fillet. Place the flounder on the spinach. Lay the shallots on top.

Squeeze the oranges into a small bowl and stir in the cumin. Pour this over the flounder and sprinkle the whole thing with a little pepper, and salt if desired.

(continued)

Fold up the edges the long way and roll down, then roll up the ends, making tight packets. Bake for 12 to 15 minutes. We serve this right from the foil, 'cause it's easy.

YIELD: 4 servings

Nutritional Analysis
Per serving: 198 calories; 2 g fat; 34 g protein; 10 g carbohydrate; 2 g dietary fiber; 8 g net carbs

Flounder in Creamy Curry Sauce

24 ounces (680 g) flounder fillets
Salt and black pepper
⅓ cup (77 g) Cocoyo (page 28)
2 tablespoons (28 g) Mayonnaise in the Jar (page 278)
1 teaspoon curry powder
¼ lemon
2 scallions

Preheat oven to 350°F (180°C, or gas mark 4). Grease a baking pan big enough to hold your fish fillets rolled up.

Salt and pepper your fish and roll your fillets up into nice neat bundles. Arrange them in the pan.

Mix together everything else but the scallions. Spoon over the fillets. Put 'em in the oven and bake for 25 to 30 minutes.

In the meanwhile, mince the scallions, including the crisp part of the green shoot.

When the fish is done, plate it, spooning any sauce that has escaped to the bottom of the pan back over the fish.

Top with the scallions to make it look pretty and serve.

YIELD: 4 servings

Nutritional Analysis
Per serving: 583 calories; 48 g fat; 36 g protein; 6 g carbohydrate; trace dietary fiber; 6 g net carbs

Simple Perch

6 slices bacon
1 large onion
Black pepper to taste
Coconut oil
24 ounces (680 g) perch fillet, in 4 servings

Chop the bacon or snip it into your skillet. Either way, fry it in your big, heavy skillet, over medium heat, until you've got nice crunchy bacon bits.

While the bacon bits are cooking, slice your onion thin.

When the bacon is crisp, scoop it out and reserve. Throw the onion in the skillet and sauté till it's translucent. Add it to the plate where you're holding the bacon. Sprinkle the whole thing with a bit of pepper.

Now add a little coconut oil if there's not enough grease left to prevent sticking. Get it hot and pan-fry your perch. Let them cook about 3 to 4 minutes per side, turning very carefully.

Plate the fillets, top with the bacon and onions, and serve.

YIELD: 4 servings

Nutritional Analysis
Per serving: 220 calories; 6 g fat; 36 g protein; 2 g carbohydrate; trace dietary fiber; 2 g net carbs

Blackened Catfish

If you've got the blackening spice on hand, this is super-quick and easy, and it's not much harder if you have to mix up the spice (see page 286)! I confess mine didn't actually get black, but it was darned good.

24 ounces (680 g) catfish fillets (6 ounces each)
1 lemon
4 tablespoons (24 g) Blackening Spice (page 286), divided
2 tablespoons (26 g) lard or fat of choice, or more as needed

Lay your fish on a plate. Squeeze the juice of the lemon evenly over the fish, both sides. Let it sit for 5 minutes to soak up the lemon juice.

Put your big, heavy skillet over medium-high heat and let it start getting hot while you . . .

Sprinkle half the Blackening Spice evenly on one side of the fish.

Skillet's hot! Add the lard to the skillet, enough to coat the bottom. Throw in the fish seasoned side down. While it's cooking, sprinkle the side of the fish that's up with the rest of the Blackening Spice. (Why didn't you just season both sides on the plate? Because some of the spice would be washed off in the juice remaining on the plate when you turned it, that's why.)

Give your fish about 3 to 4 minutes, then flip carefully, adding more fat to the skillet if you need to. Give it another 3 to 4 minutes, then serve.

YIELD: 4 servings

Nutritional Analysis
Per serving: 222 calories; 11 g fat; 28 g protein; 2 g carbohydrate; trace dietary fiber; 2 g net carbs

NOTE

Catfish is generally farmed, making it less than ideal. However, it's also one of those fish that's popular with fishermen. So if you have an angler or two in the family, send 'em off to get you a couple of cats—and tell them that since you're cooking the fish, they get to clean 'em.

Pecan Catfish

24 ounces (680 g) catfish fillet (6 ounces each)
2 lemons
4 tablespoons (60 ml) olive oil, divided
½ cup (56 g) chopped pecans
2 tablespoons (8 g) minced fresh parsley
2 teaspoons Paleo Worcestershire (page 293)

Preheat oven to 400°F (200°C, or gas mark 6). Grease a shallow baking dish.

Lay the catfish fillets in the baking dish. Cut 1 lemon in quarters and squeeze 1 each over the catfish fillets, turning to get both sides. Drizzle with half the olive oil. Cover loosely with foil and put in the oven, setting the timer for 10 minutes.

While the fish is baking, put your heavy skillet over low heat and start toasting the pecans in the rest of the olive oil. When they're toasty—maybe 4 to 5 minutes—squeeze in the juice from the other lemon. Stir in the parsley and the Worcestershire, too.

(continued)

When the timer beeps, uncover the fish, spread the pecan mixture on top, and put it back in the oven for another 3 to 5 minutes, then serve.

YIELD: 4 servings

Nutritional Analysis
Per serving: 389 calories; 28 g Fat; 29 g protein; 6 g carbohydrate; 1 g dietary fiber; 5 g net carbs

Wholly Mackerel!

Mackerel has a whole lot going for it: It's virtually always wild-caught; it's fatty, so it's full of omega-3s; and it's quite cheap. Some people say it's "too fishy," but as Mark Sisson points out, that's like complaining your steak is "too beefy."

1 pound (455 g) mackerel
2 teaspoons olive oil
Salt (optional) and black pepper
1 teaspoon paprika
1 small onion
Lemon

Preheat oven to 350°F (180°C, or gas mark 4). Grease a roasting pan big enough to hold your fish.

My mackerel came whole, not even gutted. I let That Nice Boy I Married do the honors of taking Mr. Fishy's insides out, but you could ask the guys at the grocery store to do it instead. Either way, wash the body cavity.

Use a sharp, thin-bladed knife to slash the mackerel to the bone at about 1-inch (2.5 cm) intervals, down both sides. This will let heat in to let it cook more quickly. Rub your mackerel all over with the olive oil.

Pepper your mackerel on either side, and salt if you wish. Sprinkle the paprika evenly over the whole thing.

Slice your onion paper-thin. Take half of it and lay it in the prepared roasting pan in a layer the length and width of your mackerel. Lay the mackerel on the row of onion and cover with the rest of the onion.

Put your mackerel in the oven and roast for 20 to 25 minutes. Plate carefully to avoid breaking it, scooping all the onions from the bottom of the pan to the top of the fish. Divide into 2 servings and serve with a wedge of lemon.

YIELD: 2 servings

Nutritional Analysis
Per serving: 302 calories; 9 g fat; 47 g protein; 5 g carbohydrate; 1 g dietary fiber; 4 g net carbs

Broiled Sardines

Fast, simple, classic. Not to mention inexpensive and nutritious. I got my fresh sardines at the local specialty fish market, ordering them a few days in advance.

32 ounces (905 g) sardines
Olive oil
Salt (optional) and black pepper
1 lemon

If your sardines haven't been gutted, you'll need to do that; mine came that way. Hold them under running water and rub gently to flake the scales off—this is very easy. Wash out the body cavity while you're at it.

Preheat broiler, with the rack as high as it can get and still allow for your roasting pan.

I have a nonstick roasting pan, but if you don't, line the pan with nonstick foil. Lay your sardines side by side in the roasting pan, drizzle them with olive oil (I used a couple of tablespoons' [28 ml] worth), and turn them till they're coated.

Now slide your sardines under the broiler. I gave mine 7 minutes, but check them by 5—how long it takes for them to be cooked through will depend on how big they are. You don't need to turn them; they're little enough that they'll cook through anyway, and they're fragile, so they may break if you try.

When they're done, plate and serve with pepper, salt if desired, and a lemon wedge.

YIELD: 4 servings

Nutritional Analysis
Per serving: 472 calories; 26 g fat; 56 g protein; 0 g carbohydrate; 0 g dietary fiber

NOTE

Be aware that these little fishies are pretty boney. They are, however, very flavorful, full of omega-3s, unlikely to be mercury contaminated, and not endangered. That's a pretty good list of attributes, if you ask me. If you'd like to fillet them, it's not that hard: Slit them down the belly, open them up like a book, pinch the spine, and pull. Most of the bones will come right out with the spine.

Crispy Smelts

Smelts are so little you eat them skin, bones, and all. That makes them super-nutritious!

1½ cups (135 g) finely ground pecans
3 tablespoons (21 g) coconut flour
2 teaspoons Creole seasoning
2 eggs
8 ounces (225 g) smelt, gutted and heads removed
Fat for frying
1 lemon

Put your pecans, the coconut flour, and the Creole seasoning in your food processor with the *S* blade in place. Run till the pecans are ground to a fine meal. Dump onto a rimmed plate.

On another rimmed plate, beat the eggs with a tablespoon of water till they're evenly mixed (no slippery globs of white).

Now dip your smelts in the egg, then roll them in the pecan meal. Put them all on a big plate as they're coated. Let them sit 20 minutes or so.

In a big, heavy-bottomed saucepan, heat an inch (2.5 cm) of fat quite hot. I don't own a frying thermometer, but you want your smelts brown and crispy within 3 to 4 minutes of hitting the fat. Just drop one in and see. I used a combination of coconut oil, lard, and bacon grease for flavor.

Now fry your smelts, 5 or 6 at a time, until brown and crisp. Add more fat to the pan as you need it. Serve the smelts good and hot, with a wedge of lemon to squeeze over them.

YIELD: 2 to 3 servings

(continued)

Nutritional Analysis

Per serving: Assuming 2 servings, each will have: 826 calories; 65 g fat; 36 g protein; 36 g carbohydrate; 16 g dietary fiber; 20 g net carbs. (The carb count comes from the "breading," which sticks pretty thickly. And I can't vouch for the calorie count, since it doesn't take the frying fat into consideration.)

Rebecca's Baked Cod with Lemon-Anchovy Sauce

Our recipe tester Rebecca loved the lemon-anchovy sauce so much she made up her own recipes using it. She said her family loved this.

24 ounces (680 g) cod fillets, in 4 servings
¼ cup (60 ml) olive oil
¼ cup (60 g) Lemon-Anchovy Sauce (page 280)

Preheat oven to 375ºF (190ºC, or gas mark 5).

Grease a baking dish the right size for your fillets. Lay them in the baking dish and drizzle each with olive oil.

Bake for 10 minutes. Then spread a tablespoon (15 g) of Lemon-Anchovy Sauce over each fillet. Let your fish bake another 7 to 10 minutes, or until flaky. Plate and serve with more sauce if desired.

YIELD: 4 servings

Nutritional Analysis

Per serving: 351 calories; 24 g fat; 31 g protein; 1 g carbohydrate; trace dietary fiber;1 g net carbs

NOTE

Rebecca says to tell you that she did this with salmon, too, and it was great. Different, but great.

Cod with Spinach and Tomatoes

I made this in individual gratin dishes, and it looked so pretty!

2 cups (60 g) fresh spinach
4 teaspoons (20 ml) olive oil
1 pound (455 g) cod fillet
1 lemon
Salt (optional) and black pepper
4 pinches cayenne
2 small tomatoes

Preheat oven to 350ºF (180ºC, or gas mark 4). If you've got 'em, grease individual baking dishes that will fit your fillets. If not, grease 1 larger roasting pan that will fit them all.

Either way, make beds with the spinach about the same size as your fillets. Now oil your fillets and lay 'em on the spinach. Squeeze the lemon over the fish. Pepper lightly, and salt if you wish, and sprinkle the fish with the cayenne.

Slice the tomato fairly thin, and cover the fish fillets with tomato slices.

Bake for 15 minutes and serve.

YIELD: 4 servings

Nutritional Analysis
Per serving: 152 calories; 6 g fat; 21 g protein; 5 g carbohydrate; 1 g dietary fiber; 4 g net carbs

Pan-Fried Cod with Chermoula

Lightly "floured" fish fillets, fried golden and topped with a flavorful sauce.

2 batches Chermoula (page 283)
24 ounces (680 g) cod fillet
⅓ cup (38 g) coconut flour
¼ teaspoon black pepper
⅛ teaspoon salt
¼ teaspoon paprika
8 tablespoons (104 g) lard, or as needed

Make your chermoula first! This is quick and easy.

Put your big, heavy skillet over medium-high heat.

Cut your fish into 4 servings.

In a rimmed plate, combine the coconut flour, pepper, salt, and paprika. Stir the whole thing together to combine.

Roll your cod fillets in the seasoned flour—you're just looking for a dusting.

By now your skillet is hot. Add a few tablespoons (39 g) of the fat, let it melt, and slosh it around.

Pick out the thickest bits of fish, and throw them in. Pieces a good inch thick (2.5 cm) will take at least 3 minutes per side, while the really thin ones may take less than a minute per side, so you need to start cooking the thick pieces first.

Pan-fry your fish, adding more fat as needed, until it's browned on both sides, and flaky clear through. Plate and top each serving with a couple of tablespoons (15 ml) of chermoula, then serve immediately.

YIELD: 4 servings

Nutritional Analysis
Per serving: 581 calories; 43 g fat; 34 g protein; 16 g carbohydrate; 9 g dietary fiber

Deviled Cod

That Nice Boy I Married gave the Cod with Chermoula a perfect 10. Then I made this the next night, and he said it was even better. Of course, he is awfully fond of anchovies.

2 tablespoons (14 g) coconut flour
2 pinches salt
2 pinches black pepper
2 pinches paprika
12 ounces (340 g) cod fillet
4 tablespoons (52 g) lard, for frying
6 anchovy fillets
2 teaspoons olive oil
½ lemon
1 teaspoon dried oregano
½ teaspoon dry mustard
2 pinches cayenne
4 tablespoons (60 ml) dry white wine

(continued)

On a rimmed plate combine the coconut flour, salt, pepper, and paprika. Roll the cod fillets in the seasoned flour, dusting them all over.

Put your big, heavy skillet over medium-high heat and melt the lard. When the skillet is hot, throw in your fish. You want to give it about 3 minutes per side, more or less, depending on thickness—you want it browned on both sides and flaky clear through.

In the meanwhile, mince the anchovies and put them in a small bowl. Add the olive oil, the juice of the lemon, the oregano, mustard, and cayenne. Mix it all up.

When the fish is done, plate it. Add the wine to the skillet and stir it about, scraping up all the nice browned bits. Now add the anchovy mixture and stir it into the wine. Let the mixture cook for a minute or two, just to reduce it a little. Then pour over the fish and serve.

YIELD: 2 servings

Nutritional Analysis
Per serving: 527 calories; 34 g fat; 36 g protein; 13 g carbohydrate; 7 g dietary fiber; 6 g net carbs

Baked Sea Bass

Roasting a whole fish is so incredibly simple and makes for an impressive presentation. Plus you have the head and skeleton to save for fish stock!

1 pound (455 g) sea bass, whole
2 tablespoons (28 ml) olive oil
Salt (optional) and black pepper
1 lemon
1 tablespoon (4 g) minced fresh oregano

Pick out a roasting pan big enough for your fish. Preheat your oven to 350°F (180°C, or gas mark 4).

We'll assume that Mr. Sea Bass has been cleaned. Wash him if he seems to need it and pat him dry with paper towels. Lay him in the roasting pan.

Now give your fish a nice massage with the olive oil. Get all over the outside and inside the body cavity. Sprinkle him with a little salt, if you use salt, and a little pepper—again, inside and out.

Slice half of your lemon paper-thin and mince your oregano. Sprinkle half of the oregano inside the body cavity of your bass. Lay a nice overlapping layer of lemon slices over that, then sprinkle the rest of the oregano on top of that.

Squeeze the remaining lemon half over your bass. Now lay a decorative row of lemon slices on top of your fish. Put the whole thing in the oven. Bake for 20 minutes, then check. Give your fish another 5 if he seems to need it, but don't overcook. (If you do, your fish will still taste good but fall apart when you serve it.)

YIELD: 2 servings

Nutritional Analysis
Per serving: 346 calories; 18 g fat; 42 g protein; 3 g carbohydrate; trace dietary fiber; 3 g net carbs

NOTE

My sea bass weighed in at 1.18 pounds, but there are certainly bigger sea bass in the world. If you've got a 2-pounder, just chop more oregano and slice another lemon, that's all. And bake a little longer.

Pink Grapefruit Skillet Shrimp

Okay, I admit it: Bourbon is made from corn. Leave it out if you must, but it definitely adds something to the dish.

24 ounces (680 g) shrimp
1 bunch scallions, sliced thinly
2 tablespoons (26 g) fat (I used lard, but coconut oil would be good, too.)
½ cup (125 g) Grapefruit Barbecue Sauce (page 276)
2 tablespoons (28 ml) bourbon

Your shrimp should be shelled, though I like to leave the tails on. Slice your scallions, including the crisp part of the green shoot.

Put your big, heavy skillet over medium-high heat. Add the fat and let it get hot.

Now throw in the shrimp and scallions and sauté, stirring frequently, until the shrimp are just pink and firm. Add the Grapefruit Barbecue Sauce and bourbon. Keep cooking for a few minutes, then plate the shrimp and spoon all the sauce over them. Serve with extra barbecue sauce, if you like, and plenty of napkins!

YIELD: 4 servings

Nutritional Analysis
Per serving: 295 calories; 12 g fat; 35 g protein; 5 g carbohydrate; trace dietary fiber; 5 g net carbs

Shrimp Stir-Fry

6 tablespoons (90 ml) coconut aminos, divided
2 pieces star anise
4 pinches ground cloves
4 cups (400 g) green beans, trimmed
1 large onion, 1-inch (2.5 cm) dice
1 pound (455 g) shrimp, shelled
2 tablespoons (16 g) grated gingerroot
¼ cup (52 g) coconut oil, or as needed, divided

In a small, nonreactive saucepan, combine the coconut aminos, star anise, and cloves. Bring to a simmer, turn off the heat, and let it steep, while you . . .

Trim your green beans and cut them into 2-inch (5 cm) lengths. Dice your onion, too, and if your shrimp isn't peeled, peel it. Grate your gingerroot and have it standing by.

Okay, prepped and ready to stir-fry! Put a wok (ideally) or a big, heavy skillet over highest heat. Add a few tablespoons (39 g) of coconut oil and let it get good and hot.

Throw in the shrimp and stir-fry till it's pink. Remove to a plate and hold while you . . .

Add another tablespoon (13 g) of oil to the skillet, then throw in the green beans and onion. Stir-fry till they're tender-crisp.

Return the shrimp to the wok, along with the ginger and the coconut amino–spice blend. Stir-fry for another minute or so, then serve.

YIELD: 4 servings

Nutritional Analysis
Per serving: 318 calories; 16 g fat; 26 g protein; 18 g carbohydrate; 5 g dietary fiber; 13 g net carbs

Asian Pepper Shrimp

3 tablespoons (39 g) coconut oil

4 cloves garlic

1 ½ pounds (710 g) shrimp, raw, peeled, tails on

1 tablespoon (15 ml) coconut aminos

1 tablespoon (15 ml) fish sauce

1 teaspoon black pepper

¼ cup (8 g) chopped fresh cilantro

Put your big, heavy skillet over low heat and melt the coconut oil. Mince or crush the garlic and throw it in. Stir it around in there for 2 to 3 minutes, keeping the heat low—you don't want the garlic to brown.

Now throw in your shrimp and sauté until pink through, probably 4 to 5 minutes, depending on how big they are. Now stir in the coconut aminos, fish sauce, and pepper. Sauté another minute or so.

Plate the shrimp and turn up the burner under the skillet. Heat the combined oil and liquid in the pan, letting it cook down for a minute or two. Pour this over the shrimp.

Top each serving with a tablespoon (2 g) of chopped cilantro and serve.

YIELD: 4 servings

Nutritional Analysis
Per serving: 280 calories; 13 g fat; 35 g protein; 4 g carbohydrate; trace dietary Fiber; 4 g net carbs

Ceviche

Don't go to the store with a particular fish in mind for your ceviche. Instead, go and ask the fish guys for the freshest, best fish they've got today. You could use shrimp or bay scallops, too.

2 pounds (900 g) fish fillets, cubed

10 limes

8 garlic cloves

1 tablespoon (1 g) minced fresh cilantro

1 habanero chile (Cheat and use a jalapeño if you're heat phobic.)

1 small red onion, sliced paper-thin

Salt and black pepper

16 large romaine lettuce leaves

2 avocados, diced

2 tomatoes, diced

Hot sauce

Cube your fish and put it in a nonreactive dish.

Juice the limes into a food processor. Squeeze them well, but avoid the membrane which can cause bitterness. Add the garlic and cilantro. Seed your hot pepper, remove the white ribs, and whack it into a few pieces; throw it into the processor. Pulse until the garlic cloves and pepper are finely minced. Pour this mixture over the fish. Slice the onion and add it to the fish.

Refrigerate and let your fish marinate overnight. Stir it up once or twice during the marinating process.

Next day, drain off most of the lime juice, leaving enough to keep the fish moist. Salt and pepper to taste.

Line plates with lettuce. Spoon the fish onto the lettuce, arrange the avocado and tomato dice over and around it, and serve with hot sauce for those who want it.

YIELD: 8 servings

Nutritional Analysis
Per serving: 221 calories; 9 g fat; 23 g protein; 17 g carbohydrate; 3 g dietary fiber; 14 g net carbs

"Linguine" with Clam Sauce

The almond meal here is seasoned similarly to Italian bread crumbs and makes a nice crunchy topping for the spaghetti squash. You could shell the clams before serving, but I think it makes a cool presentation this way.

24 clams, in the shell
1 cup (235 ml) water
6 cups (1.5 kg) cooked spaghetti squash
16 tablespoons (160 ml) olive oil, divided
1 cup (160 g) diced onion
20 cloves garlic, crushed (This seems like a lot of
· garlic, but this dish is traditionally garlicky.
   Use less if you insist.)
1 cup (60 g) minced fresh parsley
4 tablespoons (60 ml) lemon juice
½ cup (60 g) almond meal
4 pinches garlic powder
4 pinches onion powder
1 tablespoon (3 g) dried oregano

Put your clams in a big flat pan or skillet and add the water. Cover the pan, put it over a medium-high burner, bring to a simmer, and cook for 7 to 10 minutes, or until the clams are open.

While that's happening, cook your spaghetti squash and scrape it into strands if you don't have some on hand. (If you like spaghetti squash and eat it often, it's a great idea to cook it in advance, scrape it into strands and keep it in a zipper-lock bag in the fridge, ready to use.) I like to microwave my spaghetti squash—I just stab it all over with a carving fork and nuke it on high for 12 to 15 minutes, or sometimes more, depending on how big it is. If you've got cooked spaghetti squash on hand, you'll want to heat it through.

You'll need another skillet, 'cause you're going to sauté the onion and garlic in 8 tablespoons (120 ml) of olive oil. When the onion is translucent, scrape all of the oil and garlic and onion into the hot spaghetti squash, add the parsley and lemon juice, and keep it hot.

Somewhere in here your clams will be cooked! Turn off the burner and uncover the skillet so they don't overcook and become rubbery.

On the home stretch! Sauté the almond meal in the remaining olive oil until it's golden, adding the garlic powder, onion powder, and oregano while it toasts.

Now! Divide the spaghetti squash between plates. Top it with the toasted, seasoned almond meal, then put 6 clams on each serving. Done!

YIELD: 4 servings

Nutritional Analysis
Per serving: 567 calories; 41 g fat; 22 g protein; 34 g carbohydrate; 5 g dietary fiber; 29 g net carbs

Baked Clams

That Nice Boy I Married has long raved about the baked clams he used to get in an Italian restaurant in the Chicago suburbs. He said these were close, even without butter or bread crumbs!

1 cup (235 ml) extra-virgin olive oil
16 cloves garlic, crushed
24 clams, fresh, in the shell
1 cup (115 g) almond meal
4 tablespoons (16 g) minced fresh parsley
1 teaspoon paprika
4 pinches black pepper
Salt (optional)

Preheat oven to 350ºF (180ºC, or gas mark 4).

Measure the oil into a cup or bowl and crush the garlic into it. Let it sit and steep while you . . .

Bring a pot of water big enough to hold your clams to a boil. When it's boiling, throw in your clams, saying a short prayer for their wee mollusk souls. Let them boil for 5 minutes, until the shells open.

Use a slotted spoon to fish (Fish, get it?) your clams out of the water onto a plate and let them cool till you can handle them.

While they're cooling, pour about a third of the garlicky olive oil into a skillet, leaving the garlic in the cup, and put the skillet over medium heat. Add the almond meal and stir until it's toasty and golden, maybe 5 minutes. Stir in the parsley, paprika, and pepper, and salt if using. Remove from heat.

Use a knife or kitchen shears to remove the half of the shell that doesn't have the actual clam in it. Arrange them in a roasting pan—dump out any excess water first.

Now spoon some of that oil and crushed garlic into each clam, using it all up as you go.

Spoon the almond meal mixture over the clams—you'll have roughly a tablespoon (15 g) of almond meal per clam. Try to cover the meat of each clam.

Put 'em in the oven and bake for 10 minutes. Serve hot, with plenty of napkins.

YIELD: 4 servings

Nutritional Analysis
Per serving: 704 calories; 61 g fat; 26 g protein; 17 g carbohydrate; 1 g dietary fiber; 16 g net carbs

Roasted Oysters

Oysters—fresh in the shell
Lemon

Preheat oven to 400ºF (200ºC, or gas mark 6).

While it's heating, scrub your oysters if they need it. If any are open, tap them sharply. If they do not immediate close up tight, discard them—they are dead and unsafe to eat. Put your oysters in a roasting pan big enough to hold them, deep side of the shell down.

Now roast them for about 15 minutes, until they open slightly. Don't expect them to open wide—about ¼ to ½ inch (6 mm to 1 cm) is about it. If they don't open, again, they were dead going into the oven and are unsafe. Discard them. (Or do as I do, and feed them to chickens!) Serve them with a wedge of lemon, and don't forget to slurp the liquor out of the shells after you eat the meat. By the way, you may find tiny little crabs in your oysters. I find the little dead crabs kind of sad, 'cause they're cute, but it's just the way it goes with oysters. They're edible, but you'd be hard pressed to separate any appreciable quantity of meat from the shells.

Nutritional Analysis
According to the USDA, each oyster will have approximately 51 calories, 6 g protein, 2 g fat, 3 g carbohydrate, 0 g fiber, 3 g net carbs.

Crab Legs in Coconut Milk

You'd pay big bucks for this in a restaurant! You'll want to serve this with nutcrackers, nutpicks, or teeny seafood forks and lots of napkins. And save the shells for stock!

24 ounces (680 g) Alaskan king crab legs
1 cup (235 ml) coconut milk, divided
1 cup (235 ml) seafood stock (Kitchen Basics makes this, or you can make your own.)
1 lime
½ teaspoon Sriracha (page 276)
4 teaspoons (1.3 g) minced fresh cilantro

You'll need to choose a shallow pan big enough to hold your crab legs—I use my big, big sauté pan, which is considerably larger than my cast-iron skillet. You just need something wide and shallow that can go on the stove top.

In the pan, combine ½ cup (60 ml) of the coconut milk and all of the seafood stock. Bring this to a simmer, then squeeze in the juice from your lime. Give it a quick stir, then lay your crab legs as flat as you can in this bath. Cover the pan, set it to low, and let your crab legs simmer/steam for about 10 to 12 minutes, depending on how big they are.

Use a tongs to pull the cooked legs out of the pan, plate 'em, and keep them warm while you . . .

Turn up the heat under the pan a bit and cook down the sauce till it's getting syrupy. Whisk in the final ½ cup (60 ml) of coconut milk and the Sriracha, heat through, and pour into a little dish for dipping. Sprinkle the minced cilantro on top and serve with the legs.

YIELD: 2 servings

Nutritional Analysis
Per serving: 572 calories; 31 g fat; 65 g protein; 10 g carbohydrate; 3 g dietary fiber; 7 g net carbs

NOTE

Why only two servings? Because I can't fit more crab legs in my big sautéuse, that's why. If you've got a bigger pan, or are willing to do two batches, go ahead and double this. Or this could serve four as a first course.

Scallops with Vermouth

Super-fast, super-elegant!

3 tablespoons (39 g) coconut oil or lard, divided
24 ounces (680 g) sea scallops
4 medium shallots, minced
2 medium onions, diced
4 teaspoons (4 g) minced fresh mint,
4 tablespoons (60 ml) dry vermouth

Put your big skillet over medium-high heat and let it get hot.

Have everything prepped and waiting; the cooking itself goes very fast. Pat your scallops dry with a paper towel, have your shallot minced and onion diced, and your mint ready to go. Place your bottle of vermouth by the stove (you can take a snort on the way, if you like).

Okay, everything's prepped and waiting, and the skillet is hot. Melt half the coconut oil, throw in the scallops, and fry them golden on both sides. Remove to plates and keep warm.

Add the rest of the oil if it looks like you need it and sauté the shallot and onions for just a few minutes, till softened. Add the mint and the vermouth and let it continue to cook until the vermouth is about half cooked away. Pour over the scallops and serve.

YIELD: 4 servings

Nutritional Analysis
Per serving: 284 calories; 12 g fat; 29 g protein; 11 g carbohydrate; 1 g dietary fiber; 10 g net carbs

Tomato-Mint Scallops

It's so easy to impress people with scallops. A gimme, really.

4 shallots, minced
2 tablespoons (28 ml) olive oil
2 medium tomatoes, ¼-inch (6 mm) dice
1 tablespoon (6 g) minced fresh mint,
¼ cup (60 ml) dry vermouth
24 ounces (680 g) scallops

Put your skillet over medium-low heat while you mince the shallot. Pour in the olive oil and start the shallot sautéing while you dice your tomato. Throw that in, too, and stir it up. Mince your mint, and stir it in.

Sauté for a few minutes till the tomatoes have softened and given off some liquid. Stir in the vermouth, then the scallops. Cover the pan, turn the burner to its lowest setting, and let the scallops poach in the sauce till done—maybe 5 minutes, depending on the size of your scallops. Turn them halfway through the cooking time. Serve the scallops on a bed of the sauce.

YIELD: 4 servings

Nutritional Analysis
Per serving: 248 calories; 8 g fat; 29 g protein; 9 g carbohydrate; 1 g dietary fiber; 8 g net carbs

Simplest Shad Roe

Shad roe is a seasonal delicacy—the eggs of the shad fish, available only for a few weeks in the spring. These teeny, teeny fish eggs come in a membrane, with two lobes, each lobe making a serving.

1 shad roe
¼ cup (52 g) lard or fat of choice
2 tablespoons (8 g) minced fresh parsley
½ lemon

In a heavy-bottomed skillet the right size for your roe, melt the lard over very low heat. Add the roe, cover, and cook very gently for about 15 minutes, turning once, very carefully. Do your best not to rupture the membrane the roe is in.

When the roe feels firm—like a medium-rare steak—separate the lobes. Serve each with 1 tablespoon (4 g) of parsley scattered on top and a wedge of lemon to squeeze over it.

YIELD: 2 servings

Nutritional Analysis
Per serving: 235 calories; 26 g fat; trace protein; 2 g carbohydrate; trace dietary fiber; 2 g net carbs

Slightly More Complicate Shad Roe

Just as the title says, this is only a teeny bit more complicated than the Simplest Shad Roe.

1 shad roe
¼ cup (52 g) lard or fat of choice
2 teaspoons lemon juice
2 teaspoons Paleo Worcestershire (page 293)
2 teaspoons anchovy paste
2 tablespoons (8 g) minced fresh parsley

Cook your roe as in Simplest Shad Roe. While it's cooking, mix together the lemon juice, Worcestershire, and anchovy paste till smooth. Might as well mince the parsley while you're at it.

When your roe is done, again, separate the lobes and plate them. Divide the sauce between them, scatter the parsley on top, and serve.

YIELD: 2 servings

Nutritional Analysis
Per serving: 251 calories; 26 g fat; 2 g protein; 2 g carbohydrate; trace dietary fiber; 2 g net carbs

Chapter 9

CHICKEN AND OTHER POULTRY

I have this mental image of early man, newly migrated to Asia, noticing the jungle fowl who walked around, flying only short distances. They no doubt also noticed that these birds fell asleep at sunset, making them easy to grab. (As a keeper of chickens, I can tell you that they become quite docile in the dark. If a chicken is making a fuss, all you have to do is tuck its head under your jacket, and it will calm right down.) Our ancestors surely started hunting these birds immediately, and it can't have taken much longer to realize that the same birds laid a lot of tasty eggs. Jackpot!

No wonder chickens were among the earliest domesticated animals and have become one of the most widespread. There are now more chickens in the world than any other species of bird. May as well eat them!

Keep in mind, though, that chickens not only often are given antibiotics and/or hormones but also are often soaked in salt water. This increases the weight, but you're paying chicken prices for water. Too, factory chicken farms are not known for their discriminating choice of feed.

Local pasture-raised chickens are your best bet. If you've never eaten a chicken that was actually allowed to walk around in the sunshine, eating grass and bugs, you'll be surprised at the richer flavor and the somewhat darker color of the meat. This is the chicken your great grandparents ate. No wonder everyone remembers great grandma's fried chicken so fondly!

If you're stuck with grocery store chicken, read the label and look for the cleanest brand. My local grocery stores have started selling chicken raised without hormones or antibiotics.

In particular: If you, like me, are a fan of chicken liver, pony up the bucks for organically raised chicken liver. The old wheeze about the liver being "the filter of the body" is inaccurate; the liver processes toxins so they can be eliminated from the body. The junk doesn't just build up in there, like sludge in your car's oil filter. (The liver also does a whole lot of other things. And truly, I can't think of a more nutritious food than liver.) Still, toxins do go to the liver to be processed, so you should buy the ones from chickens fed the fewest possible toxins.

Walnut Roasted Chicken

4 pounds (1.8 kg) whole chicken
¼ cup (60 ml) olive oil, divided
1 garlic clove, crushed
¼ cup (30 g) finely chopped walnuts
½ teaspoon minced fresh rosemary
1 tablespoon (4 g) minced fresh parsley
1 lemon, quartered

Preheat oven to 375°F (190°C, or gas mark 5).

In a small bowl, mix 3 tablespoons (45 ml) of the olive oil, garlic, walnuts, rosemary, and parsley.

With your hands, gently loosen the skin on the chicken breast. Spread the walnut mixture evenly under the skin. Quarter the lemon and put it in the body cavity.

Rub the chicken all over with the rest of the olive oil. Put it on a rack in a roasting pan and put it in the oven.

Roast for 1½ to 1¾ hours, or until the drumstick moves easily and the juice runs clear when the thigh is pierced to the bone.

Remove the chicken to a platter. Remove the lemon wedges but put them on the platter with the chicken. Let it rest for 10 to 15 minutes before carving.

If you like, make pan gravy with the drippings, but this is not essential. (See Simple Pan Gravy, page 289.)

Carve the chicken and serve with the lemon wedges to squeeze over it.

YIELD: 5 servings

Nutritional Analysis
Per serving: 671 calories; 52 g fat; 48 g protein; 3 g carbohydrate; trace dietary fiber; 3 g net carbs

Tandoori Chicken

The flavor of this marinade is to die for!

4 pounds (1.8 kg) chicken pieces (cut-up chicken, bone in, skin on)
1 cup (230 g) Cocoyo (page 28)
3 tablespoons (45 ml) lemon juice
3 tablespoons (24 g) grated gingerroot
4 garlic cloves, crushed
1 tablespoon (15 ml) white wine vinegar
1 tablespoon (15 ml) garam masala
1 tablespoon (7 g) ground cumin
1 tablespoon (7 g) paprika
½ teaspoon cayenne
¼ teaspoon ground nutmeg
½ teaspoon turmeric (optional)
½ teaspoon salt
2 tablespoons (28 ml) olive oil
2 tablespoons (26 g) coconut oil, melted

In a mixing bowl, whisk together the Cocoyo, lemon juice, gingerroot, garlic, vinegar, garam masala, cumin, paprika, cayenne, nutmeg, turmeric if using, salt, and olive oil. Put this mixture in a big darned zipper-lock bag, and add the chicken. Seal the bag, pressing out the air as you go. Turn the bag and squish everything around until you're certain the chicken pieces are coated all over—don't skimp on this step. Throw the bag in the fridge and let the chicken marinate overnight. Should you open the refrigerator, give the bag a little more squishing.

When you're ready to cook your chicken, preheat your oven to 425ºF (220ºC, or gas mark 7). Line a roasting pan with foil and put a rack in it—this is important, as you want dry heat to reach all sides of the chicken, instead of it cooking in the drippings.

Arrange the chicken on the rack, pieces not touching. If by chance any part of any piece of chicken is uncoated with the marinade, use a brush to touch it up with marinade from the bag.

Put your chicken in the oven and roast for 20 to 30 minutes—20 minutes if your chicken parts are on the small side, 30 minutes if they're big. Leave the oven closed during this time.

Now use a tongs to turn the chicken and let it roast another 10 minutes. Turn off the oven and leave it in there for 20 to 30 minutes. Don't open the oven and let the heat out.

Remove from the oven, transfer to a platter, and serve.

YIELD: 6 servings

Nutritional Analysis

Per serving: 623 calories; 49 g fat; 40 g protein; 5 g carbohydrate; 1 g dietary fiber; 4 g net carbs. This assumes that you'll be eating all the marinade, which you won't.

NOTE

Garam masala is a traditional Indian spice blend. Look in the international aisle of your big grocery store, at a good health food store, or order online. If you can't find it, add:

¼ tablespoon ground cumin
¼ tablespoon ground coriander
¼ tablespoon ground cardamom
⅛ tablespoon black pepper
½ teaspoon ground cinnamon
1 tablespoon (6.5 g) ground cloves
⅛ teaspoon ground nutmeg

Adding some turmeric to taste is optional because it is not strictly traditional in tandoorin marinades. I like it and it appears to have numerous health benefits.

Grapefruit Chicken Kabobs

My sister Kim served these to party guests and tells me everyone wanted the recipe.

½ ruby red grapefruit
1 tablespoon (15 ml) dry sherry
3 tablespoons (45 ml) coconut aminos
¼ cup (60 ml) chicken broth
2 tablespoons (28 ml) white balsamic vinegar or use the Grapefruit Balsamic Vinegar on page 283
1 teaspoon tomato paste (You can buy this in tubes, so you don't have to open a whole can for this.)
2 tablespoons (28 ml) olive oil
1 teaspoon grated gingerroot
Garlic clove, crushed
2 pounds (900 g) boneless, skinless chicken breast
1 medium onion, chunked
1 red bell pepper, cut in squares
1 green bell pepper, cut in squares

Juice the half grapefruit into a bowl, getting every drop you can. Add the sherry, coconut aminos, chicken broth, white balsamic, tomato paste, olive oil, ginger, and garlic. Mix thoroughly.

Cut up your chicken and vegetables. Put them in a big zipper-lock bag, pour in the marinade, and seal it, pressing out the air as you go. Turn the bag to coat everything, then toss it in the fridge for at least a half hour.

If you're going to cook these outside, get your grill going. If the weather's bad, use your broiler.

(continued)

Drain the marinade into a small, nonreactive saucepan and bring to a boil. Boil for a minute or two to kill any germs.

Thread the chicken and vegetables on skewers (if you're using bamboo skewers, soaking them in water for a half hour first will keep them from catching fire during cooking). Don't pack stuff too tightly.

Now grill or broil, turning often, for 10 to 12 minutes, or until done through. Baste a few times while cooking with the reserved marinade.

Serve kabobs with what remains of the marinade poured over them.

YIELD: 6 servings

Nutritional Analysis

Per serving: 257 calories; 9 g fat; 35 g protein; 8 g carbohydrate; 1 g dietary fiber; 7 g net carbs

Asparagus, Shiitake, and Chicken Skillet

Once I'd made the Asparagus and Shiitake Sauté, I found myself thinking of other things to do to it. Like this.

½ medium onion, diced
8 ounces (225 g) boneless, skinless chicken breast, diced
Asparagus and Shiitake Sauté (page 98)
1 tablespoon (15 ml) coconut aminos

This is easy—add the onion and chicken breast to the skillet while preparing the Asparagus and Shiitake Sauté. Stir in the coconut aminos at the end, with the orange. Serve as-is, or over Cauli-Rice (page 87).

YIELD: 3 servings

Nutritional Analysis

Per serving: 275 calories; 7 g fat; 23 g protein; 36 g carbohydrate; 7 g dietary fiber; 29 g net carbs

Baked Oriental Chicken

Make this easy by buying precut pineapple chunks in a tub.

3 pounds (1.5 kg) chicken pieces
Salt and black pepper
1 clove garlic
3 tablespoons (39 g) coconut oil
1 teaspoon paprika
2½ ounces (70 g) pineapple
1 tablespoon (15 ml) coconut aminos
1 tablespoon (15 ml) reduced chicken broth
¼ medium onion
1 tablespoon (8 g) grated gingerroot

Salt and pepper the chicken all over, and lay it, skin side down, in a roasting pan just big enough to hold it.

Put everything else in a blender or food processor and run until you have a paste. Spread it all over the bottom side of the chicken, which is up.

Bake at 375ºF (190ºC, or gas mark 5) for half an hour. Turn the chicken over, baste with the combined sauce and pan juices, and bake for another half an hour. Serve with the pan drippings spooned over it, and over any Cauli-Rice dish you might serve with it.

YIELD: 5 servings

Nutritional Analysis

Per serving: 483 calories; 36 g fat; 35 g protein; 3 g carbohydrate; trace dietary fiber; 3 g net carbs

Chicken Satay

Classic Thai street food. The serving size assumes that you're having these as a snack or appetizer; figure it'll serve three as a main course.

1 pound (455 g) skinless, boneless chicken breast
1 stalk lemon grass
1 large shallot
2 garlic cloves
1½ teaspoons Sriracha (page 276)
1½ inches (3.5 cm) gingerroot, peeled and chopped
1½ teaspoons ground coriander
1 teaspoon turmeric
2 teaspoons ground cumin
3 tablespoons (45 ml) coconut aminos
3 tablespoons (45 ml) fish sauce
2 tablespoons (28 ml) olive oil (I used light olive oil—EVOO *doesn't* have that Asian flavor.)
3 tablespoons (60 g) honey
3 drops liquid stevia

Put a package of bamboo skewers in water to soak. (If you've got plenty of metal skewers, you can use those instead.)

One at a time, put your chicken breasts in a zipper-lock bag and seal it, pressing out the air as you go. Use a heavy, blunt object to pound the chicken out to ¼-inch (6 mm) thick. Remove from the bag and repeat until all your chicken is pounded.

Now cut your chicken into strips about ¾-inch (2 cm) wide. Put 'em back in that zipper-lock bag—unless it's developed a hole. If it has, you need a new bag.

Put the rest of the stuff in your food processor and run until you've got something between a lumpy sauce and a paste. Pour/scrape the sauce into the bag with the chicken. Seal it up, again, pressing out the air as you go. Then turn and massage the whole thing till the paste is evenly worked through the chicken strips. Let them sit for at least an hour, and all day while you're at work is great.

When cooking time comes, fire up the grill. Thread your chicken strips, accordion-fashion, on your now fireproof bamboo skewers. Figure about 5 minutes per side should do it. Serve with Not-Peanut Sauce, page 277.

You can broil these instead, if the weather is not conducive to grilling.

YIELD: 6 servings

Nutritional Analysis
Per serving: 202 calories; 7 g fat; 19 g protein; 16 g carbohydrate; 1 g dietary fiber; 15 g net carbs

Chicken-Chutney Spread/ Stuffing

I made this to stuff mushrooms, but it made a great omelet, too. Or you could stuff it into celery stalks. Whatever.

1 cup (140 g) cooked chicken, diced (I used dark meat.)
1 tablespoon (15 g) brown mustard
1 ½ tablespoons (24 g) Peach Chutney (page 280)
3 scallions
1 tablespoon (4 g) chopped fresh parsley
¼ cup (60 g) Mayonnaise in the Jar (page 278)
⅛ teaspoon salt

Assemble everything in your food processor and pulse till you've got a rough paste. This will keep a day or two in a snap-top container in the fridge.

YIELD: 4 servings

Nutritional Analysis
Per serving: 293 calories; 14 g fat; 14 g protein; 35 g carbohydrate; 7 g dietary fiber; 28 g net carbs

Chicken Taco Filling

A simple, inexpensive family-pleaser. I used bone-in chicken thighs because I had them, but boneless, skinless thighs would work great.

4 chicken thighs, skinned
½ cup (120 ml) water
1 lime
2 garlic cloves, crushed
1 tablespoon (7.5 g) chili powder
Salt to taste

Arrange your chicken thighs in a medium-size skillet—you don't want too much extra room. Add the water and squeeze in the lime juice. Bring to a simmer, turn the burner down, and cover the pan. Simmer for 25 to 30 minutes, or until the chicken is done through. Turn off the burner. Remove the chicken from the pan, retaining the liquid, place on a cutting board, and let it cool.

When the chicken is cool enough to handle, pick the meat off the bones (if you used bone-in thighs), then chop the meat into ½-inch (1 cm) chunks.

Return the chopped chicken to the pan and turn the burner back on to low heat. Stir in the garlic and chili powder.

Let the chicken mixture cook, stirring now and then, until the liquid has evaporated. Salt and pepper to taste. Use for all your taco-meat-y needs!

YIELD: 4 servings

Nutritional Analysis
Per serving: 211 calories; 15 g fat; 17 g protein; 3 g carbohydrate; 1 g dietary fiber; 2 g net carbs

Chicken Soft Tacos

Who doesn't like this? You'll get 6 tacos out of this, but it's up to you whether there are 1 or 2 to a serving.

1 batch Chicken Taco Filling (opposite)
Eggy Wraps (page 78)
1 small red onion, diced fine
1 medium tomato, ¼-inch (6 mm) dice
¼ cup (4 g) minced fresh cilantro
1 avocado, diced
¼ head iceberg lettuce, shredded
½ cup (115 g) Coconut Sour Cream (page 29)
Hot sauce

This is an every-man-for-himself sort of meal. Just put everything out and let people construct their own soft tacos. These quantities are variable, of course; I just eyeballed it for the nutritional count.

YIELD: 6 servings

Nutritional Analysis
Per serving: 354 calories; 26 g fat; 19 g protein; 12 g carbohydrate; 3 g dietary fiber; 9 g net carbs

Dill Chicken

An example of how a few simple ingredients can add up to a really delicious dish. I would recommend serving on a bed of Cauli-Rice (page 87), to soak up the extra sauce.

6 chicken thighs
2 tablespoons (26 g) fat (I used lard.)
1 cup (235 ml) low-sodium chicken broth
1 teaspoon dried or 2 teaspoons fresh dill
½ teaspoon black pepper
½ medium onion, diced fine
2 tablespoons (8 g) minced fresh parsley

Put your heavy skillet over medium-high heat and start browning the chicken thighs in the fat. I started mine skin-side down to make sure the skin got a nice golden color, but you want them lightly browned all over.

In the meanwhile, measure the chicken broth and stir the dill and pepper into it. Dice your onion, too.

When your thighs are golden all over, remove them to a plate and add the onion to the skillet, turning the heat down a tad. Sauté the onion in the fat in the skillet until it's translucent. Now put the chicken thighs back in on top of the onion and pour the broth over it all. Scatter the parsley over the whole thing.

Turn the heat down to low and put a lid on the skillet. Set your oven timer for 25 minutes.

When the timer beeps, take the lid off the skillet and let the thighs keep simmering until the sauce reduces down to a nice syrupy consistency. Serve the thighs with the sauce.

YIELD: 6 servings

Nutritional Analysis
Per serving: 250 calories; 19 g fat; 18 g protein; 1 g carbohydrate; trace dietary fiber; 1 g net carbs

Creamed Curried Chicken

Serve over Cauli-Rice (page 87), with crumbled bacon and Peach Chutney (page 280).

1 ½ pounds (710 g) skinless, dark meat chicken
1 cup (235 ml) chicken broth
2 teaspoons coconut oil

1 teaspoon curry powder
1 cup (235 ml) unsweetened coconut milk
½ cup (120 ml) water, or as needed
Salt (optional)

Put your skinned chicken leg-and-thigh in a big saucepan and add the broth. Cover and put over low heat. Let the whole thing simmer till the chicken is done and tender, about 45 minutes. Fish out the chicken with a tongs, and put it on a plate to cool.

In the meanwhile, let the broth continue simmering until it's reduced to about ⅓ cup (80 ml). How will you know? Pour it into a Pyrex measuring cup—you have other plans for that saucepan.

Rinse the saucepan and put it back on the low burner. Add the coconut oil. When it melts, add the curry powder and sauté it, stirring constantly, for just a minute or two. Add the broth, coconut milk, and water. Whisk it all up.

By now the chicken has cooled enough for you to handle it, we hope. Strip the chicken off the bones and chop it up, or snip it up with a kitchen shears. Stir the chicken into the sauce and it's ready to use!

YIELD: 3 servings

Nutritional Analysis
Per serving: 295 calories; 24 g fat; 18 g protein; 3 g carbohydrate; trace dietary fiber; 3 g net carbs

Crunchy Deviled Chicken

A simple way to vary "chicken again."

4 chicken legs (leg and thigh quarters)
½ cup (60 g) almond meal
1 teaspoon curry powder
1 teaspoon cayenne
1 teaspoon dry mustard
4 tablespoons (60 ml) olive oil

Preheat oven to 350ºF (180ºC, or gas mark 4).

Cut the drumsticks from the thighs.

On a rimmed plate, combine the almond meal with the seasonings.

Rub each piece of chicken with a little olive oil, then roll in the seasoned almond meal. Arrange in a roasting pan.

Roast for an hour or so, until juices run clear when pierced to the bone, and the coating is crunchy.

YIELD: 5 servings

Nutritional Analysis
Per serving: 405 calories; 30 g fat; 30 g protein; 4 g carbohydrate; trace dietary fiber; 4 g net carbs

Deviled Roast Chicken

I love whole chickens! Somehow they seem more special to me than cut-up chicken. They are usually cheaper, too.

2 tablespoons (28 ml) olive oil
2 tablespoons (28 ml) lemon juice
1 teaspoon coconut aminos
3 anchovy fillets
1 teaspoon brown mustard
½ teaspoon red-pepper flakes
5-pound (2 kg) whole chicken

Preheat oven to 350ºF (180ºC, or gas mark 4).

Put everything but the chicken in your blender and run till the anchovies are pulverized. Pour this into a dish, using a rubber scraper to get it all.

Put your chicken on a rack in a roasting pan. When the oven's hot, slide the chicken in and set your timer for 20 minutes.

Baste your chicken with the sauce you've made, getting every inch of skin you can. Put the chicken back in and give it another 20 minutes. Baste again.

After another 20 minutes, baste one more time—by now you'll be running out of sauce. Give the chicken another 20 to 30 minutes, or until the juices run clear when the thigh is pierced to the bone.

Remove the chicken from the oven and let it rest for 10 minutes before carving.

YIELD: 8 servings

Nutritional Analysis
Per serving: 548 calories; 44 g fat; 35 g protein; 1 g carbohydrate; trace dietary fiber; 1 g net carbs

Orange-Herb Chicken

This takes a little doing, but it looks really cool and tastes wonderful. Turns a simple whole chicken into a company meal.

5-pound (2 kg) whole chicken
2 oranges
2 tablespoons (28 ml) olive oil
5 garlic cloves, divided
Poultry seasoning
Salt (optional) and black pepper
1 large onion
2 celery ribs
1 carrot
1½ cups (355 ml) chicken broth

Preheat oven to 350°F (180°C, or gas mark 4).

To start, halve one of the oranges and grate the rind of one half into a small dish. Squeeze in the juice, too. Add the olive oil, a clove of garlic, crushed, and ½ teaspoon of poultry seasoning. Set this aside while you . . .

Slice the remaining half orange paper thin. It's okay if you wind up with some partial slices; that's better than cutting them too thick. Sprinkle your orange slices lightly on one side with poultry seasoning.

Using clean hands, loosen the chicken's skin while leaving it intact. Work orange slices, seasoned side down, up under the skin, keeping them flat against the flesh. Cover as much of the flesh as you practically can. I managed to cover the breast and most of the outer thighs.

Salt and pepper the inside of the chicken (skip the salt if you like) and dust it with more poultry seasoning. Use your hands to rub it around a bit. Now . . .

Cut your second orange in eighths. Peel and halve a couple of the garlic cloves. Whack the onion into chunks. Now stuff the body cavity of the chicken as full as you can with onion chunks and orange wedges, and those halved garlic cloves, too.

Whack the celery ribs into chunks somewhere around 3 to 4-inches (7.5 to 10 cm) long. Peel the carrot and whack it into similar lengths. Throw both of these in a roasting pan, along with the rest of the onion chunks and orange wedges, and the last couple of garlic cloves, peeled, but whole.

Back to your chicken. Salt and pepper him all over if you like, then use about half the orange juice/olive oil mixture to give him a nice massage. Cover every millimeter of the skin of your chicken. Place him on top of the veggies in the roasting pan—they'll be your rack. Put Mr. Chicken in the oven. Set your timer for 30 minutes.

When the timer beeps, baste the chicken with some of the remaining orange juice mixture. Put it back in the oven, and give it another 20 to 30 minutes. You want the juices running clear when you pierce the thigh joint, and the leg moving easily. Baste it again, if you've got some baste left, give it another 5, then pull it out of the oven and put it on a platter to rest.

Pick the orange slices out of the pan, squeezing the juice into the vegetables as you do so. Now scoop out the vegetables and put 'em in your blender. Pour the broth into the roasting pan and stir it around for a minute, dissolving all of the nice brown bits, then pour the broth into the blender, too. Run till the vegetables are puréed, and you've got a smooth, creamy gravy. Pepper, and salt if desired, and serve with the chicken.

Some Cauli-Rice (page 87) to absorb the gravy would be a great go-along with this.

(continued)

Roasted Chicken with Creamy Apple-Horseradish Sauce

This recipe started with a hunch that the roasted apples and onion would make a good sauce. It worked out even better than I hoped.

1 apple
½ large onion
2 pounds (900 g) chicken, cut up
Salt (optional)
Black pepper (for seasoning), plus ¼ teaspoon for sauce
1 teaspoon lemon juice
1 teaspoon horseradish
½ teaspoon Paleo Worcestershire (page 293)
½ teaspoon brown mustard

Preheat oven to 350ºF (180ºC, or gas mark 4). Grease a roasting pan just big enough to hold your chicken.

Quarter your apple, cut out the core, and slice it about ⅛-inch (3 mm) thick. Peel and slice your onion about the same thickness. First make a layer of apples in the bottom of the roasting pan, then top with the onion.

Sprinkle your chicken lightly with pepper, and with salt if desired. Arrange on top of the apples and onions. Put the whole thing in your oven. Set your timer for 30 minutes.

When the timer beeps, baste the chicken with the liquid that will have started accumulating in the bottom of the pan and put it back in for another 30 minutes. Check then to see if it's golden and done, and the edges of the apple and onion layers browning a bit. If it's looking good, baste it again and give it just 10 more minutes. If it needs longer, hey, give it a little longer.

Once crisp and golden, place chicken on a platter to keep it warm.

Dump everything from the bottom of the pan into your blender. Turn the sucker on, and add the lemon juice, horseradish, Worcestershire, mustard, and ¼ teaspoon pepper. You will now have a gorgeously creamy and irresistibly flavorful sauce. Taste it and see if it needs just a suspicion of salt—I used a scant ¼ teaspoon—and pour into a sauce boat. Serve with the chicken.

Orange-Ginger Chicken Stir-Fry

1½ pounds (710 g) boneless, skinless chicken thighs
1 navel orange
¼ lemon
3 tablespoons (39 g) coconut oil
1 tablespoon (8 g) grated gingerroot
½ cup (120 ml) chicken stock
1½ pounds (710 g) bok choy, trimmed and
   roughly chopped

1 bunch scallions, trimmed and cut in 1-inch
  (2.5 cm) pieces
Salt and black pepper
4 teaspoons (11 g) toasted sesame seeds, to
  garnish (optional)

Cut your chicken into 1½-inch (3.5 cm) chunks. Grate a teaspoon of orange zest, then squeeze all the juice from the orange and the quarter lemon into a small dish.

Put your wok or big, heavy skillet over high heat and add the coconut oil. Let it get hot before you add the chicken in batches, stir-frying for 3 to 4 minutes, till golden.

Add all the chicken back to the skillet. Add the ginger and orange–lemon juice mixture, plus the chicken stock. Let the whole thing simmer for a couple of minutes.

Stir in the bok choy and scallions and stir-fry till the bok choy is just barely wilted.

Salt and pepper to taste, then plate and top each serving with 1 teaspoon of sesame seeds.

YIELD: 4 servings

Nutritional Analysis
Per serving: 328 calories; 20 g fat; 28 g protein; 9 g carbohydrate; 3 g dietary fiber; 6 g net carbs

Rosemary Chicken with Lemon and Peppers

Serve this on a bed of Cauli-Rice (page 87), with a crisp salad on the side, and the family will ask, "What's the occasion?"

2 pounds (900 g) chicken thighs, bone in, skin on
Salt and black pepper
4 tablespoons (60 ml) olive oil, divided
1 large onion, sliced
3 banana peppers
8 cloves garlic, minced
4 sprigs rosemary or 1 tablespoon (3.3 g) dried
  rosemary needles
1 cup (235 ml) chicken broth
1 large lemon

Salt and pepper the chicken all over. Put 2 tablespoons (28 ml) of the olive oil in your big, heavy skillet, over medium-high heat, and start browning the chicken. You want it golden all over.

In the meanwhile, peel and slice your onion about ¼-inch (6 mm) thick. Remove the stem and seeds from your peppers, and slice them cross-wise, again, ¼-inch (6 mm) thick.

When the chicken is golden all over, remove it from the skillet. Add the rest of the oil and sauté the vegetables. When they've softened, add the garlic to the skillet, along with the rosemary.

Measure the chicken broth. Grate a couple of teaspoons (3 g) of zest from the lemon into a little dish and reserve. Halve the lemon and squeeze the juice into the broth.

(continued)

Pour the broth/lemon juice mixture over the vegetables. Now place the chicken thighs on top. Cover the skillet, but leave a crack for some steam to escape. (I call this the "tilted lid" technique.) Let the whole thing simmer for 40 minutes or so. Check to see if you need more broth and add a couple of tablespoons (28 ml) if you need to.

When your chicken is very tender, remove it from the skillet. Turn up the heat and let the remaining broth reduce till it's getting a little syrupy. Taste it and add a little more salt and pepper if you think it needs it. Spoon the peppers, onions, and sauce over the chicken, sprinkle a little lemon zest over each portion, and serve.

YIELD: 6 servings

Nutritional Analysis
Per serving: 406 calories; 32 g fat; 23 g protein; 7 g carbohydrate; 2 g dietary fiber; 5 g net carbs

NOTE

If you can't get banana peppers, you could use green bell peppers. Or hot Hungarian wax peppers. Or Anaheims, the mildly hot chiles usually used for Chiles Rellenos. You don't want to use something seriously hot, though—no jalapeños, much less habaneros!

Moroccan Chicken

Wendy McCullough, who tested this, tells us, "I did not pay my family to say anything nice and I heard things from 'I'm not a fan of lemon but this is good' to 'the flavors blended nicely together' to 'Mom, may I have the last piece? This is good!'" I'd call that a big thumbs-up.

4 chicken legs, cut into drumsticks and thighs
Salt and black pepper
3 tablespoons (45 ml) olive oil
1 large onion
3 carrots
2 teaspoons paprika
1 teaspoon black pepper
1 teaspoon ground ginger
¼ teaspoon turmeric
¼ teaspoon ground cinnamon
1 garlic clove, crushed
1 cup (235 ml) chicken broth
1 lemon

Cut the thighs from the drumsticks and salt and pepper them lightly.

Put your big, heavy skillet over medium-high heat, add the olive oil and let it get hot. Now add the chicken and brown it all over—you will probably have to do this in a couple of batches. When it's browned all over, transfer to a casserole. Turn your oven on to 350°F (180°C, or gas mark 4).

Turn the burner to medium low and add the onion to the skillet. Sauté till it's translucent. While that's happening, peel the carrots and slice them thin. Add them to the skillet and sauté a few more minutes.

Add the spices and garlic and keep sautéing, stirring, for another 3 or 4 minutes. Now add the chicken broth. Bring to a boil, stirring all the while.

Cut the lemon in eighths and arrange them around the chicken pieces in the casserole. Pour the mixture from the skillet over the whole thing. Cover—foil works fine—and bake for 30 minutes. Uncover and give it another 15. Serve with the pan liquid and vegetables spooned over the chicken, and the baked lemon wedges on the side.

A bed of Cauli-Rice would be wonderful under this, to soak up the broth!

YIELD: 4 servings

Nutritional Analysis
Per serving: 456 calories; 31 g fat; 33 g protein; 11 g carbohydrate; 3 g dietary fiber; 8 g net carbs

Orange-Pecan Chicken Skillet

Lisa C. tested this recipe and sends these notes from her husband: Mixing it up well is important because it tastes REALLY good when you get a hit of each of the flavors— the pecans, orange, chicken, veggies. Great mouthfeel. You see the cauliflower and you expect risotto and you just want to eat more.

½ **head cauliflower**
3 **tablespoons (39 g) lard or fat of choice, divided**
¼ **cup (28 g) chopped pecans**
1 **pound (455 g) boneless, skinless chicken breast**
½ **medium onion, chopped**
½ **red bell pepper, diced**
½ **orange**
1 **lemon**
2 **tablespoons (28 ml) chicken Broth Concentrate (page 27)**
¼ **cup (15 g) minced fresh parsley**
Salt and black pepper

Trim the leaves and the very bottom of the stem from your cauliflower. Whack it into chunks and run them through the shredding blade of your food processor (see page 87). Steam your Cauli-Rice lightly—I give mine 6 minutes on high in the microwave.

Prep everything first: Chop your pecans (if you didn't buy them that way). Dice your chicken—go for ½-inch (1 cm) cubes. Chop your onion and dice your red pepper.

Put your big, heavy skillet over medium heat and melt a couple of teaspoons (4 g) of the fat. Add the pecans and stir until they smell toasty. Don't walk away! Those pecans would as soon burn as look at you. Just stir them till they're done. Remove to a plate and reserve.

Turn up the burner to medium high. Add another tablespoon of the fat, let it melt, then add the chicken. Stir-fry it till the pink is gone. Remove it from the skillet and reserve it, too.

Melt the rest of the fat! Add the onion and red pepper. Stir-fry till the onion is translucent.

Somewhere in here your Cauli-Rice will be done. Uncover it immediately to stop the steaming!

Add the chicken back to the onion and pepper, then dump in the Cauli-Rice. Grate in the zest of your half orange and squeeze in the juice. Squeeze in the juice of the lemon, too, and add the concentrated chicken broth. Stir everything up really well.

Now stir in the pecans and the parsley. Salt and pepper to taste, and serve.

YIELD: 4 servings

Nutritional Analysis
Per serving: 307 calories; 18 g fat; 28 g protein; 10 g carbohydrate; 3 g dietary fiber; 7 g net carbs

Salsa-Mustard Chicken

This combination of salsa and mustard is terrific. Try it with pork chops, too.

3 pounds (1.3 kg) chicken legs, cut in pieces
2 tablespoons (26 g) coconut oil
½ cup (130 g) salsa
¼ cup (60 g) brown mustard
3 tablespoons (45 ml) unsweetened coconut milk
1 tablespoon (15 ml) chicken Broth Concentrate
  (page 27)

Put your big, heavy skillet over medium-high heat and start browning the chicken in the coconut oil. When it's golden on both sides, remove to a plate and hold it while you . . .

Add the salsa to the skillet and sauté it in the coconut oil and drippings, scraping up the browned stuff from the bottom. Cook till the onion and tomatoes have softened.

Stir in the mustard, coconut milk, and chicken broth concentrate, stirring till it's all well blended. Turn the burner down to low.

Put the chicken back in the skillet on top of the sauce. Cover the skillet and let the whole thing simmer for about 40 minutes. Serve the chicken with the sauce.

YIELD: 3 servings

Nutritional Analysis
Per serving: 752 calories; 54 g fat; 62 g protein; 3 g carbohy-drate; 1 g dietary fiber; 2 g net carbs

Coconut Chicken

Saskia, who tested this recipe, says that she and her husband were skeptical about the idea of mustard with this, but that they found it tasted great.

2 pounds (900 g) boneless, skinless chicken breast
2 teaspoons ground cumin
¾ teaspoon ground coriander
½ teaspoon cayenne
¼ teaspoon salt
⅛ teaspoon black pepper
2 eggs
2 cups (160 g) finely shredded coconut meat
Coconut oil, to grease
Spicy brown mustard or Dijon mustard

Cut your chicken into 6 servings.

Mix the seasonings together. Now sprinkle them evenly all over the chicken. Let this sit for 10 minutes or so.

Break your eggs into a rimmed plate, add a tablespoon (15 ml) of water, and beat them till they're well-blended—no big strings of white. Spread your coconut on another rimmed plate.

Now dip each piece of chicken into the eggs, coating both sides, then dredge it in the coconut, coating it completely. Put 'em all on a big plate, put 'em in the fridge, and let 'em sit for an hour or so, for the coating to solidify a bit. (You can do this a day in advance if you like.)

Preheat your oven to 400°F (200°C, or gas mark 6). Grease a shallow baking tin liberally with coconut oil and lay the chicken in it.

Bake for 7 minutes, then use a pancake turner to flip the pieces, being careful not to dislodge the coconut. Add a little more coconut oil if the pan seems to need it. Give the breasts another 7 minutes, or until golden all over. Now cover with foil and let them cook another 15 to 20 minutes, or until done through. (Timing will depend on the thickness of your chicken breasts.

Serve with mustard for dipping.

YIELD: 6 servings

Nutritional Analysis
Per serving: 298 calories; 15 g fat; 37 g protein; 5 g carbohydrate; 3 g dietary fiber; 2 g net carbs

Not-Quite-Mexican Chicken

Our recipe tester Arleen said, "Don't dare change a thing!!!!!" She rated this an 11.

3½ pounds (1.5 kg) chicken—breasts and thighs are best. Bone in, skin on.
Salt and black pepper
1 tablespoon (13 g) lard
½ onion—chopped
1 medium tomato, seeded and in ¼-inch (6 mm) dice
2 tablespoons (28 ml) chipotle chile canned in adobo (or see Chipotles in Adobe, page 294)
1 tablespoon (7.5 g) chili powder
1½ tablespoons (25 ml) balsamic vinegar
1 teaspoon ground cumin
½ teaspoon salt
⅛ teaspoon ground cinnamon

Preheat oven to 350ºF (180ºC, or gas mark 4).

Salt and pepper your chicken and arrange it in a roasting pan. Start it roasting, while you . . .

Put your big, heavy skillet over medium heat and melt the lard. Sauté the onion until it's soft and caramelized. While that's happening, slice your tomato across the equator and squeeze out the seeds. Then dice 'er up.

When the onion is soft and golden, add the tomato to the skillet. Continue cooking, stirring often, until it softens enough that you can mash it easily with a fork. Mash up the tomato, turn the burner down, and keep simmering for 5 minutes, stirring often to prevent scorching.

Transfer the onions and tomatoes to your blender or food processor and add the chipotle. Run till you have a smooth purée.

Add the chili powder, balsamic vinegar, cumin, salt, and cinnamon and run the processor to blend.

Let the chicken roast for about an hour, basting occasionally with the juices collecting in the pan.

When the chicken is golden brown and the juices run clear when a joint is pierced, coat with the sauce. Let it roast just another 5 to 10 minutes. Serve with any remaining sauce.

YIELD: 5 servings

Nutritional Analysis
Per serving: 534 calories; 39 g fat; 40 g protein; 4 g carbohydrate; 1 g dietary fiber; 3 g net carbs

NOTE

Arleen does suggest doubling the sauce, just so you'll have some left over the next day to dip chicken wings in.

Spring Chicken

If you like, you could swap out the mint for fresh oregano, for a different take on the same dish.

5 pounds (2 kg) chicken pieces
Salt and black pepper
2 pounds (900 g) asparagus
1 bunch scallions
½ cup (48 g) fresh mint
1 garlic clove, peeled and chopped
2 lemons
¼ cup (60 ml) olive oil

Preheat oven to 350°F (180°C, or gas mark 4).

If your chicken's not in serving pieces, do that first—cut legs from thighs, wings from breasts. Salt and pepper it lightly, then arrange it in a roasting pan.

Snap the ends off your asparagus spears where they want to break naturally. Arrange them over and around the chicken pieces. Slice up the scallions and scatter them over the whole thing, too.

Put the mint and garlic in your food processor, with the S blade in place. Squeeze in the juice of the lemons and add the olive oil. Run till the garlic is pulverized. Now pour this mixture evenly over the chicken.

Cover the pan with foil. Bake for 40 minutes, uncover, and give it another 10. Pierce to the bone at a place where the meat is thick; if the juices run clear, your chicken is done. If not, give it another few minutes. Then serve!

YIELD: 6 servings

Nutritional Analysis
Per serving: 663 calories; 48 g fat; 50 g protein; 7 g carbohydrate; 2 g dietary fiber; 5 g net carbs

Sweet-and-Sour Chicken

Sweet-and sour chicken without the sugar or cornstarch! You'll notice this is substantially similar to the Sweet and Sour Pork recipe (page 237).

1 pound (455 g) boneless, skinless chicken breast—in
  1-inch (2.5 cm) cubes
½ large onion, in 1-inch (2.5 cm) chunks
1 green bell pepper, in 1-inch (2.5 cm) chunks
6 ounces (170 g) fresh pineapple chunks
2 tablespoons (28 ml) coconut aminos
2 tablespoons (28 ml) cider vinegar
1 tablespoon (8 g) grated gingerroot
2 drops liquid stevia extract (optional)
3 tablespoons (39 g) coconut oil, divided
Glucomannan, if desired

Have everything cut up and standing by the stove. In a small dish, mix together any juice from the pineapple chunks with the coconut aminos, vinegar, gingerroot, and stevia, if using. Put this by the stove as well.

Put a wok or big skillet over highest heat. When it's good and hot, put in about half the coconut oil and let it melt. Throw in the chicken and stir-fry for 4 to 5 minutes, or till done through. Scoop out onto a plate and reserve.

Add the rest of the oil to the wok or skillet. Throw in the onion and pepper and stir-fry till they're tender-crisp.

Now add the chicken back to the skillet along with the pineapple chunks. Stir it up, then stir in the sauce. Keep stir-frying for another minute or two. Thicken the sauce slightly with glucomannan if desired, and serve.

YIELD: 3 servings

Nutritional Analysis
Per serving: 354 calories; 18 g fat; 34 g protein; 14 g carbohydrate; 2 g dietary fiber; 12 g net carbs

Easy Curried Chicken

This is a paleo riff on a dish I came up with the first year I was low carbing, and I think the coconut milk improves it. If ever a dish cried out for Cauli-Rice (page 87) to serve it on, this is it. The sauce is way too good to waste a single drop.

3 pounds (1.3 kg) chicken pieces, skinned
1 medium onion, chopped
4 cloves garlic, crushed
2 tablespoons (12.6 g) curry powder
1 cup (235 ml) unsweetened coconut milk
½ cup (120 ml) chicken broth

Preheat oven to 350ºF (180ºC, or gas mark 4).

Skin your chicken, cut the legs from the thighs if they're not already cut apart, and arrange in a roasting pan.

Chop the onion and scatter it around the chicken.

Crush the garlic and mix it in with the curry powder, coconut milk, and chicken broth. Pour this all over the chicken.

Roast for an hour, turning the chicken pieces over every 20 minutes or so, so that both sides soak in the sauce.

After an hour, pull your chicken out of the oven and transfer to a platter.

Now, look at the stuff in the pan. Looks awful, doesn't it? But it smells amazing, no? Pour and scrape it all into your blender or food processor and run the thing. Your sauce will magically smooth out, becoming creamy, golden, and beautiful. Serve the chicken with this sauce.

YIELD: 6 servings

Nutritional Analysis
Per serving: 424 calories; 31 g fat; 30 g protein; 5 g carbohydrate; 1 g dietary fiber; 4 g net carbs

Creamy Tarragon Chicken

Our tester Michelle recommends serving this over spaghetti squash instead of the Cauli-Rice. Sounds good to me!

1½ pounds (710 g) boneless, skinless chicken breast
Salt and black pepper
2 tablespoons (28 ml) olive oil
1 tablespoon (4 g) finely chopped fresh tarragon
1 cup (235 ml) unsweetened coconut milk
¼ lemon
2 teaspoons chicken Broth Concentrate (page 27)

Cut your chicken into ½-inch (1 cm) slices. Salt and pepper lightly.

Put your big, heavy skillet over medium-high heat and slosh the oil around. When the oil it hot, add the chicken in batches—don't crowd it. Sauté till it's done through and has a little golden color.

Return all the chicken to the skillet and stir in the tarragon.

Pour in the coconut milk, and Broth Concentrate and stir it up. Let it simmer for a few minutes to cook down a little. Now squeeze in the juice from your lemon half and stir it in. Salt and pepper to taste, and serve.

This might also be good over a bed of Cauli-Rice (page 87), but that's up to you.

YIELD: 4 servings

Nutritional Analysis
Per serving: 373 calories; 23 g fat; 39 g protein; 2 g carbohydrate; trace dietary fiber; 2 g net carbs

Chicken Livers en Brochette

1 ½ pounds (710 g) chicken livers
¾ teaspoon dried marjoram
¾ teaspoon dried thyme
½ teaspoon salt (optional)
⅛ teaspoon black pepper
10 slices bacon
8 ounces (225 g) mushrooms
1 onion, in 1-inch (2.5 cm) chunks
¼ cup (60 ml) olive oil
¼ cup (60 ml) dry white wine

Cut your livers in two where the two lobes naturally separate. (If you have a smallish one without lobes, it's already separated.)

Mix together the marjoram, thyme, salt if using, and the pepper. Sprinkle the livers all over with the seasonings.

Cut your bacon slices in half crosswise. Now wrap each liver chunk in a half slice of bacon and spear it on a skewer, piercing through the overlapped ends of the bacon. In between bacon-wrapped liver chunks, add a mushroom and a couple of leaves of onion. Aim for 6 evenly loaded skewers.

Now you can grill your livers over a charcoal fire, should you have one, or you can broil 'em a good 4 to 5 inches (10 to 13 cm) from your broiler's flame. Either way, mix together the oil and the wine and baste the skewers before cooking, and every few minutes while broiling. Give them no more than about 5 minutes per side; overcooked liver is an abomination, but you do want your bacon done.

Serve hot!

YIELD: 6 servings

Nutritional Analysis
Per serving: 306 calories; 19 g fat; 25 g protein; 7 g carbohydrate; 1 g dietary fiber; 6 g net carbs

Guatalote en Mole Poblano

This is classic Mexican cuisine, and amazing. You'll want to make the mole in advance; it's time consuming. So make the sauce some rainy Saturday and stash it in the freezer. Roasting the turkey is simple, and you can just heat the sauce up.

2 turkey thighs
Salt and black pepper
3 tablespoons (39 g) lard
2 cups (500 g) Mole Poblano (page 291)
Fresh cilantro (optional)

Salt and pepper your turkey thighs. Melt the lard in the bottom of a Dutch oven and start browning the thighs in it. In the meanwhile, preheat the oven to 325ºF (170ºC, or gas mark 3).

When the thighs are golden all over, cover the Dutch oven and put it in the oven. Let it cook for 60 to 90 minutes, till it's good and tender.

Ten minutes or so before the turkey is done, heat the mole. Carve the turkey and serve the mole spooned over it. A little snipped cilantro on top is pretty, but not essential.

YIELD: 6 servings

Nutritional Analysis
Per serving: 238 calories; 18 g fat; 14 g protein; 7 g carbohydrate; 2 g dietary fiber; 5 g net carbs

Turkey Chili

This is "proper" chili, which is to say, it has no tomatoes. Well, that's what's proper in Texas, anyway. I don't know how they feel about the turkey.

¼ cup (52 g) lard, or bacon grease or olive oil
3 pounds (1.3 kg) ground turkey
1 quart (946 ml) unsalted chicken broth
6 tablespoons (45 g) chili powder
10 cloves garlic, crushed
1½ teaspoons ground cumin
1 teaspoon dried oregano
1 teaspoon cayenne, or more or less, to taste
½ teaspoon black pepper
1 tablespoon (6 g) unsweetened cocoa powder
2 teaspoons honey
3 tablespoons (21 g) paprika
⅓ cup (47 g) shelled pumpkin seeds (pepitas)
Salt to taste

Put a big, heavy kettle on the stove—a Dutch oven would be ideal. Melt the lard and start browning and crumbling the ground turkey. When all the pink is gone, add the chicken broth, chili powder, garlic, cumin, oregano, cayenne, pepper, cocoa powder, honey, and paprika. Bring to a simmer and let it cook slowly for an hour.

In the meanwhile, run the pepitas through your food processor until they're the texture of corn meal.

After an hour, stir in the ground pepitas. Let it simmer another 15 to 20 minutes, then serve.

YIELD: 6 servings

Nutritional Analysis
Per serving: 522 calories; 31 g fat; 49 g protein; 13 g carbohydrate; 4 g dietary fiber; 9 g net carbs

Asian-American Lettuce Wraps

1 pound (455 g) ground turkey
1 medium onion, minced
2 garlic cloves
1 teaspoon five-spice powder
3 tablespoons (45 ml) coconut aminos
1 teaspoon dark sesame oil
1 teaspoon grated gingerroot
3 tablespoons (50 g) Not-Peanut Sauce (page 277)
1 tablespoon (6 g) chopped fresh mint
1 tablespoon (1 g) chopped fresh cilantro
1 head butter lettuce

In a big, heavy skillet, start browning and crumbling the turkey. Mince the onion and garlic and stir them in—add a touch of oil if you need to, to keep the turkey from sticking.

When the pink is gone from the turkey, stir in the five-spice powder, the coconut aminos, the dark sesame oil, the ginger, and the Not-Peanut Sauce and let the whole thing cook another few minutes, until the liquid that has cooked out of the turkey cooks down. Now stir in the mint and cilantro.

(continued)

Serve with lettuce leaves to wrap it in and more Not-Peanut Sauce. A little chopped cucumber and scallion is nice with this, too, but not essential.

YIELD: 3 servings

Nutritional Analysis
Per serving: 264 calories; 14 g fat; 28 g protein; 5 g carbohydrate; 1 g dietary fiber; 4 g net carbs

Poultry Hash

Roast extra chicken and make this later in the week, or use up leftover turkey. Figure this for four servings alone, or six servings if you top it with fried eggs.

1 medium turnip, diced about ¼ inch (6 mm)
½ medium celery root, diced ¼ inch (6 mm)
1 large onion, diced
2 tablespoons (26 g) lard or chicken fat, or other fat
2 cups (280 g) diced chicken or turkey, already cooked
1½ tablespoons (10.8 g) poultry seasoning
½ teaspoon salt (optional)

Dice the turnip and celery root and start them steaming together—mine took about 6 minutes on high in the microwave. (If you plan to steam on the stove top first, get the water heating in your steamer before you start dicing vegetables.)

In the meanwhile, dice your onion. Put your big, heavy skillet over medium-low heat, melt the lard in it, and start the onion sautéing.

Now cut up your chicken or turkey—I actually snipped mine into bits with a poultry shears, rather than dicing it with a knife. Just reduce it to bits similar in size to your bits of vegetable.

When the turnip and celery root are al dente, add them to the skillet. Add the diced chicken or turkey and the poultry seasoning and salt and stir it all up. Now spread your hash in an even layer in your skillet, cover with a tilted lid, and let it cook for 7 to 8 minutes. (Set a timer!)

Stir your hash up and spread it in an even layer again. Give it another 7 to 8 minutes with a tilted lid. Repeat one more time.

Now uncover the skillet, stir the hash up, spread it out, pat it down a little with the flat of your spatula, and turn up the heat just a tad—don't go crazy and crank it way up, just increase it a little. All you want is to get a little browned crust on the bottom of your hash. Give it maybe 5 minutes.

If you plan to serve your hash with fried eggs on top, this is the time to start frying 'em. If not, just let your hash brown a little, then serve.

YIELD: 4 servings

Nutritional Analysis
Per serving: 327 calories; 24 g fat; 22 g protein; 6 g carbohydrate; 1 g dietary fiber; 5 g net carbs

Thanksgiving Weekend Hash

I really did make this the day after Thanksgiving. Worth roasting extra brussels sprouts for.

1 cup (160 g) diced onion
2 cups (280 g) diced turkey
2 tablespoons (26 g) bacon grease
3 cups (270 g) leftover roasted brussels sprouts
Salt and black pepper

Dice your onion and turkey. Put your big, heavy skillet over medium-low heat and melt the bacon grease. Sauté the onion in it until it's translucent.

Add the turkey and brussels sprouts and turn the burner down to medium low. Stir everything together and use the edge of your spatula to break up the brussels sprouts a bit.

Spread in an even layer in the bottom of your skillet and let it sit for 5 minutes. Turn the mixture over, pat it out in an even layer again, and let it cook another 5 minutes. Salt, pepper, and serve.

YIELD: 3 servings

Nutritional Analysis
Per serving: 283 calories; 15 g fat; 25 g protein; 12 g carbohydrate; 4 g dietary fiber; 8 g net carbs

Turkey, Mushroom, and Pea Pod Stir-Fry

1 pound (455 g) turkey breast, boneless and skinless
2 medium onions, halved and sliced
2 cups (140 g) sliced mushrooms
2 cups (150 g) snow peas or sugar snap peas
6 tablespoons (90 ml) coconut aminos
1 teaspoon white balsamic vinegar
1 tablespoon (8 g) grated gingerroot
2 garlic cloves, minced
6 tablespoons (78 g) coconut oil, divided

Cut your turkey in bite-size pieces. Halve and slice your onions. Slice your mushrooms if they didn't come that way. Pinch the ends off your pea pods and pull off any strings.

In a small dish, stir together the coconut aminos, white balsamic, gingerroot, and garlic. Set this by the stove.

Put a wok or big skillet over highest heat and melt half the oil. When it's hot, add the turkey and stir-fry till the pink is gone. Remove to a plate or bowl.

Melt the rest of the oil in the wok or skillet and throw in the onion. Stir-fry for a minute or so, then add the mushrooms and pea pods. Stir-fry for another minute or two, until the pea pods have turned brilliantly green.

Add the turkey back to the skillet and add the coconut amino mixture. Stir-fry for another minute, then serve.

YIELD: 3 servings

Nutritional Analysis
Per serving: 504 calories; 29 g fat; 41 g protein; 20 g carbohydrate; 4 g dietary fiber; 16 g net carbs

NOTE

Feel free to use chicken breast in this instead. For that matter, you could use leftover roasted turkey—just skip the step of stir-frying the turkey. Instead, dice it up and add it at the end with the seasoning mixture, and then stir-fry long enough to heat through.

Pan-Seared Duck Breast with Plum Sauce

Regina, our tester, says that the combination of taste and ease of preparation make this a 10!

24 ounces (680 g) duck breast, boneless, skin-on
  (4 breast halves.)
½ teaspoon salt
¼ teaspoon black pepper
¼ teaspoon dry mustard
1 pinch ground rosemary
1 tablespoon (13 g) bacon grease
2 tablespoons (28 ml) olive oil
Plum Sauce (page 282)

Preheat oven to 375°F (190°C, or gas mark 5). Using a very sharp, thin-bladed knife, score the skin on each duck breast into 1½-inch (3.5 cm) diamonds.

Mix together the salt, pepper, mustard, and rosemary. Rub the breasts with the seasoning mixture.

Put your big, heavy skillet over medium-high heat. Let it get good and hot before you . . .

Add the bacon grease and olive oil. Swirl them together and let them heat a minute. Then add the duck, skin-side down. Let it cook without disturbing it until the skin is brown and crunchy, about 5 minutes.

Now put the skillet in the oven and let it cook another 12 minutes or so. Timing will depend a bit on how thick your breasts are and how rare you like your duck.

Plate skin-side up and let rest 5 minutes. Now slice, and serve with the Plum Sauce.

YIELD: 4 servings

Nutritional Analysis
Per serving: 643 calories; 62 g fat; 15 g protein; 6 g carbohydrate; 1 g dietary fiber; 5 g net carbs

NOTES

This is calculated on 6-ounce (170 g) duck breasts, but that's not a big deal—if your butcher has bigger ones, so much the better!

That calorie count is predicated on the inaccurate notion that you'll eat all the pan drippings. You won't be getting that many calories. But save the drippings to cook with—I mean, bacon/olive/duck fat? How great is that?

Regina didn't have an ovenproof skillet, so she transferred the duck and the grease from her skillet into a glass baking dish before putting it in the oven, and she said it worked fine.

Basic Roast Duck

6 pounds (2.8 kg) duck, whole
1 medium onion
1 large carrot
1 large celery rib
Herbs, if desired
1 garlic clove (optional)

Preheat oven to 450°F (230°C, or gas mark 8).

Prick your duck's skin all over, especially the areas with a thick layer of fat underneath. Don't pierce the meat, just the skin. Prick liberally—you're letting the excess fat cook out, so your duck won't be greasy. Use the tip of a sharp knife for this, or the tines of a carving fork. I find my dinner forks are not sharp enough for this job.

Peel and chunk the onion and carrot and chunk the celery. Stuff these into the body cavity. If you have some fresh herbs on hand—rosemary and/or sage are good—put a few sprigs in there, too. You can rub your duck with a cut clove of garlic, too, if you like.

Truss your duck—tuck the wing tips underneath and tie the legs together. Put it on a rack in a roasting pan.

When the oven's up to 450°F (230°C, or gas mark 8), put the duck in, turning the temperature down to 350°F (180°C, or gas mark 4). Now roast your duck 20 minutes to the pound or 2 hours for a 6-pounder. Every half hour or so, pull your duck out and repeat the pricking of the fatty areas.

When your duck is done, remove the duck to a platter and let it rest for 10 to 20 minutes. In the meanwhile, take the rack out of the roasting pan and pour off the duck fat to use for cooking. Pull the veggies out of the body cavity and discard.

If you like, you can make Giblet Gravy according to the recipe on page 290. More traditionally, you can serve it with a fruit-based sauce, the Plum Sauce on page 282, the Grapefruit Barbecue Sauce on page 276, or the Raspberry Barbecue Sauce, page 275.

YIELD: 6 servings

Nutritional Analysis
Per serving: 1,334 calories; 129 g fat; 38 g protein; 3 g carbohydrate; 1 g dietary fiber; 2 g net carbs

NOTES

The calorie count and fat count do not reflect all the fat that will cook off your duck. 1 cup (208 g) of duck fat will have about 1,600 calories, so figure the actually calorie count will be considerably lower than this. That said, duck is rich. That's why it's so good.

If you like, swap that carrot in the body cavity for a quartered orange.

Unsightly but Delicious Duck

This takes FOREVER, but it did yield an extremely tender and tasty duck.

6 pound (2.8 kg) duck, whole
Salt and pepper, or other preferred seasonings

Preheat your oven to 300°F (150°C, or gas mark 2).

Using a very sharp, thin, straight-bladed knife, slash the breast skin of your duck into roughly 1-inch (2.5 cm) diamonds. Be careful—you want to cut the skin and fat, but not the flesh of the duck. This is a little tricky. Turn the duck over and do the same wherever the skin is thick, with a goodly layer of fat under it.

Use the point of your knife to pierce the skin all over.

Truss your duck—tuck the wing tips underneath and tie the legs together. Put it on a rack in a roasting pan, placing it breast down. Put the duck in the oven and set a timer for 1 hour.

When the timer goes off, pull your duck out of the oven. Pierce the skin all over again and turn the duck breast-side-up. Put the duck back in the oven and set the timer for another hour.

Repeat this performance twice more: Remove the duck from the oven, pierce the skin all over, turn it over, and put it back. You're roasting it for a total of 4 hours.

Remove the duck from the oven and turn it up to 400°F (200°C, or gas mark 6). While the oven is heating . . . Lift the rack, duck and all, out of the pan and set it somewhere safe—I think the sink is ideal, because drips are easy to clean up. Carefully pour the accumulated duck fat into an old glass jar. (If you want to know how much you get, you could pour it into a Pyrex measuring cup instead. I got a bit more than a cup.) Save the fat for cooking; it's delicious!

Put the rack back in your roaster, with the duck breast-side-up. You can now salt and pepper or otherwise season your duck—you didn't do it earlier because you wanted that duck fat to be pristine. I sprinkled mine with Chicken Seasoning Redux (page 285), which is great on any poultry. Put the duck back in the now-400°F (200°C, or gas mark 6) oven. Let him crisp for 10 minutes.

You can then glaze your duck if you like. The original recommendation was for a soy-sauce-and-molasses glaze, but we're not doing that. I used the Grapefruit Barbecue Sauce on page 276. Baste the duck liberally with whatever sauce you choose and give it a final 10 minutes.

Remove to a platter, let it rest for 10 minutes, then carve and serve with any remaining sauce.

YIELD: 6 servings

Nutritional Analysis

Per serving: 1,321 calories; 129 g fat; 38 g protein; 0 g carbohydrate; 0 g dietary fiber, 0 g net carbs. I got a little more than a full cup of duck fat from this, over 1,600 calories' worth. That has to be subtracted from these nutritional calculations. But I intend to add that duck fat to other foods!

NOTES

I read about this method of cooking a duck and always wanted to try it. It takes forever and involves turning the sucker over a few times, but, as advertised, it does yield a very moist, flavorful, ungreasy duck with crispy skin. It also yields a whole lot of duck fat, which is exceedingly delicious for cooking with.

However, unlike the illustrations I saw when I read about this, my duck did not come out picture perfect. Instead, it was so tender that the wings had started coming off. Still, it tasted so good, and I got so much yummy duck fat, I thought I'd tell you about it.

Chapter 10

BEEF

We've been scolded so long for eating beef that it's good to consider that ruminant herd animals, of which cows are a prime example, for millennia formed the backbone of the human diet. Even grocery store beef is an excellent source of protein, B6, B12, and zinc. Switch to grass-fed beef, and it's a prime source of omega-3 fatty acids as well. Eat quality beef without guilt.

Let's start with a couple of the most paleo recipes you'll ever find!

Steak Tartare

An old-time classic. Some serve this on a bed of greens, but I like the look of the rings of garnish surrounding the beef.

Every chef from Anthony Bourdain to Emeril Lagasse is adamant that steak tartare must be hand chopped. So sharpen up your chef's knife and get out your cutting board! Slice your beef very thin one direction, then the other. Keep chopping—you want a texture that's not as mushy as ground beef but definitely something you can make a patty with. I spent about 5 minutes chopping.

8 ounces (225 g) beef tenderloin (filet mignon)

¼ teaspoon salt

¼ teaspoon black pepper

1 tablespoon (15 ml) Paleo Worcestershire (page 293), plus extra for serving

2 teaspoons hot sauce, such as Tabasco, plus extra for serving

1 shallot, minced

2 tablespoons (17.2 g) capers

2 tablespoons (8 g) minced fresh parsley

2 egg yolks, whole

2 tablespoons (30 g) Dijon mustard

Put your lovely chopped beef in a bowl and add the salt, pepper, Worcestershire, and hot sauce. Those measurements are what I used, but feel free to season your beef to taste. Mix it up well!

Form your beef into 2 patties and place them on plates. Make a hollow the diameter of an egg yolk in the middle of each patty.

Mince your shallot and surround each patty with a circle of it. Drain the capers and add that to the shallot, again, ringing the patty. Mince your parsley and add to the Rings of the Beef Patty.

Separate your egg yolks from the whites—save the whites for some other use or just feed 'em to the dog. Slip a raw egg yolk into each of the hollows you made in the beef patties.

Put a tablespoon (15 g) of mustard on each plate, and serve.

To eat, each diner mixes his egg yolk with his beef, then takes a little of the garnishes on each forkful of meat. Pass additional Worcestershire and hot sauce for those who want them.

YIELD: 2 servings

Nutritional Analysis
Per serving: 405 calories; 32 g fat; 24 g protein; 4 g carbohydrate; 1 g dietary fiber; 3 g net carbs

NOTE

It's hard to get more paleo than raw meat and eggs. This means, however, that your meat and eggs must be of the best quality. This is no place for second-rate foodstuffs. I paid $28/pound for filet mignon from the local specialty butcher, and it was worth every penny.

Marrow Bones

Wild animals go for the marrow first. If you haven't tried it, it's time to get over being squicked out. Not only is marrow as paleo as it gets, it tastes like meat-flavored butter. How can you resist that? (Me, I was eating marrow before I knew it was supposed to be "gross." I always sucked the marrow out of the bones in my lamb chops. Yum.)

Beef or lamb marrow bones, in 2-inch (5 cm) lengths

Preheat your oven to 350°F (180°C, or gas mark 4). Arrange your bones on end in a pan just about the right size to hold them. (Obviously, they'll stand up more easily if you put them thick-end down.)

Roast your bones for about 20 minutes. Then scoop out the marrow—Victorian households had narrow spoons for just this purpose, but you'll probably have to use a butter knife—salt, pepper, and eat. That's it.

I'm afraid I have no nutritional stats for this recipe, but you can figure it's mostly fat with a bit of protein. Get those bones from grass-fed stock, and you'll get plenty of omega-3s and CLA (a fat with anticancer and antiobesity properties).

Filet Mignon with Creamy Mustard Sauce

Want to impress a special someone on date night? Here's how.

2 beef filet mignon, 1½-inches (3.5 cm) thick
Salt and black pepper
1 tablespoon (12.5 g) lard or other fat (bacon grease would be good!)
2 tablespoons (20 g) minced shallot
2 tablespoons (30 g) mustard, whole grain or Dijon (The whole grain would look pretty!)
¼ cup (60 g) Coconut Sour Cream (page 29)
1 tablespoon (4 g) minced fresh parsley (A nice variation would be to add about a half teaspoon of minced fresh tarragon to the sauce, instead.)

Pepper your filets mignon liberally and salt them lightly.

Put your big, heavy skillet over high heat and add the lard. When it's good and hot, throw in the steaks. Give them maybe 4 to 5 minutes per side—if you like your meat well done, pick another recipe! They should be pink-to-red in the middle. Plate the steaks and keep them warm.

Turn the burner down to medium low and add the shallot. Sauté for a couple of minutes, then turn the burner very low.

Now add the mustard and coconut sour cream. Stir until warmed through, but do not boil. Taste and add a little more salt and pepper if needed. Spoon over the steaks, top with the chopped parsley, and serve.

YIELD: 2 servings

Nutritional Analysis
Per serving: 454 calories; 40 g fat; 20 g protein; 4 g carbohydrate; trace dietary fiber; 4 g net carbs

Marinated Chuck

Commercial meat tenderizer is made with papaya enzyme. Unsurprisingly, the fresh stuff works just as well. This turns a chuck roast into a grillable steak.

2 pounds (900 g) chuck roast, 2-inches (5 cm) thick
⅛ papaya, seeded
½ cup (120 ml) olive oil
¼ cup (60 ml) coconut aminos
½ cup (120 ml) dry red wine
1 tablespoon (8 g) grated gingerroot
2 teaspoons curry powder
2 tablespoons (30 g) Caveman Ketchup (page 273)
¼ teaspoon black pepper
1 teaspoon hot sauce, such as Tabasco

Put everything but your chuck in your food processor. Don't peel your papaya—that's the part that's richest in the tenderizing enzyme.

Put your chuck in a nonreactive pan just big enough to hold it. Using a fork, pierce it all over with ruthless abandon. Flip, and repeat on the other side.

Now pour the marinade on your chuck, flipping it a few times to make sure it's thoroughly coated.
Let your chuck marinate for an hour, maybe two, but no more—the papaya is such a powerful tenderizer you might end up with mushy steak!

Get your charcoal going. When your charcoal is well ashed, grill to your preference—I like about 10 minutes per side, but it'll depend on your tastes and how far your grill is from your charcoal.

YIELD: 6 servings

Nutritional Analysis
Per serving: 507 calories; 42 g fat; 24 g protein; 4 g carbohydrate; trace dietary fiber; 4 g net carbs. This analysis includes all the marinade, and you'll be throwing some away.

Marinated Flank Steak

Commercial meat tenderizer is extracted from papaya. This marinade uses fresh papaya to get the same tenderizing effect.

3 pounds (1.3 kg) flank steak
1 papaya wedge, 1-inch (2.5 cm) wide
1 tablespoon (7 g) smoked paprika
2 garlic cloves, peeled
1 teaspoon dried rosemary
1 tablespoon (15 ml) chipotle chile canned in adobo, minced
¼ cup (60 ml) water
1 teaspoon honey
2 tablespoons (26 g) lard or other fat

Use a knife with a very sharp, thin blade to lightly score the surface of your steak in squares or diamonds about 2 inches (5 cm) apart. Put it in a big zipper-lock bag.

Put everything else in the food processor. Don't remove the skin from the papaya; it's the richest source of papain, the tenderizing enzyme. Run the processor till you have a purée. Pour it into the bag with the steak and seal it up, pressing the air out as you go. Turn the bag several times to coat.

Throw the bag with the steak into the fridge and let it marinate for an hour or so—the papaya is a very powerful tenderizer and don't let it go too long. The first time I used the papaya, I wound up with a mushy steak!

When it's time to cook, put your big, heavy skillet over highest heat and let it get good and hot. Melt the lard and slosh it around. Now pull your steak out of the marinade and throw it in the skillet—be careful, it will spit! Pan-broil

(continued)

it quickly till seared on both sides but still pink in the center. Time will depend on the thickness of your steak, but it shouldn't take more than 3 to 5 minutes per side.

Remove to a platter and slice thin across the grain to serve.

YIELD: 8 servings

Nutritional Analysis
Per serving: 351 calories; 21 g fat; 33 g protein; 5 g carbohydrate; 1 g dietary fiber; 4 g net carbs

Walnut-Anchovy Steak

This sauce really points up the flavor of a good steak.

1 tablespoon (15 ml) olive oil
1 pound (455 g) beef rib eye or sirloin, or another good broilable steak, 1-inch (2.5 cm) thick
¼ recipe Anchovy Dip/Sauce (page 283)
¼ cup (30 g) chopped walnuts

Preheat oven to 350°F (180°C, or gas mark 4).

Put your big, heavy skillet over high heat and get it good and hot. Pour in the olive oil, slosh it around to coat, and throw in your steak. Set your timer for 5 to 6 minutes.

In the meanwhile, make your anchovy dip or sauce if you haven't yet—me, I make this when I have leftover anchovy dip in the fridge.

Chop your walnuts and spread them on a shallow baking pan. Slide them into the oven. You're already using your timer for the steak, but take note of the time—you want your walnuts to roast for 8 to 10 minutes.

When the timer beeps, flip your steak and give it another 5 minutes—yes, set the timer.

Okay, your steak's done. Spread it with the anchovy dip, sprinkle the toasted walnuts over that, and serve.

YIELD: 3 servings

Nutritional Analysis
Per serving: 553 calories; 47 g fat; 29 g protein; 2 g carbohydrate; 1 g dietary fiber; 1 g net carbs

Herb Sauce for Steak

I could have put this in the sauces and seasonings chapter, but since this is specifically for steak, I thought I'd put it here.

1 teaspoon dried basil or 1 tablespoon (2.5 g) fresh, minced
1 teaspoon black pepper
1 garlic clove
2 tablespoons (20 g) minced onion
1 teaspoon dried thyme or 1 tablespoon (2.4 g) fresh thyme leaves, stripped from the stems
1 pinch cayenne
½ cup (120 ml) olive oil

Just put everything in the blender and run till the garlic and onion are pulverized.

Rub either side of a steak liberally with this before pan-broiling or grilling, then drizzle a little more over the steak when it's done. This is enough for two good-size steaks.

YIELD: 1 batch

Nutritional Analysis
Total: 980 calories; 108 g fat; 1 g protein; 6 g carbohydrate; 2 g dietary fiber; 4 g net carbs

Blackened Steak

1½ pounds (710 g) steak (rib eye, sirloin, something good for grilling or broiling, at least 1-inch (2.5 cm) thick, at room temperature)
1 teaspoon Blackening Spice (page 286), or to taste
1 tablespoon (13 g) bacon grease or lard

Put your big, heavy skillet—preferably cast iron—over highest heat.

Sprinkle the Blackening Spice evenly over both sides of the steak, using your palm to gently press the spice into the meat to help it adhere.

When the skillet is hot, add the bacon grease or lard and throw in your steak. I'd give a 1-inch thick (2.5 cm) rib eye 5 minutes on the first side, but your timing will depend on the thickness of your steak and how well done you like it. (Gray steak, phooey!) I set a timer to be sure I don't overdo mine.

Flip your steak and set your timer again. Keep an eye on your steak, though; I fairly commonly find the second side is done more quickly than the first. When it's crusty on the outside and pink in the middle, plate and serve very hot.

Creamy coleslaw is a great match for this.

YIELD: 4 servings

Nutritional Analysis
Per serving: 403 calories; 33 g fat; 24 g protein; 0 g carbohydrate; 0 g dietary fiber; no net carbs

Balsamic-Glazed Beef Ribs

You can tell I came up with this recipe in the winter, because in the summer I would have slow-smoked those ribs. Still, this oven method yields excellent results.

4 pounds (1.8 kg) beef spareribs
Salt and black pepper
¼ cup (60 ml) balsamic vinegar
¼ cup (60 ml) beef broth
½ small onion
2 garlic cloves
1 teaspoon brown mustard
½ teaspoon black pepper
2 tablespoons (30 g) tomato sauce

Preheat your oven to 300°F (150°C, or gas mark 2).

While that's happening, salt and pepper your rack of beef ribs all over. Place them in a roasting pan that holds them without too much extra room. Put 'em in the oven and set the timer for 30 minutes.

In the meanwhile, put everything else in your blender and run it till the onion and garlic are pulverized. This is your sauce.

When the timer beeps, baste the ribs liberally with the sauce. Turn them over and baste the other side. Leave that side up and put them back in. Set the timer for 20 minutes this time.

When it beeps, repeat basting and turning. Put them back in the oven, and set the timer for 20 minutes. Keep doing this until your ribs are tender when you stick a fork in 'em, and the meat is pulling away from the ends of the bones.

(continued)

Use a kitchen shears to cut them into individual ribs—you could use a sharp knife, but I think a shears is easier—and serve with a little extra drizzle of the sauce.

YIELD: 8 servings

Nutritional Analysis
Per serving: 719 calories; 61 g fat; 38 g protein; 2 g carbohydrate; trace dietary fiber; 2 g net carbs

Scandinavian Beef Stew

Perfect for a snowy evening!

2 pounds (900 g) beef chuck, in 1-inch (2.5 cm) cubes
3 tablespoons (39 g) lard or other fat
3 large carrots, peeled and in 1-inch (2.5 cm) lengths
1 small rutabaga, peeled and in 1-inch (2.5 cm) cubes
1 large parsnip, peeled and cut in 1-inch (2.5 cm) pieces (The top is likely to be thicker than the bottom, so cut those slices up to make more even.)
1 medium onion, chopped
1 tablespoon (6 g) ground coriander
2 teaspoons ground ginger
¼ teaspoon ground nutmeg
1½ cups (355 ml) beef broth
1 tablespoon (15 ml) beef Broth Concentrate (page 27), if you have it on hand
½ teaspoon dried thyme
Salt and black pepper to taste
¼ cup (15 g) minced fresh parsley

Put your big, heavy skillet over medium-high heat and brown the beef in the lard, turning to get all sides. Do this in batches, so as not to crowd your beef cubes.

While that's happening, cut up all your root vegetables. Put them in the bottom of your slow cooker.

Your beef cubes are browned. Transfer them to the slow cooker, putting them on top of the root vegetables. Put the skillet back on the heat and add the onion (and a little more fat, if needed). Sauté till it's translucent. Add the coriander, ginger, and nutmeg and stir well.

Now stir the beef broth concentrate into the beef broth, pour the mixture into the skillet, and stir it around, scraping up all the nice brown stuff till it dissolves. Stir in the thyme, then pour and scrape onions and broth into the slow cooker.

Cover your slow cooker and set it for low. Let it cook for 6 hours.

Uncover the pot, stir up your stew, and salt and pepper to taste. Ladle into bowls, top with parsley, and serve.

YIELD: 8 servings

Nutritional Analysis
Per serving: 340 calories; 23 g fat; 21 g protein; 12 g carbohydrate; 3 g dietary fiber; 9 g net carbs

Beef, Mushroom, and Daikon Stew

Fragrant with Asian spices, this smells like heaven when you walk in the door.

1 pound (455 g) beef chuck
2 tablespoons (26 g) lard or coconut oil
1 large onion
1 daikon
1 large carrot
8 ounces (225 g) sliced mushrooms
1 piece gingerroot, the size of a walnut in the shell
3 garlic cloves

1 piece star anise
1 cup (235 ml) beef broth
¼ cup (60 ml) coconut aminos
1 teaspoon honey
½ teaspoon black pepper

Cut your beef into 1-inch (2.5 cm) cubes. In your big, heavy skillet, over medium-high heat, melt the lard or coconut oil and start browning the beef cubes. Don't crowd them; better to do 2 batches.

While the beef is browning, peel your onion and cut it into 1-inch (2.5 cm) chunks. Peel the daikon and carrot and slice diagonally, about ¼-inch (6 mm) thick. Up by the thick end of each, you'll get big slices, of course, so halve or quarter them to get stuff in similarly sized pieces. Put all these vegetables, plus the mushrooms, in your slow cooker. By the way, remember to turn your beef cubes while you're cutting all that stuff up!

Using a sharp knife, slice the gingerroot as thinly as possible, across the grain. Peel the garlic and slice it paper thin, too. Add these to the vegetables and stir them in. Throw in the star anise, too.

Your beef chunks should be nicely browned now. Put them on top of the vegetables in the slow cooker.

Now stir together the beef broth, coconut aminos, honey, and pepper. Pour it over everything, cover the pot, set it to low, and forget about it for 8 to 10 hours.

That's it! Serve with soup spoons to get all the super-tasty broth.

YIELD: 4 servings

Nutritional Analysis
Per serving: 403 calories; 25 g fat; 24 g protein; 21 g carbohydrate; 4 g dietary fiber; 17 g net carbs

Mexican-oid Shredded Beef Stew

This is done in two stages—cooking the meat ahead of time, then assembling the stew the next day.

1 ½ pounds (710 g) beef round
½ large onion, chopped, plus 1 medium onion, sliced thin
1 large carrot, peeled and sliced
1 bay leaf
1 cup (235 ml) beef broth
½ red bell pepper
½ yellow bell pepper
½ green bell pepper
2 jalapeño peppers
2 tablespoons (26 g) lard
4 garlic cloves, crushed
2 teaspoons ground cumin
2 teaspoons dried oregano
½ teaspoon ground cinnamon
2 tablespoons (28 ml) beef Broth Concentrate (page 27)
3 medium tomatoes, divided
Salt and black pepper

Do this part ahead: Put your beef in the slow cooker. You don't need to cut it up or brown it or anything; just throw it in there. Add the half onion, carrot, bay leaf, and beef broth. Cover the pot, set to low, and let it cook for a good 10 hours. Turn off the slow cooker and let the mixture cool.

Next day, remove the beef from the pot, and turn the slow cooker back on to high to reheat the broth. (If you've refrigerated your beef and broth, you may want to bring it up to temperature on the stove or in the microwave to save time.) Add the medium onion, slice the bell peppers, and mince the jalapeños. Put your big, heavy skillet over medium-high heat, add the lard, and throw in the veggies.

(continued)

Go wash your hands really well with soap and water after handling the jalapeños. Now go back and stir your vegetables!

When the vegetables are getting a little tender, transfer them to the slow cooker. Stir in the garlic, cumin, oregano, cinnamon, and beef broth concentrate. Cover the pot to keep in the heat, while you . . .

Cut two of the tomatoes into ¼-inch (6 mm) dice. Stir them into the stew. Run the third through your food processor to pulp it and stir that in, too.

Now, for that meat: Use two forks, or clean hands, to pull it apart into shreds. (I tried forks, but abandoned them to use my hands. Still, you may be tidier than I.) Shred it pretty fine. Stir your beef shreds back into the stew.

When the stew is good and hot, take the lid off and cook for another 30 to 45 minutes to let the flavors blend and a little. Salt and pepper to taste, then serve.

YIELD: 6 servings

Nutritional Analysis
Per serving: 324 calories; 19 g fat; 27 g protein; 11 g carbohydrate; 3 g dietary fiber; 8 g net carbs

Spiced Pot Roast

Our tester, Arleen, asked if she would make this again, said, "Apparently I HAVE to. Hubby is saying it's the best roast I EVER made."

4 pounds (1.8 kg) beef chuck
Salt
½ teaspoon black pepper
½ teaspoon allspice
¼ teaspoon ground nutmeg
4 medium tomatoes

1 medium onion
3 tablespoons (45 ml) olive oil
3 tablespoons (45 ml) lemon juice
1 ½ tablespoons (25 ml) cider vinegar
2 tablespoons (26 g) lard
⅔ cup (160 ml) beef broth, divided
2 bay leaves

Sprinkle your roast lightly all over with salt, if using. In a small bowl, mix together the pepper, allspice, and nutmeg. Sprinkle over both sides of the roast and rub in well. Stab it all over with a fork.

Core your tomatoes, cut 'em in chunks, and put them in your food processor. Peel your onion and cut it in chunks, too, and throw them in the food processor with the tomatoes. Pulse till they're chopped. Now add the olive oil, lemon juice, and vinegar. Run the processor till you've got a slurry.

Put your roast in a big zipper-lock bag and pour in the mixture from the food processor. Seal the bag, pressing out the air as you go. Refrigerate both for at least 8 hours, and a day is great.

Okay, you're done waiting. Pull out your roast and drain and reserve the marinade. In a Dutch oven, over medium-high heat, melt the lard and sear the roast on both sides.

Now add the marinade, the beef broth, and the bay leaves. Bring to a boil, then turn down to a simmer. Cover and let it cook for a good 2½ to 3 hours, until the meat is fork-tender.

Remove the roast to a platter and keep warm. Now turn up the heat and reduce the juices in the pot until they're starting to thicken up. You could add a little glucomannan or arrowroot at this point, if you like, but it's not essential. Pour the sauce into a gravy boat and serve with the pot roast.

Fauxtatoes would be perfect with this.

YIELD: 6 servings

Nutritional Analysis

Per serving: 763 calories; 59 g fat; 50 g protein; 7 g carbohydrate; 1 g dietary fiber; 6 g net carbs

Slow-Cooker Horseradish Beef

Horseradish and beef are a very traditional pairing.

2 tablespoons (26 g) lard or other fat
2 pounds (900 g) beef chuck roast
Salt and black pepper
¼ cup (60 g) Prepared Horseradish (page 288)
3 garlic cloves, crushed
1 medium onion, chopped
4 medium carrots, peeled and chunked
2 medium turnips, peeled and chunked
1 ½ cups (355 ml) beef broth or stock
3 tablespoons (45 ml) beef Broth Concentrate (page 27) (Slow-Cooker Demi-Glace [page 27] would work, too.)
¼ cup (15 g) minced fresh parsley
Glucomannan

Put your big, heavy skillet over medium-high heat and melt the lard. Salt and pepper your roast lightly all over and start searing it in the lard—you want it browned on both sides.

Measure the horseradish and crush the garlic into it. Stir them together. Probably time to turn your beef!

Peel and cut up your veggies and put them in your slow cooker. Our tester, Lynda V.V., reminds you to peel off the fibrous layer right under the surface of your turnips.

When the roast is seared on both sides, use a spoon to spread the horseradish evenly over both sides. Place the roast on top of the vegetables.

Stir the beef broth concentrate into the beef broth and pour the mixture around the roast—not over it, so as not to wash off the horseradish. Cover the pot, set to low, and cook 5 to 6 hours.

When time's up, fish out your roast and put it on a platter. Use a slotted spoon to fish out the vegetables and pile them around the roast. Sprinkle with the parsley.

Thicken the liquid in the pot a little with your glucomannan shaker—not too thick. Salt and pepper to taste. Ladle into a gravy boat and serve with the roast and vegetables. Serve with extra horseradish on the side, if you like.

YIELD: 4 to 5 servings

Nutritional Analysis

Per serving: Assuming 4, each will have 619 calories; 42 g fat; 42 g protein; 17 g carbohydrate; 4 g dietary fiber; 13 g net carbs

NOTE

Lynda says she's going to try this with a different cut of beef. I'm very fond of chuck, but I'm betting this would be good with a brisket.

Crispy Shredded Beef

I found this simple recipe in an old, very authentic Mexican cookbook. The results are wonderful and versatile.

**1½ pounds (710 g) beef chuck, in 1-inch
   (2.5 cm) cubes**
1 onion, divided
Salt
Water
2 tablespoons (26 g) lard

You'll want to start well ahead of time, because you have to simmer the beef and then cool it before frying it crisp. I simmered my beef the night before, which worked very well.

Cut up your beef chuck and put it in a big, heavy saucepan with half of the onion, diced. Add water to cover and about a half teaspoon of salt and bring to a boil. Turn the burner down so the water is barely simmering, cover the pot, and let your beef cook for an hour, or until it shreds easily. Let cool in the broth. (You could do this step in your slow cooker, if you like. I'd give the beef at least 5 to 6 hours on low.)

When the beef is cool, use a slotted spoon to fish it out and put it on a big plate or pie plate. Use 2 forks to tear the beef into little shreds.

Dice the rest of your onion. Put your big, heavy skillet over low heat, melt the lard, and add the onion. Cook it gently—you don't want it to brown—until the onion is translucent.

Now add the shredded beef and turn the burner up to low medium. Fry, turning everything over every 3 to 5 minutes or so, until you've got quite a lot of the beef shreds browned and crispy. Use in omelets, on salads, all sorts of things!

YIELD: 6 servings

Nutritional Analysis
Per serving: 282 calories; 22 g fat; 18 g protein; 2 g carbohydrate; trace dietary fiber; 2 g net carbs

Crispy Beef Soft Tacos

You know the family is going to like this!

Eggy Wraps (page 78)
Crispy Shredded Beef (opposite)
Coconut Sour Cream (page 29)
**Salsa (page 281—though I promise not to tell
   if you use store-bought organic salsa)**
½ red onion, diced
1 avocado, sliced
1 medium tomato, diced
2 cups (110 g) shredded lettuce, iceberg or romaine

A lot of this stuff can and should be made in advance—the Eggy Wraps, the Crispy Shredded Beef, the Coconut Sour Cream, and possibly the Salsa. Warm the beef; dice the onion, avocado, and tomato; and shred the lettuce.

Now just set everything out and let people build their own soft tacos!

YIELD: 6 servings

Nutritional Analysis
Per serving: 576 calories; 46 g fat; 27 g protein; 17 g carbohydrate; 4 g dietary fiber; 13 g net carbs

Tangerine Beef Stir-Fry

Zingy!

1 pound (455 g) beef tenderloin, lean
½ navel orange
1 tablespoon (15 ml) white balsamic vinegar
4 tablespoons (60 ml) coconut aminos, divided
4 shallots, thinly sliced
3 tangerines, peeled and sectioned
2 tablespoons (28 ml) dry sherry
1 clove garlic
1 teaspoon Sriracha (page 276), or to taste
3 tablespoons (39 g) coconut oil, divided
¼ cup (4 g) minced fresh cilantro

Slice your beef thin, across the grain—it's easiest to do this if it's half frozen. Put the strips in a dish.

Grate the zest of your half orange (we'll be using the juice in a bit) and mix with the white balsamic vinegar and 2 tablespoons (28 ml) of the coconut aminos. Pour this over the beef, toss so all the strips are coated, and let the beef sit for at least a half an hour, to marinate. In the meanwhile, peel and slice your shallots and peel and section your tangerines.

Time to squeeze that half orange! Mix the juice with the rest of the coconut aminos, the sherry, the garlic, crushed, and the Sriracha. Put this by the stove.

Drain the beef. Put your wok (or a big skillet) over highest heat. Add 1 tablespoon (13 g) of the coconut oil and let it get good and hot. Add half the beef to the wok and stir-fry till the pink is gone, about 3 minutes. Remove from the wok to a plate and throw another tablespoon of coconut oil into the wok. Stir-fry the rest of the beef the same way and remove it, too, from the wok.

Put the last tablespoon of coconut oil in the wok and let it get hot. Throw in the shallots and stir-fry for just a minute or two. Add the tangerine sections and stir-fry another minute or two.

Return the beef to the wok and add the sauce you made earlier. Toss it all together for just a minute, then serve topped with the cilantro.

YIELD: 4 servings

Nutritional Analysis
Per serving: 426 calories; 24 g fat; 33 g protein; 16 g carbohydrate; 2 g dietary fiber; 14 g net carbs

Braised Oxtails

I love oxtails. They're the kind of tough, bony meat that properly cooked is more flavorful than tenderer cuts could ever be.

2 pounds (900 g) beef oxtails
1 tablespoon (13 g) beef fat or coconut oil
½ cup (65 g) chopped carrot
½ cup (55 g) chopped parsnip
1 onion
½ cup (50 g) chopped celery
2 sundried tomato halves
2 cloves garlic, crushed
1 ½ cups (355 ml) beef broth
Salt and black pepper to taste

In your big, heavy skillet, over a medium-high burner, brown the oxtails in the fat—sear them well.

In the meanwhile, chop up all your veggies, including snipping the sundried tomato halves into little bits.

When the oxtails are well seared, scoop 'em out and set them on a plate. Throw the carrot, parsnip, onion, and celery in the skillet and sauté them for 5 minutes or so—add a little more fat if you think you need it.

Now stir in the snipped sundried tomatoes and the garlic. Nestle the oxtails down amidst the veggies and pour in the beef broth. Turn the burner to low and cover the skillet. Let the whole thing simmer for a good 90 minutes.

Now you have a decision to make! Choice one: Take the oxtails out and reserve them in a warm place, while you use your stick blender to purée the veggies into the broth, making a nice gravy. Serve the oxtails with the gravy.

Or… Choice two: Scoop out the oxtails and the vegetables, both, and reserve. Now turn up the burner and boil the liquid in the skillet down to about half its volume. Now serve the oxtails on a bed of vegetables, with the reduced pan juices poured over it all.

YIELD: 4 servings

Nutritional Analysis
Per serving: 682 calories; 36 g fat; 75 g protein; 10 g carbohydrate; 2 g dietary fiber; 8 g net carbs

Chiles Not-Quite Rellenos

I found stuffing limp, roasted peppers annoying enough that I did them this way. And you know what? They were great!

4 poblano peppers
1 pound (455 g) ground chuck
4 tablespoons (40 g) minced onion
2 medium tomatoes, ¼-inch (6 mm) dice
2 garlic cloves, crushed
¼ teaspoon ground cloves
½ teaspoon ground coriander
2 teaspoons chili powder
½ teaspoon black pepper
2 cups (475 ml) beef broth
4 tablespoons (36 g) raisins
2 tablespoons (14 g) slivered almonds
4 eggs
Black pepper
Salt (optional)

Broil your poblanos about 5 inches (13 cm) from the heat, turning often, till the skin blisters. In the meanwhile . . .

In your big skillet, start browning and crumbling your ground chuck. As it cooks down a bit, add the onion.

When the pink is gone from the meat, pour off any excess fat that has accumulated.

Somewhere in here, your poblanos will be blistered all over. Pull 'em out and put 'em in a plastic sack to sit for a few minutes.

Add the diced tomato, garlic, cloves, coriander, chili powder, pepper, and beef broth to the ground chuck and stir them in. Now stir in the raisins and almonds. Turn the burner to low and let the whole thing simmer. You're going to let it cook till the broth is almost all cooked away.

While that's happening, grab your poblanos. Peel the now-loosened skin off them, at least as much as you can. Pull out the stems and seeds and discard. Slit 'em down the side.

Your beef's still simmering, but it's getting there. Turn on your oven to 350°F (180°C, or gas mark 4) and grease a baking dish just big enough to hold half your poblanos spread out flat. Do that—lay half your poblanos flat in the baking dish.

Pile your meat mixture on top, making an even layer. Now cover it with the remaining opened-up poblanos.

Separate your eggs. Beat the whites till they're stiff but not dry. Now beat the yolks with a little pinch of pepper, and a pinch of salt if you like, till they're creamy. Fold the yolks into the whites.

Spread the whole fluffy eggy mixture on top of the big meat-and-poblano sandwich, covering it evenly. Slide the whole thing into the oven and bake it for 20 to 25 minutes, or until the eggs are just getting golden. Cut into portions and serve immediately.

YIELD: 4 servings

Nutritional Analysis
Per serving: 497 calories; 31 g fat; 34 g protein; 21 g carbohydrate; 3 g dietary fiber; 18 g net carbs

Creamy Chipotle Beef

Good as an omelet filling, especially with some avocado slices slipped in. Also good over Cauli-Rice or fauxtatoes.

12 ounces (340 g) ground chuck
1 small onion, diced small
2 cloves garlic, crushed
2 medium tomatoes, diced small
4 tablespoons (60 ml) Chipotle Free-Range Dressing (page 142)
1 teaspoon chili powder
2 tablespoons (28 ml) chipotle chile canned in adobo, or Chipotles in Adobo (page 294) minced

Put your big, heavy skillet over medium heat and start browning and crumbling your ground chuck. As some fat cooks out of it, add the onion, garlic, and tomato and stir together. Keep cooking till the pink is gone from the beef.

Drain any excess grease from the beef mixture. Now stir in the dressing, chili powder, and minced chipotle. Let it cook for another 3 to 4 minutes. Ready to use!

YIELD: 3 servings

Nutritional Analysis
Per serving: 337 calories; 24 g fat; 22 g protein; 8 g carbohydrate; 2 g dietary fiber; 6 g net carbs

NOTE

If you don't want to use the canned chipotles in adobo, there's a recipe for making your own, sans sugar, on page 294.

Condiment Burgers

We're used to putting condiments on burgers. Here I've put condiments in burgers!

1 pound (455 g) ground chuck
¼ cup (60 g) Caveman Ketchup (page 273)
2 tablespoons (30 g) brown mustard
1 tablespoon (15 g) Prepared Horseradish (page 288)
1 tablespoon (15 ml) coconut aminos
¼ teaspoon anchovy paste
¼ teaspoon black pepper
¼ cup (40 g) minced onion
¼ cup (30 g) Pork Rind Crumbs (page 30)
1 egg
Lettuce
Tomato
¼ red onion

Assemble everything through the egg in a mixing bowl, then use clean hands to smoosh everything together very well. Form into 3 patties, place on a plate, and refrigerate for half an hour or so.

Now pan-fry or grill, then serve wrapped with lettuce, sliced tomato, and maybe some paper-thin red onion!

YIELD: 3 servings

Nutritional Analysis
Per serving: 458 calories; 34 g fat; 30 g protein; 7 g carbohydrate; 1 g dietary fiber; 6 g net carbs

Umami Burgers

The point here was to use high-umami flavorings to intensify the flavor of the beef. It works!

⅓ cup (55 g) minced onion
⅓ cup (60 g) minced tomato
1 tablespoon (12.5 g) lard— or coconut oil
2 cloves garlic, minced
¾ teaspoon Liquid Umami (see page 288)
½ teaspoon anchovy paste
½ teaspoon pepper
1 pound (455 g) ground chuck

In a heavy-bottomed skillet with a good, not-sticky surface, start sautéing the onion and tomato in the lard over low heat, stirring often. You want to soften them, brown them a little, and evaporate much of the liquid, concentrating the flavor. When the mixture's getting to that point, stir in the garlic, umami liquid, anchovy paste, and pepper and sauté just another minute or two. Then turn off the burner and let it cool for 5 minutes or so, so you can handle it.

Put your ground chuck in a big mixing bowl and add the stuff from the skillet. Using clean hands, smoosh it all together really well. Now form into 3 hamburger patties At this point, it's a nice idea to refrigerate them for a while, but sometimes one simply doesn't have the time. No matter.

You can grill these, of course. Inside, I like to cook them in a skillet over low heat—I don't want the outsides to dry out before the insides are done.

Serve these with the condiments of your choice, if you like, but they don't really need anything.

YIELD: 3 servings

Nutritional Analysis
Per serving: 461 calories; 35 g fat; 31 g protein; 2 g carbohydrate; trace dietary fiber; 2 g net carbs

Adobo Burgers with Chipotle Onions

So there I was, staring at a pound of ground chuck, thinking, "Geez, what to do with it this time?" Then I remembered I'd made adobo seasoning that day, and these were born. If you're not going to make the chipotle onions (though you should!), consider adding ¼ cup (40 g) minced onion to this, too.

1 pound (455 g) ground chuck
1 tablespoon (7.2 g) Adobo Seasoning (page 285)
¼ cup (30 g) Pork Rind Crumbs (page 30)
1 egg
Chipotle Onions (page 104)
3 cups (165 g) shredded romaine lettuce
1 avocado, sliced

In a big mixing bowl, combine your ground chuck, adobo seasoning, pork rind crumbs, and egg. Use clean hands to squish everything together really well. If you plan to grill them, form into 3 patties, put them on a plate, and chill for 30 minutes or so. If you're cooking them in a skillet, you can start right away. Either way, cook your burgers to your liking, though I'd keep them a bit pink in the center.

While the burgers are cooking, make your Chipotle Onions. (If you're going to grill your burgers outside, do this first—you can't be running back and forth between the grill and the stove!)

Make beds of romaine on 3 plates. Arrange the sliced avocado on top of the lettuce. Now put a burger on each, top with the chipotle onions, and serve.

YIELD: 3 servings

Nutritional Analysis
Per serving: 635 calories; 50 g fat; 36 g protein; 11 g carbohydrate; 4 g dietary fiber; 7 g net carbs

Super Burgers

There is a burger place that is upping the ante by adding ingredients such as these to create something that doesn't need ketchup, pickles, or anything else. So I gave it a shot, and this is the result.

1½ pounds (710 g) ground chuck
2 teaspoons coconut aminos
1 teaspoon anchovy paste
½ teaspoon Celery Salt (page 285, or use store-bought)
⅛ teaspoon dry mustard
⅛ teaspoon black pepper
1½ tablespoons (15 g) minced onion

Throw the meat in a mixing bowl and add everything else. With clean hands, moosh it all up till it's really well mixed. Form into 4 patties no more than 1-inch (2.5 cm) thick. It's nice to make these in advance and chill before cooking.

Put your big, heavy skillet over medium-low heat and get it hot before throwing in your Super Burgers. Let 'em cook brown on one side before flipping them and cooking the other, then serve. These don't need a thing, but add lettuce and tomato if you like.

YIELD: 4 servings

Nutritional Analysis
Per serving: 458 calories; 35 g fat; 31 g protein; 1 g carbohydrate; trace dietary fiber; 1 g net carbs

Chile-Basil Burgers

1 ½ pounds (710 g) ground chuck

1 red bell pepper

½ small onion

2 garlic cloves

2 small red chile peppers

1½ tablespoons (4 g) plus 1 teaspoon minced
   fresh basil

½ teaspoon ground cumin

¼ teaspoon salt

¼ teaspoon black pepper

6 tablespoons (84 g) Mayonnaise in the Jar (page 278)

½ lime

Sriracha (page 276; optional, to taste)

Place the hamburger in a large bowl.

Seed your red bell pepper, chunk it, and put it in your food processor with the *S* blade in place. Peel and chunk the onion and put it in there, too. Crush in one of the garlic cloves. Stem and seed the peppers and add them. Now wash your hands very thoroughly! (And we're going to wash them again later. Don't mess around with hot peppers.)

Pulse the food processor till everything's chopped pretty fine. Dump this in with the hamburger.

Mince the basil and add it to the bowl, along with the cumin, salt, and pepper. Use clean hands to smoosh it all together really well, then form into 4 patties. Put 'em on a plate and chill for a half hour if you've got the time.

Grill if it's cookout weather. If not, put your big, heavy skillet over medium-low heat and pan fry them.

While the burgers are cooking, mix together the mayo, a little zest and the juice of the lime half, the extra teaspoon of basil, the second clove of garlic, crushed, and a little Sriracha, if you like. Spoon this sauce over the burgers to serve.

YIELD: 4 servings

Nutritional Analysis
Per serving: 629 calories; 53 g fat; 32 g protein; 8 g carbohydrate; 1 g dietary fiber; 7 g net carbs

Philippa's Distant Ancestor's Meatloaf

This is based on my grandmother's meatloaf, the one my mother made when I was growing up. I adapted it for low carb years ago, and now I've paleoized it. And it's still good. Lynda, our tester, says, "WOW! I wouldn't change a thing in this recipe . . . This could easily become my new favorite meatloaf recipe!" She also says she served halved cherry tomatoes on the side and thought they went perfectly.

1½ pounds (710 g) ground chuck

⅔ cup (77 g) Pork Rind Crumbs (page 30)

½ cup (120 ml) unsweetened coconut milk

2 eggs

1 large onion, diced

1 ½ tablespoons (10.8 g) poultry seasoning

1 teaspoon salt

Just plunk everything into a big mixing bowl and use clean hands to smoosh it all together very well. Pack it into a loaf pan, then turn it out onto your broiler rack. (If you prefer, you can just plunk it on your broiler rack and pat it into a loaf shape.) Bake at 400°F (200°C, or gas mark 6) for 40 minutes. Let it cool for 10 minutes before slicing and serving.

If you'd like an accompaniment, consider Caveman Ketchup (page 273) or Steak Sauce (page 274).

YIELD: 6 servings

Nutritional Analysis

Per serving: 368 calories; 29 g fat; 23 g protein; 3 g carbohydrate; trace dietary fiber; 3 g net carbs

NOTE

Lynda had trouble turning her meatloaf out of the pan onto the broiler rack. Rinsing the pan with cold water first should help some.

Lascaux Meatloaf

This was inspired by a French meatloaf recipe, so I named it after the home of the famous cave paintings. If you can make this of ground buffalo, so much the better!

1 pound (455 g) ground chuck
½ pound (225 g) mild pork sausage
⅓ cup (40 g) Pork Rind Crumbs (page 30)
½ cup (80 g) chopped onion, fairly fine
1 clove garlic, minced
¼ cup (15 g) chopped fresh parsley
¼ cup (60 ml) dry red wine
1 egg
1 tablespoon (15 g) Dijon or spicy brown mustard
½ teaspoon dried savory
½ teaspoon dried thyme
¼ teaspoon dried ground rosemary
½ teaspoon salt or 1 teaspoon Vege-Sal
¼ teaspoon black pepper

Preheat oven to 350°F (180°C, or gas mark 4).
Dump all your ingredients in a big bowl. Use clean hands to squish it all together until it's really well mixed.

Now pack your meatloaf mixture into a loaf pan and bake for 50 to 60 minutes. Remove from the oven, drain the fat out of the pan, and let the loaf sit for 5 to 10 minutes before slicing and serving.

YIELD: 6 servings

Nutritional Analysis

Per serving: 411 calories; 33 g fat; 22 g protein; 3 g carbohydrate; 1 g dietary fiber; 2 g net carbs

Many-Vegetable Meatloaf

Lots of seasonings, too!

½ green bell pepper
½ medium onion
½ large celery rib
1 medium tomato
½ large carrot
½ pound (225 g) ground beef
½ pound (225 g) ground pork
1 egg
½ cup (60 g) Pork Rind Crumbs (page 30)
½ teaspoon dried sage
¼ teaspoon dry mustard
¼ teaspoon dried thyme
¼ teaspoon salt or to taste
¼ teaspoon black pepper
⅛ teaspoon ground nutmeg
⅛ cup (30 g) Caveman Ketchup (page 273)
1 tablespoon (15 ml) balsamic vinegar
½ tablespoon (10 g) honey
½ tablespoon (7.5 g) brown mustard

Preheat oven to 350ºF (180ºC, or gas mark 4).

Remove the stem and seeds from your green pepper and chop it fine—I did all my chopping in the food processor. Dump it into a big darned mixing bowl.

Do the same with your onion—peel it and chop it fine. Chop your celery, too. Tomatoes are the ingredient where a food processor really helps, because chopping them fine on a cutting board is so messy! Anyway, dump all your chopped vegetables in your mixing bowl.

Use the shredding blade of your processor or your box grater to shred your carrot and add it to the veggie party.

Now add everything through the nutmeg. Use clean hands to work it all together well. It will seem too wet to begin with—keep kneading it for a few minutes, and it will start to thicken up a bit, thanks to the Pork Rind Crumbs.

Turn the mixture out onto your broiler rack and form into a nice, smooth, even loaf. Bake for an hour.

Okay, mix together the ketchup, vinegar, honey, and brown mustard. Spoon this evenly over the meatloaves. Let 'em bake another 5 minutes to glaze, then serve.

YIELD: 5 servings

Nutritional Analysis
Per serving: 346 calories; 26 g fat; 22 g protein; 6 g carbohydrate; 1 g dietary fiber; 5 g net carbs

Venison Chili

This is for all of you hunters out there. I had to buy my ground venison at the specialty butcher for $13/pound, but one trusts you'll pay far less. Feel free to make this with ground beef chuck instead, if you like.

2 tablespoons (26 g) bacon grease
1 pound (455 g) ground venison
1 medium onion, chopped
2 medium tomatoes, ¼-inch (6 mm) dice
¼ cup (60 ml) dry red wine
½ cup (120 ml) beef broth
2 garlic cloves, crushed
1 green bell pepper, diced

1½ tablespoons (11 g) chili powder

1 chipotle chile canned in adobo, minced

1 teaspoon ground cumin

1 teaspoon paprika

3 tablespoons (45 g) Caveman Ketchup (page 273)

1 teaspoon dried oregano

½ ounce (15 g) bitter chocolate

Put your big, heavy skillet over medium-low heat. Melt the bacon grease and start browning and crumbling the venison. Throw in the onion, too.

When the pink is gone from the meat and the onion is translucent, add everything else. Stir it up well. Turn the burner to low and let the whole thing simmer for 45 minutes to an hour. That's it!

YIELD: 4 servings

Nutritional Analysis
Per serving: 279 calories; 12 g fat; 30 g protein; 12 g carbohydrate; 4 g dietary fiber; 8 g net carbs

Paleo Joe

Yet another version of the venerable "Joe's Special." I persistently offer variations of this because I know of no simple skillet supper that I like so well.

1 ½ pounds (710 g) ground beef

4 ounces (115 g) mushrooms

1 medium onion

⅓ cup (37 g) oil-packed sundried tomatoes, drained

3 garlic cloves, crushed

10 ounces (280 g) spinach

5 eggs

Salt and black pepper to taste

In your big, heavy skillet, over medium heat, start the ground beef browning.

In the meanwhile, chop your mushrooms and onion. Chop your sundried tomatoes, too, but keep 'em separate from the mushrooms and onions.

Go back and start breaking up and turning your ground beef. You want it crumbled into medium-size bits. When most of the pink is gone, add the mushrooms, onions, and garlic, and stir it up. Keep sautéing, stirring often, till the pink is all gone from the meat, and the onion is translucent. At this point, pour off the excess fat if you wish—I keep it, myself.

Now add the sundried tomatoes and the spinach and stir 'em in. Regarding the spinach: A box of frozen chopped spinach, thawed and squeezed dry, works well here, and has no nonpaleo additives. However, you can use fresh spinach that you've chopped. It will just have a lot more volume to start with (it will cook down fast) and take a minute or two longer to cook.

While that's all getting acquainted, crack your eggs into a bowl and scramble 'em up with a fork. Pour them over the whole mass of stuff and let it cook, stirring and turning the mixture over, until the eggs are set. Salt and pepper to taste, and serve.

YIELD: 6 servings

Nutritional Analysis
Per serving: 444 calories; 35 g fat; 26 g protein; 6 g carbohydrate; 2 g dietary fiber; 4 g net carbs

Picadillo Unstuffed Cabbage

This Latin American–inspired skillet supper is a meal in itself. I love that!

⅔ pound (303 g) ground chuck
⅔ pound (303 g) ground pork
1 ½ ounces (43 g) raisins (This is the quantity in many snack-size boxes of raisins.)
3 tablespoons (45 ml) boiling water
1 onion, diced
3 medium tomatoes, diced
1 jalapeño pepper
2 garlic cloves, crushed
½ head cabbage
1 cup (235 ml) beef broth
8 fluid ounces (235 ml) tomato sauce
1 teaspoon dried oregano
½ teaspoon dried thyme

In your biggest, heavy skillet, over medium-low heat, start browning and crumbling the beef and pork together.

Put the raisins in a small dish and add the boiling water. Let them sit to puff while you continue with the recipe.

In the meanwhile, dice up your onion and tomatoes. Halve the jalapeño and remove the seeds, then mince it fine. When most of the pink is gone from the meat, add the onions and let them sauté till they're just turning translucent, then add the diced tomatoes, minced jalapeño, and crushed garlic and stir it all up. Sauté for 5 minutes or so. While it's sautéing, wash your hands really well with soap and water to get the jalapeño off them!

Chop your cabbage coarsely into 1- to 2-inches (2.5 to 5 cm) bits. Add to the skillet and stir in everything else, including the raisins and their soaking water. Use your spatula to turn everything over, working the cabbage and the meat mixture together. Then cover the skillet, turn the burner to low, and set the timer for 20 minutes.

When the timer beeps, take the lid off the skillet, turn it up a bit—medium or so—and let the whole mixture simmer for another 5 to 10 minutes, to reduce the liquid, then serve in bowls.

YIELD: 5 servings

Nutritional Analysis
Per serving: 401 calories; 26 g fat; 25 g protein; 18 g carbohydrate; 3 g dietary fiber; 15 g net carbs

Chapter 11

PORK AND LAMB

Ogg and his friends were very brave to hunt wild pigs. They're among the most dangerous prey. But, man, do they taste good! Pork is one of the most popular meats in the world. Every scrap of a pig is edible and delicious and—despite so many people feeling guilty about eating pork—it is also highly nutritious. Pork is a great source of protein, but also an outstanding source of thiamin, niacin, B6, and zinc. Pork is also a good source of potassium. It will surprise you to know that a 6-ounce (170 g) pork chop has more potassium than a banana.

Like us, pigs make vitamin D in their skin in response to sunlight; that vitamin D is stored in their fat. That means that pasture-raised pork is also one of the rare rich dietary sources of vitamin D. Don't throw away fat from pastured pork. We call that lard, and it's one of the best and most traditional cooking fats.

As for lamb, I hope to increase its popularity. I grew up eating lamb and have always loved it, and can't figure out why so many of my countrymen have never tried it. Along with being delicious and versatile, lamb is the only meat commonly found in mainstream grocery stores that is virtually always grass-fed, making it the healthiest choice in the meat case. If you haven't tried lamb, you really need to. If you're already a lamb fan, you'll find some new things to do with it here.

Carnitas

One of the most wonderful cheap meals I have ever had was at an unassuming little joint in San Diego called Carnitas Urupan. They sell these crisp but meltingly tender chunks of pork by the pound. We bought green salads, carnitas, and guacamole, piled the meat and guac on the salads, and dug in. Amazing.

1½ pounds (710 g) pork shoulder, exclusive of bone
Water
1 teaspoon salt (optional)

Trim any major layers of fat off your pork shoulder, but don't try to get it too lean; you'll need the fat later on. Cut your pork into chunks roughly 1½ to 2 inches (3.5 to 5 cm).

Put the pork in your big, heavy skillet—you want a single layer, but the pork cubes can be very close together; that's fine. Cover with water, add the salt, if using, and put over a burner set to medium-high heat. Bring the water to a boil, then turn the burner down to low—you want to keep the water barely simmering.

Now let your pork cubes simmer. And simmer. And simmer. Mine took a good 3 or 4 hours. That's okay; the simmering makes them tender. If you happen to be wandering through the kitchen, turn the cubes over once or twice.

Let your pork simmer till the water has completely cooked away. Continue cooking, letting the pork cubes brown in the fat that has collected in the bottom of the skillet. When they're crisply brown, they're done!

YIELD: 4 servings

Nutritional Analysis
Per serving: 301 calories; 23 g fat; 22 g protein; 0 g carbohydrate; 0 g dietary fiber; 0 g net carbs

NOTE

I mentioned eating carnitas on a salad, but try making a soft taco with one of the Eggy Wraps on page 78.

Balsamic Pork Steak

A simple way to vary my favorite cut of pork.

1 pound (455 g) pork shoulder steak, ½-inch
(1 cm) thick
1 tablespoon (15 ml) olive oil
Black pepper
1 garlic clove
2 tablespoons (28 ml) balsamic vinegar

Put your big, heavy skillet over medium heat and add the olive oil. Add the pork steak, browning it on both sides.

In the meanwhile, mix together the pepper, garlic, and balsamic vinegar.

When your steak is nice and brown on both sides, pour the vinegar mixture into the skillet. Flip the steak a couple of times to coat it. Now cover the skillet, turn the heat down to low, and let it cook for another 5 minutes, then serve.

YIELD: 3 servings

Nutritional Analysis
Per serving: 311 calories; 25 g fat; 20 g protein; 1 g carbohydrate; trace dietary fiber; 1 g net carbs

Chermoula Chops

Chermoula is from North Africa, around Morocco and Tunisia. I have no idea if they use it on pork, but it sure does taste good this way.

1½ pounds (710 g) pork loin chops, ½-inch (1 cm) thick
1 tablespoon (15 ml) olive oil
1 batch Chermoula (page 283)

Very simple. In your big, heavy skillet, over medium-high heat, sauté your chops in the oil till they're golden on both sides, and done through, but not a minute longer!

While they're cooking, make the Chermoula.

When the chops are done, plate them and top them with the Chermoula, dividing it evenly between them. Serve immediately.

YIELD: 3 servings

Nutritional Analysis
Per serving: 314 calories; 21 g fat; 28 g protein; 1 g carbohydrate; trace dietary fiber; 1 g net carbs

Pan-Braised Pork Chops with Plum Sauce

When I was growing up, my mother always served applesauce with pork, which led me to a broader principle: Pork tastes great paired with fruit. Just about any fruit.

1½ pounds (710 g) pork loin chops, ½-inch (1 cm) thick
Salt and black pepper
1 tablespoon (13 g) lard
¼ cup (60 ml) chicken broth
¼ batch Plum Sauce (page 282)

Put your big, heavy skillet over a medium-high burner. While it's heating, season your chops lightly on both sides with salt and pepper. Melt the lard in the skillet and start browning the chops in it.

While the chops are browning, stir together the chicken broth and Plum Sauce.

When the chops are golden on both sides, pour in the broth-and-sauce mixture. Cover the pan, turn the burner to low, and set your timer for 10 minutes.

Then uncover the skillet, turn the chops over to make sure both sides are well acquainted with the sauce, and let them simmer another 5 to 7 minutes uncovered. You want the sauce to reduce till it's getting slightly syrupy.

Serve the chops with the pan liquid spooned over them and more plum sauce on the side if you like.

YIELD: 3 servings

Nutritional Analysis
Per serving: 291 calories; 18 g fat; 28 g protein; 2 g carbohydrate; trace dietary fiber; 2 g net carbs

NOTE

A pound and a half (710 g) of ½-inch (1 cm) thick pork chops should be three chops. Why three? Because that's what I could fit in my skillet. If you've got a bigger skillet, feel free to increase this recipe.

Pork Burgers with Apples and Onions

Quick, easy, good.

1½ pounds (710 g) ground pork
2 cloves garlic, crushed
2 teaspoons coconut aminos, divided
½ teaspoon salt, divided
¾ teaspoon black pepper, divided
1 apple (I used a Granny Smith.)
1 medium onion
1 tablespoon (13 g) coconut oil

Put your big, heavy skillet over low heat. While that's heating, put the ground pork, garlic, 1 teaspoon of the coconut aminos, and the first salt and pepper in a mixing bowl. Use clean hands to smoosh it all together really well, then form it into 4 patties. Don't make them too thick or you'll overcook the outsides while trying to get the middles done—maybe a little more than ½-inch (1 cm) thick.

Throw your burgers into your now-hot skillet. (Do heat the skillet first—it makes a difference.) While they're cooking, cut the apple into quarters and cut out the core, then slice it quite thin. Slice your onion thin, too. Somewhere in here you'll need to flip your burgers.

When your burgers are done just through, remove them from the skillet to a plate and put a pot lid over them to keep them warm. Melt the coconut oil in the skillet (you can skip this if your pork has left enough grease in the skillet), add the apple and onion, and sauté until the apples are soft and golden and the onion translucent. Stir in the remaining teaspoon of coconut aminos, and salt and pepper to taste.

Serve the burgers with the onion and apple mixture piled on top.

YIELD: 4 servings

Nutritional Analysis
Per serving: 514 calories; 40 g fat; 29 g protein; 9 g carbohydrate; 2 g dietary fiber; 7 g net carbs

Pork with Apples

Did I mention I like pork with apples?

24 ounces (680 g) pork chops
Salt and black pepper
1 tablespoon (13 g) fat
1 apple
1 medium onion
1 teaspoon poultry seasoning
1 cup (235 ml) chicken broth

Put your big, heavy skillet over medium-high heat. While that's heating, season your chops lightly on both sides with the salt and pepper. Slash the edges to help them lie flat.

Add the fat to the skillet—I used lard, but bacon grease would be good here, and olive oil or coconut oil would work fine—slosh it around to coat, and add the chops. You want them golden on both sides. You may need to do this in 2 batches, depending on the size of your chops.

While your chops are browning, cut your apple into quarters, remove the core, and slice fairly thin. Peel your onion and slice it, too. Stir your poultry seasoning into the broth and reserve.

When the chops are browned, remove them from the skillet and add the apples and onions. Toss them together in the skillet, then spread them evenly over the bottom of the skillet.

Place the chops on top of the apples and onions, overlapping if necessary. Now pour the broth over everything. Cover the skillet, turn the burner to low, and let the whole thing simmer for an hour.

Remove the chops from the skillet to plates. If there's still quite a lot of broth in the skillet—this will depend on how tightly your skillet's lid fits—turn up the burner and cook it down. You want just a few tablespoons (45 ml) of liquid left.

When the liquid in the skillet is reduced, spoon the apples and onions over the chops and serve.

YIELD: 4 servings

Nutritional Analysis
Per serving: 333 calories; 20 g fat; 28 g protein; 8 g carbohydrate; 1 g dietary fiber; 7 g net carbs

Strawberry Pork Chops

18 ounces (510 g) pork loin chops, fairly thin
Salt and black pepper
1½ tablespoons (25 ml) olive oil, or more if needed
6 strawberries
1 clove garlic, crushed
¼ cup (60 ml) chicken broth
¼ teaspoon dried thyme, or a teaspoon of fresh
¾ teaspoon brown mustard

Season the chops lightly on both sides and start sautéing them in the olive oil—use medium-low heat to give them time to cook through before they burn on the outside.

While your chops are cooking, hull and chop your strawberries, and crush your garlic.

When your chops are done through, remove from the pan, plate them, and keep them warm while you . . .

Throw your strawberries in the pan, along with the garlic, chicken broth, thyme, and mustard. Simmer, stirring to scrape up the nice brown bits from the bottom of the skillet. Cook till the strawberries soften a bit and the broth cooks down, so the whole thing has a slightly syrupy consistency. Spoon over the chops and serve.

YIELD: 3 servings

Nutritional Analysis
Per serving: 218 calories; 13 g fat; 22 g protein; 2 g carbohydrate; 1 g dietary fiber; 1 g net carbs

Southeast Asian Pork Burgers

12 ounces (340 g) ground pork, not too lean
1 clove garlic
1½ teaspoons dried basil
1 tablespoon (8 g) grated gingerroot
½ teaspoon black pepper
½ teaspoon salt
1 tablespoon (15 ml) lime juice

Simply use clean hands to smoosh everything together, and make into 2 or 3 patties—I made 2. Chill them for a minute or two while you . . .

Put your big, heavy skillet over medium-low heat. When it's hot, throw in the burgers and cook 'em slowly—you don't want the outsides to scorch before the insides are done.

Serve with Paleo Nuoc Cham (page 276).

YIELD: 2 servings

Nutritional Analysis
Per serving: 458 calories; 36 g fat; 29 g protein; 3 g carbohydrate; 1 g dietary fiber; 2 g net carbs

Pork with Ras Al Hanout

Simple pork chops with a Middle Eastern savor.

3 tablespoons (45 ml) olive oil
1 ½ pounds (710 g) pork chops, ½-inch (1 cm) thick
3 teaspoons (15 g) Ras Al Hanout (page 286)
2 garlic cloves, minced
½ lemon
3 tablespoons (12 g) minced fresh parsley

Put your big, heavy skillet over medium-low heat and add the olive oil. Slosh it around to coat the skillet, then throw in your chops. Sauté them till they're good and brown on the bottom—maybe 8 to 10 minutes.

Flip 'em and sprinkle the done side with the ras al hanout. Let them keep sautéing till they're done on the other side and the juice runs clear, but don't overcook—you don't want to dry them out.

Plate the chops. Add the garlic to the oil left in the skillet and stir it around for just 20 seconds or so. Now squeeze in the juice from the lemon half and stir that in, too, scraping up the brown tasty bits from the skillet. Pour the lemon-garlic mixture over the chops.

Sprinkle the parsley over the chops and serve.

YIELD: 3 servings

Nutritional Analysis
Per serving: 514 calories; 37 g fat; 37 g protein; 9 g carbohydrate; 3 g dietary fiber; 6 g net carbs

Chili Verde de Puerco

Our tester Lisa says, "Definitely a keeper. I already told several folks at work about it!"

2 tablespoons (26 g) lard
3 pounds (1.3 kg) lean, boneless pork loin,
    in 1-inch (2.5 cm) cubes
1 onion, chopped
1 red bell pepper, diced
1 green bell pepper, diced
2 Anaheim chile peppers, diced
1 jalapeño, seeded and minced
5 tomatillos, papery skin removed, and chopped
1 teaspoon dried oregano
1 teaspoon ground cumin
¼ cup (60 ml) chicken broth
1 tablespoon (15 ml) cider vinegar
½ cup (8 g) chopped fresh cilantro, divided
Salt (optional)

A Dutch oven is best for this. Put it over medium heat, melt the lard, and brown the pork cubes. You'll need to work in batches, to avoid crowding. As each batch is done, remove to a plate with a slotted spoon.

Add the onions and the peppers—wash your hands really well with soap and water once you're done handling the Anaheim and jalapeño!—tomatillos, oregano, and cumin to the pan and sauté them, stirring often, until the vegetables soften.

Return the pork to the pot and add the broth, vinegar, and half the cilantro to the pot. Turn the burner to its lowest setting and let it simmer for an hour or so.

Salt to taste. Serve with lime wedges the rest of the cilantro, and Cocoyo (page 28) or Coconut Sour Cream (page 29) if you want a creamy note.

YIELD: 6 servings

Nutritional Analysis

Per serving: 347 calories; 15 g fat; 43 g protein; 10 g carbohydrate; 2 g dietary fiber; 8 g net carbs

Slow-Cooker Pork Chili-Stew

Is it chili? Is it a stew? Who cares? It's great!

1 pound (455 g) pork shoulder, exclusive of bone
1 tablespoon (13 g) lard
2 medium tomatoes
1 green bell pepper
1 onion
2 garlic cloves
1 cup (235 ml) chicken broth
1 tablespoon (7 g) paprika
1 teaspoon ground cumin
2 teaspoons dried oregano
1 piece chipotle chile canned in adobo, or more or less, to taste, minced

Cut your pork into 1-inch (2.5 cm) cubes. Put your big, heavy skillet over a medium burner and start browning the pork cubes in the lard. You don't have to brown them all over, just get a couple of sides, to get that good rich flavor in the finished dish. You'll need to do this in more than one batch—in my skillet it took three.

In the meanwhile, dice your tomatoes, pepper, onion, and mince the garlic.

As a batch of pork cubes is browned, start layering in your slow cooker: A layer of veggies, a layer of pork, a layer of veggies, a layer of pork—if you do three batches of cubes, you will have three layers of veggies and pork. (Like you couldn't figure that out.)

When all the pork is browned and layered in the slow cooker, pour the excess fat off from the skillet. Put it back on the burner, pour in the broth, and add the seasonings. Stir it all around, scraping up the nice browned bits from the bottom. Now pour this over the meat and vegetables. Slap on the cover, set it to low, and let it go for 8 hours.

YIELD: 4 servings

Nutritional Analysis

Per serving: 282 calories; 20 g fat; 18 g protein; 10 g carbohydrate; 3 g dietary fiber; 7 g net carbs

Sweet-and-Sour Pork

Sweet-and-sour pork without the sugar or cornstarch!

1 pound (455 g) pork loin, in 1-inch (2.5 cm) cubes
½ large onion, in 1-inch (2.5 cm) chunks
1 green bell pepper, in 1-inch (2.5 cm) squares
6 ounces (170 g) fresh pineapple chunks
2 tablespoons (28 ml) coconut aminos
2 tablespoons (28 ml) cider vinegar
1 tablespoon (8 g) grated gingerroot
2 drops stevia (optional)
3 tablespoons (39 g) coconut oil, divided
Glucomannan, if desired

Have everything cut up and standing by the stove. In a small dish, mix together any juice off the pineapple chunks with the coconut aminos, vinegar, gingerroot, and stevia, if using. Put this by the stove as well.

Put a wok or big skillet over highest heat. When it's good and hot, put in about half the coconut oil and let it melt. Throw in the pork and stir-fry for 4 to 5 minutes, or till done through. Scoop out onto a plate and reserve.

(continued)

Add the rest of the oil to the wok or skillet. Throw in the onion and pepper and stir-fry till they're just a little short of tender crisp.

Now add the pork back to the skillet along with the pineapple chunks. Stir it up, then stir in the sauce. Keep stir-frying for another minute or two. Thicken the sauce slightly with the glucomannan if desired, and serve.

YIELD: 3 servings

Nutritional Analysis
Per serving: 304 calories; 19 g fat; 20 g protein; 14 g carbohydrate; 2 g dietary fiber; 12 g net carbs

NOTE

You could serve this over Cauli-Rice (page 87), if you like, but we just ate it plain.

Dry-Rub Ribs

Smoking ribs takes time, but not a lot of work. It's a perfect choice for a summer Saturday when you're working around the yard—and what a reward for your hard work!

4 tablespoons (28 g) hot smoked paprika
8 teaspoons (21 g) chili powder
2 teaspoons salt
1 teaspoon dry mustard
1 teaspoon garlic powder
½ teaspoon black pepper

4 pounds (1.8 kg) pork spareribs
1 cup (235 ml) chicken broth
⅓ cup (80 ml) olive oil

You can oven roast your ribs if you want, following the directions for Spareribs Adobo (page 240), but for a rack of ribs that will make a grown man weep, slow smoke them. These directions are for a propane grill:

You'll need wood chips—any store that carries barbecue grills will have these, often in a variety of woods. Put a big bowl by your grill and start soaking several handfuls of wood chips in water—they'll need to soak for at least a half hour before you use them. Put a drip pan under one side of your grill, then light only the burner on the other side. Close the lid to let it heat. It helps to have an oven thermometer—some grills have them built in, but if yours doesn't, you can grab one for a couple of bucks in the housewares aisle of any grocery store. You want your internal grill temperature to be 250ºF (120ºC).

While the chips are soaking and the grill is heating, you're going to prepare your slab for smoking. In a small bowl, mix together all the seasonings. Set aside a couple of tablespoons (15 g) of this mixture in a cereal bowl.

Using the rest of the spice mixture, sprinkle your ribs liberally all over. (If you've got a little more rub than you need, save it for sprinkling on any dish that needs a little zip.)

Bear your mighty slab out to the backyard, taking along a square of heavy-duty foil, as well. Put the slab of ribs over the drip pan, on the side away from the lit burner.

Turn up the edges of your foil a bit and put it over the lit burner. Put a handful of those soaked wood chips on it. Now close the lid. Soon, smoke should be seeping out of your grill.

Go make your mopping sauce by mixing the chicken broth and olive oil with the reserved rub.

When your ribs have smoked for a half hour or so, take the mop, a basting brush, and a tongs out to your grill. Baste your slab all over with the mopping sauce, turning them over in the process. Put another handful of wood chips on the foil, and close the grill.

Now repeat this process—baste, turn, add more wood chips—every 30 minutes or so for a good 6 hours, or until your ribs are meltingly tender.

Serve with coleslaw, fauxtato salad, and plenty of napkins!

YIELD: 6 servings

Nutritional Analysis
Per serving: 676 calories; 58 g fat; 34 g protein; 5 g carbohydrate; 2 g dietary fiber; 3 g net carb

Oven-Barbecued Ribs

Tender, juicy, and delicious, with a real barbecue flavor.

4 pounds (1.75 kg) pork spareribs
Salt and black pepper
2 onions, finely minced
2 cups (480 g) Caveman Ketchup (page 273)
2 cups (475 ml) water
¼ cup (60 ml) Paleo Worcestershire (page 293)
½ cup (120 ml) Habanero-Lime Balsamic (page 284)
2 tablespoons (15 g) dry mustard
1 tablespoon (15 ml) liquid smoke flavoring (optional; Read the labels—some have sugar, some don't.)

Preheat oven to 350°F (180°C, or gas mark 4).

Salt and pepper your ribs lightly all over. Lay them, meaty side up, in a big, nonreactive roasting pan—Pyrex is ideal.

Put everything else in your food processor or blender—this may take 2 batches, depending on the size of your food processor. Pulse till the onion is finely minced. Spoon/pour half the sauce mixture over the ribs, turning to get all sides.

Put your ribs in the oven. Roast for 3 hours, basting every 30 minutes with the remaining sauce and turning the ribs over when you do.

Serve like any barbecued ribs: Cut into individual ribs and serve with lots of napkins. The Classic Coleslaw on page 122 would be perfect with these!

YIELD: 6 servings

Nutritional Analysis
Per serving: 618 calories; 45 g fat; 34 g protein; 20 g carbohydrate; 2 g dietary fiber; 18 g net carbs

NOTE

You may not have a Pyrex or other nonreactive roaster big enough for a full slab of ribs. No reason not to cut the slab in two, between the bones, to help them fit—or even to put them in two pans. Just divide the onions and sauce between them.

My Favorite Oven Ribs

When I want ribs and don't feel like slow-smoking them outside, this is my most-used recipe. I promise you, you won't miss the sugar sauce at all.

5 garlic cloves, crushed, divided
¼ cup (60 ml) olive oil, divided
4 pounds (1.8 kg) pork spareribs
1½ tablespoons (10.5 g) paprika
1½ teaspoons ground cumin
1½ teaspoons dried oregano
¾ teaspoon salt
¾ teaspoon black pepper
¾ cup (175 ml) chicken broth

Preheat oven to 325°F (170°C, or gas mark 3).

Mix 4 crushed cloves of garlic with 2 tablespoons (28 ml) of olive oil. Let it sit for 10 minutes. Rub this mixture all over the ribs, coating both sides. Put 'em in a roasting pan.

In a small dish, stir together the seasonings. Remove 1½ tablespoons (21 g) of the mixture to a cereal-size bowl and reserve.

Sprinkle the ribs all over with the seasoning mixture that you didn't reserve in the cereal bowl. Get all sides. Then stick 'em in the oven and set your timer for 25 minutes (or 20, or 30. Timing is not extra-sensitive here.)

While the ribs are roasting, stir the chicken broth, last clove of garlic, and the remaining olive oil into the reserved rub.

When the timer goes off, baste your ribs with the broth/olive oil mop, turning them over as you do so. Stick 'em back in the oven and set the timer for another 20 minutes.

Repeat, for a good 90 minutes to 2 hours; you want your ribs sizzling brown all over and tender when you pierce them with a fork. Cut into individual ribs to serve.

YIELD: 6 servings

Nutritional Analysis
Per serving: 633 calories; 54 g fat; 33 g protein; 3 g carbohydrate; 1 g dietary fiber; 2 g net carbs

Spareribs Adobo

4 pounds (1.8 kg) spareribs
¼ cup (29 g) Adobo Seasoning (page 285), divided
¾ cup (175 ml) chicken broth
¼ cup (60 ml) olive oil

Preheat oven to 325°F (170°C, or gas mark 3).

Put 1 tablespoon (15 g) of your adobo seasoning in a bowl. Sprinkle the rest all over your ribs, both sides. Put them in a roasting pan—if you have to cut your slab in half to make it fit, that's fine.

Put your ribs in the oven and set your timer for 30 minutes. In the meanwhile, mix the chicken broth and olive oil with the reserved adobo seasoning.

When the timer beeps, baste your ribs. Turn them over and baste the other side, too. Put them back in the oven.

Repeat this process—roast 30 minutes, baste the ribs, and turn them over—for 2 hours, or until the ribs are tender and the meat is pulling away from the bone. (How long this will take will depend on the thickness and meatiness of your ribs.) When your ribs are so tender you can't bear it, pull 'em out of the oven. Let them cool 5 minutes, cut them apart, and serve with plenty of napkins.

YIELD: 6 servings

Nutritional Analysis
Per serving: 631 calories; 54 g fat; 33 g protein; 2 g carbohydrate; 1 g dietary fiber; 1 g net carbs

Slow-Cooker Ribs

What a great choice for a day when you're going to a local football game. Let dinner cook while you're all out in the crisp autumn air. Then bring the fans home to ribs, with no more than 10 minutes' work before serving. Make some slaw the day before, and you've got a meal.

4 pounds (1.8 kg) pork spareribs
Salt and black pepper
½ cup (120 g) Caveman Ketchup (page 273)
1 orange
3 tablespoons (45 ml) Grapefruit Balsamic Vinegar
    (page 286) (Habanero-Lime Balsamic [page 284]
    would be good here, too.)
2 tablespoons (28 ml) coconut aminos
1 tablespoon (20 g) honey
1 teaspoon ground cumin
1 tablespoon (8 g) grated gingerroot
3 garlic cloves, crushed
1 tablespoon (15 ml) hot sauce or to taste (Tabasco's
    good, but chipotle hot sauce would work here, too.)

Salt and pepper your slab on both sides, then cut into individual ribs. Put 'em in your slow cooker.

Measure your Caveman Ketchup into a bowl. Grate the zest from the orange into it, then squeeze in the juice. Add everything else and stir it up. Pour over the ribs, stirring to make sure they're coated with the sauce.

Cover the pot, set to low, and cook for 6 hours.

When the ribs are done, remove them to a platter. Now pour the liquid from the slow cooker into a nonreactive sauce pan. Over a medium-high burner, cook it down until it thickens up and looks like barbecue sauce. Serve with the ribs.

YIELD: 6 servings

Nutritional Analysis
Per serving: 635 calories; 45 g fat; 33 g protein; 31 g carbohydrate; 2 g dietary fiber; 29 g net carbs. This figure will vary with how much of the sauce you consume. Less sauce, fewer carbs.

Definitely Not Pork Pad Thai

This is so seriously not authentic, but it is inspired by pad Thai. It tastes great, it's filling, and you don't need another thing with it, except maybe sriracha.

4 cups (1 kg) cooked spaghetti squash
2 tablespoons (28 ml) fish sauce
¼ cup (60 ml) lime juice
4 drops liquid stevia extract
1 pound (455 g) pork loin, cut in strips
3 garlic cloves, minced
2 large shallots, sliced thin
2 tablespoons (26 g) coconut oil, divided
8 ounces (225 g) mung bean sprouts, divided
¼ cup (4 g) minced fresh cilantro
¼ cup (10 g) minced fresh basil

Boil your spaghetti squash until tender, or pierce several times with a fork and microwave 6 to 8 minutes.

(continued)

In a small dish, mix together the fish sauce, lime juice, and liquid stevia extract. Set by the stove.

Slice your pork, mince your garlic, and slice your shallots.

Put a wok or big skillet over highest heat and melt half the oil. When it's hot, add the pork and stir-fry until it's just done through. Remove to a plate and hold.

Add the rest of the oil to the pan and let it get hot. Now throw in the garlic and shallots and stir-fry for just 30 seconds or so. Now add the spaghetti squash to the skillet and toss to combine it well with the garlic and shallots. Return the pork to the pan and add half the bean sprouts. Stir-fry for a minute.

Now add the fish sauce/lime juice mixture and toss to coat. Add the minced herbs and toss again. Toss in the rest of the sprouts and turn off the pan. Serve immediately.

YIELD: 4 servings

Nutritional Analysis

Per serving: 235 calories; 12 g fat; 18 g protein; 18 g carbohydrate; 3 g dietary fiber; 15 g net carbs

Asian Braised Pig's Feet

I'd never had pig's feet before, but really wanted to try them, and thought this book the right place for them. They're full of gelatin, which makes them great for your joints, hair, nails, and skin. Also makes them sticky— and tasty!

4 pig's feet
2 tablespoons (26 g) lard
1 medium onion, chopped
3 cloves garlic, sliced thin
1 piece gingerroot, about the size of a whole walnut
3 cups (710 ml) chicken broth, divided
¼ cup (60 ml) coconut aminos
½ teaspoon dry mustard
1 tablespoon (20 g) honey
1 piece star anise

Scrub your pig's feet well under running water. If they need it, grab a disposable razor and shave off any hair. (No, I am not joking.)

In your big, heavy skillet, over medium-high heat, melt the lard. Now throw in the pig's feet and brown them well on every surface you can get into actual contact with the bottom of the skillet—since they're irregular, there are spots that just won't brown, but do your best. While this is happening, chop the onion. Peel the garlic and slice it as thinly as possible. Do the same with the gingerroot. In a Pyrex measuring cup, mix together 1½ cups (355 ml) of the chicken broth, the coconut aminos, mustard, and honey, stirring till the honey dissolves.

Remove the pig's feet from the skillet and throw in the chopped onion. Sauté for a minute or two. Now put the pig's feet back in. Add the garlic and ginger, distributing them evenly around the skillet. Pour in the broth mixture and tuck the star anise down amid the whole thing.

Turn the burner to low. Now let the whole thing simmer for 3 to 4 hours, adding chicken broth as the mixture cooks down.

Serve with the pan liquid spooned over them. Don't bother with napkins—put a whole roll of paper towels on the table instead. You'll need them!

YIELD: 4 servings

Nutritional Analysis

Per serving: 656 calories; 44 g fat; 47 g protein; 16 g carbohydrate; 1 g dietary fiber; 15 g net carbs

Breakfast Sausage

No sugar, no MSG! If your family loves sausage for breakfast, or if you use it in meatloaf and other recipes, triple this recipe.

1 pound (455 g) lean pork shoulder, 80 percent lean
½ pound (225 g) pork fat, trimmings
5 scallions
1 pinch ground cinnamon
1 pinch ground cloves
1 pinch ground nutmeg
1 teaspoon black pepper
1½ tablespoons (3 g) dried sage
1 tablespoon (2.7 g) dried thyme leaves
1 tablespoon (1.7 g) dried marjoram
1½ teaspoons salt

Have the meat guys grind the lean pork and pork fat together. If you're buying pastured pork from a local small farmer, tell him or her that you need ground pork for sausage, and it shouldn't be too lean. I got them both and had them ground together, because so much pork is so lean. To start, put the pork in a big mixing bowl.

Trim your scallions, whack them into a few chunks, and put them in the food processor. Run till the scallions are very finely minced. Add them to the pork.

Measure all the other seasonings into a small dish and stir them together. Now sprinkle about ¼ of this mixture over the meat and knead it in. Repeat until you've worked in all the spices.

Form into 16 patties. One assumes you're not going to eat all of them at once, so freeze them, separated by a double layer of waxed paper. Thaw and cook like any standard sausage patty.

YIELD: 16 servings

Nutritional Analysis
Per serving: 116 calories; 11 g fat; 4 g protein; 1 g carbohydrate; trace dietary fiber; 1 g net carbs

NOTES

It's important not to use very lean pork for this recipe; that's why the combination of pork shoulder and fat trimmings.

If you wet your hands with cold water before handling the meat, it will stick to them far less.

Sausage Skillet Supper

One of my favorite skillet suppers. If you're planning to make this, don't bother forming your sausage meat into patties. I mean, what's the point?

1 batch Breakfast Sausage (page 243)
1 green bell pepper
2 celery ribs
½ medium onion
1 cup (235 ml) chicken broth
½ head cauliflower
2 tablespoons (28 ml) Paleo Worcestershire (page 293)
Salt and black pepper

Put your big, heavy skillet over medium-high heat and start browning and crumbling the sausage while you dice your veggies.

When the sausage is about halfway cooked, throw in the vegetables. Sauté, stirring frequently, till the pink is gone from the sausage. Drain off any excess grease.

Stir in the chicken broth. Leave the heat at medium high and let the whole thing cook till the broth has cooked way down—you want just a film of liquid left on the bottom of the skillet.

While the meat and veggies are simmering, turn your cauliflower into Cauli-Rice (see page 87).

Okay, your Cauli-Rice is cooked and your broth has reduced. Stir the Cauli-Rice into the stuff in the skillet, combining everything well. Stir in the Worcestershire, salt and pepper to taste, and serve.

YIELD: 4 servings

Nutritional Analysis
Per serving: 515 calories; 43 g fat; 20 g protein; 12 g carbohydrate; 4 g dietary fiber; 8 g net carbs

Italian Sausage

Great crumbled and sautéed with peppers and onions, in an omelet, lots of ways!

1½ teaspoons fennel seeds
1 teaspoon salt
1½ teaspoons black pepper
1 teaspoon paprika
1 teaspoon red-pepper flakes
2 pounds (900 g) ground pork, shoulder
2 cloves garlic, crushed

Put a small, heavy skillet over medium heat and stir the fennel seeds in it for just a few minutes. Put 'em in a your food processor, along with the salt, pepper, paprika, and red-pepper flakes. Pulse to grind the spices together.

Put the ground pork in a big mixing bowl and sprinkle the seasonings over it. Crush the garlic and add it, too. Now use clean hands to squish it all together really, really well. Make into 16 patties and freeze, if you're not going to use immediately.

YIELD: 8 servings

Nutritional Analysis
Per serving: 303 calories; 24 g fat; 19 g protein; 1 g carbohydrate; trace dietary fiber; 1 g net carbs

The Easter Lamb

You don't have to serve this for Easter, obviously. I did, because I grew up with leg of lamb for Easter, but this is a classic festive spring dish.

5 pounds (2 kg) leg of lamb
6 garlic cloves
⅓ cup (80 ml) olive oil
½ lemon

1½ tablespoons (2.5 g) minced fresh rosemary,
1½ tablespoons (6 g) minced fresh oregano,
¼ teaspoon black pepper

Start several hours before you want to serve your lamb, so you can give it time to marinate before the roasting time, which is also a few hours.

First, peel the garlic cloves and slice them thinly lengthwise.

Now put your lamb on the cutting board and, using a paring knife, go all serial killer on it. Stab it about 2 inches (5 cm) apart, all over, both sides. Insert a sliver of garlic into each hole—push them well in. Put your garlic-studded lamb in a nonreactive pan—I used Pyrex.

Mix together the olive oil, the juice of your half lemon, the minced herbs, and the pepper. Rub this mixture evenly over both sides of your lamb. Now let it sit for at least 2 to 3 hours.

About 3 hours before dinnertime, preheat your oven to 400°F (200°C, or gas mark 6). Put the lamb on a rack in a roasting pan. Insert a meat thermometer into the thickest part, but not touching the bone.

When the oven is up to temperature, put the lamb in and immediately turn the oven down to 325°F (170°C, or gas mark 3). Now let it roast for about 30 minutes per pound, a bit less if you prefer your lamb rare. (I like mine medium to medium well.) Check the meat thermometer to be sure—145°F to 150°F will be rare, 160°F well done.

Remove to a platter and let the lamb rest for 15 minutes while you make your gravy (see Simple Pan Gravy, page 289). Then carve and serve.

YIELD: At least 6 servings

Nutritional Analysis
Per serving: 800 calories; 63 g fat; 54 g protein; 2 g carbohydrate; trace dietary fiber; 2 g net carbs—but remember that the calorie and carb count assumes you'll be eating all that olive oil, which you won't.

Next, a couple of things to do with your leftover roast lamb.

Lamb Not-Biryani

I'm a chatty sort and was talking recipes with one of the cashiers at my neighborhood grocery store. He said his favorite dish was biryani, an Indian dish, and asked if I'd made one. I hadn't, since they usually involve rice, but thought it would be interesting to play with the idea. The result was this beautifully spiced skillet supper that uses up leftover leg of lamb.

1 head cauliflower
1 cup (230 g) Cocoyo (page 28)
2 garlic cloves, crushed
⅛ teaspoon cayenne
½ teaspoon ground cumin
¼ teaspoon black pepper
1 teaspoon salt or to taste
12 ounces (340 g) leftover lamb, cubed
1 onion, chopped
2 tablespoons (26 g) coconut oil
¼ teaspoon turmeric
⅛ teaspoon ground cloves
½ teaspoon ground cinnamon
⅓ cup (50 g) raisins
⅓ cup pistachio nuts, shelled and roasted

(continued)

First, turn your cauliflower into Cauli-Rice (page 87)—you want about 6 cups. While it's steaming, mix the Cocoyo with the garlic, cayenne, cumin, pepper, and salt. Dice up your lamb, too, and chop your onion.

Put your big, heavy skillet over medium heat and melt the coconut oil. Sauté the onion until it's translucent, then stir in the turmeric, cloves, and cinnamon. Cook another minute or so.

By now your Cauli-Rice should be ready. Add it to the skillet and stir it up. Stir in the lamb, the Cocoyo mixture, and the raisins. Let the whole thing cook a few more minutes.

Stir in the pistachios, and serve.

YIELD: 3 to 4 servings

Nutritional Analysis
Per serving: Assuming 3, each will have 681 calories; 53 g fat; 25 g protein; 34 g carbohydrate; 8 g dietary fiber; 26 g net carbs

NOTE

If you don't happen to have any leftover lamb on hand, there's no reason you couldn't dice up a lamb steak and sauté the bits before putting together the rest of this dish.

Sheep-Hunter's Pie

Because before there were shepherds there were sheep-hunters.

Proper Shepherd's Pie is made with leftover lamb, not hamburger—it's a traditional way to use up Sunday's leftovers. (The one with hamburger is properly called Cottage Pie. Yes, I'm a pedant.) A great reason to buy a good, big leg of lamb.

1 batch UnSour Cream Fauxtatoes (page 85)
1½ pounds (710 g) leftover lamb leg, cooked
1½ medium onions, peeled and chunked
1 cup (235 ml) Simple Pan Gravy (page 289)
   (or leftover lamb gravy)
2 tablespoons (28 ml) Paleo Worcestershire (page 293)
1 teaspoon black pepper
Salt (optional)
Paprika

Make your fauxtatoes and have them standing by. Preheat the oven to 350ºF (180ºC, or gas mark 4).

Cut your lamb and onions into chunks and put 'em in the food processor with the S blade in place. Pulse to grind the two together.

When the lamb mixture is still medium coarse, add the gravy, Worcestershire, and pepper. Now pulse to grind them into the mixture. Taste and add salt if you feel it needs it.

Grease an 8-cup (1.8 kg) casserole and put the lamb mixture in it, spreading it evenly. Top with the fauxtatoes, also spreading it evenly, as if you were "frosting" the lamb. Sprinkle lightly with paprika.

Put 'er in the oven and bake for an hour, then serve.

YIELD: 6 servings

Nutritional Analysis
Per serving: 497 calories; 42 g fat; 21 g protein; 12 g carbohydrate; 3 g dietary fiber; 9 g net carbs

Greek Lamb Shanks, Slow-Cooker Style

Lamb shanks are exactly the kind of tough, bony cut of meat that shines with slow cooking.

2½ pounds (1 kg) lamb shank (2 shanks)
3 tablespoons (45 ml) olive oil
1 carrot
1 medium onion
1 celery rib
½ medium tomato
¼ cup (60 ml) dry white wine
¼ cup (60 ml) chicken broth
2 garlic cloves
½ teaspoon dried oregano
¼ cup (15 g) chopped fresh parsley

First put your big, heavy skillet over medium heat and start browning the shanks in the olive oil. You want 'em brown all over.

While that's happening, peel your carrot and slice it thin. Ditto your onion. Slice your celery thin, too, including any fresh-looking leaves. Cut your tomato half in ¼-inch (6 mm) dice. Put all of this in the slow cooker. Don't forget to turn your shanks during all of this peeling and slicing!

Measure the wine and chicken broth and crush the garlic into it. Stir in the oregano.

Okay, your shanks are browned all over. Nestle them down into the vegetables as far as you can—mine stood up diagonally against the wall of the pot, thick ends down. Pour the wine and broth mixture over them and sprinkle the parsley over everything.

Cover and cook on low for 6 to 7 hours, or on high for 2 hours and low for another 2 to 3.

Serve the shanks with the vegetables and pot juices.

YIELD: 2 servings

Nutritional Analysis
Per serving: 1,171 calories; 82 g fat; 87 g protein; 13 g carbohydrate; 3 g dietary fiber; 10 g net carbs

NOTE

Obviously, this is a darned big serving at 1,171 calories. I just like the way a whole lamb shank looks on the plate. Feel free to carve these into smaller portions.

I'm very fond of lamb chops but not so fond of their price. Instead, I wait until whole legs of lamb go on sale around Easter (this year, lamb went down to $5.99/pound) and buy a few legs, having the nice meat guys slice them into ½-inch (1 cm) steaks for me. Then I stock the freezer. These are meatier than lamb chops, too.

Island Lamb Steak

Find tamarind sauce (a.k.a. tamarind extract) in a grocery store with a comprehensive international section, or order it online. It's a jarred product but contains nothing but tamarind, so I thought it acceptable. My jar has been living in my refrigerator for several years now and is still going strong.

24 ounces (680 g) lamb leg, in steaks, about ½-inch (1 cm) thick (This should be 2 steaks.)
1 garlic clove, crushed
1 tablespoon (15 g) brown mustard
1 teaspoon Tamarind Sauce (or substitute, see Note, page 294)
1 medium onion, sliced
1 tablespoon (13 g) coconut oil
1 large tomato

In a small dish, mix together the garlic, mustard, and Tamarind Sauce. Spread on one side of each of your lamb steaks.

Halve, peel, and slice your onion, a little thinner than ¼-inch (6 mm) thick.

Put your big, heavy skillet over low heat and melt the coconut oil, then slosh it around. Separate your onion slices and spread them in an even layer in the skillet. Lay your lamb steaks on the onion, coated side up. Cover the skillet and set the timer for 40 minutes.

YIELD: 2 servings

Nutritional Analysis
Per serving: 733 calories; 54 g fat; 50 g protein; 12 g carbohydrate; 2 g dietary fiber; 10 g net carbs

Maple-Glazed Lamb Steaks

So I saw this recipe for leg of lamb glazed with maple syrup and apple cider. That seemed like way too much time and trouble, not to mention too much sugar. But I was intrigued by the whole lamb-maple thing, and I made this up instead. Good thing, too; it's terrific.

1 pound (455 g) lamb leg steaks, ½-inch (1 cm) thick
2 tablespoons (28 ml) olive oil
2 tablespoons (20 g) minced shallot
2 teaspoons maple syrup
1 tablespoon (15 ml) balsamic vinegar
½ lemon
1 garlic clove, crushed
Salt and black pepper

Put your big, heavy skillet over medium heat and pan-broil the lamb steaks in the olive oil till they're done to your liking. Remove them from the pan.

Sauté the minced shallot in the pan drippings for a couple of minutes, till it's softened a bit.

Add the maple syrup and balsamic vinegar to the pan and squeeze in the juice from the half lemon. Crush in the garlic, too. Stir it up and salt and pepper to taste.

Put the lamb steaks back in the pan, flipping them to coat both sides. Let the whole thing simmer a minute or two, to reduce the sauce. Then serve the steaks with the sauce spooned over them.

YIELD: 2 servings

Nutritional Analysis
Per serving: 562 calories; 44 g fat; 33 g protein; 9 g carbohydrate; trace dietary fiber; 9 g net carbs

Lamb Steak with Sundried Tomatoes and Capers

One of those "Hmmm, what's in the house?" recipes, and boy, did it work out! I'd be happy to pay for something like this at a restaurant.

16 ounces (455 g) lamb leg, separable lean and fat
  (steak about ½-inch [1 cm] thick)
2 tablespoons (28 ml) olive oil
2 tablespoons (14 g) oil-packed sundried tomatoes,
  minced
2 anchovy fillets, minced
1 garlic clove, minced
4 teaspoons (11.5 g) capers, chopped
2 tablespoons (28 ml) balsamic vinegar
2 tablespoons (28 ml) water

Put your big, heavy skillet over medium heat and start pan-broiling the lamb steaks in the olive oil. Give them a good 7 to 8 minutes on each side. In the meanwhile, mince your sundried tomatoes, anchovy, and garlic and rough-chop your capers.

When the steaks are browned on both sides, but still pink in the center, plate them.

Add the stuff you chopped up to the skillet and sauté it for a minute. Then add the balsamic vinegar and water and stir it all around, deglazing the pan. Let it boil down till the liquid's getting syrupy, spoon over the steaks, and serve.

YIELD: 2 servings

Nutritional Analysis
Per serving: 411 calories; 32 g fat; 28 g protein; 3 g carbohydrate; trace dietary fiber; 3 g net carbs

Lemon-Garlic-Mint Lamb Steaks

Lamb and mint are a time-honored combination, and I like this a whole lot better than the gooey green mint jelly my mom used to eat with her lamb chops. I never did like that stuff.

2 pounds (900 g) lamb leg steaks
1 tablespoon (13 g) lard
1 large garlic clove crushed, or a couple of smaller ones
1 tablespoon (6 g) minced fresh mint
1 tablespoon (15 ml) extra-virgin olive oil
¼ lemon

Slash the edges of your lamb steaks to prevent curling.

In your big, heavy skillet, over high heat, melt the lard and start pan-frying the lamb steaks. You want them brown on both sides and done through, but not dried out.

In the meanwhile, peel your garlic and mince your mint.

Okay, we're figuring your lamb steaks are brown on both sides and done through. Remove them to a platter.

(continued)

You should have lots of nice brown stuff in the pan. Use a spatula to scrape it up, stirring it around. If you need to, add a tablespoon (15 ml) or two of water to dissolve the brown stuff, but I didn't need it.

Now add the olive oil and crush in the garlic. Sauté for a couple of minutes, stirring all the while.

Now squeeze in the juice from the lemon and stir that in well. Pour the stuff from the pan over the steaks.

Sprinkle the mint over everything and serve while it's still hot.

YIELD: 4 servings

Nutritional Analysis
Per serving: 474 calories; 37 g fat; 32 g protein; 1 g carbohydrate; trace dietary fiber; 1 g net carbs

Caribbean Dreams Lamb Steak

Though not authentic by any means, this is inspired by Jamaican jerk. One of the best things I've ever done with a lamb steak

1 pound (455 g) lamb leg steak
1 teaspoon liquid smoke flavoring (Read the labels—some have sugar, some don't.)
1 teaspoon hot sauce (Habanero or Scotch bonnet sauce)
1 tablespoon (13 g) coconut oil
2 tablespoons (20 g) minced onion
1 scallion, minced

½ teaspoon dried thyme or 1 tablespoon fresh
1 teaspoon black pepper
1 teaspoon ground allspice
¾ teaspoon ground ginger
1 tablespoon (15 ml) Habanero-Lime Balsamic (page 284)
1½ teaspoons coconut aminos
1 tablespoon (15 ml) water

Rub your steak on both sides with the smoke flavoring, then with the habanero or scotch bonnet sauce. If you used your hands for this—I did—go wash them right away!! You don't want them booby trapped with super-hot peppers.

Put your big, heavy skillet over medium-high heat and melt the coconut oil. Now throw in the steak, and brown it nicely, maybe 5 to 6 minutes per side. Use the time to mince your onion and scallion!

Remove the steak to a plate while you . . .

Turn the heat down, and add the onion and scallion to the skillet. Sauté for just a couple of minutes. Now add everything else and stir it all up.

Put your steak back in the skillet, turning to coat with the sauce. Let it simmer for a couple of minutes, till the sauce reduces to a syrupy consistency. Serve the steak with the sauce over it!

YIELD: 2 servings

Nutritional Analysis
Per serving: 495 calories; 38 g fat; 33 g protein; 6 g carbohydrate; 1 g dietary fiber; 5 g net carbs

Lamb Stroganoff

Creamy, savory, and comforting.

1 pound (455 g) lamb leg steak
¼ cup (60 ml) olive oil, divided
1 medium tomato, ¼-inch (6 mm) dice
1 medium onion, chopped
8 ounces (225 g) sliced mushrooms
1 tablespoon (15 g) brown mustard
1 teaspoon dried thyme
½ teaspoon hot smoked paprika
13½ ounces (400 ml) unsweetened coconut milk
Salt and black pepper to taste

Put your big, heavy skillet over high heat. When it's good and hot, start browning your lamb steak in 1 tablespoon (15 ml) of the olive oil. Give it about 6 to 7 minutes per side.

In the meanwhile, dice your tomato, chop your onion, and slice your mushrooms, if you foolishly bought them unsliced.

When your steak is well seared on both sides, but still pink in the middle, pull it out of the skillet to a plate and set it aside.

Add another tablespoon (15 ml) of oil to the skillet and start sautéing the diced tomato. As it softens, mash the tomato with a fork. When it's been reduced to a pulp in the bottom of the skillet, let your tomato simmer for about 3 to 4 minutes, then scoop it out into a bowl.

Now put the rest of the oil in the skillet and start sautéing the onion and mushrooms. If you'd like the mushrooms in somewhat smaller pieces, use the edge of your spatula to break them up some, but it's not essential.

When the onions are soft and translucent and the mushrooms have darkened, add the tomato pulp back to the skillet. Add the mustard, thyme, and paprika to the skillet, too, and stir it all up.

Now stir in the coconut milk. Bring the whole thing to a simmer, turn the burner down, and let it cook while you . . .

Throw your lamb on the cutting board and slice it thin, across the grain. Cut the slices in 1-inch (2.5 cm) lengths or so. Then stir all your lamb bits into the stuff in the skillet. Pour in any lamb juices that have gathered on the plate and/or cutting board.

Keep simmering for another 5 to 7 minutes or so. Salt and pepper to taste, then serve.

You can serve this in bowls, as-is; as a thick, creamy stew; or you can serve it over Fauxtatoes, Cauli-Rice, or spaghetti squash.

YIELD: 3 servings

Nutritional Analysis
Per serving: 758 calories; 70 g fat; 25 g protein; 13 g carbohydrate; 2 g dietary fiber; 11 g net carbs. Four servings if you serve it over something!

Chapter 12

SOUPS

Soup is such a wonderful, versatile food! It can be a light first course or a hearty meal-in-a-bowl. It can be mellow and comforting or spicy and stimulating, casual or elegant. And few foods are more nutritious—because of how soup is cooked, it conserves water-soluble vitamins.

It is also, of course, the main way we eat bone broth, and bone broth is magical, healing stuff. It's a great source of calcium in its most readily absorbed form, and that's valuable enough. It's also a terrific source of gelatin. This is why soup made from homemade broth or stock jellies when you chill it.

Why is this important? Gelatin is simply a form of the connective tissue *collagen*. The protein in the average animal carcass is roughly 50 percent collagen by weight, but that collagen is disproportionately distributed in the bones, joints, skin, and tough, sinewy cuts. Because of the American preference for tender, skinless, boneless cuts of muscle meat, our intake of collagen has dropped dramatically, and this, in turn, has skewed our amino acid balance, just as eating separated vegetable oils and restricting animal fats has skewed our fatty acid balance.

Gelatin is soothing to the intestinal tract, which is why your mother gave you soup when you had an upset stomach. (That mom probably gave you Campbell's doesn't change the fact that mom was acting on ancient wisdom.) It helps build strong and healthy joints and indeed will help strengthen all of your connective tissue. That's why it's great for your skin. You've heard of collagen cream? Taking the stuff internally will do a whole lot more for your face than rubbing it on the surface. Gelatin also builds strong, healthy hair and nails, so consider soup a frontline beauty treatment.

There is some evidence that gelatin also improves insulin response in diabetics, no small thing. Just as impressive, it's generally anti-inflammatory. No wonder soup has long been considered a cure-all!

Accordingly, this chapter begins with recipes both for broth and stock. The difference? Broth is simply made from boiling up bones, often completely naked bones, and little else. It's a way to get all of the nutrition out of any meat, poultry, or fish you eat. Stock is a richer product, made from cooking bony but meaty cuts, plus seasoning vegetables, specifically to create a wildly flavorful and nutritious final result.

If you find yourself wanting soup when you have no homemade broth or stock in the house, there are some decent packaged broths out there, but read the labels. I like Kitchen Basics brand, which comes in several varieties, including chicken, beef, vegetable, and seafood. Kitchen Basics is widely distributed in grocery stores. Your health food store, too, is bound to have a selection of organic broths. To improve the nutritional profile of packaged broth, dissolve a tablespoon (7 g) or two of unflavored gelatin powder in your pot of hot soup. Improves the texture, too—gives it a wonderful silky quality.

So! First to the broth and stock, then to the soups!

Bone Broth

One of the most important healing and strengthening foods, from something most people throw away. This is more a rule than a recipe.

Whenever you eat meat that has bones, save the bones in an old plastic grocery sack in the freezer. (Or some other plastic bag. Or another container. That part doesn't matter.) Save chicken bones in one sack, beef bones in another, and fish bones in a third—throw in lobster, crab, and shrimp shells, too. Don't worry if the bones are picked clean; they'll still make great broth. When you have enough to fill your stockpot or slow cooker, it's time to make broth.

I like to make broth in my slow cooker, but a stockpot is great, too. Just dump in the bones, cover with water, add about ¼ cup (60 ml) of any kind of vinegar—this helps draw calcium out of the bones, making the broth more nutritious—and about a teaspoon of salt, unless you're dead set against it. The salt helps draw flavor out of the bones, and a teaspoon in a whole pot of broth isn't much.

Now cover your slow cooker or kettle. If you're using your slow cooker, set it on low, and if you're using a kettle, put it over a low burner.

Now just let it sit. And sit. And sit. I've been known to let mine slow cook for two solid days; I wouldn't give it a second less than 12 hours, and that actually seems skimpy to me. This is why a slow cooker is good—you can just let it play quietly in a corner by itself, while you may be understandably reluctant to leave a stove burner on all night or while you're away from home.

(continued)

(If you're making your broth on the stove: Tightly cover your pot and bring the broth to a good hard boil before turning it off for the night or leaving the house, and you should be able to safely leave it on the stove overnight. I've never had a problem with this. But, I repeat, I'm a daredevil. Do what you're comfortable with—and I sure wouldn't leave it for a lot longer than 12 hours, and you should be sure to finish the whole project within two days' time.)

Now strain out the bones, throw 'em away, and make a killer pot of soup with your broth. Or freeze it. Or use it to make Broth Concentrate, page 27, a very useful thing to have in your freezer.

It's impossible to get an accurate nutritional count on this, but you know a few things: It'll have virtually no carbs, some protein (that gelatin, remember?), and a good deal of calcium in its most readily absorbed form.

Chicken Stock

Oh my gosh. Pure gold.

10 chicken backs (good, big meaty ones)
3 celery ribs
1 large carrot
1 large onion
¼ cup (60 ml) vinegar (I used cider vinegar.)
Salt, just a little (I used about a teaspoon to the whole
   pot. It helps draw flavor out of the bones and meat.)
1 bay leaf

I think it's easiest to do this in your slow cooker. I use my big 5½-quart (5 kg) Crock-Pot. Throw in the chicken backs. Whack the celery into chunks about 3- to 4-inches (7.5 to 10 cm) long. Peel the carrot and cut it in chunks, too. Same with the onion. Throw 'em all in the pot.

Now add water to just cover and add the vinegar, and the salt if you're using it. Throw in the bay leaf. Cover the pot, set it to low, and let the whole thing cook 12 to 18 hours. (I generally start mine one day and finish the next.)

Turn off the pot and let your stock cool with the lid in place. Now put a colander in a great big bowl and strain your stock. You can throw away the bones and veggies, if you like, though I feed mine to my chickens. (Yes, my chickens eat chicken. No, they haven't gotten Mad Chicken Disease.) I often pick some of the meat off and eat it myself; it's wildly moist and flavorful.

Now chill your stock. I don't have room in my overstuffed fridge for my biggest bowl. Since I wrote this book in winter, I put mine on a high shelf in an unheated storage room, where the temperature hovers in the low forties. In the summer I'd transfer it to a number of smaller containers that would fit in the fridge. You're just cooling the stock long enough for the fat that rises to the top to solidify, so you can easily skim it off. This, by the way, is schmaltz, one of the most popular fats in Jewish cookery—very much worth keeping.

You have now achieved truly gorgeous stock. You may use it to make soup, in sauces, or cook it down to make concentrate for flavoring all sorts of things.

YIELD: I get about 2½ to 3 quarts (2½ to 3 L) of stock.

Nutritional Analysis
MasterCook can't account for the skimmed fat so I can't get an accurate nutritional count. This will have a few grams of carb per serving, because of the vegetables, and again, plenty of calcium and protein.

Beef Stock

Because the bones and vegetables need roasting, this is a bit more complicated than chicken stock, but it's so very worth it.

5 pounds (2 kg) meaty beef soup bones
Olive oil (a few tablespoons)
2 large onions
2 carrots
1 large parsnip
12 large celery ribs
Salt and pepper
1 bay leaf

Preheat oven to 350°F (180°C, or gas mark 4).

Rub your beef bones lightly with olive oil and lay them in a large roasting pan. Peel and chunk the onions, carrots, and parsnip; wash and chunk the celery; and scatter them around the bones. (If your pan doesn't have enough room for both, you can roast the vegetables in a separate, oiled pan.) Roast everything slowly, turning everything over now and again with a spatula, until the bones are well browned and the vegetables caramelize—but don't let anything scorch. You don't want any black spots.

Now transfer it all to a stockpot and cover with water. Add just a teaspoon or so of salt, a half teaspoon of pepper, and a bay leaf. Bring to a simmer, then turn it down so it's just below a simmer and let it cook, uncovered or loosely covered (you want steam to escape, to let the stock concentrate a bit), for at least 6 hours. During the first hour or so, scum will rise to the top; skim this off and discard.

After a good 6 hours, turn off your burner and let the stock cool. Now strain it into a big darned bowl. You can discard the bones and vegetables, though I can't resist picking off bits of the meat and eating any marrow.

Chill the stock till it gels and the fat is hardened on top, then skim off the fat. Now you can freeze your stock in containers to have on hand for soups and sauces, or you can make Broth Concentrate (page 27) or Slow-Cooker Demi-Glace (page 27), both fabulous things to have in your freezer.

YIELD: Makes roughly 3 quarts (3 L).

Nutritional Analysis
One more time: MasterCook was no help here; it doesn't know from beef soup bones, and we don't know how much carbohydrate cooks out of the seasoning vegetables. The best I can do is to tell you that the vegetables have about 90 grams of carb with 30 grams of fiber to start with.

Now, to do something with your broth and stock! Because I make broth more often than stock, most of these recipes call for it, though you can use stock instead to great effect.

Mulligatawny

This is our favorite soup by far. That Nice Boy I Married calls it "Smell-I-Ga-Yummy," because the fragrance is so heavenly.

1 medium onion, chopped

1 carrot, shredded

2 celery ribs, diced

2 tablespoons (26 g) coconut oil

1½ tablespoons (9.4 g) curry powder (or more, to taste)

2 cloves garlic, crushed

2 quarts (2 L) chicken broth

3 cups (420 g) diced chicken (leftover, or you can dice up boneless, skinless breasts and/or thighs)

1 bay leaf

1 tart apple, diced

½ teaspoon black pepper

½ teaspoon dried thyme

Zest of 1 fresh lemon, grated

14 fluid ounces (425 ml) unsweetened coconut milk

Salt to taste

In a large, heavy-bottomed pot, over low-medium heat, sauté the vegetables in the coconut oil. When they're soft, add the curry powder and garlic and sauté for another couple of minutes.

Add the chicken broth, diced chicken, bay leaf, diced apple, pepper, thyme, and lemon zest to the pot and stir it all up. Bring to a simmer and let it cook for 30 to 45 minutes.

Stir in the coconut milk, salt to taste, and serve.

YIELD: 6 servings

Nutritional Analysis
Per serving: 496 calories; 38 g fat; 30 g protein; 10 g carbohydrate; 2 g dietary fiber; 8 g net carbs

NOTE

We usually make this out of chicken, but it's good with turkey broth and diced leftover turkey and particularly fabulous made from the remains of a leg of lamb— simmer the meaty lamb bone till you have a broth and proceed from there.

Almond-Coconut Soup

This is so good! All I did was take my favorite recipe for peanut soup and swap almond butter for the peanut butter, coconut oil for the butter, and coconut milk for the heavy cream. If anything, I like this better than peanut soup!

1 large celery rib

½ medium onion

1 tablespoon (13 g) coconut oil

1 quart (946 ml) chicken broth

¾ cup (195 g) almond butter

1 cup (235 ml) coconut milk

Salt and black pepper to taste

Glucomannan (optional)

Dice your celery and chop up any leaves, too—they're really good in the soup. Dice your onion. In a big, heavy saucepan, over medium heat, melt the coconut oil and sauté the celery and onion till the onion is translucent.

Add the chicken broth, bring to a simmer, and let it cook until the vegetables are quite soft—30 minutes or so.

Grab your stick blender! Use it to purée the onion and celery into the broth. Now add the almond butter and keep blending till it's incorporated. Blend in the coconut milk, and salt and pepper to taste.

If you want, you can use your glucomannan shaker to thicken this up a little—I made mine a little thicker than heavy cream—but it's awfully good as-is. If you wanted to garnish this, some toasted slivered almonds would be pretty. So would some snipped chives or scallion tops. But honestly, we just ate it plain, and it was awesome.

YIELD: 4 servings

Nutritional Analysis
Per serving: 498 calories; 45 g fat; 17 g protein; 15 g carbohydrate; 8 g dietary fiber; 7 g net carbs

Grainless Avgolemono

This iconic Greek egg-lemon soup traditionally includes rice or orzo. I just left that part out. Still tastes great.

6 cups (1.4 L) chicken stock (Quality really counts here.)
1 teaspoon minced fresh dill weed
8 ounces (225 g) boneless, skinless chicken breast in ½-inch (1 cm) cubes (Use thighs if you prefer.)
1 carrot, shredded
4 eggs
½ cup (120 ml) fresh lemon juice, or more, to taste
Salt and black pepper

In a big, heavy saucepan over medium heat, bring the chicken stock to a simmer and add the dill. Stir in the chicken cubes—don't just dump them in, stir them in, or they'll congeal into a clump in the bottom of the pot. Shred the carrot and add it, too.

While that's simmering, put the eggs and lemon juice in your blender and run till they're well-blended. Turn the blender off but leave the mixture in it.

When the chicken and carrot are done, turn the blender back on and slowly add one ladleful of the hot broth to the egg-lemon mixture. When that's smooth, add another.

Now take your blender container over to your pot. Turn the heat down to just below a simmer, and start whisking the soup. Slowly add the mixture from the blender, whisking the whole time. Keep cooking another 30 seconds, whisking the whole time, then serve.

YIELD: 4 servings

Nutritional Analysis
Per serving: 178 calories; 6 g fat; 20 g protein; 5 g carbohydrate; 1 g dietary fiber; 4 g net carbs

NOTES

Some people prefer their Avgolemono completely smooth. If you're one of them, skip the chicken chunks, and use your stick blender to purée the carrot shreds into the stock. Don't skip the step of "tempering" the eggs by blending a little of the hot broth into them before whisking them into the main body of the soup, or you'll get a lemony egg drop soup, not the creamy mixture you're looking for.

Chicken Gumbo

If you prefer, you can use 8 ounces (225 g) of boneless, skinless chicken thighs and just dice them and stir them in. I use the stuff on the bone because I always have it on hand and I feel the bones enrich the broth.

1 large onion, diced

1 large green bell pepper, diced

1 large celery rib, diced

1 tablespoon (13 g) lard or fat of choice

3 large tomatoes, ¼-inch (6 mm) dice

1½ cups (82.5 g) sliced okra

1 quart (946 ml) chicken broth

2 garlic cloves, crushed

1 teaspoon dried thyme or 1 tablespoon (2.4 g) fresh

¼ teaspoon cayenne or to taste

¼ teaspoon black pepper

2 bay leaves, whole

12 ounces (340 g) skinless chicken, dark meat (One big leg-and-thigh quarter, or a couple of smaller ones.)

Dice your onion, pepper, and celery. Put a big, heavy saucepan over medium heat, melt the lard, and start sautéing.

Dice your tomatoes and slice your okra. When the onion is turning translucent, stir in the tomatoes and okra and let them sauté a couple of minutes.

Stir in the chicken broth, garlic, thyme, cayenne, and pepper. Add the bay leaves. Plunk in your skinned chicken legs and thighs, the whole thing. Bring to a simmer, cover, turn the burner down to low, and let the whole thing cook for an hour.

Use a tongs to fish your chicken out of the soup and put it on a plate till they're cool enough to handle. Strip the meat off, snip it up, and stir it back in. Now serve.

YIELD: 3 servings

Nutritional Analysis

Per serving: 287 calories; 12 g fat; 26 g protein; 18 g carbohydrate; 5 g dietary fiber; 13 g net carbs

Lemony Pumpkin Soup

Our tester Mary made this with canned pumpkin, because she couldn't find fresh, and said it worked fine. Another tester, Rebecca, made the same recipe, substituting fresh butternut squash for the pumpkin, and said it worked great. She also said to tell you her husband thinks this soup is really good cold, too.

2 tablespoons (26 g) coconut oil

1 medium onion, chopped

1 pound (455 g) pumpkin cubes, peeled (Fresh would be best, but use canned if fresh is not available.)

1 medium celery root (10 to 12 ounces [280 to 340 g])

2 garlic cloves, crushed

2 sprigs fresh thyme or ½ teaspoon ground dried thyme

½ teaspoon Celery Salt (page 285, or use store-bought)

5 cups (1.2 L) chicken stock

½ cup (120 ml) unsweetened coconut milk

1 lemon

Salt and black pepper

In a big, heavy saucepan, over medium-low heat, melt the coconut oil and sauté the onion gently until it's translucent.

If you're using fresh pumpkin, now's the time to seed, peel, and cube it. It's definitely time to peel your celery root—removing the tough layer under the skin, too. This is easiest if you whack the celery root into quarters or slices first. Cut it in small cubes. Put both pumpkin and celery root cubes in the saucepan, along with the garlic, thyme, celery salt, and chicken stock. (If you're using canned pumpkin, we'll put that in later.) Bring to a simmer and cook 30 minutes, or until the vegetables are soft.

Remove the thyme sprigs. Now use your stick blender to purée everything. If you're using canned pumpkin, blend it in now and bring the whole thing back to a simmer, before you . . .

Stir in the coconut milk. Halve your lemon, and squeeze in the juices. Stir it in.

Salt and pepper to taste, and serve.

YIELD: 6 servings

Nutritional Analysis
Per serving: 123 calories; 9 g fat; 2 g protein; 10 g carbohydrate; 1 g dietary fiber; 9 g net carbs. Calculated for pumpkin.

Broccoli-Apple Soup

Unusual and good. And how nutritious is this?!

2 pounds (900 g) broccoli
1 small Granny Smith apple
1 medium onion
6 cups (1.4 L) chicken broth
1 pound (455 g) skinless chicken legs and thighs
1 cup (235 ml) unsweetened coconut milk
Salt and pepper to taste

Peel the tough skin off the broccoli stems and chop the stems and flowers coarsely. Throw it in your slow cooker. Chop your apple and onion and do the same. Pour in the chicken broth and plunk the leg-and-thigh on top. Cover the pot and set it to low if you're going out for several hours, or high if you want it done within 4 or 5.

Now use a tongs to pull out the chicken. Put it on a plate and let it cool, while you . . .

Use your stick blender to purée the broccoli, apple, and onion right there in the slow cooker. Add the coconut milk and blend that in, too.

Pick the chicken off the bones and snip or chop it into bite-size bits—I use my kitchen shears. Stir back into the soup, salt and pepper to taste, and serve.

YIELD: 6 servings

Nutritional Analysis
Per serving: 209 calories; 11 g fat; 18 g protein; 11 g carbohydrate; 4 g dietary fiber; 7 g net carbs

Beef Tomato Bisque

This soup depends on the stock. If you have broth instead, it's worth the time to start with 6 cups (1.4 L) and cook it down to 4 before adding the other ingredients. Or, if you have some concentrated broth or demi-glace on hand, add a heaping spoonful!

4 cups (950 ml) beef stock
3 medium tomatoes, diced
1 small onion, diced
1 clove garlic
1 bay leaf
¼ teaspoon black pepper
3 whole cloves
13½ fluid ounces (400 ml) unsweetened coconut milk
Salt to taste
2 tablespoons (5 g) minced fresh basil

In a big, heavy saucepan, combine the stock, tomatoes, onion, garlic, bay leaf, and pepper. Put your cloves in a tea ball before throwing them in, so they'll be easy to remove later on. Bring to a simmer and let the whole thing cook for a half hour or more, till the vegetables are quite soft.

(continued)

Remove the bay leaf and the tea ball with the cloves in it. Now use your stick blender to purée the soup until smooth. Stir in the coconut milk and bring back to a simmer. Salt to taste, stir in the basil, and serve.

YIELD: 6 servings

Nutritional Analysis
Per serving: 196 calories; 14 g fat; 9 g protein; 11 g carbohydrate; 2 g dietary fiber; 9 g net carbs

Oxtail Soup

Don't wrinkle your nose! The meat on oxtails is just voluntary muscle, the same as a steak or a roast. But it's bonier and more flavorful and makes this soup taste astoundingly rich. And don't panic at this list of instructions—I'm explaining how to do this either in a Dutch oven or a slow cooker, so it takes up a lot of space. But it's not hard.

3½ pounds (1.5 kg) beef oxtails (good meaty ones, cut in sections)
2 tablespoons (26 g) lard or tallow, divided
1 leek
1 onion
1 celery rib
2 carrots
1 turnip
1 quart (946 ml) beef broth
2 teaspoons dried thyme
2 medium tomatoes, diced
2 tablespoons (28 ml) balsamic vinegar
Salt and black pepper

I made my soup in my Dutch oven, but you could use a slow cooker if you like. If you're using a Dutch oven, do your browning in it. For the slow cooker, use your big, heavy skillet.

Either way, melt a tablespoon (13 g) of the lard or tallow in the pot of choice, over medium-high heat, and when it's hot, throw in the oxtails. You want to sear them well all over.

While that's happening, trim the leaves and root off your leek and split it lengthwise. Wash it to get out any dirt between the layers. Then slice into nice half rounds, a little thinner than ¼ inch (6 mm). Go turn your oxtails!

Dice your onion and celery, including any celery leaves. Peel and slice your carrots, too, and peel your turnip and cut into ½-inch (1 cm) cubes.

When your oxtails are nicely browned, remove them to a plate. (If you're using a slow cooker, you don't want to put them in there yet.)

Melt the rest of the fat in your pan and throw in the leek, onion, and celery. Sauté till the onion is translucent.

If you're using your slow cooker, transfer the vegetables into it. Pour your broth into the skillet and stir it around to loosen up any browned bits. If you're cooking your soup in a Dutch oven, leave the vegetables in it and add the broth to the kettle. Again, stir it around a bit. Add the thyme to the broth.

Now add the carrots and the turnips to the soup, either in the Dutch oven or slow cooker. Throw the oxtails on top of that. (Having the oxtails on top of the veggies is important in a slow cooker, less so in a kettle.) Pour the broth over the veggies and oxtails.

Dice the tomatoes and put them on top. Pour in the balsamic vinegar. Add salt and pepper to taste.

Cover. If you're using the Dutch oven, put it on a low burner. If you're using a slow cooker, set it to low. For a Dutch oven, let it simmer 4 to 5 hours; in a slow cooker I'd give it at least 6 to 8.

Done? Use a tongs to pull out the oxtails and put them on a plate. (You may as well use the plate you used earlier, to save on dishwashing.) Let them cool till you can handle them.

In the meanwhile, take a look at your soup and see how much fat there is on top. If there's quite a lot, you'll want to skim it a bit. The easiest way is to cool and chill the soup overnight, then spoon off the hardened fat, but that will hardly do if you want to eat it for tonight's supper. In that case, just use a deep-bellied spoon or a turkey baster to skim.

When your broth is skimmed and your oxtails cool enough to handle, pick the meat off the bones. Discard the bones, chop the meat, and throw it back into the soup.

If you've chilled your soup, you'll want to bring it back to a simmer of course. Either way, when your soup is hot, ladle into bowls and serve.

YIELD: At least 5 servings

Nutritional Analysis
MasterCook says they'll break down as follows, but, once again, that doesn't take into account the fact that you'll skim the fat off the soup.

Per serving: 812 calories; 42 g fat; 90 g protein; 13 g carbohydrate; 2 g dietary fiber; 11 g net carbs

Cauliflower Soup

Thick and rich-tasting, good on a chilly night.

2 celery ribs
½ large onion
1 medium carrot
1 tablespoon (13 g) coconut oil
1 medium head cauliflower
2 quarts (2 L) chicken broth
2 cloves garlic, crushed
¼ teaspoon ground nutmeg
Salt and black pepper to taste

Dice your celery and onion and shred your carrot.

In a really big saucepan with a heavy bottom, over medium heat, melt the coconut oil. Throw in the celery, onion, and carrot and start them sautéing.

While that's happening, trim the leaves and the bottom of the stem off your cauliflower and whack the rest into chunks.

When your seasoning vegetables have softened, add the cauliflower, garlic, chicken broth, and nutmeg to the pot.

Bring to a simmer, turn the burner to low, and let it cook until the cauliflower is soft, about 40 to 45 minutes.

Now use your stick blender to purée the whole thing right there in the pot. Salt and pepper to taste, and serve.

YIELD: 6 servings

Nutritional Analysis
Per serving: 106 calories; 4 g fat; 9 g protein; 9 g carbohydrate; 3 g dietary fiber; 6g net carbs

Purée Mongole

I saw an old recipe that called for blending canned green pea and tomato soups. It sounded interesting, so I decided to try it with actual peas and tomatoes. Good!

2 cups (300 g) frozen green peas, thawed, or fresh ones if you can get 'em.

4 medium tomatoes, diced

½ cup (40 g) diced onion

½ cup (60 g) diced celery

2 cups (475 ml) chicken broth

1 teaspoon curry powder

2 cups (475 ml) unsweetened coconut milk

Salt to taste

This is quite simple: Combine the peas, tomatoes, onion, celery, chicken broth, and curry powder in a big saucepan. Put over medium heat and bring to a simmer. Turn down to keep it just simmering and let it cook for 45 minutes, till everything's soft.

Use your stick blender to purée everything quite thoroughly. You want this smooth. Now blend in the coconut milk, salt to taste, and serve.

YIELD: 4 servings

Nutritional Analysis
Per serving: 334 calories; 25 g fat; 10 g protein; 22 g carbohydrate; 6 g dietary fiber; 16 g net carbs

After-Thanksgiving Cabbage Soup

When I was growing up, the only thing better than Thanksgiving dinner was the soup my mother made the following Monday from the nearly stripped carcass. But Mom's soup included the leftover stuffing, plus rice, so I needed to come up with my own after-Thanksgiving soup.

1 medium onion, chopped

2 celery ribs, diced

1 medium carrot, shredded

2 tablespoons (26 g) chicken fat or coconut oil

6 cups (1.4 L) turkey broth

2 bay leaves

1 teaspoon dried thyme

2 cloves garlic, crushed

½ teaspoon ground cinnamon

½ teaspoon ground nutmeg

1 14.5 ounce (410 g) can tomatoes or three medium tomatoes, diced

¼ head cabbage, sliced thin

1 ½ cups (210 g) cooked diced turkey

Salt and black pepper

Chop your onion and celery. If your celery has leaves, chop 'em up and use them—they're wonderful. Shred your carrot—I used my box grater, but you could run it through the shredding blade of your food processor instead. Come to think of it, you could throw all three in the food processor and pulse till they're chopped medium fine. Just reduce them to little bits somehow.

In a big, heavy saucepan, over low heat, melt the fat or oil and sauté the onion, celery, and carrot until they're starting to soften.

Add the turkey broth, bay leaves, thyme, garlic, cinnamon, nutmeg, and tomatoes and bring it to a simmer. Let it cook at a low simmer for a half hour or so, then stir in the cabbage and diced turkey. Simmer till the cabbage is just tender, maybe another 15 to 20 minutes.

Salt and pepper to taste, and serve.

YIELD: 4 servings

Nutritional Analysis
Per serving: 175 calories; 10 g fat; 13 g protein; 8 g carbohydrate; 2 g dietary fiber; 6 g net carbs

NOTE

This recipe assumes that you have a turkey carcass to dispose of and have therefore used it to make Bone Broth, and, furthermore, picked all the meat off the boiled-up bones and diced it up. This actually used about half the broth and less than half the meat I got from my carcass—which is why another turkey soup recipe follows.

Sopa de Guatalote y Calabaza

Here's another way to use up that turkey carcass. This Mexican soup is wonderful.

1½ pounds (710 g) pumpkin cubes, peeled, about ½ inch (1 cm)
1 medium onion, diced
3 chipotles canned in adobo (or Chipotles in Adobo, page 294)
10 cups (2.4 L) turkey broth
3 cloves garlic
2 bay leaves
1 tablespoon (7 g) ground cumin
2 teaspoons ground coriander
½ teaspoon ground cinnamon
Salt and black pepper
2 cups (280 g) cooked diced turkey
½ cup (70 g) shelled pumpkin seeds (pepitas), toasted

In your slow cooker, combine your pumpkin cubes, onion, chipotles, turkey broth (we're assuming here you've boiled up your turkey carcass. If not, use chicken broth), garlic, bay leaves, cumin, coriander, and cinnamon. Cover the pot, set to low, and let it cook 5 hours, or until the pumpkin is very tender.

Use your stick blender to purée the whole thing right there in the pot. Salt and pepper to taste. Stir in the diced leftover turkey and serve with toasted pepitas on top.

YIELD: 6 servings

Nutritional Analysis
Per serving: 288 calories; 14 g fat; 27 g protein; 16 g carbohydrate; 2 g dietary fiber; 14 g net carbs

Egg Drop Soup

Made with homemade bone broth and pastured eggs, it's hard to think of a more nourishing soup than this.

1 quart (946 ml) chicken broth
1 tablespoon (15 ml) coconut aminos
1 tablespoon (15 ml) white wine vinegar
1 teaspoon grated gingerroot
1 scallion, sliced thin, including the crisp part
  of the green
2 eggs

Put your broth in a saucepan over medium-high heat and bring to a simmer. While it's heating, stir in the coconut aminos, vinegar, gingerroot, and scallion.

While the soup is heating, break your eggs into a measuring cup with a pouring lip and scramble 'em up.

When your broth reaches a boil, turn it down to a bare simmer. Then stir slowly with a fork while you equally slowly pour in the eggs, a little at a time, drawing them out into shreds. The egg will cook instantly, and your soup is ready to serve!

YIELD: 3 servings

Nutritional Analysis
Per serving: 103 calories; 5 g fat; 10 g protein; 3 g carbohydrate; trace dietary fiber; 3 g net carbs

Mushroom Soup

Canned mushroom soup is mostly used in gooey casseroles, but this is actually soup! Makes a nice first course before a simple roast.

¼ cup (52 g) lard or olive oil
1 cup (160 g) chopped shallots
16 ounces (455 g) sliced mushrooms
6 cups (1.4 L) chicken stock
4 tablespoons (16 g) minced fresh parsley
4 tablespoons (60 ml) sherry, medium to dry
Salt and black pepper

In your big, heavy saucepan, over medium heat, melt the lard and start sautéing the shallots and mushrooms, stirring often.

When the mushrooms have softened and changed color, add the chicken stock. Bring to a simmer and let the whole thing cook for 30 to 40 minutes.

Use your stick blender to purée the soup right in the pot. Stir in the parsley and sherry, then salt and pepper to taste, and serve.

YIELD: 6 servings

Nutritional Analysis
Per serving: 152 calories; 9 g fat; 3 g protein; 10 g carbohydrate; 1 g dietary fiber; 9 g net carbs

Winter Squash Chipotle Bisque

You can make this with butternut, acorn, buttercup, pumpkin—any winter squash.

1 small onion, chopped
1 tablespoon (13 g) coconut oil, or more if needed
1 pound (455 g) winter squash
6 cups (1.4 L) chicken broth
1 teaspoon ground cumin
2 garlic cloves, crushed
1 piece chipotle chile canned in adobo (or Chipotles
  in Adobo, page 294)
14 fluid ounces (425 ml) unsweetened coconut milk
Salt and black pepper (optional)
Glucomannan (optional)

In a big, heavy saucepan, start sautéing the onion in the coconut oil. While it's sautéing, remove the seeds from your squash—I used half a buttercup, but butternut, acorn, or pumpkin would work fine, too—peel and cut into 1-inch (2.5 cm) chunks.

When the onion is translucent, add the squash, chicken broth, cumin, garlic, and chipotle to the pan. Bring to a boil, then turn down to a simmer, cover, and cook till the squash is soft—at least 90 minutes.

Now purée everything—easiest is to use your stick blender and purée it in the pan. Add the coconut milk and continue blending for another minute. Pepper, and salt if desired. If you like, thicken it a tad more with some glucomannan—just blend it in—and serve.

YIELD: 5 servings

Nutritional Analysis
Per serving: 265 calories; 21 g fat; 9 g protein; 14 g carbohydrate; 2 g dietary fiber; 12 g net carbs

Senagalese Soup

Unusual and wonderful, this soup can be served hot or cold. Either way, if you'd like to make it look really spiffy, you could toast some coarsely shredded coconut meat and float it on top.

1 onion, chopped
1 celery rib, diced
1 tablespoon (13 g) coconut oil
1 tablespoon (6.3 g) curry powder
1 Granny Smith apple, cored and diced
1 quart (946 ml) chicken broth
1 avocado
1 cup (235 ml) unsweetened coconut milk
Salt

In a big, heavy saucepan, over medium heat, start sautéing the onion and celery in the oil. When they've softened, add the curry powder and sauté another minute or so.

Add the apple and the chicken broth. Bring to a simmer, and let the whole thing cook until the apple is quite soft, at least an hour.

Now use your stick blender to purée your soup. Halve your avocado, remove the pit, and use a spoon to scoop the flesh into the pot, then use the stick blender to purée again.

Stir in the coconut milk, salt to taste if you like, and either serve hot or chill for a cold first course.

YIELD: 6 servings

Nutritional Analysis
Per serving: 195 calories; 16 g fat; 5 g protein; 9 g carbohydrate; 2 g dietary fiber; 7 g net carbs

NOTE

If you'd like this soup to be perfectly smooth, simply strain it before serving. Not worth the trouble to me, but you might want to serve this for a fancy dinner; it's certainly good enough!

Manahata Clam Chowder

That's the aboriginal name of Manhattan, if you're wondering.

No canned clams here—whole littlenecks in the shell! If you're uncomfortable with that, ask your fish guys to shuck your clams. I think the whole clams on top of the soup make a dramatic presentation.

4 slices bacon

1 large onion

2 small carrots

2 celery ribs

1 green bell pepper

4 garlic cloves, crushed

2 quarts (2 L) fish stock, or chicken, if you don't have fish stock (I used Kitchen Basics brand seafood stock.)

6 medium tomatoes, diced

1 small turnip, diced

2 bay leaves

2 teaspoons dried oregano

1 teaspoon dried thyme

½ cup (30 g) minced fresh parsley

½ teaspoon red-pepper flakes

1 teaspoon hot smoked paprika

½ teaspoon black pepper

Salt

30 littleneck clams in the shell

Snip or chop up the bacon. Put a big, heavy pot over medium-low heat and start frying the bacon bits—you want to fry out all the fat, leaving crispy bacon bits, plus fat in the pan for sautéing.

While the bacon is cooking, peel and chunk the onion and carrot and chunk the celery, keeping any unwilted leaves. Put 'em all in your food processor and pulse till they're all chopped pretty fine.

When the bacon bits are crisp, scoop them out and reserve, leaving the fat in the pan.

Now start sautéeing the onion/carrot/celery mixture in the bacon grease. Put the food processor bowl back on the base. Chunk the pepper and throw it in. Pulse to chop it, too.

When the onion/carrot/celery mixture has softened, add the green pepper and crush in the garlic. Keep sautéing for another 4 to 5 minutes.

Add the fish stock, diced tomatoes, diced turnip, and all the seasonings, except the salt.

Bring to a simmer, cover, and let the whole thing cook for 45 minutes to an hour, until the turnips are soft. Salt to taste. If you like, you can stop here, let the soup cool, and hold it for quick finishing later.

Ten minutes before serving time, bring the soup to a boil and add the clams in the shell. Make sure they're all submerged. Boil for 10 minutes, or until the clams open. Serve, topped with the bacon and those picturesque clams-in-the-shell.

YIELD: 5 servings

Nutritional Analysis

Per serving: 334 calories; 13 g fat; 16 g protein; 25 g carbohydrate; 6 g dietary fiber; 19 g net carbs

Shrimp, Mushroom, and Snow Pea Soup

Our tester Heather says this packs a lot of flavor for pretty minimal effort and rates it a 10.

4 ounces (115 g) mushrooms, sliced
1 tablespoon (13 g) coconut oil
5 cups (1.2 L) chicken broth
2 tablespoons (28 ml) coconut aminos
1 tablespoon (15 ml) dry sherry
1 garlic clove, crushed
½ pound (225 g) fresh snow pea pods
4 scallions, sliced, including the crisp part of the green
¾ pound (340 g) shrimp, shelled (Get the littlest you can find, and—bonus!—they're usually cheaper than the big ones.)
½ teaspoon dark sesame oil
Sriracha (optional; page 276)

In your big, heavy saucepan, sauté the mushrooms in the coconut oil until they soften and change color. If you'd like them in smaller bits, you can use the edge of your spatula to break them up a bit in the process, but the whole slices are prettier. Up to you.

Add the chicken broth, coconut aminos, sherry, and garlic. Bring to a simmer and cook for 10 minutes or so.

In the meanwhile, pinch the ends and pull the strings off your snow peas and snip them into thirds. Slice your scallions, separating the white part from the crisp green part. I'm assuming you bought your shrimp already shelled, but if you didn't, do that, too.

Stir the snow peas, the white part of the scallions, and the shrimp into the soup and let it cook another few minutes, just until the shrimp turn pink and firm up. Add the sesame oil and the Sriracha if using. Ladle into bowls and garnish with the green scallion tops.

YIELD: 3 servings

Nutritional Analysis
Per serving: 279 calories; 10 g fat; 33 g protein; 11 g carbohydrate; 2 g dietary fiber; 9 g net carbs

Sopa de Coco y Aguacate

3 cups (710 ml) chicken broth
¼ large onion, diced
1 chipotle canned in adobo (or Chipotles in Adobo, page 294)
1 clove garlic
13½ fluid ounces (400 ml) unsweetened coconut milk
1 avocado
Salt to taste

Put your chicken broth and onion in a large saucepan and put them over medium heat. Use your kitchen shears to snip in the chipotle, then crush the garlic and add it, too. Bring to a simmer and let it cook until the onion is soft, maybe 20 minutes.

Use your stick blender to purée the onions and chipotle into the chicken broth. (I had some visible bits of chipotle. Don't sweat it, it adds character.)

Now blend in the coconut milk. Let the whole thing come back to a boil.

Whack your avocado in half, remove the pit, and use a spoon to scoop it into the soup. Now blend the whole thing up—I quit while there were still some small bits of avocado, again, for texture and character. Salt to taste.

(continued)

Serve immediately. This soup will not keep well. Awfully good, though.

YIELD: 4 servings

Nutritional Analysis
Per serving: 305 calories; 29 g fat; 7 g protein; 9 g carbohydrate; 2 g dietary fiber; 7 g net carbs

NOTE

For some reason, that chipotle didn't make my soup hot at all; it was mellow and very flavorful. You could pass hot sauce for those who want it, but we liked it this way. You could also add a little minced cilantro as garnish, but really, this doesn't need a thing.

Chilled Asparagus Soup

Our tester Arleen says you can serve this hot, too.

2 pounds (900 g) asparagus
1 tablespoon (15 ml) olive oil
1 medium onion, chopped
5 cups (1.2 L) chicken broth or stock, if you have it
¼ teaspoon ground nutmeg
½ lemon
13½ fluid ounces (400 ml) unsweetened coconut milk, chilled (That's one can.)
Salt and black pepper

Snap the ends off your asparagus where they want to break naturally. Steam them quite lightly—about 4 minutes in the microwave—then uncover them immediately to stop the cooking. Let them cool a bit while you . . .

Put a big, heavy saucepan over medium-low heat. Add the olive oil and onion and sauté the onion till it's soft.

Add the chicken broth or stock to the onion.

By now you can handle your asparagus. Trim the tips and reserve (they're going to be your garnish). Whack the rest into 1-inch (2.5 cm) lengths and add to the pot, along with the nutmeg. Let it simmer till the asparagus is soft. Then turn off the burner and let it cool.

You can transfer this to your blender or food processor if you like, but I'd probably purée it in the pot with my stick blender. Whatever, render it nice and smooth. (If you want it to be super-smooth, you could sieve it, but I doubt I'd bother.) Now add every drop of juice from the half lemon and chill the whole thing well. (You can do all this the day before, if you like.)

When you're ready to serve, whisk the coconut milk into the soup and salt and pepper to taste. Ladle into bowls, top with the asparagus tips, and serve.

YIELD: 6 servings

Nutritional Analysis
Per serving: 234 calories; 20 g fat; 8 g protein; 10 g carbohydrate; 4 g dietary fiber; 6 g net carbs

Caldo de Pollo

Chicken soup with a Mexican accent. Our tester Rebecca called this "very tasty, very easy."

2 medium carrots, peeled and chopped
1 medium zucchini, diced
1 medium onion, diced
2 jalapeños, seeded and minced
2 tablespoons (26 g) lard or other fat
3 medium tomatoes, ¼-inch (6 mm) dice
4 cloves garlic, crushed
1 teaspoon dried oregano
1 teaspoon ground cumin
6 cups (1.4 L) chicken broth
1½ pounds (710 g) boneless, skinless chicken thighs
Salt and black pepper
¼ cup (4 g) minced fresh cilantro
1 lime

Peel and chop (or shred) your carrots, dice your zucchini and onion, and seed and mince your jalapeños.

Put your big, heavy skillet over medium-high heat, melt the lard and start sautéing the vegetables. Now wash your hands very well, to get the hot pepper off 'em.

While the veggies are sautéing, dice your tomatoes and peel your garlic.

When the sautéing vegetables have softened, add the tomatoes to the pot and crush in the garlic. Stir it up, add the oregano and cumin, and sauté for another few minutes.

Pour in the chicken broth and bring the whole thing up to a simmer, while you dice up your chicken into bite-size bits.

When the broth is simmering, add the chicken, stirring all the while. (Do NOT just dump it in without stirring. It will congeal into a clump at the bottom of the pot. Stir it in.)

Let your soup simmer for 30 to 45 minutes. Salt and pepper to taste. Serve sprinkled with cilantro, with a wedge of lime to squeeze in.

YIELD: 5 servings

Nutritional Analysis
Per serving: 216 calories; 11 g fat; 17 g protein; 13 g carbohydrate; 3 g dietary fiber; 10 g net carbs

Quasi-Italian Chicken Vegetable Soup

Look at all those vegetables!

1 large onion, chopped
1 large carrot, peeled and sliced
2 celery ribs, diced (Chop up any unwilted leaves and throw them in, too.)
1 fennel bulb, chopped
2 tablespoons (28 ml) olive oil
1 large zucchini, diced
4 medium tomatoes, diced
2 tablespoons (5 g) minced fresh basil
½ teaspoon black pepper
4 garlic cloves, crushed
2 quarts (2 L) chicken broth
1 pound (455 g) boneless, skinless chicken thighs
1 pound (455 g) fresh spinach, chopped
Salt to taste

(*continued*)

Peel and chunk the onion and carrot, chunk the celery, and trim and chunk the fennel bulb. Put 'em all in your food processor with the S blade in place. Pulse till everything's pretty finely chopped.

Put a big darned pot over medium-low heat, add the olive oil, and start sautéing the vegetable mixture, stirring fairly often.

While that's happening, dice your zucchini and tomatoes. Mince your basil, too.

When the veggies in the pot are getting soft, add the zucchini, tomatoes, basil, and pepper. Add the garlic, too. Stir them in and sauté for another 5 minutes or so.

Add the chicken broth and bring to a simmer. While it's heating, cut your chicken into ½-inch (1 cm) cubes.

When the broth is simmering, stir in the chicken. Don't just plunk it in! Stir it in, or it will congeal into a lump at the bottom of the pot.

Let the soup simmer for 30 to 45 minutes.

Chop the spinach and stir it in. Cook till the spinach is wilted. Salt to taste, and serve.

YIELD: 4 servings

Nutritional Analysis
Per serving: 298 calories; 14 g fat; 23 g protein; 23 g carbohydrate; 8 g dietary fiber; 15 g net carbs

Chicken-Avocado Soup

If you have chicken stock on hand, this is super-fast and easy. By the way, this would be a great place to use the Paleo Umami Seasoning on page 288—just put a couple of teaspoons in a tea ball and put it in the pot while it simmers.

6 cups (1.4 L) chicken broth
1 teaspoon Sriracha or to taste (page 276, or use store-bought)
1 pound (455 g) boneless, skinless chicken breast
1 avocado
4 scallions
1 clove garlic, crushed
Salt and black pepper

Pour your broth into a big, heavy saucepan and place over medium-high heat. Stir in the Sriracha. Let it heat, while you . . .

Cut the chicken in bite-size dice; ditto the avocado. Slice the scallions, separating the white and the crisp green part.

When the broth is simmering, stir in the chicken and the white part of the scallions. (Don't just drop the diced chicken in without stirring! It'll congeal into a lump in the bottom of the pot. Stir it in.) Crush in the garlic. Bring back to a simmer, turn the burner down to low, and let it simmer for 10 minutes.

Salt and pepper the soup to taste. Ladle into bowls. Now divide the avocado dice and the sliced green scallion shoots among the bowls, and serve.

YIELD: 4 servings

Nutritional Analysis
Per serving: 277 calories; 13 g fat; 34 g protein; 6 g carbohydrate; 2 g dietary fiber; 4 g net carbs

Shrimp and Coconut Milk Soup

This is Thai-ish, with a fair amount of substituting for hard-to-find ingredients. Our tester Gina called this "a 10 by far!"

1 quart (946 ml) fish stock
1 tablespoon (8 g) grated gingerroot, peeled
2 tablespoons (28 ml) lemon juice
½ teaspoon lime zest
1 garlic clove, crushed
1 bunch scallions
⅓ cup (5 g) minced fresh cilantro, divided
1 tablespoon (13 g) coconut oil
4 shallots, minced
14 fluid ounces (425 ml) unsweetened coconut milk
3 tablespoons (45 ml) fish sauce (nuoc mam or nam pla)
1 pound (455 g) shrimp (small ones, shelled)
1 lime, quartered

In a big, heavy saucepan, over medium heat, start warming the fish stock. Add the ginger, lemon juice, lime zest, and garlic.

While the broth is heating, slice up the scallions, separating the white from the crisp part of the green shoot. Add the white part to the broth along with ¼ cup (4 g) of the cilantro, then let it simmer for 20 minutes.

In a small skillet, sauté the shallots in the coconut oil until they're beginning to brown. Add them to the soup.

Stir in the coconut milk and the fish sauce. Bring back to a simmer and let it cook for 5 to 10 minutes.

Stir in the shelled shrimp and let the soup cook for 5 minutes, till the shrimp is pink and firm.

Ladle the soup into bowls, topping with the rest of the cilantro and the sliced green scallion tops. Serve with lime wedges. Pass the fish sauce for those who want it. Sriracha wouldn't come amiss either, come to think of it.

YIELD: 4 servings

Nutritional Analysis
Per serving: 478 calories; 33 g fat; 28 g protein; 14 g carbohydrate; 1 g dietary fiber; 13 g net carbs

Chapter 13

CONDIMENTS, SEASONINGS, AND SAUCES

Ketchup, Barbecue Sauce, Paleo Worcestershire, Sriracha, and other condiments have two things in common: They add tremendous variety and appeal to our menus, and they generally contain sugar or corn syrup, and often bad fats as well. Spice blends, too, often have sugar, artificial flavors, and occasionally bad fats. The recipes in this chapter, of course, do not.

Some of these recipes are more important than others. Many recipes call for as much as a half cup (120 g) of ketchup. Commercial ketchup contains more sugar per ounce than ice cream. Accordingly, I've been making my own ketchup for years. Barbecue sauce is even more sugary than ketchup, and who sticks to the supposed 2-tablespoon (32 g) serving listed on the label? I've made a lot of barbecue sauce, too.

On the other hand, while Worcestershire contains enough sugar to have 3 grams of carbohydrate per tablespoon (15 ml), it's a rare recipe that calls for much more than 1 tablespoon (15 g). Sriracha, the wildly popular Asian hot sauce, has a gram of sugar per teaspoon, but it's so hot most people won't use much more than that. I wouldn't blame you if you decided that such minor sources of sugar aren't worth worrying about.

However, some of you will want to eliminate even these sources of junk in your diet. This is why I have worked hard on a wide array of condiments, seasonings, and sauces for you. I have, for the most part, used my own versions of these condiments in developing these recipes. So I know they work! (An exception is sriracha, since I didn't learn how to make it until a few weeks before I was done with recipe development.)

Consider asking your friends who use commercial condiments and spice blends to save bottles for you. It's so much more convenient to have your Worcestershire in a shaker-top bottle, you know?

Budget tip: If you can find a source of bulk spices, you will pay vastly less for them than you will for the spices in shaker bottles at the grocery store. My local health food stores carry a wide variety of herbs and spices, many of them organically raised. These are so much cheaper and so much fresher than the stuff at the grocery store that there's simply no comparison.

We'll start with the most popular condiment in America. I'm really proud of this recipe.

Caveman Ketchup

You know that commercial ketchup is loaded with corn syrup, right? Here an apple provides most of the sweetness, bolstered by a little honey and stevia. This is less syrupy than the commercial stuff, but the flavor is pure ketchup.

12 ounces (355 ml) tomato paste
1½ cans water (use tomato paste can)
1 apple, sweet variety
½ small onion
1 garlic clove, crushed
¾ cup (175 ml) cider vinegar
¼ teaspoon ground cloves
¼ teaspoon black pepper
1 tablespoon (20 g) honey
12 drops liquid stevia or to taste

Combine the tomato paste and water in a nonreactive saucepan over medium heat. Use a deeper pan than you think you need for this. Simmering ketchup splatters.

In the meanwhile, peel, core, and chunk your apple and peel and chunk your half onion. Throw them in your food processor and run till they're reduced to a purée. Stir them into the tomato paste mixture, along with the garlic, vinegar, cloves, pepper, and honey.

Bring the mixture to a simmer and let it cook for 30 minutes, uncovered.

Transfer the mixture to your blender—you could let it cool first, though I didn't—and run till any stray bits of apple and onion are pulverized. Blend in the stevia at this point, too.

Let it cool, and store in a clean old jar in the fridge.

(continued)

YIELD: 1 quart (960 g), 32 servings

Nutritional Analysis
Per serving: 15 calories; trace fat; trace protein; 4 g carbohydrate; 1 g dietary fiber; 3 g net carbs

NOTE

This is one of the few recipes where I've used tomato paste. If you want to cook down a couple of pounds of tomatoes, you certainly may. Me, I'll settle for organic tomato paste.

Presidential Cocktail Sauce

I cribbed this recipe from a book by the White House chef during the Kennedy Administration, using my own ketchup, of course. Serve with shrimp or any seafood.

½ cup (120 g) Caveman Ketchup (page 273)
2 tablespoons (28 ml) lemon juice
2 tablespoons (28 ml) dry sherry
2 tablespoons (20 g) minced onion

Put everything in your blender or food processor and run for 30 seconds or so—that's all.

YIELD: 4 servings

Nutritional Analysis
Per serving: 25 calories; trace fat; 1 g protein; 4 g carbohydrate; 1 g dietary fiber; 3 g net carbs

Florida Cocktail Sauce

Perfect with cold poached shrimp, clams or oysters on the half shell, or any other seafood you've got on hand.

½ cup (120 g) Caveman Ketchup (page 273)
1 tablespoon (10 g) minced onion
1 teaspoon Paleo Worcestershire (page 293)
2 tablespoons (30 g) Prepared Horseradish (page 288)
½ lime
½ teaspoon coconut aminos
1 teaspoon Celery Salt (page 285, or use store-bought)

Run it all through the blender till smooth. That's all! Serve with cold shrimp, crab, clams or oysters on the half shell, whatever.

YIELD: About ⅔ cup (160 g), 5 servings

Nutritional Analysis
Per serving: 19 calories; trace fat; 1 g protein; 5 g carbohydrate; 1 g dietary fiber; 4 g net carbs

Steak Sauce

You know that A-1 and Heinz 57 are full of sugar, right? I love this with steak and eggs.

¼ cup (60 g) Caveman Ketchup (page 273)
1 tablespoon (15 ml) Paleo Worcestershire (page 293)
1 teaspoon lemon juice
1 teaspoon brown mustard
2 drops liquid stevia extract (optional)

While your steak is broiling, stir everything together. That's it!

YIELD: 2 servings

Nutritional Analysis
Per serving: 26 calories; trace fat; 1 g protein; 6 g carbohydrate; 1 g dietary fiber; 5 g net carbs

Barbecue Sauce

This is a classic barbecue sauce along the Kansas City line. It's not syrupy like commercial sauce, because it doesn't have all that sugar. But the flavor passes muster with my Kansas-born-and-raised husband.

½ medium onion, minced

1 tablespoon (13 g) lard

1½ cups (360 g) Caveman Ketchup (page 273)

4 tablespoons (30 g) chili powder

3 tablespoons (45 ml) Paleo Worcestershire (page 293)

1 tablespoon (11 g) Celery Salt (page 285, or use store-bought)

1 tablespoon (15 g) yellow mustard

10 drops liquid stevia

2 tablespoons (40 g) honey

1 clove garlic

¼ cup (60 ml) water or as needed

In a heavy-bottomed saucepan, sauté the onion in the lard until it's soft. Add everything else. Bring to a simmer and let it cook for a good 15 minutes.

Transfer your sauce to the blender or food processor and run till it's smooth. If it's too thick, add a little more water, a tablespoon at a time. Store in a snap-top container in the fridge and use like any barbecue sauce.

YIELD: 2½ cups (20 standard 2-tablespoon [32 g] servings)

Nutritional Analysis
Per serving: 21 calories; 1 g fat; trace protein; 3 g carbohydrate; 1 g dietary fiber; 2 g net carbs

Raspberry Barbecue Sauce

Great for chicken or pork!

6 ounces (170 g) raspberries

¼ cup (60 ml) water

1 tablespoon (15 ml) raspberry vinegar

1 tablespoon (15 ml) white balsamic vinegar

½ cup (125 g) Barbecue Sauce (opposite)

2 tablespoons (40 g) honey

1 tablespoon (15 g) brown mustard

In a nonreactive saucepan over medium-low heat, simmer the raspberries in the water until they're soft. Now rub them through a sieve, right back into the pan. Given the choice between a little more raspberry pulp and a few less seeds, err on the side of more pulp, though you do want to sieve out the majority of the seeds.

Now add everything else. Stir well and let it simmer for 5 to 10 minutes. Done!

YIELD: 1 cup (235 ml)

Nutrition Analysis
Per cup: 313 calories; 6 g fat; 4 g protein; 70 g carbohydrate; 14 g dietary fiber; 56 g net carbs

Grapefruit Barbecue Sauce

Especially good with fish and chicken, but try it with pork, too.

1 cup (235 ml) ruby red grapefruit juice
1 clove garlic, crushed
2 tablespoons (28 ml) olive oil
6 tablespoons (90 g) Caveman Ketchup (page 273)
4 teaspoons (20 g) brown mustard
½ teaspoon ground cumin
6 dashes chipotle hot sauce

Combine everything in a nonreactive saucepan. Bring to a simmer and cook till it's reduced enough to thicken up to barbecue sauce consistency. Store in a snap-top container in the fridge.

YIELD: 1⅓ cups (320 g), 12 servings

Nutritional Analysis
Per serving: 33 calories; 2 g fat; trace protein; 3 g carbohydrate; trace dietary fiber; 3 g net carbs

Paleo Nuoc Cham

This tart-sweet-salty dipping sauce is an essential part of Vietnamese cuisine. Try it on chicken or fish, or even as a salad dressing.

2 tablespoons (28 ml) lime juice
2 tablespoons (28 ml) fish sauce
15 drops liquid stevia extract, or to taste
1 garlic clove, minced
1 teaspoon Sriracha (page 276)
1 ½ teaspoons white balsamic vinegar

Just stir everything together, and use.

YIELD: 4 servings, 1 tablespoon (30 ml) each

Nutritional Analysis
Per serving:14 calories; 1 g fat; 1 g protein; 3 g carbohydrate; trace dietary fiber; 3 g net carbs

Sriracha

Sriracha, an Asian hot sauce, has become so popular that a couple of years ago Bon Appétit *magazine declared it "the ingredient of the year." However, the commercial stuff has sugar and preservatives in it that you may not want to eat, even in small quantity. It's not hard to make your own, and this recipe makes enough to last you for—well, a while, depending on how much of a chile-head you are.*

12 jalapeños, red and ripe (or Fresnos if you can't get jalapeños)
8 garlic cloves, minced
1 teaspoon salt
2 tablespoons (40 g) honey or sucanat
1 cup (235 ml) cider vinegar or white wine vinegar

Remove the stems from your jalapeños. Throw the jalapeños in the food processor with the garlic, salt, and honey. Pulse to chop to a coarse purée. Spoon into a jar, cap it, and let it ferment at room temperature for a week.

Now dump your purée into your blender or food processor, add the vinegar, and run for a few minutes.

Sieve your sriracha into a nonreactive saucepan, bring to a simmer, and let it cook for 5 minutes—or more, if you like it a little thicker. Store in an old shaker-top hot sauce bottle and use just as you would commercial sriracha.

YIELD: About 10 fluid ounces (20 ml, or 60 servings of 1 teaspoon)

Nutritional Analysis
Per serving: 4 calories; trace fat; trace protein; 1 g carbohydrate; trace dietary fiber; 1 g net carbs

NOTES

Sriracha, including the popular "rooster" sauce, is properly made with red jalapeños, so find 'em if you can. Red jalapeños are just green jalapeños that have been allowed to ripen; if you garden you could grow your own. If you don't, try your local farmer's market in the late summer. If you can't find red jalapeños for love nor money, you can use Fresno peppers, but your sauce will be a little hotter. Or you can use green jalapeños, but it will be slightly less sweet, and, of course, green.

Commercial Sriracha is made with distilled white vinegar, but that struck me as unpaleo, so I tried this with both cider vinegar and white wine vinegar. Both tasted good to me.

My Sriracha came out a little less sweet than the commercial stuff. Rather than add more sucanat or honey, I added a few drops of liquid stevia, but do as you please.

Not-Peanut Sauce

Asian peanut sauce is very popular, but of course it contains peanuts. (Duh.) I figured I'd try it with almond butter instead, and it was yummy!

½ cup (130 g) almond butter
3 tablespoons (45 ml) water
1 garlic clove, peeled and chopped
2 teaspoons coconut aminos
1 teaspoon dark sesame oil
1 tablespoon (15 ml) fish sauce
1 tablespoon (15 ml) lime juice
3 tablespoons (45 ml) unsweetened coconut milk
½ teaspoon (10 g) honey or 3 drops liquid stevia extract
½ teaspoon Sriracha (page 276)

Just assemble everything in your blender and run till it's smooth. Store in a snap-top container in the fridge and use as you would peanut sauce.

YIELD: 1 cup (225 g), 8 servings

Nutritional Analysis
Per serving: 117 calories; 10 g fat; 4 g protein; 4 g carbohydrate; 2 g dietary fiber; 2 g net carbs

Mayonnaise in the Jar

This is so easy, I never buy nasty, soy-oil-laden mayonnaise anymore. Don't make more than this unless you're going to use it all up right away. Because of those raw egg yolks, this is more perishable than commercial mayo. A week, maybe 10 days, is about as long as you can keep this.

2 egg yolks
1 tablespoon (15 ml) lemon juice
1 tablespoon (15 ml) wine vinegar or another
  tablespoon lemon juice
1 teaspoon (3 g) dry mustard
2 dashes hot sauce, such as Tabasco
¼ teaspoon salt
1 cup (235 ml) olive oil (I use extra light.)

Put everything but the oil in a clean old jar with a good tight lid—I use an old salsa jar. Have your oil measured and standing by in a measuring cup with a pouring lip.

Now take your stick blender and insert it all the way down to the bottom of the jar. Turn it on, and give it a few seconds to blend the egg yolks with the seasonings.

Keep the blender running. Now slowly start pouring in the oil; you want a stream about the diameter of a pencil lead. Work the blender up and down in the jar as you go.

When you can't get any more oil to incorporate, and it's puddling on the surface, stop! You're done. Any leftover oil can go back in the bottle. Cap your jar of mayo and stash it in the fridge.

YIELD: 1 cup (225 g), 8 servings

Nutritional Analysis
Per serving: 255 calories; 28 g fat; 1 g protein; trace carbohydrate; trace dietary fiber; trace net carbs

NOTE

If you're scared of raw egg yolks, see page 15 for how to pasteurize them.

Lemon-Balsamic Mayonnaise

2 egg yolks
1 tablespoon (15 ml) white balsamic vinegar
1 tablespoon (15 ml) lemon juice
½ garlic clove, chopped
¼ cup (60 ml) extra-virgin olive oil
⅔ cup (160 ml) light-flavored olive oil (perhaps
  as much as ¾ cup [180 g])

Put the egg yolks, vinegar, lemon juice, and chopped garlic in the bottom of a clean glass jar. Have both oils measured and standing by. Add the extra-virgin olive oil. Submerge your stick blender, turn it on, and blend till it's incorporated. Now, keeping the stick blender on, slowly drizzle in the light olive oil until the mixture is thickened and the oil starts puddling on the surface. Done! Use right away or cap the jar and stash it in the fridge for up to a week or so. (Okay, I've been known to keep mine a little longer, but I'm a dare-devil—and get my eggs from my own backyard.)

YIELD: ¾ cup (168 g), 6 servings

Nutritional Analysis
Per serving: 313 calories; 35 g fat; 1 g protein; 1 g carbohydrate; trace dietary fiber; 1 g net carbs

Lemon Aioli

Perfect with any simple fish dish, or as a dip for cold shrimp.

½ lemon
2 egg yolks
4 cloves garlic, peeled
2 dashes hot sauce
½ teaspoon salt
1 cup (235 ml) olive oil
2 tablespoons (8 g) minced fresh parsley

Grate half a teaspoon zest from the lemon and reserve. Squeeze 2 tablespoons (28 ml) of lemon juice into your blender. Add the egg yolks, garlic, hot sauce, and salt if using. Turn on the blender and run it until the garlic is pulverized.

Measure the olive oil into a glass measuring cup with a pouring lip. Now, with the blender running, pour the oil into the egg yolk mixture quite slowly, in a stream about the diameter of a pencil lead. If the aioli thickens enough that the oil starts to pool on the surface, stop adding oil; otherwise add all the oil. Now quickly blend in the parsley, and serve.

YIELD: 8 servings

Nutritional Analysis
Per serving: 257 calories; 28 g fat; 1 g protein; 1 g carbohydrate; trace dietary fiber; 1 g net carbs

Hollandaise for Sissy Cavemen

In 500 More Low-Carb Recipes, I had a recipe for "Hollandaise for Sissies," made from sour cream, egg yolks, and lemon juice. This is the paleo version.

½ cup (115 g) Coconut Sour Cream (page 29)
3 egg yolks
1 tablespoon (15 ml) lemon juice
2 dashes hot sauce, such as Tabasco

This needs very gentle heat; a double boiler is a good idea. That said, I used a heavy-bottomed saucepan over very low heat. Simply whisk everything together and keep whisking until it thickens up a bit.

That's it! Use as you would hollandaise—with vegetables, over eggs, over poached fish, take your pick! Keeps for a few days in a snap-top container in the fridge, so feel free to double this.

YIELD: 5 servings

Nutritional Analysis
Per serving: 36 calories; 3 g fat; 2 g protein; trace carbohydrate; trace dietary fiber; trace net carbs

NOTE

You can use Cocoyo (page 28) instead of the Coconut Sour Cream. You'll just get a slightly thinner result.

Peach Chutney

We love curry, and we love chutney with our curry! I like this better than commercially bottled Major Grey's Chutney.

2 pounds (900 g) peach slices (that's weight after you've peeled 'em and removed the stones)
⅓ cup (33 g) gingerroot, peeled and in paper-thin slices
3 garlic cloves, peeled and in paper-thin slices
1 teaspoon (2 g) whole cloves
1 cinnamon stick
1 cup (235 ml) white balsamic vinegar
16 drops liquid stevia or to taste

Put everything in a nonreactive saucepan over low heat. Let it cook just below a simmer for a good hour, or until you can easily mash it up with a fork and the liquid's getting syrupy. Mash it all coarsely with a fork—you want it to have some texture, not be like a purée. Let it cool, and store in a tightly lidded jar in the fridge.

YIELD: 32 servings, 2 teaspoons (11 g) each

Nutritional Analysis
Per serving: 16 calories; trace fat; trace protein; 4 g carbohydrate; 1 g dietary fiber; 3 g net carbs

Paleonzu

This citrusy condiment is a riff on the popular Japanese dipping sauce called ponzu, without the soy or the rice vinegar. Try it with fish, pork, or poultry.

⅓ cup (80 ml) white balsamic vinegar
¼ cup (60 ml) coconut aminos
½ lime
¼ navel orange

In a small, nonreactive saucepan over medium-low heat, combine the white balsamic vinegar and the coconut aminos. Squeeze in the juice from the lime and orange and throw the wedges in there. Bring the whole thing to a simmer and let it cook just 3 to 5 minutes.

Let your Paleonzu cool, then squeeze all remaining sauce and juice out of the citrus wedges as you remove them from the pan. Store in in the fridge in an airtight container—an old shaker-top bottle would be perfect.

YIELD: ⅔ cup (160 ml), 6 servings

Nutritional Analysis
Per serving: 12 calories; 0 g fat; 0 g protein; 3 g carbohydrate; 0 g dietary fiber; 3 g net carbs

Lemon-Anchovy Sauce

I found this in a 30-year-old Bon Appétit *cookbook. It didn't need a lot of tweaking to be paleo, just better oil. Oh, and I added garlic. It's basically a riff on mayonnaise. Our tester Rebecca liked this so much, she developed two recipes using it all on her own!*

2 egg yolks
3 tablespoons (45 g) brown mustard
2 ounces (55 g) canned anchovies
1 lemon
1 shallot
1 clove garlic, peeled
1 cup (235 ml) olive oil
1 tablespoon (8.5 g) capers, drained
Salt and black pepper to taste

Put your egg yolks, mustard, anchovies (including the oil, so make sure they're canned in olive oil), the grated zest and the juice of the lemon, the shallot, and the garlic in your food processor. Run till the shallot and garlic are pulverized. In the meanwhile, measure your oil into a measuring cup with a pouring lip.

Now, with the processor running, very slowly pour in the oil. You want a stream about the diameter of a pencil lead. When the sauce is thickened up like mayonnaise and the oil starts to puddle on the surface, quit, even if it's not all in—you can pour it back in the bottle. Turn off the processor.

Add the capers and pulse just to mix them in—you don't want to chop them too much.

Scrap into a serving dish, cover, and refrigerate for at least a few hours, and of course keep refrigerated until serving.

YIELD: About 1½ cups (24 servings of 1 tablespoon [16 g] each)

Nutritional Analysis
Per serving: 92 calories; 10 g fat; 1 g protein; 1 g carbohydrate; trace dietary fiber; 1 g net carbs

Paleo Pizza Sauce

I first made this to put in the Portobello Not-Pizzas, but discovered it was good on burgers, chicken, and omelets, too.

8 ounces (235 ml) tomato sauce
¼ small onion
2 cloves garlic
2 teaspoons (2 g) Italian seasoning
¼ teaspoon black pepper

Put everything in the blender—cut the quarter onion into a few chunks first—and run till the onion and garlic are pulverized. Pour mixture into a small, nonreactive saucepan, bring to a low simmer, and let it cook for about 7 to 8 minutes. That's it!

YIELD: 8 servings

Nutritional Analysis
Per serving: 12 calories; trace fat; trace protein; 3 g carbohydrate; 1 g dietary fiber; 2 g net carbs

Salsa

Fresh salsa is a whole different thing than the stuff out of a jar. Great over omelets, on a chicken breast, on a steak—use your imagination.

2 cups (360 g) diced tomatoes
¼ cup (37.5 g) diced red bell pepper
¼ cup (37.5 g) diced green bell pepper
¼ cup (40 g) diced red onion
½ large jalapeño, minced, or a whole one if they're small
1 clove garlic, crushed
½ lime
Salt
¼ cup (4 g) minced fresh cilantro

Dice up the tomatoes, peppers, and onion, and combine 'em in a nonreactive bowl. Remove the seeds and white ribs from your half jalapeño and mince it quite fine, then add it to the bowl as well. Now go wash your hands really well with soap and water, or you'll regret it the next time you touch your eyes or nose!

Crush in the garlic, and stir the whole thing up. Now squeeze in about half the juice from your lime half and stir it in. Taste, and see if you think it needs more—if it does, squeeze in the rest of the juice. Salt to taste, then stir in the cilantro. (You can leave it out if you hate the stuff, I suppose. Just don't let me know. I love cilantro.)

YIELD: 3 cups (675 g), 10 servings

Nutritional Analysis
Per serving: 13 calories; trace fat; trace protein; 3 g carbohydrate; 1 g dietary fiber; 2 g net carbs

Plum Sauce

Great with pork or chicken! Your plums need to be really ripe for this. Don't bother with second-rate plums!

¼ cup (40 g) onion, diced small
1 tablespoon (13 g) coconut oil or fat of choice
2 whole plums, red or purple, good and ripe
1 tablespoon (15 ml) sherry
¼ teaspoon ground rosemary
1 garlic clove, crushed
¼ cup (60 ml) water

In a heavy saucepan, over medium-low heat, start the onion sautéing in the oil.

In the meanwhile, halve your plums, remove the stones, then dice the flesh. Don't peel them! The peel adds a lot of flavor.

When the onions have softened, add the plums to the pan and sauté until they're starting to soften, too. Now add the sherry, rosemary, and garlic and keep stirring for a couple of minutes. Your plums should be mostly dissolving into a sauce by now, with some bits of flesh and skin for texture.

Now stir in the water, turn the burner down to the lowest heat, and let it cook for another 5 minutes. Use immediately, or keep in a tightly lidded container in the fridge for a few days.

YIELD: 1 cup (250 g), 4 servings

Nutritional Analysis
Per serving: 58 calories; 4 g fat; trace protein; 6 g carbohydrate; 1 g dietary fiber; 5 g net carbs

Creamy Garlic and Herb Sauce

The seasonings in this sauce are based on the popular Boursin cheese. Good over chicken or fish, burgers, lots of things!

14 fluid ounces (425 ml) unsweetened coconut milk
2 cloves garlic
½ teaspoon dried basil
½ teaspoon dried marjoram
½ teaspoon black pepper
¼ teaspoon dried thyme
1 scallion
1 teaspoon (1 g) dried dill
½ teaspoon salt (optional)
½ teaspoon anchovy paste

Just throw everything in the blender or food processor and run till the garlic and scallion are pulverized.

YIELD: 2 teaspoons (12 g) each, 14 servings

Nutritional Analysis
Per serving: 60 calories; 6 g fat; 1 g protein; 1 g carbohydrate; trace dietary fiber; 1 g net carbs

NOTE

The seasonings in this are based on the popular Boursin cheese. Good with lots of things!

Anchovy Dip/Sauce

That Nice Boy I Married is kinky for anchovies. I came up with this sauce for him.

2 ounces (55 g) anchovy fillets, canned in olive oil
¼ cup (60 ml) extra-virgin olive oil
1 teaspoon (5 ml) lemon juice
¼ cup (10 g) fresh basil
5 garlic cloves, peeled

Throw everything in your food processor and run it till the garlic is pulverized. Use as a dip for vegetables or a sauce over meat, fish, or eggs.

YIELD: 6 servings

Nutritional Analysis
Per serving: 104 calories; 10 g fat; 3 g protein; 1 g carbohydrate; trace dietary fiber; 1 g net carbs

Chermoula

This traditional North African marinade and seasoning is simple and bursting with flavor!

2 tablespoons (8 g) minced fresh parsley
2 tablespoons (2 g) minced fresh cilantro
½ lemon, grated zest and juice
2 tablespoons (28 ml) olive oil
¼ teaspoon smoked paprika
¼ teaspoon ground cumin

Just mix everything together! Use as a marinade or serve over pork, chicken, fish, you name it.

YIELD: ½ cup (130 ml), 4 servings

Nutritional Analysis
Per serving: 63 calories; 7 g fat; trace protein; 1 g carbohydrate; trace dietary fiber; 1 g net carbs

Grapefruit Balsamic Vinegar

This is my attempt to clone some fabulous balsamic vinegar I found at the Key West Olive Oil Company. Sweet, tangy, and delicious.

2 cups (475 ml) balsamic vinegar
½ ruby red grapefruit

Pour your balsamic vinegar into a nonreactive saucepan. Cut your half grapefruit in half again, into quarters, and squeeze all the juice into the pan. Drop the squeezed-out grapefruit quarters into the pan, too.

Now set the pan over a very low burner, and let it cook just below a simmer until the vinegar is reduced by half—you should have just over a cup of liquid when you're done. Eyeball it by the level on the side of the pan.

Fish the grapefruit rinds out of the mixture, and squeeze all the extra vinegar and juice out of them, back into the pan. Let it cool, and store in a tightly-capped nonreactive container.

YIELD: 1 cup (235 ml), 16 servings

Nutritional Analysis
Per serving: 7 calories; trace fat; trace protein; 3 g carbohydrate; trace dietary fiber; 3g net carbs

NOTE

Because you're reducing the balsamic vinegar, the quality you start with matters. I use Colavita Organic, and it works very well.

Habanero-Lime Balsamic

This is my attempt to come up with something like the Habanero-Lime Balsamic I bought in Key West, really good syrupy stuff. This comes darned close, and once I had it on hand I found myself using it in all sorts of things. Bet you will, too!

2 cups (475 ml) balsamic vinegar
½ lime
½ habanero chile
1 tablespoon (20 g) honey, if needed

Put the balsamic in a small, nonreactive saucepan. Squeeze in the lime and drop it in. Remove the seeds and ribs from the half habanero, cut it into a few pieces, and throw it in, too. Now wash your hands really, really well! That habanero is more than 100 times as hot as a jalapeño, you know.

Put this over a very low burner and let it cook super-slowly till it's reduced by half. Taste it and decide if it needs to be a little sweeter. If it does, stir in the honey. Either way, use a fork to pick out the lime quarter and the bits of habanero and let it cool before pouring into a tightly lidded container for storage.

YIELD: 1 cup (240 ml), 16 servings

Nutritional Analysis
Per serving: 9 calories; trace fat; trace protein; 3 g carbohydrate; trace dietary fiber; 3 g net carbs

NOTE

Use the smoothest grocery store balsamic you can get for this; it will make a difference in the finished product. I like Colavita Organic.

Habanero-Lime Sauce

This is a mayonnaise-type sauce with some extra bits added. Adjust the heat by the size of chile you choose—or you could cheat and go for a milder chile.

1 egg yolk
2 tablespoons (28 ml) lime juice
⅛ teaspoon lime zest
¼ habanero chile, or more or less to taste
1 pinch salt (optional)
½ cup (60 ml) light-flavor olive oil
1 scallion, minced
1 tablespoon (4 g) minced fresh cilantro

Put the egg yolk, lime juice, and zest in a clean glass jar. Seed the habanero (or rather, piece of a habanero, unless you like things VERY hot) and remove the ribs. Cut it in bits and add to the jar. Immediately wash your hands very well with soap and water! Then put the salt in the jar, too, if you're using it.

Measure your oil into a glass measuring cup with a pouring lip and have it standing by. Insert your stick blender, all the way to the bottom of the jar with the egg and lime, and turn it on. Blend up the stuff in the jar, then slowly start to pour in the oil in a stream about the diameter of a pencil lead. When it's all in, and the sauce is the texture of mayonnaise—which is really what it is, a variant of mayonnaise—turn off the blender.

Now mince your scallion and cilantro and stir them into the sauce. Done!

I created this to go with steamed crab legs, but it's nice on sliced avocado, too, and would be good in a wide variety of salads.

YIELD: 4 servings

Nutritional Analysis
Per serving: 258 calories; 28 g fat; 1 g protein; 1 g carbohydrate; trace dietary fiber; 1 g net carbs

Celery Salt

I needed celery salt one day and didn't have any on hand, so I made my own. I was startled at how much more flavorful than it was than the stuff I'd purchased. This has half the salt of—well, of salt—and roughly a third less sodium than commercial celery salt. You can make it with good-quality salt, too.

2 tablespoons (36 g) salt
2 tablespoons (13 g) celery seed

Put the salt and celery seed in your food processor and run till the celery seed is pulverized. Transfer to a shaker jar with a tight lid, and cap.

YIELD: ¼ cup (80 g), 12 servings

Nutritional Analysis
Per serving: 4 calories; trace fat; trace protein; trace carbohydrate; trace dietary fiber; trace net carbs

Adobo Seasoning

Adobo seasoning in myriad varieties is ubiquitous in Caribbean and Hispanic cooking. This one has no sugar, MSG, or other junk. Tastes good, too!

1 tablespoon (9 g) garlic powder
2 tablespoons (14 g) ground cumin
2 tablespoons (12 g) black pepper
1 tablespoon (1.3 g) dried parsley
1 teaspoon dried sage, rubbed

1 teaspoon (1 g) dried thyme
1 tablespoon (7 g) paprika
1 tablespoon (18 g) salt

Just stir everything together and store in an old spice shaker.

YIELD: 8 servings

Nutritional Analysis
Per serving: 11 calories; trace fat; 1 g protein; 2 g carbohydrate; 1 g dietary fiber; 1 g net carbs

Chicken Seasoning Redux

Years and years ago, I picked up something simply called "Chicken Seasoning" for a buck at Big Lots. I loved it, but you know how it is with Big Lots—they never had it again. I set about cloning it, and I did pretty well. Over the years, I've bumped up the paprika, changing to the hot smoked stuff. I've also reduced the salt. This is my favorite seasoning for simple roasted chicken.

3 tablespoons (54 g) salt
1 tablespoon (7 g) hot smoked paprika
2 teaspoons (6 g) onion powder
2 teaspoons (6 g) garlic powder
2 teaspoons (2 g) curry powder
1 teaspoon (2 g) black pepper

Just stir everything together and store in an old spice shaker. Sprinkle over chicken before roasting or use as a table seasoning. Also fabulous on roasted nuts.

YIELD: 18 servings, 1 teaspoon (3 g) each

Nutritional Analysis
Per serving: 4 calories; trace fat; trace protein; 1 g carbohydrate; trace dietary fiber, 1 g net carbs

Cajun Seasoning

All the spiciness of traditional Cajun seasoning, with half the salt.

3 tablespoons (21 g) paprika
1 tablespoon (18 g) salt
2 tablespoons (18 g) garlic powder
1 tablespoon (6 g) black pepper
1 tablespoon (6.9 g) onion powder
1 tablespoon (6.7 g) cayenne
1 tablespoon (3 g) dried oregano
1 tablespoon (2.7 g) dried thyme

Just measure everything into a bowl, stir it up, and store it in an old spice shaker. Sprinkle it over chicken and chops, add it to salads and egg dishes, you name it.

YIELD: 33 servings, 1 teaspoon (4 g) each

Nutritional Analysis
Per serving: 6 calories; trace fat; trace protein; 1 g carbohydrate; trace dietary fiber; 1 g net carbs

Blackening Spice

Make blackened fish, blackened steak, blackened pork chops . . .

2 teaspoons (4 g) black pepper
½ teaspoon garlic powder
½ teaspoon onion powder
¼ teaspoon cayenne, or more or less to taste
½ teaspoon ground cumin
½ teaspoon dried oregano
½ teaspoon dried thyme
½ to 1 teaspoon (6 g) salt

Just mix everything together. Keep in an old spice shaker bottle.

YIELD: 1 batch (How many servings this is will depend on how hot you like your food. Figure this is enough for a couple of steaks or a few fish fillets.)

Nutritional Analysis
1 batch: 29 calories; 1 g fat; 1 g protein; 6 g carbohydrate; 2 g dietary fiber; 4 g net carbs

Ras Al Hanout

This Moroccan spice blend is good on all sorts of things—fish, poultry, stews, vegetables. I could probably buy this locally—we have a good international grocery in town—but you may not be able to, so I figured I'd tell you how to mix some up.

4 teaspoons (8 g) ground coriander
4 teaspoons (10 g) ground cumin
2 teaspoons (2.5 g) turmeric
2 teaspoons (2.5 g) ground cinnamon
1 teaspoon (2 g) cardamom
1 teaspoon (2 g) black pepper
½ teaspoon ground cloves
½ teaspoon cayenne
½ teaspoon ground nutmeg
1 teaspoon (2 g) ground ginger

Just mix it all together, then store in a spice shaker.

YIELD: ⅓ cup (27 g), 16 servings

Nutritional Analysis
Per serving: 7 calories; trace fat; trace protein; 1 g carbohydrate; trace dietary fiber; 1g net carbs

Taco Seasoning

Commercial taco seasoning usually has some sort of flour or other grain added, and sometimes sugar. This is easy to make and tastes great. It's stronger than commercial taco seasoning, because it's not diluted with starch.

2 tablespoons (14 g) ground cumin
2 tablespoons (14 g) paprika
2 teaspoons (6 g) onion powder
1 tablespoon (5.5 g) cayenne or to taste
½ teaspoon salt
1 teaspoon (2 g) black pepper or to taste

Simply stir everything together. Store in an old spice jar, one with a shaker top.

YIELD: 6 servings (1 tablespoon [2.65 g] each)

Nutritional Analysis
Per serving: 19 calories; 1 g fat; 1 g protein; 3 g carbohydrate; 1 g dietary fiber, 2 g net carbs

What Is Umami?

You may remember from junior high school science that your tongue has taste buds for only four tastes: sweet, salty, sour, and bitter. Turns out there's a fifth: umami.

A Japanese word, *umami* translates as "deliciousness" or "savoryness." It's actually the flavor of free glutamates, and it makes virtually all savory foods taste better.

Many foods are rich in umami, but many of them, including sharp, aged cheeses and soy sauce, are not paleo. So what are some paleo sources of umami? Coconut aminos are actually richer in umami than soy sauce and can be used in exactly the same way. Anchovies are loaded with umami, and so is the Asian fish sauce brewed from them. But coconut aminos, soy sauce, and anchovies all have very distinct flavors and don't blend with every recipe.

Three paleo foods that are rich sources of umami are mushrooms, especially shiitake mushrooms, tomatoes, and kelp. This gave me an idea: Why not combine the three into a general umami seasoning? It works beautifully. The two seasonings that follow do not taste good on their own, any more than fish sauce does. They do, however, make all sorts of dishes taste better. Indeed, I've rapidly come to reach for my shaker bottle of liquid umami three and four times a day, adding a few dashes to most everything. While it's not an essential ingredient in this book, I added it to most of the savory dishes that follow.

Paleo Umami Seasoning

My local health food store carries all three of these ingredients in bulk; I can buy just what I need. Maybe yours does, too? You will likely have to go to a health food store for the granular kelp, at any rate.

6 dried shiitake mushrooms
6 sundried tomato halves, dry pack
¼ cup (75 g) kelp seaweed granules

Use a big knife or a kitchen shears to cut the shiitake into small bits; ditto the sundried tomatoes.

Put the mushrooms and tomatoes, plus the kelp—or double or triple the quantities of everything, doesn't matter—in your food processor with the *S* blade in place. Turn it on and let it run till everything's ground fine, which will take a while.

When you've got something resembling a granular/powder consistency, store it in an airtight container. I don't like this as a sprinkle-on seasoning, but I do like to put a tablespoon (7 g) or so of this combination in a tea ball and add it to soups and stews, anything moist that will be simmering a while. Adds a certain *je ne sais quoi.*

You can also use this to make Liquid Umami (opposite), which I find myself using in everything!

YIELD: 6 servings

Nutritional Analysis
Per serving: 20 calories; trace fat; 1 g protein; 5 g carbohydrate; 1 g dietary fiber; 4 g net carbs

Liquid Umami

Like the granular Paleo Umami Seasoning (page 290), this is not appealing on its own, but it improves all sorts of things when added with a sparing touch. I find myself adding a few dashes to most savory dishes and made three batches by the time I was done with this book.

1 cup (235 ml) water, divided
¼ cup (28.8 g) Paleo Umami Seasoning (opposite)

In a small saucepan, bring ½ cup (120 ml) of the water to a simmer, then stir in the Paleo Umami Seasoning. Turn off the heat, cover, and let the whole thing cool.

Stir in another ½ cup (120 ml) water, then pour through a fine-mesh strainer, pressing with the back of a spoon to get all the liquid. Store in an old hot sauce or soy sauce bottle—anything with a shaker top.

YIELD: About ½ cup

Nutritional Analysis
Per batch: 30 calories; trace fat; 1 g protein; 7 g carbohydrate; 1 g dietary fiber; 6 g net carbs. The nutritional content per dash, for good or ill, will be negligible.

Prepared Horseradish

Why make your own horseradish? Because commercial prepared horseradish often has sugar. This is a lot more flavorful—and pungent!—too.

1 horseradish root, about 8 to 10 inches (20 to 25 cm)
1 tablespoon (15 ml) water
2 tablespoons (28 ml) apple cider vinegar or a little more, if the root is large

First things first: BE CAREFUL. You think onions are hard on the eyes? You haven't played with fresh horseradish root yet. Have plenty of ventilation and do not hang over the food processor. Work at arm's length as much as possible.

Peel your horseradish root and cut off any soft brown patches. Now run it through the shredding blade of your food processor.

Working at arm's length, swap out the shredding disc for the S blade. Add the water and vinegar and pulse till your horseradish is ground fine.

Now for the hard part: transferring it to a jar. I took mine out on the front stoop to get maximum ventilation, and I still had to work at arm's length and turn away every so often. Anyway, transfer the stuff into a clean jar with a tight lid. Cap and store in the fridge. Should keep 3 to 4 weeks. If you won't use it up that quickly, feel free to freeze it.

YIELD: Your yield will depend a bit on the size of your root, but this is the estimate for the whole batch

Nutritional Analysis
Per Batch: 11 calories; trace fat; trace protein; 3 g carbohydrate; trace dietary fiber; 3 g net carbs

NOTE

The horseradish really does fight back—read the labels on all the prepared horseradish in your grocery store. I've seen a few brands without sugar.

Simple Pan Gravy

Many people seem to think that making gravy is a difficult, arcane skill, but I was doing it when I had to stand on a step stool to reach the stove top. You can do it, too!

I can't give exact measurements, because it will depend on the size of your roast, how many drippings you have, and how many people you're serving. So this is more a rule than a recipe.

When your roast—whether it's beef, pork, lamb, chicken, whatever—is done, pull the pan out of the oven. Remove the roast to a platter and put it in a warm place while you make the gravy.

Next you skim the excess fat off your drippings. The easiest way to do this is to pour them into a zipper-lock bag, seal it, and hold it by one corner. Dangle it for a minute or two, until the drippings separate into the dark layer at the bottom and the fat layer at the top. Hold the bag over the roasting pan and snip a little bit off that bottom corner of the bag, let all the dark stuff run back into the pan, then, as you get to the grease, pinch the corner to stop the flow. You can either toss the fat or keep it to cook with.

Add some broth or stock to the roasting pan—for a 5-pound (2 kg) leg of lamb, I used about 2½ cups (570 ml). You'll want to use beef broth for a beef roast, chicken broth for poultry or pork. For lamb I've been known to use either one, or even a 50/50 mixture of the two. Turn on a low burner under the pan and stir the broth around, scraping up all the nice browned bits in the bottom of the pan. This is where your real flavor is coming from.

Taste this mixture. Does it have a good, meaty flavor? If it's a little frail flavored, let it simmer for 5 to 10 minutes to reduce it a bit.

(continued)

Now you need to thicken your gravy. I like to use glucomannan, because it has no impact on blood sugar, but you can use arrowroot if you prefer. Either way, the most important thing to remember is to start whisking your dripping-broth mixture before you add your thickener. If you add the thickener and then stir, you will get lumps.

To use the glucomannan, start whisking, then lightly sprinkle the glucomannan over the liquid. Go slowly—fiber thickeners get gummy if you overdo it. It's far easier to add a little more than it is to fix gummy gravy. When your gravy is a little thinner than heavy cream, quit adding glucomannan!

To use arrowroot, put a little cold broth—about a ½ cup (120 ml)—in a measuring cup. Add a couple of tablespoons of arrowroot. Now whisk this mixture till it is smooth—don't skimp on this step. A lumpy arrowroot mixture will make lumpy gravy.

When your arrowroot slurry is smooth, start whisking the dripping/broth mixture and slowly add the slurry, a little at a time. Again, as soon as your gravy is thick enough, quit, and serve it as soon as possible. Arrowroot loses its thickening properties with extended exposure to heat. (This means that if you're going to hold your gravy over a warm burner for an hour or more—for example, during Thanksgiving dinner—glucomannan is the better choice.) Add salt and pepper to taste.

Giblet Gravy

This is a painless way to get a few organ meats into the family. It basically goes like the Simple Pan Gravy (page 289), with this addition:

Before you ever put your turkey or chicken in to roast, tend to that little bag of giblets. Put the neck, heart, and gizzard in a saucepan and cover them with water. Bring to a simmer and let them cook till the gizzard is tender—likely to be at least an hour. Add water as needed. DO NOT ADD THE LIVER AT THIS POINT. Overcooked liver is dreadful.

Once your giblets are simmering, you'll get your bird in to roast, of course.

When the gizzard is easily pierced with a fork, add the liver to the pan, turn off the burner, and cover the pan. Let the residual heat poach the liver. After about 10 minutes, uncover the pan again and let the giblets cool.

Fish the cooled giblets out of the broth—don't pour that broth down the drain! You're going to be using it in the gravy. Put the giblets on your cutting board.

Trim the cartilage off the gizzard and dice the rest fine. Pick as much meat as you can off the neck and mince it, too. The heart and liver can be diced without any further trimming.

When you make your gravy according to the Simple Pan Gravy rule, use the giblet broth, with additional broth as needed. When the gravy is thickened, stir in the diced giblets.

Since giblet gravy is, of course, of poultry, I should add: I like a touch of poultry seasoning in the gravy and a teeny smidge—maybe ¼ teaspoon—of coconut aminos. I also add just a suspicion of garlic, by peeling a clove, cutting it in half, impaling one of the halves on a fork, and stirring the gravy with it for a minute or so. Salt and pepper to taste, of course.

Mole Poblano

This is not a quick-and-easy sauce. But I am crazy about mole poblano, so when I found a seriously authentic old Mexican cookbook, I decided I had to try this, substituting for the nonpaleo ingredients, like ground tortillas. The recipe makes quite a lot, so I consider it amply rewarding. Pollo con Mole Poblano is the national dish of Mexico, so try this on chicken, as well as the turkey recipes you'll find in chapter 9. I also have used it on and in omelets—but then, I put everything on or in omelets!

5 ancho chiles

3 chipotle chiles

3 New Mexico chiles

3 tablespoons (27 g) raisins

3 tablespoons (45 ml) boiling water

¾ cup (105 g) shelled pumpkin seeds (pepitas)

1 medium onion

4 cloves garlic

1 medium carrot, peeled and chopped

3 tablespoons (39 g) lard

3 cups (710 ml) chicken broth

½ teaspoon ground cloves

2 teaspoons (5 g) ground cinnamon

1 teaspoon (2 g) black pepper

¼ teaspoon ground coriander

2 large tomatillos

2 tablespoons (32 g) almond butter

1 ounce (28 g) bitter chocolate

Salt

The night before you plan to make your mole, put the chiles in a heat-proof bowl and add enough boiling water to cover them. Cover the bowl—I just set a plate on top—and let them sit overnight.

Next day comes the serious cooking. First, put your raisins in a custard cup and pour the 3 tablespoons (45 ml) of boiling water over them. Let them sit while you . . .

Put your pepitas in your big, heavy skillet over medium heat and stir them until they're golden—they'll puff a bit, too. Put your toasted pepitas in your food processor with the S blade in place and run it till they're the texture of cornmeal. Dump your pepita meal in a bowl and reserve.

Take the chiles out of the soaking water, but reserve the water. Pull the cores out of your chiles, removing as many of the seeds as you easily can. Put 'em in your food processor. Peel your onion and cut it in chunks, and throw it in, too, along with the garlic. Peel your carrot and chop it into smallish bits, and add it to the processor as well. Now run the processor until you have a purée. (If you have a small processor, you may need to do this in batches.)

Melt the lard in the biggest heavy skillet you can lay your hands on. Scrape in the purée and sauté for about 10 minutes, stirring often. (This will not be like the usual sautéing, since your mixture will be a soft paste.)

Add the chicken broth and the spices and stir it up. Bring your sauce back to a simmer and let it cook for 15 minutes.

While that's happening, remove the papery skins from the tomatillos and wash the stickiness off their skin, then chunk them and add them to the processor along with the raisins and their soaking water. Run the food processor till you have a purée. Add this to the skillet, too, during that 15 minutes of simmering time.

Now stir in the almond butter, making sure it dissolves into the sauce. Stir in the pumpkin seed meal and let it keep simmering while you . . .

(continued)

Grate the bitter chocolate. Stir it into the sauce until it's melted and well incorporated.

Keep simmering! Give it another 15 to 20 minutes. If it gets too thick, add some of that chile water you saved to thin it out—it should be about the consistency of jarred spaghetti sauce.

Now salt to taste. I used about a teaspoon and a half for the whole batch.

You can now turn off your sauce and let it sit for an hour or two, cooling in the pan. The flavors will develop during this time, and the grainy bits of pumpkin seed will soften. Don't bother to wash your food processor, though, because after the sauce cools, you're going to come back and . . .

Put the sauce back in the food processor. Run till your sauce smooths out. It's done!

YIELD: 1½ quarts (375 g), 18 servings

Nutritional Analysis
Per serving: 112 calories; 8 g fat; 5 g protein; 7 g carbohydrate; 2 g dietary fiber; 5 g net carbs

Raspberry Purée

So simple it's barely a recipe, but I've already come up with a few ways to use it, so in it goes. You can strain this if you want, but I didn't bother.

6 ounces (170 g) fresh raspberries
½ teaspoon lemon juice
3 drops liquid stevia (optional, or to taste)

Throw everything into your food processor. Run till it's puréed. Store it in a snap-top container. Voilà.

YIELD: 1 batch

Nutritional Analysis
Per batch: 81 calories; 1 g fat; 1 g protein; 19 g carbohydrate; 11 g dietary fiber; 8 g net carbs

Rum Vanilla Extract

Why make your own vanilla? A lot of commercial vanilla extract has sugar in it. Why rum? Because sugarcane is paleo, though extracted sugar is not. Frankly, I'm not sure enough grainy-ness or potato-ness is left in the alcohol used in standard vanilla extract to be a problem, but, hey, rum tastes good. And this is cheaper than standard vanilla, too.

1 pint (475 ml) white or dark rum, your choice
3 vanilla beans, or more, if you like

Simplicity itself: Split the vanilla beans lengthwise and halve them crosswise if they're longer than the rum bottle. Put the beans into the rum. Now stash it in a dark, cool cupboard and shake it every now and then, when you think of it. Let it steep for at least 6 to 8 weeks before using, then use like any vanilla.

YIELD: 96 servings (1 teaspoon each)

Nutritional Analysis
Per serving: 11 calories; 0 g fat; 0 g protein; 0 g carbohydrate; 0 g dietary fiber

NOTE

You can make this with vodka instead of rum, for a more neutral vanilla flavor.

Paleo Worcestershire

Commercial Worcestershire has high fructose corn syrup and molasses in it. This really is very close in flavor to top-quality Worcestershire, without the nonpaleo ingredients.

1 medium onion, chopped

3 tablespoons (33 g) mustard seed

½ teaspoon red-pepper flakes

2 garlic cloves, crushed

1 teaspoon (2 g) peppercorns

1 tablespoon (8 g) grated gingerroot

1 cinnamon stick

1 teaspoon (2 g) whole cloves

1 ½ cups (355 ml) cider vinegar

½ cup (120 ml) balsamic vinegar

2 tablespoons (40 g) honey

½ cup (120 ml) coconut aminos or 3 tablespoons (45 ml) lemon juice

¼ cup (30 g) tamarind pulp

½ teaspoon curry powder

2 anchovy fillets, minced

½ cup (120 ml) water

Salt

In a large, nonreactive saucepan, combine everything. Put over low heat and bring to a simmer. Keep it on a very low flame until the onions are soft—45 minutes to an hour. Taste it and decide if you think it needs more salt—I added about a teaspoon.

Put your sauce in a tightly lidded container and refrigerate it for a week or two, to let the flavors blend. Then strain, put it in an old shaker bottle or a squeeze-top bottle, and refrigerate. Use it just as you would commercial Worcestershire.

NOTE

"Tamarind pulp?" I hear you cry. This is a syrupy, sweet-and-sour concentrate of a tropical fruit, used as a seasoning in Caribbean, Hispanic, and Southeast Asian cuisines. Mine—Tamicon brand, purchased in the international aisle at a local grocery store—contains nothing but tamarinds. I don't use a lot of it, but then the stuff appears to never go bad. So it lives in the back of my fridge, and every now and then I haul it out for something like this. If you can't buy tamarind pulp locally, you can order it online—even Amazon.com carries it. Or, if you prefer, you can run equal quantities of dates, prunes, dried apricots, and lemon juice through your blender or food processor till you have a paste. One tablespoon of each will give you the ¼ cup (30 g) of paste the recipe calls for.

YIELD: 36 servings (1 tablespoon each)

Nutritional Analysis

Per serving: 19 calories; trace fat; trace protein; 4 g carbohydrate; trace dietary fiber; 4 g carbohydrate

Chipotles in Adobo

For the hard-core, here are chipotles in adobo sauce without the sugar you often find in the canned ones.

10 dried chipotle peppers
½ cup (80 g) onion, chopped fine
4 tablespoons (60 ml) cider vinegar
4 garlic cloves, crushed
⅓ cup (80 g) Caveman Ketchup (page 273)
3 cups (710 ml) water
¼ teaspoon salt (optional)
Liquid stevia extract, if desired

Stem and seed your peppers first.

Combine everything but the salt and stevia in a nonreactive saucepan. Put over a low burner, bring to a boil, then turn down to very low. (Go wash your hands! You've been handling hot peppers!) Let it simmer. And simmer. And simmer. You want the peppers to be soft and the sauce to cook down to about 1 cup (250 g). If the peppers start to go dry before they're soft, add a little more water, about ¼ cup (60 ml) at a time.

When your peppers are soft and your sauce thick but not cooked away, taste. Need salt? Add it. Need a teeny bit more sweetness? Do not just add the stevia to the pot. Scoop out about ¼ cup (63 g) of the sauce, add a drop or two of stevia to that, and stir it up. Add it back to the pot and stir it in.

NOTE

My dried chipotles were considerably larger—two to three times the size—of the chiles I find in the canned version. I find it easy to eyeball about the same quantity as a smaller pepper, though, and just return the rest to the container.

Store your peppers in a snap-top container in the freezer and use as you would canned chipotles in adobo.

YIELD: 10 servings

Nutritional Analysis
Per serving: 27 calories; trace fat; 1 g protein; 7 g carbohydrate; 1 g dietary fiber; 6 g net carbs

Chapter 14

DESSERTS

As in my previous books, I offer these recipes with a degree of trepidation. All of these recipes are delicious. None contain table sugar or corn syrup, grains, dairy, or damaged fats. That makes them considerably better than your standard desserts. But I must warn you that the sugars in honey, maple syrup, and fruit are, indeed, sugar. They can spike your blood sugar, release insulin, jack up triglycerides, all that stuff.

So please, consider these an occasional treat, something to be eaten on a holiday, a birthday, or at a dinner party, but definitely not something to be eaten daily. Not even weekly, unless you have a very robust carbohydrate metabolism, no weight problem, and a rigorous exercise schedule.

But on those special occasions? Oh, boy, are you going to thank me.

Coconut Whipped Cream

I'll start with an exception to the rule: This topping over fresh, organic berries is a dessert you can afford to eat on a regular basis.

14 fluid ounces (425 ml) unsweetened coconut milk
Liquid stevia, if desired
Vanilla extract, if desired

Put your coconut milk in the fridge overnight. Then carefully open it and scoop out the thickened part that's risen to the top. Put it in a deep mixing bowl. Now use your electric mixer to whip it till it's fluffy—mine didn't get stiff like dairy cream does, but it got nicely fluffy and mounded away from the beaters. The coconut milk is mildly sweet, so you may not want any extra sweetening, but you could add a few drops of liquid stevia, or of vanilla extract, or both—or, for that matter, French vanilla liquid stevia, which is what I used.

Coconut Milk Topping

After making the Coconut Whipped Cream (above), I wanted to come up with a way to whip the undrained coconut milk. This is soft and almost a little marshmallowy.

14 fluid ounces (425 ml) unsweetened coconut milk
¼ teaspoon French vanilla liquid stevia
2 teaspoons unflavored gelatin

Put your coconut milk and stevia in a heavy saucepan over low heat. Sprinkle the gelatin powder on top. Heat slowly.

When the coconut milk is hottest-tap-water temperature, whisk the gelatin in very well, making sure it's all dissolved.

Put this mixture in a snap-top container to chill. If possible, use a round one big enough to double as a bowl for whipping in.

Chill this mixture well, at least overnight.

Now use your electric mixer to whip it for several minutes. Like the Coconut Whipped Cream (at left) it will not get stiff, but it should expand and become fluffy.

Serve with berries, or over any dessert.

YIELD: 8 servings

Nutritional Analysis
Per serving: 102 calories; 10 g fat; 1 g protein; 2 g carbohydrate; 0 g dietary fiber; 2 g net carb

Next, two fruit desserts that are fit for company.

Pot de Framboise

This easy dessert is a glorious color and has a fabulous flavor.

1 orange
½ lemon
1 cup (235 ml) boiling water
1 to 2 tablespoons (7 to 14 g) unflavored gelatin
6 ounces (170 g) raspberries, partially frozen
6 ounces (170 g) blackberries, partially frozen
1 cup (235 ml) unsweetened coconut milk
½ teaspoon liquid stevia extract or to taste

Grate a teaspoon of orange zest, then juice your orange and half lemon. Put this in your blender with the boiling water. Turn it on and sprinkle in the unflavored gelatin powder. Let it run till the gelatin is dissolved.

Add the two kinds of berries and run till they're mostly ground up. Put your blender container in the fridge for 10 minutes or so—just till the mixture has thickened to egg white consistency.

Put the container back on the blender base, turn it on, and pour in the coconut milk. Now add ¼ teaspoon of the stevia, and taste. Does it need the other ¼ teaspoon? This will depend on your berries, not to mention your sweet tooth. Add the rest of the stevia if you need it.

Pour into 6 pretty little dessert cups and chill for several hours. You could top this with Coconut Whipped Cream (opposite) or Coconut Milk Topping (opposite) if you like, and garnish with a whole berry or two.

YIELD: 6 servings

Nutritional Analysis
Per serving: 123 calories; 8 g fat; 2 g protein; 13 g carbohydrate; 4 g dietary fiber; 9 g net carbs

NOTES

One tablespoon (7 g) of gelatin will give you a soft, pudding consistency. Two tablespoons (14 g) will result in a more jelled texture. It's up to you.

You can, if you like, use frozen mixed organic berries, partially thawed. Or you can just throw your containers of berries in the freezer for an hour or so.

Pot de Strawberry

1 lemon
1 cup (235 ml) boiling water
1 to 2 tablespoons (7 to 14 g) unflavored gelatin
12 ounces (340 g) strawberries, hulled and partially frozen (You can freeze then partially thaw them, or simply use frozen, unsweetened organic strawberries.)
1 cup (235 ml) unsweetened coconut milk
½ teaspoon liquid stevia extract, or to taste

First juice your lemon and grate a half teaspoon of lemon zest. Put this in your blender with the boiling water. Turn it on and sprinkle in the unflavored gelatin powder. Let it run till the gelatin is dissolved.

Add the strawberries and run till they're mostly ground up, but you still have some pretty red bits of strawberry in the mixture. Put your blender container in the fridge for 10 minutes or so—just till the mixture has thickened to egg white consistency.

(continued)

Put the container back on the blender base, turn it on, and pour in the coconut milk. Now add ¼ teaspoon of the stevia, and taste. Does it need the other ¼ teaspoon? This will depend on your strawberries, not to mention your sweet tooth. Add the rest of the stevia if you need it.

Pour into 5 or 6 pretty little dessert cups and chill for several hours. You could top this with Coconut Whipped Cream (page 296) if you like and garnish with a strawberry fan.

YIELD: 6 servings

Nutritional Analysis
Per serving: 101 calories; 8 g fat; 1 g protein; 8 g carbohydrate; 1 g dietary fiber; 7 g net carbs

NOTE

Like the Pot de Framboise, you can use less gelatin for a softer, pudding consistency, or more for a firmer, more jelled consistency.

Pot de Chocolat

Very easy. Very, very good—rich, velvety, and chocolaty beyond belief.

1 ½ cups (355 ml) unsweetened coconut milk
6 ounces (170 g) bitter chocolate
2 tablespoons (40 g) honey
20 drops chocolate liquid stevia
2 egg yolks

In a saucepan, over low heat, warm the coconut milk and the chocolate together, till the chocolate is completely melted and the coconut milk is steaming. Whisk this together, right there in the pan.

Pour this into your blender and turn it on. Now add everything else and let the blender run for about 5 minutes.

Pour into little teeny cups—I used little Chinese teacups. This is very rich, so servings should be quite small. Chill for 6 to 8 hours.

Garnish with a raspberry, or perhaps a strawberry fan, or a mint leaf, should you be feeling spiffy. Though I doubt anyone will turn this down ungarnished. You could, I suppose, top this with Coconut Whipped Cream (page 296), but personally I think this stands alone quite brilliantly.

YIELD: 8 servings

Nutritional Analysis
Per serving: 225 calories; 22 g fat; 4 g protein; 12 g carbohydrate; 3 g dietary fiber; 9 g net carbs

Chocolate Pudding

Avocado is the stealth ingredient here! It makes for a fantastic texture. This recipe has been going around online, but I halved the honey, replacing it with stevia.

2 ripe avocados
1 cup (96 g) cocoa powder
½ cup (170 g) honey
¼ teaspoon French vanilla liquid stevia, or more if needed
8 strawberries, sliced

Halve your avocados, remove the stones, and use a spoon to scoop the flesh into your food processor, with the S blade in place. Add everything else but the strawberries. Now run the food processor until the whole thing is super-smooth, and all the cocoa powder is incorporated—you may want to scrape down the walls of the processor once or twice.

Spoon into 4 dessert dishes, and top each serving with a few strawberry slices. That's it!

YIELD: 4 servings

Nutritional Analysis
Per serving: 347 calories; 18 g fat ; 6 g protein; 56 g carbohydrate; 10 g dietary fiber; 46 g net carbs

Lime-Vanilla Honeydew

A simple, cooling summer dessert.

2 limes
5 drops French vanilla liquid stevia, or to taste
4 cups (720 g) honeydew melon balls or chunks

Grate the zest from the limes into a small dish and squeeze in every drop of juice. Stir in the French vanilla liquid stevia.

Put your melon balls or chunks in a nonreactive serving bowl (glass is pretty). Pour the lime mixture over the melon and toss to coat. Refrigerate until well-chilled, stirring now and then if you think of it.

Serve garnished with thin slices of lime, if you like.

YIELD: 6 servings

Nutritional Analysis
Per serving: 54 calories; trace fat; 1 g protein; 15 g carbohydrate; 1 g dietary fiber; 14 g net carbs

Gussied-Up Cherries

Fresh Bing cherries are scrumptious just as they are. But if you'd like to dress them up for a party, here's how.

½ cup (55 g) finely chopped pecans
1 cup (230 g) Coconut Sour Cream (page 29)
1 teaspoon grated lemon rind
¼ teaspoon French vanilla liquid stevia
1 pound (455 g) Bing cherries

Stir your pecans in a dry skillet over medium heat until they smell toasty—maybe 3 to 4 minutes. Take them off the heat and reserve.

Whisk together the coconut sour cream, lemon rind, and stevia till well blended.

Now: Arrange the cherries on a platter, with a dish of the sweetened coconut sour cream in the center. Give everyone a little dish of pecans. People pick up cherries by the stem, dip in the coconut sour cream, then in their pecans, and eat 'em right off the stem.

YIELD: 4 servings

Nutritional Analysis
Per serving: 152 calories; 10 g fat; 2 g protein; 15 g carbohydrate; 3 g dietary fiber; 12 g net carbs

Gingered Melon Balls

Pretty!

2 limes
2 teaspoons grated gingerroot
5 drops liquid stevia extract, or to taste
2 cups (320 g) cantaloupe balls
2 cups (360 g) honeydew melon balls

Grate a half teaspoon of lime rind into a small dish and squeeze in all the juice from both limes. Stir in the gingerroot and stevia.

Combine the melon balls in a nonreactive serving dish—glass will show off the pretty colors. Pour on the lime-ginger mixture and toss to coat. Chill for a few hours, stirring now and then when you think of it. Then serve.

YIELD: 6 servings

Nutritional Analysis
Per serving: 49 calories; trace fat; 1 g protein; 13 g carbohydrate; 1 g dietary fiber; 12 g net carbs

Baked Plums

4 whole plums
½ cup (115 g) Coconut Sour Cream (page 29)
4 drops French vanilla liquid stevia, or to taste
2 teaspoons coconut oil
¼ cup (28 g) slivered almonds
1 teaspoon honey

Preheat oven to 350°F (180°C, or gas mark 4).

Halve the plums and remove the stones. Place them in a shallow baking dish, cover with foil, and bake for 30 minutes or until getting soft. Timing will depend on the type of plums you use and how ripe they are.

In the meanwhile, flavor the coconut sour cream with the French vanilla liquid stevia and beat with a whisk or electric mixer until it's fluffy. Don't expect it to get stiff like whipped cream—you're just looking for it to get a bit fluffy.

Put a medium-size skillet over low heat, melt the coconut oil, and add the almonds. Sauté them, stirring often, until they're pale gold. Stir in the honey to coat and remove from the heat.

When the plums are soft, you can serve them right away, topped with the coconut sour cream and a sprinkle of almonds—if you serve them hot like this, the cream will melt instead of staying fluffy. Super-tasty this way. Or you can make the plums in advance, then chill them before serving. In that case, your cream will stay fluffy. Take your pick!

YIELD: 4 servings

Nutritional Analysis

Per serving: 213 calories; 18 g fat; 3 g protein; 14 g carbohydrate; 2 g dietary fiber; 12 g net carbs

Honey-Rum Grilled Pineapple

You can make these packets well ahead of time if you like. Then throw them on the grill while you're eating your steak or chicken. Our tester Arleen says her 15-year-old son made this, and it was "fantastic."

2 tablespoons (40 g) honey
2 tablespoons (28 ml) dark rum
½ teaspoon ground cinnamon
4 teaspoons (17 g) coconut oil (extra-virgin is best here, to get the coconut flavor.)
12 ounces (340 g) fresh pineapple, in chunks

In a small dish, stir together the honey, rum, and cinnamon.

Tear four 12-inch (30 cm) squares of foil. Turn up the edges a little. Put a teaspoon of coconut oil on each.

Divide the pineapple between the squares of foil. Drizzle 1 tablespoon (15 ml) of the honey-rum mixture over each, folding each into a packet as you go. (Fold the foil so the long edges come together, fold them down, then roll up the ends.)

When all your packets are done, throw them on the grill for 10 minutes, turning once.

YIELD: 4 servings

Nutritional Analysis

Per serving: 87 calories; 5 g fat; trace protein; 9 g carbohydrate; trace dietary fiber; 9 g net carbs

Maple-Cinnamon Baked Pears

A very special autumn dessert. Keep in mind that pears are a high-carb fruit.

2 pears (I used d'Anjou, but use whatever looks best, and be sure they're ripe!)
2 tablespoons (40 g) maple syrup
½ teaspoon ground cinnamon
¼ cup (30 g) chopped walnuts

Preheat oven to 350°F (180°C, or gas mark 4). Grease an 8 x 8-inch (20 x 20 cm) baking dish.

Halve your pears and use the tip of a spoon to scoop out the cores. Remove the stems and the little tough bit at the blossom end, too. Place your pears in the greased baking dish.

Put ½ tablespoon (10 g) maple syrup in the hollow of each pear—if it doesn't all fit, that's fine, because you're also going to . . .

Take your spoon and smear a little syrup all over the cut surfaces.

Now sprinkle the cinnamon evenly over your pears. Put the pan in the oven and bake 'em for an hour, or until soft.

(continued)

During the last 10 minutes of the baking time, spread your chopped walnuts in a small, ovenproof pan and put them in the oven to toast.

When the walnuts are toasted, remove both them and the pears from the oven. Plate the pears, sprinkle with the walnuts, and serve.

YIELD: 4 servings

Nutritional Analysis
Per serving: 123 calories; 5 g fat; 2 g protein; 20 g carbohydrate; 3 g dietary fiber; 17 g net carbs

---

NOTES

My husband called these "stellar" served just like this. But if you'd like to gild the lily, you could:

- Put them in bowls, and pour a little coconut milk over them.
- Top them with Coconut Whipped Cream (page 296).
- Top them with Coconut Sour Cream (page 29).
- Serve them with Vanilla Frozen Custard (page 310).

Poached Pears with Raspberry Sauce

Our tester Michelle says, "I made this for my dad's birthday dessert. Three men loved it!!!" We asked if she would make this again. Her reply? "OH FOR SURE!"

½ **lemon**
2 **teaspoons honey**
2 **pears, ripe!**
6 **ounces (170 g) raspberries, divided**
½ **orange**
¼ **teaspoon liquid stevia extract, or more if needed**

Squeeze the juice from the half lemon into a small dish and mix with the honey. Grate in just a touch of the zest, too—maybe ⅛ teaspoon.

Working from the blossom end, use an apple corer or paring knife to core the pears, leaving the top of the pear intact. Peel, but leave the skin at the very top and the stem intact. Rub your pears all over with the lemon juice mixture.

Lay your pears in a glass pie plate, with the stems toward the center. Add 2 tablespoons (28 ml) water. Microwave uncovered for 3 minutes, turn the pears over, then give them another 2 to 3 minutes, or till tender. You can do this in advance, if you like.

Set aside a few raspberries for garnish, then put the rest in a small, nonreactive saucepan. Squeeze in the juice from the half orange and grate in ½ teaspoon zest. Cover and put on a low burner for 5 minutes, then check—you want to cook till the berries are soft, but no longer. Give them another 5 minutes if they need it.

When the berries are soft, mash 'em up good with a fork. You want to reduce them to a pulp. Now pass the pulp through a strainer to remove the seeds, rubbing with a spoon to get as much of the pulp possible. Don't forget to scrape any clinging pulp off the outside of the sieve!

Stir the stevia into the raspberry pulp, and taste—does it need more? If it does, add it drop by drop—it's easy to add and impossible to remove.

To serve, stand your pears up in pretty bowls, spoon the raspberry purée over them, and garnish with the reserved raspberries.

YIELD: 2 servings

Nutritional Analysis

Per serving: 178 calories; 1 g fat; 2 g protein; 46 g carbohydrate; 10 g dietary fiber; 36 g net carbs. The high carb count is largely because pears are a high-carb fruit. Govern yourself accordingly.

Strawberries Au Savage

Remember: This is a way of eating strawberries, not a way of using strawberries to eat maple syrup. So use good, ripe, sweet strawberries! Carmen, who tested this, says she tried it both with genuine maple syrup and with sugar-free pancake syrup and liked it both ways. She felt "the maple syrup gave it a whole new dimension of flavor."

1 pound (455 g) strawberries
8 teaspoons (53 g) maple syrup

Wash your berries briefly in cold water and put them on a platter. Give everyone a little plate, with a custard cup holding a couple of teaspoons of maple syrup. Everybody picks up strawberries by the hull, dips them in just a tiny bit of maple syrup, and eats them!

YIELD: 4 servings

Nutritional Analysis

Per serving: 66 calories; trace fat; 1 g protein; 16 g carbohydrate; 2 g dietary fiber; 14 g net carbs

Orange-Rum Glazed Bananas

These are wonderful, but they're the highest-carb dessert in this book. Call this eight servings instead of four, if you like.

4 bananas, not too ripe
½ orange
8 teaspoons (52 g) honey
8 teaspoons (40 ml) dark rum or rum vanilla
¼ cup (28 g) slivered almonds
¼ cup (60 ml) unsweetened coconut milk

Preheat oven to 350°F (180°C, or gas mark 4).

Grease a baking dish with coconut oil—if you have cute little baking dishes that will each fit one banana, halved lengthwise, so much the better.

Peel your bananas and split lengthwise. Lay it in the baking dish or dishes.

Grate a teaspoon of zest and put it in a small dish. Squeeze in the juice from the half orange, too. Add the honey and the rum and stir the whole thing together till the honey dissolves. Pour this over the bananas, coating them evenly.

Bake for 20 minutes, basting two or three times with the syrup in the bottom of the dish.

(continued)

While the bananas are baking, stir the almonds over low heat in a dry skillet until they're light gold.

When the bananas are done, plate them, drizzle with coconut milk, top with the almonds, and serve.

YIELD: 4 servings

Nutritional Analysis
Per serving: 285 calories; 8 g fat; 4 g protein; 49 g carbohydrate; 5 g dietary fiber; 44 g net carbs

Barely There Meringues

These are little bubbles of crunchy sweetness that vanish in your mouth.

3 egg whites
¼ teaspoon cream of tartar
1 tablespoon (20 g) honey
8 drops French vanilla stevia extract

Be very sure there is not a single speck of yolk in your whites. The merest hint of a yolk molecule will result in whites that stubbornly refuse to whip. Your bowl and beaters also need to be absolutely grease-free. Helps to have your whites at room temperature, too.

Preheat your oven to 300°F (150°C, or gas mark 2) and line a couple of cookie sheets with baking parchment.

Put all your ingredients in a deep, narrow mixing bowl and use an electric beater to whip at high speed until they're stiff but not dry—they should hold a peak when you lift the beaters out of the bowl.

If you're feeling fancy, you may now spoon your meringue into a pastry bag with a star tip and pipe little stars of it onto the baking parchment. If not, you can do as I did and just spoon it out in roughly teaspoon-and-a-half mounds.

Bake for 90 minutes to 2 hours, until honey brown and dry through. Store in an airtight container.

YIELD: 36 servings

Nutritional Analysis
Per serving: 3 calories; 0 g fat; trace protein; 1 g carbohydrate; trace dietary fiber; 1g net carbs

Gingerbread

I've always loved gingerbread—I've even had it for my birthday cake a couple of times. This has the real flavor of gingerbread!

1 cup (115 g) almond meal
¼ cup (26 g) flaxseed meal
¼ cup (29 g) coconut flour
¼ teaspoon salt
1 teaspoon (4.5 g) baking soda
2 teaspoons (3.5 g) ground ginger
1 teaspoon (1.5 g) ground cinnamon
¼ cup (52 g) coconut oil, melted
¼ cup (85 g) honey
32 drops liquid stevia
½ cup (115 g) Cocoyo (page 28)
2 eggs

Preheat oven to 350°F (180°C, or gas mark 4). Grease an 8 x 8-inch (20 x 20 cm) baking pan.

In a mixing bowl, combine the dry ingredients—everything from the almond meal through the cinnamon. Stir them together, so everything is evenly distributed.

In a 2-cup (470 ml) measure, measure and stir together the coconut oil, honey, liquid stevia, and Cocoyo. Break in the eggs and stir them in, too.

Now pour it all into the dry ingredients and whisk until there are no pockets of dry stuff left. Pour into the prepared pan and bake for 30 to 35 minutes, or until it's pulling away from the edges of the pan and a toothpick inserted in the center comes out clean.

YIELD: 16 servings

Nutritional Analysis
Per serving: 123 calories; 7 g fat; 6 g protein; 11 g carbohydrate; 3 g dietary fiber; 8 g net carbs

Here are a few super-great cookie recipes. Don't scarf down the whole batch in a couple of days! If you don't have a houseful of people to eat them, freeze them, then thaw just enough for the moment.

Brownies!

No, really! They're fudgy and everything!

1 cup (208 g) coconut oil, melted
1 cup (96 g) cocoa powder
9 eggs
½ cup (170 g) honey
¼ teaspoon chocolate liquid stevia
¼ teaspoon French vanilla liquid stevia

¼ teaspoon salt
¾ cup (90 g) coconut flour
1 cup (120 g) chopped walnuts

Preheat oven to 350°F (180°C, or gas mark 4). Grease a 9 x 13-inch (23 x 33 cm) baking pan.

Melt the coconut oil in a saucepan and whisk in the cocoa powder.

Now, in a mixing bowl, whisk the eggs very well. Add the honey, liquid stevia, and salt and whisk again, till the honey is all dissolved.

Add the coconut flour a little at a time, whisking between additions. DON'T just dump it all in and mix—you'll get lumps.

Now add the coconut oil/cocoa powder mixture and whisk it in very well. Stir in the chopped nuts.

Spread the batter evenly in your prepared pan. Bake for 20 to 30 minutes, or until a toothpick comes out clean.

Let 'em cool and cut in bars. That's it! Store these in an airtight container in the fridge. Unlike brownies made from white flour and white sugar, these have nutritious foods in them that will spoil if not refrigerated. If, like me, you don't have enough people in the house to eat these up before they spoil, freeze them. (No eating 4 or 5 a day just to use them up! That's cheating.)

YIELD: 24 servings

Nutritional Analysis
Per serving: 196 calories; 15 g fat; 5 g protein; 14 g carbohydrate; 5 g dietary fiber; 9 g net carbs

Paleo Energy Bars

Credit where credit is due: This started with a recipe by Mark Sisson, of Mark's Daily Apple. I played with it, and my brilliant recipe testers tweaked it. It's a group effort!

½ cup (72.5 g) shelled almonds
½ cup (50 g) pecan halves
½ cup (40 g) shredded coconut meat, divided
¼ cup (65 g) almond butter
¼ cup (52 g) coconut oil
1 teaspoon vanilla extract
3 tablespoons (60 g) honey
½ teaspoon salt
½ teaspoon ground cinnamon
¼ cup (30 g) almond meal
3 tablespoons (21 g) coconut flour
3 eggs
15 drops liquid stevia extract (French vanilla if you have it, plain if not.)
¼ cup (35 g) Zante currants

Preheat oven to 325ºF (170ºC, or gas mark 3). Put your almonds and pecans in a shallow baking dish—a jelly roll pan is good—and slide 'em in. Set the timer for 5 minutes. When it goes off, shake the pan, add ¼ cup of the coconut, and shake again. Let the whole thing toast for another 5 minutes.

Dump your toasted nuts in the food processor, with the *S* blade in place. Pulse until they're chopped medium fine—some like bread crumbs, some still in chunks a little smaller than a pea.

In a microwaveable mixing bowl, combine the almond butter and coconut oil and zap 'em for about 30 seconds at 50 percent power—you just want to melt the oil and soften the almond butter a little. You can do this while your nuts are toasting. Stir the almond butter and coconut oil together.

Stir in the vanilla extract, the honey, the salt, and the cinnamon into the almond butter/coconut oil mixture. Now stir in the nut mixture, the almond meal, and the coconut flour.

Whisk the eggs with the liquid stevia, then add and mix them in.

Finally, stir in the currants. (If your currants are a bit dry—mine were—put them in a custard cup with a little water and nuke them for 30 seconds or so on high, then let them sit for a couple of minutes. They'll turn soft again.)

Turn the mixture out into an 8- x 8-inch (20 x 20 cm) baking pan you've sprayed with nonstick cooking spray. Press it firmly into an even layer.

Slide the pan into the oven and set your timer for 7 minutes. When it goes off, sprinkle the reserved ¼ cup (20 g) of coconut over the top, press it down gently, and slide 'em back in for another 7 to 10 minutes. Then remove from oven and let them cool in the pan a bit before cutting into 16 bars. Store in a snap-top container.

YIELD: 16 servings

Nutritional Analysis
Per serving: 163 calories; 12 g fat; 4 g protein; 10 g carbohydrate; 3 g dietary fiber; 7 g net carbs

Nutritional Analysis
Per serving: 90 calories; 6 g fat; 2 g protein; 8 g carbohydrate; 2 g dietary fiber; 6 g net carbs

Coconut-Almond Pokies

Gooey and oh, so good!

1 cup (224 g) Coconut Butter (page 31)
½ cup (130 g) almond butter
½ cup (170 g) honey
½ teaspoon French vanilla liquid stevia
½ teaspoon salt
2 egg whites

Preheat oven to 350ºF (180ºC, or gas mark 4) and either grease a couple of cookie sheets or line them with baking parchment. (I love baking parchment!)

Simply combine everything in a bowl and use an electric mixer to beat until you have a thick, gooey batter.

Drop by tablespoonfuls (15 g) on the prepared cookie sheets and bake for 15 minutes. Cool on wire racks.

YIELD: 24 servings

Cinnamon Spice Pokies

Just like Coconut-Almond Pokies, only cinnamony!

1 cup (224 g) Coconut Butter (page 31)
½ cup (130 g) almond butter
½ cup (170 g) honey
½ teaspoon French vanilla liquid stevia
½ teaspoon salt
2 egg whites
1½ teaspoons ground cinnamon
¼ teaspoon ground nutmeg
1 pinch ground cloves

Preheat oven to 350ºF (180ºC, or gas mark 4) and either grease a couple of cookie sheets or line them with baking parchment. (I love baking parchment!)

Simply combine everything in a bowl and use an electric mixer to beat until you have a thick, gooey batter.

(*continued*)

Drop by tablespoonfuls (15 g) on the prepared cookie sheets and bake for 15 minutes. Cool on wire racks.

YIELD: 24 servings

Nutritional Analysis
Per serving: 90 calories; 6 g fat; 2 g protein; 8 g carbohydrate; 2 g dietary fiber; 6 g net carbs

Ginger Pokies

I'd call them gingersnaps, but they're more chewy than snappy. Awfully good, try them with a cup of tea.

1 cup (224 g) Coconut Butter (page 31)
½ cup (130 g) almond butter
½ cup (170 g) honey
½ teaspoon French vanilla liquid stevia
½ teaspoon salt
2 egg whites
1 teaspoon ground cinnamon
1 teaspoon ground ginger

Preheat oven to 350ºF (180ºC, or gas mark 4) and either grease a couple of cookie sheets or line them with baking parchment.

Simply combine everything in a bowl and use an electric mixer to beat until you have a thick, gooey batter.

Drop by tablespoonfuls (15 g) on the prepared cookie sheets and bake for 15 minutes. Cool on wire racks.

YIELD: 24 servings

Nutritional Analysis
Per serving: 90 calories; 6 g fat; 2 g protein; 8 g carbohydrate; 2 g dietary fiber; 6 g net carbs

Eric's Birthday Cookie Pie

Dense and fudgy, this is somewhere between a truffle, a brownie, and a flourless chocolate cake. I invented this for my husband's birthday.

1 cup (224 g) Coconut Butter (page 31)
½ cup (130 g) almond butter
2 egg whites
½ cup (170 g) honey—or sugar-free imitation honey
¼ teaspoon chocolate liquid stevia
¼ teaspoon French vanilla liquid stevia
1 ½ ounces (43 g) bitter chocolate, melted
1 pinch salt
½ cup (60 g) chopped walnuts

Preheat oven to 350ºF (180ºC, or gas mark 4). Grease a springform pan—mine is 9½ inches (24 cm) in diameter, but 9 inches (23 cm) would do, and I think 10 inches (25 cm) would be okay, too, but you'd want to shorten the baking time a tad.

Put everything but the walnuts in a mixing bowl and use an electric mixer to beat it till you have a dense, sticky mixture somewhere between a batter and a dough.

Scrape the dough into the prepared pan, using a rubber scraper to get all of it and to smooth the batter out into an even layer. It won't be very thick—mine was about ½ inch (1.25 cm).

Bake for 7 minutes—set a timer! When the timer beeps, sprinkle the chopped walnuts evenly over the top and gently press them into the surface just a little. Bake for another 8 minutes.

Remove from oven and cool before cutting.

YIELD: 12 servings

Nutritional Analysis

Per serving: 187 calories; 17 g fat; 5 g protein; 7 g carbohydrate; 4 g dietary fiber; 3 g net carbs

Chocolate Sunflower Balls

Little nuggets of energy! The kids will love these. They're kind of Tootsie Roll-ish, but a whole lot more nutritious.

1 cup (145 g) sunflower seeds
⅓ cup (50 g) raisins (fresh, moist ones)
2 ounces (55 g) bitter chocolate, melted
1 tablespoon (15 ml) water

Put the sunflower seeds and raisins in the food processor with the *S* blade in place and run till they're finely ground. Add the melted chocolate and the water and run till you've got a stiff dough. Roll into little balls—maybe ¾ inch (2 cm) in diameter—and store in a snap-top container.

YIELD: 26 servings

Nutritional Analysis

Per serving: 49 calories; 4 g fat; 2 g protein; 3 g carbohydrate; 1 g dietary fiber; 2 g net carbs

Cinnamon Sunflower Balls

Going for a hike? Two or three of these in a zipper-lock bag, and you've got all the energy you need for the afternoon.

1 cup (145 g) sunflower seeds
¼ cup (35 g) raisins (fresh, moist ones)
¼ teaspoon ground cinnamon
2 tablespoons (26 g) coconut oil, melted
1 tablespoon (15 ml) water

Put the sunflower seeds, raisins, and cinnamon in the food processor with the *S* blade in place and run till they're finely ground. Add the coconut oil and water and run till you have a stiff dough. Form into little balls, about ¾ inch (2 cm) in diameter. Store in a snap-top container.

YIELD: 18 servings

Nutritional Analysis

Per serving: 65 calories; 5 g fat; 2 g protein; 3 g carbohydrate; 1 g dietary fiber; 2 g net carbs

Glazed Walnuts

Just slightly sweet, these make a nice nibble after supper. Take care when frying them—it's a quick jump from done to burnt.

1½ cups (150 g) walnuts
Boiling water
1 tablespoon (20 g) honey (Increase to 2 if desired.)
½ teaspoon vanilla
Coconut oil, for frying

(continued)

Put your walnuts in a bowl and cover with boiling water. Let them sit for just 4 or 5 minutes, then drain well.

Add the honey to the walnuts and toss they're all evenly coated. Now add the vanilla and toss till that's evenly distributed, too.

Now spread your walnuts on a plate and let them dry for an hour or two. This will minimize spitting when you fry them.

Put your big, heavy skillet over medium heat and add ¼ inch (6 mm) of coconut oil. Let it get hot, then fry your walnuts a handful at a time, till just crisp. Cool, and store in a tightly lidded container.

YIELD: 6 servings

Nutritional Analysis
Per serving: 201 calories; 18 g fat; 8 g protein; 7 g carbohydrate; 2 g dietary fiber; 5 g net carbs

Instant Strawberry Ice Cream

This takes a pretty good food processor, but oh, gosh, is it good.

1 pound (455 g) unsweetened frozen strawberries
14 fluid ounces (425 ml) unsweetened coconut milk
¼ teaspoon liquid stevia extract, or to taste
½ tablespoon (8 ml) lemon juice

Just put everything in your food processor and run it till the strawberries are ground up. This may require prying a strawberry off the blade a few times! The strawberries freeze the mixture, and you get really-truly ice cream with an insanely great strawberry flavor. Keep in mind that if you have some left over, you can store it in a snap-top container in the freezer, but because of the lack of sugar it will freeze rock-hard. Take it out of the freezer a good half hour before you want to eat it, to let it soften a bit.

YIELD: 6 servings

Nutritional Analysis
Per serving: 156 calories; 14 g fat; 2 g protein; 9 g carbohydrate; 2 g dietary fiber; 7 g net carbs

Vanilla Frozen Custard

You'll need an ice cream freezer for this.

27 fluid ounces (793 ml) unsweetened coconut milk
1 teaspoon unflavored gelatin
1 ½ tablespoons (30 g) honey
15 drops French vanilla liquid stevia
2 tablespoons (28 ml) vanilla extract
1 pinch salt (optional)
6 egg yolks

Put your coconut milk in a big saucepan and slowly heat it—use a very low burner. While it's warming, sprinkle the unflavored gelatin on top.

When your coconut milk is about as hot as the hottest possible tap water—hot enough that you can put your finger in it, but not for long—whisk in the gelatin and also the honey, the stevia, the vanilla extract, and the salt if using. Let it continue heating while you . . .

Separate out your egg yolks and put them in a mixing bowl. (You could keep the whites to make meringues, but 6 whites will make a *lot* of meringues. I gave mine to my dogs.) Whisk them very well.

Use a ladle to transfer one ladleful of the hot coconut milk into the bowl of egg yolks and whisk it all together very well. Repeat with a second ladleful of hot coconut milk, again whisking it in really well.

Now start whisking the pot of coconut milk and slowly pour the egg yolk mixture into it. Keep whisking until your custard reaches a texture a little thicker than heavy cream—it should coat a spoon.

Pour the custard back into the mixing bowl, cover, and chill thoroughly—overnight is a good idea.

Then freeze your custard according to the directions that come with your ice cream freezer.

YIELD: 6 servings

Nutritional Analysis
Per serving: 341 calories; 32 g fat; 5 g protein; 10 g carbohydrate; trace dietary fiber; 10 g net carbs

Dark Chocolate Frozen Custard

Rich and dark and oh-so-chocolaty. Remember, though, that you have to make the custard in advance, so you can chill it before you freeze it.

27 fluid ounces (793 ml) unsweetened coconut milk
4 ounces (115 g) bitter chocolate
¼ cup (85 g) honey
¼ teaspoon French vanilla liquid stevia
¼ teaspoon chocolate liquid stevia
6 egg yolks

In a big, heavy-bottomed saucepan, over very low heat, slowly warm the coconut milk with the chocolate. Whisk from time to time as the chocolate melts, as it takes a bit of whisking to incorporate the chocolate into the coconut milk.

When the coconut milk is warm and the chocolate melted, whisk in the honey and liquid stevia. Keep heating.

Separate your yolks into a medium-size bowl and whisk them up.

When the coconut milk/chocolate mixture is just below a simmer, use a ladle to transfer about ½ cup (120 ml); (that's what my ladle holds) into the bowl of egg yolks and immediately whisk very well. Transfer another ladleful into the yolks, and again, whisk very well.

(continued)

Now pour this mixture back into the main pot of coconut milk, whisking all the while. (DO NOT just try to whisk your egg yolks straight into your pot of coconut milk. You'll get scrambled egg yolk chunks in coconut milk, not what you're looking for.) Cook a bit longer, letting the mixture thicken up a bit.

Turn off the burner, let it cool, then stick it in the fridge and chill it well.

When dessert time rolls around, transfer your chilled custard to your ice cream freezer and freeze according to the directions that come with your unit. Serve—if you can bear to share it.

YIELD: 6 servings

Nutritional Analysis
Per serving: 451 calories; 42 g fat; 7 g protein; 21 g carbohydrate; 3 g dietary fiber; 18 g net carbs

Paleo Baked Custard

This is a nice dessert that would also make a lovely breakfast!

14 fluid ounces (425 ml) unsweetened coconut milk
3 tablespoons (60 g) honey
¼ teaspoon French vanilla liquid stevia, or to taste
5 eggs
⅛ teaspoon salt, scant

Just assemble everything in your blender container and run it until it's all well blended. Now taste. Do you think it needs to be a little sweeter? Add a little more liquid stevia.

Pour into a greased 1-quart (1 L) Pyrex casserole. Cover the casserole with foil and put it in your slow cooker. Now fill the space around the casserole with water, up to 1 inch (2.5 cm) from the rim of the casserole. Cover the pot, set to low, and cook for 4 hours. Turn off the slow cooker, remove the lid, and let the water cool till you can remove the casserole without scalding your fingers. Chill overnight before serving.

YIELD: 6 servings

Nutritional Analysis
Per serving: 216 calories; 17 g fat; 6 g protein; 11 g carbohydrate; trace dietary fiber; 11 g net carbs

NOTE

This calls for a big, round slow cooker—you can't fit a casserole dish in a little one, or an oval one. (If you're buying a new large-size slow cooker, buy a round one. You can do so much more with them.) If you don't have a slow cooker, put your casserole dish in a larger pan and fill the larger pan with water. Bake at 300°F (150°C, or gas mark 2) for 60 to 75 minutes. Or you could pour the custard mixture into individual custard cups and bake the same way—at 300°F (150°C, or gas mark 2) in a water bath—for an hour.

Maple Pumpkin Custard

Here's your Thanksgiving dessert!

14 ounces (400 g) pumpkin purée
14 fluid ounces (425 ml) unsweetened coconut milk
¼ teaspoon liquid stevia extract or to taste
2 tablespoons (40 g) maple syrup
4 eggs
⅛ teaspoon salt
1 tablespoon (6 g) pumpkin pie spice

Easy! Just whisk everything together. Pour it into a greased 1-quart (1 L) casserole and cover with foil.

Put the casserole into your slow cooker. Now carefully pour water around the casserole, up to 1 inch (2.5 cm) below the rim. Cover the slow cooker and set to low. Let it cook for 4 hours.

Turn off the slow cooker, uncover, and let it cool. When you can reach in there without scalding yourself, pull out your custard and put it in the fridge to chill, preferably overnight.

Serve with the Coconut Whipped Cream (page 296) or Coconut Milk Topping (page 296). If you'd like a little crunch, some chopped toasted pecans would be lovely, and look pretty too.

YIELD: 6 servings

Nutritional Analysis
Per serving: 216 calories; 17 g fat; 6 g protein; 12 g carbohydrate; 2 g dietary fiber; 10 g net carbs

NOTE

This calls for a big, round slow cooker—you can't fit a casserole dish in a little one, or an oval one. (If you're buying a new large-size slow cooker, buy a round one. You can do so much more with them.) If you don't have a slow cooker, put your casserole dish in a larger pan and fill the larger pan with water. Bake at 300°F (150°C, or gas mark 2) for 60 to 75 minutes.

Chapter 15

BEVERAGES

Undoubtedly the hunter-gatherer's usual beverage was water, and you cannot go wrong choosing filtered water when you're thirsty. Still, most of us occasionally want something else to drink. I, by way of example, go through a great deal of tea. Tea leaves are edible raw, after all, so combining them with water strikes me as innocuous. Ditto herbal teas, so long as they don't include grains or sugar. If our ancestors ate rose hips and mint leaves and licorice root, and it seems likely they did, I don't see why infusing them in water makes them unhealthy. If you like herbal tea, I say go for it.

Some herbals are medicinal, of course, and I've included a few recipes that have these effects. After all, herbs would have been the only medicine Ogg had.

Coffee is iffier, and most paleo plans ban it. Nevertheless, I suspect more than a few of you will still indulge, and coffee, like tea, is sugar free and a good source of antioxidants. Black is the best way to drink it, of course, but if you simply can't fight down the latte jones, there's a coconut-milk-based recipe in this chapter.

You'll find I've used sparkling water and club soda in this chapter. Unpaleo? I don't see why. There are naturally carbonated springs; the famous Perrier brand comes from one. Surely ancient man drank from these springs. If you're a stickler, use naturally carbonated water in these recipes, but I consider club soda, La Croix, and the like to be paleo-friendly. Be wary, though; some beverages labeled "sparkling water" are really clear diet sodas. Read the labels to find the ones with only carbonated water and natural flavor, no sweetener.

Then there's alcohol. The general attitude I've found regarding alcohol in paleo circles is "It's not paleo, but we know you're going to do it anyway—so here are some ways to do it without the sugary mixers, syrupy liqueurs, and grain-based malt beverages." I can't argue; I drink. You'll find some great cocktail recipes here, all better for you than beer, hard lemonade, or one of those sweet drinks currently masquerading as martinis.

Lemonade

This is a rough rule of thumb, since your lemon might have more or less juice than mine or be more or less acidic. This is lovely stuff, though, so do try it.

1 lemon
Ice
10 drops liquid stevia
8 ounces (235 ml) water

Warm your lemon a bit—I put mine in the oven for 5 minutes while roasting something else. Then roll it hard under your palm, really leaning on it. These two things will assure you get the most juice possible out of your lemon.

Now halve your lemon and squeeze every last drop of juice into a tall glass. I stuck my thumb in there and really reamed it out. Get all that flavor!

Add the ice and 6 to 8 drops of the stevia. Fill with the water, and taste—you'll probably want the rest of the stevia, but it's a whole lot easier to add more than it is to take it out once you've overdone it. Stir it up and drink it right away!

YIELD: 1 serving

Nutritional Analysis
Per serving: 12 calories; trace fat; 1 g protein; 6 g carbohydrate; 1 g dietary fiber; 5 g net carbs

Iced Tea

Pleasantly sweet and lemony, this is very refreshing—and vastly cheaper than sugary iced tea in bottles.

10 tea bags (I used Luzianne.)
3 tablespoons (7.5 g) dried stevia leaves, crumbled
8 cups (2 L) boiling water
2 lemons

Put your tea bags in a half-gallon pitcher. Put the stevia in a tea ball or two (depends on the size of your tea ball) and drop it in the pitcher, too.

Pour boiling water over the tea and stevia. While it steeps, drop the lemons in, whole, and let them warm for a few minutes.

Carefully pull the lemons out. Roll them firmly under the heel of your hand to loosen up the juice. Then halve the lemons, squeeze every drop of juice into the tea, and drop in the halves.

(continued)

Let the whole thing cool. If you like, you can fish out the tea bags, tea ball, and lemons before serving, though I didn't bother. (If you're not going to drink this all at once, do fish everything out. Leaving them in too long can make your tea bitter.) Chill, then pour over ice, of course.

YIELD: ½ gallon (2.3 L, or 8 servings of 1 cup [235 ml] each, though I'd generally drink more than that)

Nutritional Analysis
Per serving: 3 calories; trace fat, trace protein; 2 g carbohydrate; trace dietary fiber; 2 g net carbs

NOTE

I wanted to try simply brewing stevia leaves with the tea, which seemed to me the most paleo possible option. It worked nicely. If your local health food store doesn't carry dried stevia leaf, ask if they can order it for you; most health food stores are wonderful about special orders. Or you can order dried stevia leaf online, like everything else on the planet. Unpaid plug: Mountain Rose Herbs is my favorite Internet source for herbs.

Feel free, by the way, to use this "stevia-in-the-tea-ball" trick with any herbal tea you like, as well.

Eric's Coconut Coffee

My husband Eric has made tremendous changes in his diet over the years, but he's not willing to give up coffee, and I suspect there are a lot of people who agree. He's always had his coffee with cream, but found this version excellent

¼ cup (60 ml) unsweetened coconut milk
5 drops French vanilla liquid stevia or to taste
6 fluid ounces (175 ml) brewed coffee

Self-explanatory, really—put the coconut milk in a mug (you can warm it first if you like, but Eric didn't) and add the liquid stevia. Pour in the coffee, stir, and enjoy!

YIELD: 1 serving

Nutritional Analysis
Per serving: 114 calories; 12 g fat; 1 g protein; 2 g carbohydrate; 0 g dietary fiber; 2 g net carbs

NOTE

Eric tried this with chocolate liquid stevia, too, and thought it was great. You could use hazelnut or toffee liquid stevia, as well. And how about a dusting of cinnamon?

Coconut Latte

Disclaimer: I am not a coffee fan, and therefore have never had a traditional latte. I therefore have nothing to compare this with. However, my husband, who loves coffee with cream, thought this was great.

1½ fluid ounces (42 ml) espresso coffee, brewed
½ cup (60 ml) unsweetened coconut milk
Liquid stevia extract—French vanilla, chocolate, hazelnut, whatever flavor you like (optional)

In a small saucepan, heat the espresso and coconut milk together until simmering. Stir in liquid stevia to taste, if desired—I added a few drops of French vanilla.

Pour into your blender and run it for a couple of minutes. If you have a proper latte frother, use that instead. Pour into a mug and drink!

YIELD: 1 serving

Nutritional Analysis
Per serving: 226 calories; 24 g fat; 2 g protein; 4 g carbohydrate; 0 g dietary fiber; 4 g net carbs

Ginger Ale

Made fresh with real ginger! This is crisper and less sweet than commercial ginger ale.

2 teaspoons grated gingerroot
12 ounces (355 ml) club soda, chilled
3 drops liquid stevia, or to taste

Grate the gingerroot and pack it into a tea infuser. Put it in a tall glass and pour the club soda over it. Swish around a few times, to infuse the flavor, then leave in the glass as you add 3 drops of liquid stevia, or to taste. Drink immediately; this doesn't keep.

YIELD: 1 serving

Nutritional Analysis
Per serving: 3 calories; trace fat; trace protein; 1 g carbohydrate; trace dietary fiber; 1 g net carbs

NOTE

Licorice is a powerful tonic, stimulating the adrenals. That makes this a good choice when you're particularly stressed and run down. However, it also means that you shouldn't drink glass after glass of this on a daily basis. Really excessive licorice intake can raise blood pressure and even make you a little bloated.

Tonic Root Infusion

Why dried wintergreen, sarsaparilla, and licorice, but fresh ginger? 'Cause that's what I had, that's why. This is a flavor reminiscent of root beer, though it is less sweet and has no head.

½ cup (24 g) dried wintergreen
¼ cup (24 g) dried, chopped sarsaparilla root
¼ cup (24 g) dried, chopped licorice root
Gingerroot (Three chunks about the size of pecans, shell and all.)
1 tablespoon (15 ml) vanilla extract or half a vanilla bean
2 cups (475 ml) water
Sparkling water or club soda

(continued)

Measure your wintergreen, sarsaparilla, and licorice into a small saucepan. Peel your ginger, slice it as thinly as possible, and add it to the pot. If you're using a vanilla bean instead of extract, split it lengthwise and throw it in, too. Now add the water and put it over a very low flame. Let it stay just below a simmer for an hour. Stir now and then when you think of it.

Let the infusion cool, then strain. Press the herbs firmly with the back of a spoon to get all of the liquid you can. I got just exactly a cup of infusion. If you're using vanilla extract, add it now and stir it in.

To use, put ice in a tall glass, add 2 to 3 tablespoons (28 to 45 ml) of the infusion, and top with chilled sparkling water. Because of the licorice root, the infusion is sweet on its own, but if you'd like it a little sweeter, add a drop or two of liquid stevia extract.

YIELD: 1 serving

Nutritional Analysis
Per serving: 38 calories; 0 g fat; 0 g protein; 4 g carbohydrate; 0 g dietary fiber; 4 g net carbs

Raspberry Fizz

3 tablespoons (45 ml) Raspberry Purée (page 295)
12 ounces (355 ml) club soda or raspberry sparkling water

Put the raspberry purée in a tall glass. Fill with ice and then add the fizzy water. Drink and enjoy.

YIELD: 1 serving

Nutritional Analysis
Per serving: 81 calories; 1 g fat; 1 g protein; 19 g carbohydrate; 11 g dietary fiber; 8 g net carbs

Take-the-Edge-Off Tea

I concocted this from some of the most effective sedative herbs. It has a nice flowery-fruity flavor, but just as important, it really does take the edge off.

4 tablespoons (8 g) passion flower
4 tablespoons (8 g) rose hips
2 tablespoons (4 g) chamomile
4 tablespoons (8 g) lemon balm
1 tablespoon (2 g) bergamot
2 tablespoons (4 g) red clover blossom
1 tablespoon (2 g) dried orange peel
1 tablespoon (2 g) dried lemon peel

Mix everything together, and store in a tightly lidded container. When you're feeling unstrung, put about a tablespoon of the herbs in a tea infuser, put it in a mug, and pour 6 ounces (175 ml) of boiling water over it. Let steep for 5 minutes. I like to add a squeeze of lemon and a couple of drops of stevia to this, but suit yourself.

NOTE

The day I created this, I had two cups (470 g) and found myself drowsy. So be advised, don't drink this if you need to drive or operate any sort of dangerous equipment. On the other hand, if you need to wind down, this will do it with no alcohol.

Hot Chocolate

Very rich and thick. You could add another ½ cup (120 ml) of water and still have a creamy consistency. We just like it this way—call us decadent!

13½ ounces (400 ml) unsweetened coconut milk
½ cup (120 ml) water
2 tablespoons (12 g) cocoa powder
8 drops chocolate liquid stevia
8 drops vanilla liquid stevia
¼ teaspoon ground cinnamon

Simply combine everything in a heavy-bottomed saucepan, over low heat, and stir well. Heat through, and serve.

YIELD: 3 servings

Nutritional Analysis
Per serving: 258 calories; 27 g fat; 3 g protein; 5 g carbohydrate; 1 g dietary fiber; 4 g net carbs

Strawberry "Ice Cream" Soda

You could try making this with flavored sparkling water instead, if you like, to vary the flavor.

10 strawberries
½ cup (120 ml) unsweetened coconut milk, chilled
5 drops vanilla liquid stevia or to taste
¾ cup (175 ml) club soda, chilled

Trim the hulls from your berries and throw 'em in the blender. Add the coconut milk and stevia and run till the berries are pulverized. Pour into a tall glass, top with the club soda, stir, and serve.

YIELD: 1 serving

Nutritional Analysis
Per serving: 312 calories; 29 g fat; 3 g protein; 15 g carbohydrate; 5 g dietary fiber; 10 g net carbs

Strawberry Shake

Super-simple, and so incredibly good! If you can get frozen organic strawberries near you, go for it. I bought fresh ones, hulled them, and threw them in the freezer overnight.

8 ounces (225 g) strawberries, hulled and frozen
14 fluid ounces (425 ml) coconut milk, unsweetened
12 drops liquid stevia extract
½ teaspoon lemon juice

Just run everything through the food processor until the berries are pulverized. The frozen berries give you a frosty shake. Pour into 2 glasses and enjoy!

YIELD: 2 servings

Nutritional Analysis
Per serving: 407 calories; 40 g fat; 4 g protein; 13 g carbohydrate; 2 g dietary fiber; 11 g net carbs

Now for a few smoothies. You'll notice that all of these include raw eggs. They're there for the protein, so these smoothies will serve for a quick-and-easy meal. If you're scared of raw eggs, see the instructions for pasteurizing them on page 15.

Grapefruit Smoothie

Bright and tangy citrus flavor.

½ cup (60 ml) unsweetened coconut milk, chilled
2 eggs
¼ ruby red grapefruit
½ lemon
½ teaspoon gelatin powder
¼ teaspoon lemon liquid stevia
10 drops lemon liquid stevia, or to taste

Put the coconut milk and eggs in your blender. Peel your quarter grapefruit and make sure you've removed all the seeds. You don't need to remove all the membrane, but do pick off any white pith and any tough bits. Put the grapefruit in the blender, too. Squeeze in the juice from the half lemon and the gelatin powder. Run the blender!

Add the ¼ teaspoon lemon liquid stevia, then taste. Add more liquid stevia drop by drop, to your liking—this will vary a little not only with your taste, but with how sweet your grapefruit is.

Pour into a glass, and drink!

YIELD: 1 serving

Nutritional Analysis
Per serving: 390 calories; 33 g fat; 14 g protein; 15 g carbohydrate; 1 g dietary fiber; 14 g net carbs

Mexican Chocolate Smoothie

Chocolate, vanilla, and cinnamon are a traditional combination in Mexican cooking. This smoothie is nicely balanced between all three.

½ cup (60 ml) unsweetened coconut milk, chilled
2 eggs
4 teaspoons (8 g) cocoa powder
¼ teaspoon French vanilla liquid stevia—plus 4 drops
½ teaspoon ground cinnamon
½ teaspoon unsweetened gelatin powder

Just put everything in your blender and run it. Pour into a glass, and breakfast is served!

YIELD: 1 serving

Nutritional Analysis
Per serving: 376 calories; 33 g fat; 16 g protein; 9 g carbohydrate; 3 g dietary fiber; 6 g net carbs

Strawberry Smoothie

Our tester Rebecca says this is thick enough to eat with a spoon. She likes it that way, but if you'd rather drink it, thin it with a little water.

6 medium strawberries, frozen
½ cup (120 ml) unsweetened coconut milk
2 eggs
1 teaspoon (5 ml) lemon juice
10 drops liquid stevia extract or to taste
½ teaspoon unflavored gelatin powder

Run it all through the blender till the strawberries are pulverized. Taste, and see if it needs more stevia. Pour and drink!

YIELD: 1 serving

Nutritional Analysis

Per serving: 376 calories; 33 g fat; 14 g protein; 9 g carbohydrate; 2 g dietary fiber; 7 g net carbs

Blueberry Blender Breakfast

½ cup (75 g) blueberries, frozen
¾ cup (175 ml) unsweetened coconut milk
1 teaspoon (5 ml) lemon juice
2 eggs
30 drops French vanilla liquid stevia

You'll want to buy some organic blueberries and throw them in the freezer ahead of time. Then you're ready to make this at a moment's notice.

Just put everything in your blender and run till the berries are ground up. Pour in a glass and serve.

YIELD: 1 serving

Nutritional Analysis

Per serving: 506 calories; 45 g fat; 15 g protein; 16 g carbohydrate; 2 g dietary fiber; 14 g net carbs

Coconut Nog

That Nice Boy I Married adores eggnog and is unafraid of raw eggs. I created this for a quick breakfast for him, and he loved it.

1 cup (235 ml) unsweetened coconut milk
2 eggs
15 drops French vanilla liquid stevia or to taste
1 teaspoon (5 ml) vanilla extract
⅛ teaspoon ground nutmeg
¼ teaspoon ground cinnamon

Run it all through the blender, pour, and drink.

YIELD: 1 serving

Nutritional Analysis

Per serving: 590 calories; 56 g fat; 15 g protein; 9 g carbohydrate; trace dietary fiber; 9 g net carbs

Cocktail Hour

Alcohol is controversial in paleo circles. It occurs naturally, and I have no doubt Ogg enjoyed fermented fruit now and then, but he probably didn't have a wine cellar at the back of the cave. Bottom line: People who enjoy moderate drinking are unlikely to give it up entirely. Too, there is compelling evidence that moderate alcohol consumption has health benefits.

So what's the least damaging way to drink? I'm sorry to say we must eliminate beer. I always liked the stuff, but it's a grain product, it usually contains gluten, and the few gluten-free beers I've seen were very high in carbohydrate.

(continued)

Dry wines are a good choice—Cabernet, Merlot, Shiraz, Pinot Noir, Chardonnay, Chablis, Pinot Grigio, prosecco, brut champagne, are all dry wines, and any liquor store with a good wine section can help you discover more.

Hard liquor is distilled from a variety of sources: brandy from wine, and therefore from grapes; whiskey from grain; vodka originally from potatoes, but now largely from grain; rum from sugarcane; tequila from agave cactus. I would consider the most paleo of these sources to be grapes, agave, and sugarcane. Yes, I know that refined sugar is not paleo, but people have been chewing on raw sugarcane for—well, forever.

That said, distilled liquor is pretty pure stuff; whiskey from gluten grains contains no gluten. It's up to you how paleo kosher you want to keep your home bar.

Absolutely not paleo are malt beverages, including alcopops like hard lemonade and coolers, cordials, liqueurs, flavored rums or schnapps, anything with sugar added. Be wary of anything that wouldn't have been in a liquor store 100 years ago. If it tastes sweet, it has sugar in it. This rules out such popular drink ingredients as triple sec and curaçao, Midori, Campari, Kahlúa, crème de cacao, and Irish cream.

The mixers are at least as iffy. Obviously you'll scratch the soda, but be aware that tonic water is sugary, too. Be wary of fruit juices, since they're naturally sugary—and the popular Rose's Lime Juice has added sugar.

Here is a modest collection of cocktails that contain nothing wildly unpaleo. All of them taste good, and all of them will, consumed in moderation, encourage a convivial party atmosphere.

Wine Cooler

I like this in the heat of summer, because it's relaxing and hydrating at the same time.

4 ounces (120 ml) dry wine, red/white, as you prefer
8 ounces (235 ml) chilled sparkling water
6 drops fruit-flavored stevia extract or to taste

Fill a tall glass with ice. Add the wine and fill with chilled sparkling water. Add the lemon stevia extract, give it a quick stir, and drink.

YIELD: 1 serving

Nutritional Analysis
Per serving: 85 calories; 0 g fat; trace protein; 2 g carbohydrate; 0 g dietary fiber; 2 g net carbs

NOTE

This is endlessly variable. Just lay in a supply of different flavors of sparkling water—I like La Croix, and it comes in lemon, lime, orange, grapefruit, raspberry, and cran-raspberry. Various companies make liquid stevia in lemon, lemon-lime, orange, berry, peach, and I'm probably missing some. Make up your own combinations!

Mojito

Refreshing! The trick to the sugar-free mojito is to bruise the mint very thoroughly. In the standard version the sugar helps release the flavor oils from the mint.

2 sprigs mint
⅓ lime
5 drops liquid stevia extract
1 shot white rum
6 ounces (175 ml) chilled club soda

Pick the leaves off your mint springs and put them in a highball glass. If you have a "muddler," go ahead and use it. I used the back of a spoon. "Muddle" your mint—mash it up really well. You need to release the flavor. Squeeze in the juice from the lime and add the stevia. Stir it up. Now add a shot of rum.

Fill the glass with ice, drop in the squeezed-out lime, and fill the glass with chilled club soda.

YIELD: 1 serving

Nutritional Analysis
Per serving: 76 calories; trace fat; 1 g protein; 3 g carbohydrate; 1 g dietary fiber; 2 g net carbs—but that assumes you'll eat the mint and the lime.

Paleo Margarita Fizz

I admit it: I'm a tequila girl, but standard margaritas are awfully sugary. This combines the same flavors and is very refreshing

1 shot tequila
½ lime
4 drops liquid stevia extract or to taste
Ice
Chilled orange sparkling water to fill

Put the tequila in a highball glass and squeeze in the juice of your half lime. Add the liquid stevia and give it a quick stir.

Fill the glass with ice, then add chilled orange sparkling water. That's it!

YIELD: 1 serving

Nutritional Analysis
Per serving: 74 calories; trace fat; trace protein; 4 g carbohydrate; trace dietary fiber, 4 g net carbs

Mangorita

This is worthy of a teeny umbrella. You can change up the flavor of this tropical cocktail by using different sparkling waters—lime is good, so is lemon, but how about orange? Or tangerine?

1 ripe mango
1 lemon
1 lime
⅓ cup (80 ml) tequila
Club soda or sparkling water

Peel your mango and cut it off the stone, cutting it in chunks as you go. Put your chunks in a container and freeze 'em.

When cocktail time rolls around, put the mango chunks in your blender and add the juice of the lemon and the lime (watch out for pits!), and the tequila. Run the blender till you have a slush.

Divide the mixture between 4 glasses, fill with chilled sparkling water, and put on some mariachi music!

(continued)

YIELD: 4 servings

Nutritional Analysis
Per serving: 84 calories; trace fat; 1 g protein; 12 g carbohydrate; 1 g dietary fiber; 11 g net carbs

Mimosa

A classic for celebratory brunches

½ orange
5 fluid ounces (150 ml) brut champagne, chilled

Squeeze the juice from your orange into a champagne flute, then fill with chilled champagne and drink!

YIELD: 1 serving

Nutritional Analysis
Per serving: 156 calories; trace fat; 1 g protein; 12 g carbohydrate; 2 g dietary fiber; 10 g net carbs

Bellini

Our tester Yvonne says she added a few drops of liquid stevia to this, to good effect.

¼ fresh peach
¼ teaspoon lemon juice
5 ounces (150 ml) chilled champagne or prosecco to fill

Peel and purée your quarter peach, adding the lemon juice, then pour or spoon it into the bottom of a champagne flute. Fill with chilled champagne, and drink!

YIELD: 1 serving

Nutritional Analysis
Per serving: 136 calories; trace fat; trace protein; 7 g carbohydrate; trace dietary fiber; 7 g net carbs

NOTES

This recipe is for one, but making four, using a whole peach and a whole bottle of champagne, makes a lot of sense. Surely you can round up three friends.

The drier your champagne, the less residual sugar will be in it. "Dry" champagne is actually fairly sweet. The stuff labeled "brut" is far drier.

NeoClassic Daiquiri

The classic daiquiri has simple syrup in it, but we're not going there, are we? Our tester Saskia loved this.

1 shot white rum
½ shot fresh lime juice
4 drops liquid stevia extract or to taste

Shake over ice and strain into a cocktail glass. Add a lime wheel to be spiffy!

YIELD: 1 serving

Nutritional Analysis
Per serving: 68 calories; trace fat; trace protein; 1 g carbohydrate; trace dietary fiber; 1 g net carbs

Strawberry Daiquiri

6 fresh strawberries, hulled

2 shots light rum

¾ shot lime juice (eyeball it!)

4 drops liquid stevia extract, or more if needed—
    depends on how sweet your berries are

½ cup crushed ice

Put it all in your blender and run till you have slush. Pour and drink!

YIELD: 1 serving

Nutritional Analysis

Per serving: 156 calories; trace fat; 1 g protein; 7 g carbohydrate; 2 g dietary fiber; 5 g net carbs

Tom Collins

1½ ounces (42 ml) fresh lemon juice

1½ shots gin

4 drops liquid stevia extract or to taste

6 fluid ounces (175 ml) club soda, chilled

In a tall glass, combine the lemon juice, gin, and liquid stevia. Add ice, then club soda to fill.

YIELD: 1 serving

Nutritional Analysis

Per serving: 120 calories; 0 g fat; trace protein; 4 g carbohydrate; trace dietary fiber; 4 g net carbs

Vodka Collins

1½ ounces (42 ml) fresh lemon juice

1½ shots vodka

4 drops liquid stevia extract or to taste

6 ounces (175 ml) club soda, chilled

In a tall glass, combine the lemon juice, vodka, and liquid stevia. Add ice, then club soda to fill.

YIELD: 1 serving

Nutritional Analysis

Per serving: 120 calories; 0 g fat; trace protein; 4 g carbohydrate; trace dietary fiber; 4 g net carbs

French 75

Katy, who tested this, says, "I was a little skeptical of brandy and champagne, but it was delicious!"

Cracked ice (4 to 5 cubes' worth)

2 fluid ounces (60 ml) brandy (¼ cup)

1 fluid ounce (28 ml) lemon juice (2 tablespoons)

6 drops liquid stevia extract, or to taste

6 ounces (175 ml) chilled brut champagne

Crack the ice and put in a cocktail shaker. Add the brandy, lemon juice, and stevia. Shake it up well, then strain into a chilled highball glass.

Top with chilled champagne and drink!

YIELD: 1 serving

Nutritional Analysis

Per serving: 144 calories; 0 g fat; trace protein; 3 g carbohydrate; trace dietary fiber; 3 g net carbs

Piña Colada

Our tester Lisa Meagher said this reminded her husband of their honeymoon. Stick to plain white or dark rum—they're made from sugarcane, but all the sugar is fermented and distilled away. The flavored varieties generally have sugar added.

3 ounces (90 ml) light rum
3 tablespoons (30 g) crushed fresh pineapple
3 tablespoons (45 ml) unsweetened coconut milk, chilled
2 cups crushed ice

Just put everything in your blender and run it till the pineapple is pulverized. Pour and drink!

YIELD: 1 serving

Nutritional Analysis
Per serving: 294 calories; 9 g fat; 1 g protein; 5 g carbohydrate; trace dietary fiber; 5 g net carbs

Vodka Gimlet

Simple. Classic. You have a cocktail shaker, don't you?

1 shot vodka
⅔ shot lime juice—eyeball it!
3 drops liquid stevia extract, or to taste (no more than four or five drops)

Shake everything over ice, strain into a cocktail glass, and drink.

YIELD: 1 serving

Nutritional Analysis
Per serving: 70 calories; trace fat; trace protein; 2 g carbohydrate; trace dietary fiber; 2 g net carbs

Proper Martini

And now a public service message: If it's sweet, it ain't a martini, even in a V-shaped glass. Thanks to the brilliant Tom Lehrer, we have the canonical formula for the martini: "Hearts full of youth, hearts full of truth: Six parts gin to one part vermouth." Vodka is an acceptable alternative. Très Mad Men.

3 shots gin or vodka
½ shot dry vermouth
A twist of lemon peel or an olive

My father, were he still with us, would tell you that it is vital to use ice straight out of the freezer, because ice that's been in an ice bucket for a while will dilute your liquor. Dad knew his martinis.

So put ice cubes straight from the freezer into a cocktail shaker or martini pitcher, depending on whether you prefer shaken or stirred. Shake or stir just long enough to chill the liquor thoroughly, then pour.

A twist of lemon is more paleo than an olive, if you're feeling like a stickler.

YIELD: 2 servings

Nutritional Analysis
Per serving: 118 calories; 0 g fat; trace protein; trace carbohydrate; 0 g dietary fiber; 0 g net carbs

ABOUT THE AUTHOR

Dana Carpender is the author of six cookbooks, including the national bestseller *500 Low-Carb Recipes*. She is also the author of *How I Gave Up My Low-Fat Diet and Lost 40 Pounds*. Her books have sold over a million copies worldwide. Previously a syndicated national columnist, Dana is now managing editor of CarbSmart.com, and tries to keep up with her blog at HoldTheToast.com.

INDEX